Al fresco dining in Edinburgh

Whether you are looking for luxurious peaceful surroundings or a bustling city centre, Scotland is hard to beat. Wonderfully varied and intensely attractive, it leaves people longing to return.

folk songs round a welcoming log fire in a quaint little pub on a cold winter's night.

Whatever the time of year, wherever you decide to go, you'll find something of interest. You'll also be spoiled for choice when it comes to hotel and guesthouse accommodation. There are many wonderful places to stay from quiet country house hotels, to small family establishments to celebrated luxury destinations that are famed throughout the world.

Diversity is the key. For city travellers, the hotels offer easy access to a host of attractions, shopping and entertainment. They're popular with business travellers and conference go-ers too as Scotland's hotels offer some of the best facilities in Europe. Sometimes the hotel itself is an attraction with spas and leisure complexes, golf courses, swimming pools and other sporting facilities.

Others have their own way of delivering a taste of Scotland to their guests. You can stay at idyllic country house hotels that have hosted the rich and famous or guest houses where you can really get to know the people who run them and the community they live in.

It's your choice but whether you're choosing five-star luxury or something a little more modest, you can always look forward to a warm welcome in a country that is renowned for its hospitality.

Indeed, nobody loves a good time like the Scots. Whether it's bringing in the New Year with a wee dram, swirling your partner at a ceilidh or enjoying a sumptuous dinner for two in an exclusive restaurant, the potential for an unforgettable evening's entertainment is always there.

There's always the chance too that you'll meet some great folks – locals and other visitors – some of whom may become friends for life. That's all just part of a visit to Scotland. As they say in the Gaelic tongue that is still very much alive and spoken by many around the country, ceud mille failte – 'a hundred thousand welcomes'. Come and enjoy our beautiful country.

Don't Miss

Walking

Two walkers at Mam Ratagan, with a view across to Loch Duich, Highlands From a countryside ramble to an airy coastal walk or a trek through the forest, Scotland is perfect for walkers. There are a number of excellent long distance routes to choose from and you can really push yourself to the limits amongst the majestic mountains.

Beaches

A beach, South Harris, Outer Hebrides Scotland's coastline is long and varied and it has some of the most beautiful beaches in the world. Why not explore the white sandy beaches of East Lothian, the Silver Sands of Morar or Fife's Blue Flag beaches?

Adventure

Splash White Water Rafting, Perthshire Scotland's wonderful natural landscape lends itself beautifully to all sorts of adventure sports from white water rafting to mountain biking, canyoning and cliff jumping.

Shopping

Shopping, Glasgow From high street stores to designer boutiques, cashmere to comics, Scotland's cities have an eclectic mix of shops that make for a shopping experience like no other.

Wildlife

A boat trip on the Moray Firth, Highlands You can spot all kinds of wildlife on a visit to Scotland, from the majestic Golden Eagle to dolphins in the Moray Firth.

Hotels and Guest Houses Guide 2007

Contents

Scotland's Tourist Areas

02 — SOUTH OF SCOTLAND
Ayrshire and Arran, Dumfries and Galloway, Scottish Borders  **1**

19 — EDINBURGH and LOTHIANS  **2**

44 — GREATER GLASGOW and CLYDE VALLEY  **3**

54 — WEST HIGHLANDS & ISLANDS, LOCH LOMOND, STIRLING AND TROSSACHS  **4**

73 — PERTHSHIRE, ANGUS and DUNDEE and THE KINGDOM OF FIFE  **5**

98 — ABERDEEN and GRAMPIAN HIGHLANDS - Scotland's Castle and Whisky Country  **6**

114 — THE HIGHLANDS AND SKYE **7**

145 — OUTER ISLANDS
Outer Hebrides, Orkney, Shetland  **8**

Sunset over Loch Lomond

WELCOME TO SCOTLAND

Once you've had a holiday in Scotland, it is easy to see why so many people from all over the world visit time and again. Put simply, Scotland is a wonderful place for holidaymakers. Whether you're planning a short break or your annual vacation, Scotland has so much to offer.

A quick look through the pages of this guide will give you a flavour of Scotland's diversity. You'll soon discover that there are many fascinating places to visit, each with its own unique attractions.

Though it's a relatively small country, Scotland is remarkably varied. You can climb a mountain in the morning then relax on a beach in the afternoon. You can canoe across a remote loch and never see another soul all day long or you can sip coffee in a city centre pavement café and watch the whole world go by. You can get dressed up to the nines and go to a world premier on a balmy summer's evening or you can join in with some traditional

Golf

The golf course at Turnberry, Ayrshire The country that gave the world the game of golf is still the best place to play it. There are over 550 courses to thrill and inspire you each presenting its own unique challenges against the magnificent backdrop of the Scottish countryside.

Castles

Loch Awe and Kilchurn Castle, Argyll Step back in time with Scotland's impressive ruins and imposing fortresses, fairytale castles and country estates.

Culture & Heritage

Rosslyn Chapel, Midlothian The traces of Scotland's history are never hard to find. Why not search for the Holy Grail at Rosslyn Chapel, follow in the footsteps of Robert Burns, or visit mysterious standing stones in Orkney and the Outer Hebrides.

Highland Games

The Braemar Gathering, Aberdeenshire Hot foot it to a Highland Games where you can find the likes of pipe bands, Scottish dancers, tossing the caber and tug o' war.

Taste of Scotland

Whisky Follow the Malt Whisky Trail and try for yourself some of Scotland's finest flavours or stop off along the coast and savour the seafood that is the envy of Europe.

Top left: Jenners, Edinburgh Top middle: Kelvingrove, Glasgow Top right: Isle of Glencoe Hotel, Highlands
Bottom left: Langass Lodge, Outer Hebrides Bottom middle: The Outsider Restaurant, Edinburgh
Bottom right: Airth Castle Hotel, near Falkirk

TRAVEL TO SCOTLAND

It's really easy to get to Scotland whether you choose to travel by car, train, plane, coach or ferry. And once you get here travel is easy as Scotland is a compact country.

By Air

Flying to Scotland couldn't be simpler with airports at Edinburgh, Glasgow, Glasgow Prestwick, Aberdeen, Dundee and Inverness. Once in Scotland you can fly to a number of the islands. The following airlines operate flights to Scotland (although not all airports):

bmi
Tel: 0870 60 70 555 flybmi.com
bmi baby
Tel: 0871 224 0224 bmibaby.com
British Airways
Tel: 0870 850 9 850 ba.com
Eastern Airways
Tel: 08703 669 100 easternairways.com

easyJet
Tel: 0905 821 0905 easyjet.com
Flybe
Tel: 0871 700 0535 flybe.com
Ryanair
Tel: 0871 246 0000 ryanair.com
ScotAirways
Tel: 0870 60 60 707 scotairways.com
Aer Arann
Tel: 0800 587 2324 aerarann.com

By Rail

Scotland has major rail stations in Aberdeen, Edinburgh Waverley and Edinburgh Haymarket, Glasgow Queen Street and Glasgow Central, Perth, Stirling, Dundee and Inverness. There are regular cross border railway services from England and Wales, and good city links. You could even travel on the Caledonian Sleeper overnight train service from London and wake up to the sights and sounds of Scotland.

First Scotrail
Tel: 08457 55 00 33 firstscotrail.com

Virgin Trains
Tel: 08457 222 333 virgintrains.co.uk

GNER
Tel: 08457 225 225 gner.co.uk

By Road

Scotland has an excellent road network from motorways and dual carriageway linking cities and major towns, to remote single-track roads with passing places to let others by. Whether you are coming in your own car from home or hiring a car once you get here, getting away from traffic jams and out onto Scotland's quiet roads can really put the fun back into driving. Branches of the following car hire companies can be found throughout Scotland:

Arnold Clark
Tel: 0845 702 3946 arnoldclark.com/rental
Avis Rent A Car
Tel: 0870 606 0100 avis.co.uk
Budget
Tel: 08701 56 56 56 budget.co.uk
easyCar
Tel: 0906 333 3333 easycar.com

Enterprise Rent-A-Car
Tel: 0870 350 3000 enterprise.co.uk
Europcar
Tel: 0870 607 5000 europcarscotland.co.uk
Hertz
Tel: 08708 44 88 44 hertz.co.uk
National Car Rental
Tel: 0870 400 4560 nationalcar.com
Sixt rent a car
Tel: 0870 156 7567 sixt.co.uk

By Ferry

Scotland has over 130 inhabited islands so ferries are important. And whether you are coming from Ireland or travelling to the islands, you might be in need of a ferry crossing. Ferries to and around the islands are regular and reliable and most carry vehicles. These companies all operate ferry services around Scotland:

Stena Line
Tel: 08705 204 204 stenaline.co.uk
P&O Irish Sea
Tel: 0870 24 24 777 poirishsea.com
Caledonian MacBrayne
Tel: 08705 650000 calmac.co.uk
Western Ferries
Tel: 01369 704 452 western-ferries.co.uk
Northlink Ferries
Tel: 08456 000 449 northlinkferries.co.uk

By Coach

Coach connections include express services to Scotland from all over the UK, and there is a good network of coach services once you get to here. You could even travel on the Postbus – a special feature of the Scottish mail service which carries fare-paying passengers along with the mail in rural areas where there is no other form of transport, bringing a new dimension to travel.

National Express
Tel: 08705 80 80 80 nationalexpress.com
City Link
Tel: 08705 50 50 50 citylink.co.uk
Postbus
Tel: 08457 740 740 royalmail.com/postbus

Knowledgeable and friendly staff are on hand at Tourist Information Centres nationwide

TOURIST INFORMATION

Wherever you plan to travel in Scotland, you'll never be too far away from a Tourist Information Centre.

There are 120 centres across the country and the knowledgeable and friendly staff are there to answer all your questions and give you the advice that can turn a good holiday into an unforgettable experience.

Each centre also has a wide stock of free guides and leaflets featuring local attractions and places of interest as well as an excellent range of maps, guide books, Scottish literature and books that you can buy.

Tourist Information Centres can help you find and book accommodation throughout Scotland. You can buy tickets for local and national events and book excursions, tours and travel. Most also offer a splendid range of souvenirs and local crafts which make ideal gifts for you to take home for friends and family.

As well as providing a valuable insight into what's on locally, some centres also provide a bureau de change service and internet access. So make sure you make the most of your stay in Scotland and make your first stop the Tourist Information Centre wherever you go.

Throughout the Highlands, across Scotland and around the world, Highland 2007 is a celebration of the unique and special nature of Highland culture. Spectacular events, large and small, will showcase the best of Highland culture during this exciting year.

Spanning the arts, sport, heritage, environment, language and science, events include the launch of a national exhibition *Fonn 's Duthchas (Land and Heritage)*, the premiere of The Highland Quest, Celtic Film and Television Festival, the Big Willow project, Inverness Film Festival and music festivals such as Blas, Belladrum Tartan Heart Festival, Nairn Jazz Festival and Skye Music Festival. Also in the programme: the Tulloch Inverness Highland Games featuring the World Highland Games Championships, RBS Highland International Tattoo, Six Cities Festival of Design, Moray Firth Flotilla, Adventure Racing World Championships, the UCI Mountain Bike and Trails World Championships. Come to the Highlands in 2007 and join the celebration!

For an up to date list of events, check the Highland 2007 website.

Gaidhealtachd 2007 - bliadhna de ghreadhnachas ann an Alba...

www.highland2007.com

Principal Partner

Highland 2007, Abertarff House, Church Street, Inverness IV1 1EU Tel: 01463 702007 Email: info@highland2007.com

BE GUIDED BY THE STARS!
Know What Standards to Expect

In Scotland the vast majority of tourist accommodation – from rural hostel to city centre hotel – and most visitor attractions are independently assessed and rated by the Scottish Tourist Board, the grading arm of VisitScotland.

Using a straightforward Quality Assurance **5 star system**, the Scottish Tourist Board makes its assessment in terms of both the **overall quality** of **service** and **facilities** on offer. Assessments are constantly monitored and reviewed every year.

VisitScotland wants to make your visit as enjoyable as possible by ensuring that you know what **standard** of service, hospitality, accommodation and food to expect **wherever** you choose to go or stay in Scotland.

Every budget is catered for from camping to penthouse suites. We want all our visitors to have a good experience and get **value for money**.

THE STARS AND OTHER PLAQUES EXPLAINED.

The Quality Assurance star ratings are explained below as are a number of specialised schemes designed to help you organise your holiday to fit your interests.

A Quality Advisor's visit to and assessment of an establishment covers up to 50 areas depending on the nature and scale of the business. These include the exterior appearance, quality, comfort and décor of private and public rooms, cleanliness and, most importantly, the welcome, ambience, management efficiency and level of service. Owners' taste or whether the establishment is contemporary or otherwise in terms of fashion is not taken into account.

If an establishment scores less than 60% it will not be graded.

Assures that the establishment is clean and tidy and of an acceptable, if basic, standard.

Assures that the establishment is of a good, all-round standard.

Assures that the establishment is of a very good standard, where attention to detail is paid in every area.

Assures that the establishment is of an excellent standard from the use of high quality materials to good food* and friendly, professional service.

Assures that the establishment is of an exceptional standard where presentation, ambience, food* and service are hard to fault. *Doesn't apply to Self-Catering

WELCOME SCHEMES

A range of Welcome Schemes have been developed by VisitScotland to complement the 1-5 Star Quality Assurance ratings. These are designed to help guide visitors to those establishments who pay particular attention to specific needs.

Welcome Schemes Properties that make specific provision for walkers and cyclists.

VisitScotland have developed similar schemes for **Anglers**, **Bikers**, **Golfers**, **Children and Ancestral Tourism**.

Green Tourism Businesses making an effort to operate in a sustainable, environmentally friendly way are graded Bronze, Silver or Gold.

 BRONZE 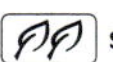 SILVER  GOLD

Bothies Bothies symbol indicates that a bothy/bod has been inspected.

Thistle Thistle symbol recognises a high standard of caravan holiday home.

Caravan Holiday Individual caravan holiday homes are inspected.

Visitors with disabilities
The following symbols are to assist you assess whether accommodation matches your requirements.

Unassisted wheelchair access

Assisted wheelchair access

Access for visitors with mobility diffculties

Our new food grading scheme assesses the presentation, quality and service of food in every kind of eating establishment in Scotland. The EatScotland logo tells you that the eating place has achieved the required standard for this new accolade.

GRADED VISITOR ATTRACTIONS

Visitor Attractions are graded with 1-5 stars according to the level of customer care they offer. The focus is on the standard of hospitality and service they provide as well as presentation, quality of shop/café etc. (if provided) and standard of toilet facilities. The wide variety of attractions graded includes: castles, museums, historic houses, leisure centres, activity centres, arts venues, tourist shops, gardens, garden centres and tours.

TYPES OF ACCOMMODATION

We grade all types of accommodation from hostels through B&Bs and self-catering properties to hotels both small and grand. We even grade Campus Accommodation and parks offering caravan holiday homes and camping. So whether you prefer to spend the night under canvas or the canopy of a four-poster bed we'll make sure you know the standard to expect.

B&B A private house offering bed and breakfast and sometimes an evening meal.

Guest House Normally larger than a B&B and run as a commercial business. Rooms usually ensuite. Breakfast and sometimes an evening meal are provided.

Small Hotel tend to reflect owners' style and normally have between 6 and 20 bedrooms (most ensuite). Meals and a drinks license (may be restricted).

Hotel A hotel with at least 20 bedrooms (most ensuite) serving breakfast and dinner and normally lunch. Drinks licence (may be restricted).

International Resort Hotel Luxury hotel with a range of leisure and sporting facilities that normally include a swimming pool, 18 hole golf course, leisure centre and country pursuits.

Self-catering House, cottage, apartment etc usually let on a weekly basis, although shorter breaks may be available.

Serviced Apartment Self-catering apartment where limited services, like cleaning or concierge, are provided. Meals and drinks may be on offer.

Lodge Travellers' accommodation near to major roads, airports or in city centres. Reception hours may be restricted and payment may be required on check-in. Sometimes with associated restaurant facilities.

Inn B&B accommodation at a traditional inn or pub. Lunch and evening meals in bar/restaurant.

Restaurant with Rooms The restaurant is the main focus of the establishment and is open to non-residents. Breakfast usually served.

Campus Accommodation College and university accommodation offered during vacation time to individuals and groups. Meals usually provided.

Hostel Accommodation often in shared rooms with bunk beds, family rooms may also be available. May have restricted access hours. All types of hostel may offer meals and other services or be self-catering; **Backpackers** tends to be for independent travellers. **Group Accommodation** is a hostel where predominantly group bookings are accepted. **Activity Accommodation** is normally provided on a group basis only and will offer activities.

Holiday Park A park that offers holiday homes and, most likely, touring and camping pitches.

Touring Park A park that offers touring pitches and probably camping pitches as well.

Camping Park A park for camping only.

SYMBOLS

	Ensuite bath and/or shower for all bedrooms
	Ensuite bath and/or shower for some bedrooms
	Private bath and/or shower for all bedrooms
	Private bath and/or shower for some bedrooms
	Ensuite bath and/or shower room(s) in self catering unit
	Washbasin in bedroom
	Hairdryer in bedrooms
	Bed linen available – free or for hire
	Towels available – free or for hire
	TV in bedrooms/in self-catering unit
	No TV
	Satellite/Cable TV
	Tea/Coffee making facilities in bedroom
	Telephone in bedrooms
	Payphone provided
	Restaurant
	Evening meal available
	Room service
	Lounge
	TV Lounge
	Full alcohol drinks licence
	Restricted alcohol drinks licence
	Non-smoking establishment
	Smoking restricted
	Laundry service
	Washing machine
	Tumble dryer
	Laundry facilities on site
	Telephone in unit
	Microwave
	Dishwasher
	Freezer
	Hi-fi
	Video
	DVD available
	CD available
	Leisure facilities
	Indoor swimming pool
	Private parking
	Limited parking
	Domestic help
	Porterage
	Not all properties have all facilities

Hostels may also provide the following:

	Meal service available
	Drying facilities
	Family rooms available
	Twin/double rooms available
	Alpine sleeping platform

FURTHER INFORMATION

Quality Assurance (at VisitScotland)
Tel: 01463 723040
Fax: 01463 717244
E-mail: qainfo@visitscotland.com

We welcome your comments on star-awarded properties.
Tel: 01463 723040
Fax: 01463 717244
E-mail: qa@visitscotland.com

SCOTLAND'S NATIONAL BOOKING AND INFORMATION CENTRE
Tel: 0845 22 55 121
E-mail: info@visitscotland.com
Call into any Tourist Information Centre for further information.

A car on the A832 road past Loch Maree, with a view to Slioch

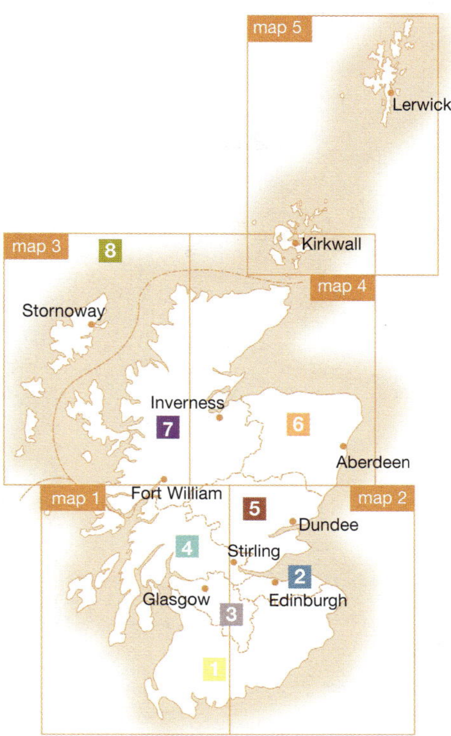

MAPS

Accommodation

MAP 1

ATLANTIC OCEAN
COLL
TIREE
MULL
COLONSAY
JURA
ISLAY
BUTE
ARRAN
Firth of Clyde
Loch Linnhe
Loch Awe
Loch Lomond
Loch Tay
CUMBRAE
Luce Bay

Arinagour
Isle of Coll
Scarinish
Isle of Tiree
Tobermory
Calgary
Dervaig
Kilchoan
Strontian
Glencoe
Loch Leven
Ballachulish
Kinloch Ranno
Lochaline
Fishnish
Craignure
Lismore
Barcaldine
Ardchattan
Connel
Oban
Killin
Isle of Iona
Pennyghael
Bunessan
Dalmally
Kilchrenan
Crianlarich
Lochearnhead
Balquhidder
Ardlui
Strathyre
Calland
Kilmelford
Cairndow
Inversnaid
Port of Menteith
Ardfern
Inveraray
Arrochar
Strachur
Tarbet
Luss
Drymen
Aberfoyl
Scalasaig
Lochgilphead
Fintry
Isle of Colonsay
Ardrishaig
Helensburgh
Balloch
Alexandria
Cardross
Port Askaig
Feolin
Ballygrant
Isle of Jura
Dunoon
Gourock
Inverkip
Wemyss Bay
Glasgow Airport
Paisley
GLASGOW
Rhubodach
Colintraive
Tighnabruaich
Tarbert
Portavadie
Kennacraig
Rothesay
Largs
Howwood
Port Charlotte
Bowmore
Claonaig
Cumbrae
Uplawmoor
Isle of Gigha
Lochranza
Kilchattan Bay
Millport
Ardminish
Seamill
Kilwinning
Port Ellen
Tayinloan
Ardrossan
Irvine
Kilmarnock
Carradale
Brodick
Troon
Prestwick
Blackwaterfoot
Whiting Bay
Ayr
Cumnock
Campbeltown
Kildonan
Dalrymple
Turnberry
Girvan
Cairnryan
Newton Stewart
Stranraer
Creetown
Wigtown
Gatehouse of Fleet
Portpatrick
Isle of Whithorn
Larne
BELFAST
To Douglas, Isle of Man
To Liverpool

Car ferries and terminals:
Brodick — Ardrossan
Scale 1:1 300 000
0   10   20 miles
© Collins Bartholomew Ltd 2006

These maps show locations of establishments appearing in the Main Advertising Section of this guide. For route planning and touring please use a current road atlas.

MAP 1   MAP 2

MAP 2
NORTH SEA
A Pitlochry
Aberfeldy
Dunkeld
Birnam
Blairgowrie
Alyth
Coupar Angus
Meikleour
Stanley
Inchture
Dundee
Wormit
Perth
Comrie
Crieff
Auchterarder
Cupar
Ceres
St Andrews
Glendevon
Milnathort
Falkland
Freuchie
Markinch
Crail
Kinross
Leslie
Lower Largo
Dunblane
Glenrothes
Lundin Link
Dollar
Ballingry
Leven
Alloa
Cowdenbeath
Kirkcaldy
tirling
Dunfermline
Grangemouth
Rosyth
Bo'ness
Inverkeithing
Burntisland
North Berwick
Falkirk
South Queensferry
Aberdour
Gullane
Dirleton
Linlithgow
Broxburn
Musselburgh
Aberlady
Dunbar
Dechmont
Uphall
EDINBURGH
Haddington
Coatbridge
Livingston
East Calder
Dalkeith
Gifford
ddingston
Harthill
Lasswade
Eyemouth
Motherwell
Penicuik
North Middleton
Chirnside
arkhall
West Linton
Lauder
Swinton
Peebles
Galashiels
Biggar
Broughton
Innerleithen
Melrose
Kelso
Abington
Selkirk
Ettrickbridge
Jedburgh
Hawick
Moffat
Thornhill
Johnstone Bridge
Langholm
Lockerbie
Crocketford
Dumfries
Ecclefechan
Gretna Green
Newcastle
Castle
Douglas
Annan
Gretna
upon Tyne
Kippford
Colvend
Auchencairn
Carlisle
Sunderland
ircudbright
Firth of Tay
Firth of Forth
Solway Firth
To Zeebrugge
Middlesbrough

MAP 3

These maps show locations of establishments appearing in the Main Advertising Section of this guide. For route planning and touring please use a current road atlas.
MAP 3
MAP 4
OUTER HEBRIDES
LEWIS
Callanish
Stornoway
Achmore
8
Ardhasaig
Tarbert
Kyles
HARRIS
Leverburgh
The Minch
Duntulm
Staffin
Uig
Lochmaddy
Locheport
Carinish
NORTH UIST
Waternish
Liniclate
BENBECULA
Creagorry
Dunvegan
Skeabost
Portree
RAASAY
Isle of Raasay
Raasay
Lochcarnan
SOUTH UIST
Portnalong
Sconser
Kyle of Lochalsh
Broadford
SKYE
Breakish
Kyleakin
Kylerhea
Glenelg
Daliburgh
(Dalabrog)
Lochboisdale
(Lochbaghasdail)
Eriskay
CANNA
Armadale
Ardvasar
Sleat
BARRA
Tangasdale
Northbay
Castlebay
RUM
Mallaig
Morar
Arisaig
EIGG
Loch Morar
Glenfinnan
MUCK
ARDNAMURCHAN
Acharacle
Ardgour
Onich
Kinlochbervie
Rhiconic
Scourie
Kylesku
Lochinver
ASSYNT
Achiltibuie
Ullapool
Aultbea
Dundonnell
Poolewe
Kinlochewe
Gairloch
Achnasheen
Shieldaig
Torridon
7
Applecross
Kishorn
Lochcarron
Ardelve
Dornie
Cannich
Glenshiel
Invergarry
Loch Lochy
Spean Bridge
Roy Bridge
Fort William
Kinlochleven

MAP 4

ORKNEY
Stromness
Scapa Flow
HOY
St Margaret's Hope
8
SOUTH RONALDSAY
Longhope
To Kirkwall
To Lerwick
To Faroes & Iceland (summer only)
Pentland Firth
Scrabster
Gills Bay
John o' Groats
Thurso
Keiss
Durness
Wick
Tongue
Lybster
Dunbeath
Lairg
Brora
Dornoch Firth
Car ferries and terminals:
Brodick
Ardrossan
Scale 1:1 300 000
0   10   20 miles
© Collins Bartholomew Ltd 2006
Dornoch
Portmahomack
Tain
Moray Firth
Lossiemouth
Buckie
Cullen
Portsoy
Macduff
Banff
Fordyce
Invergordon
Cromarty
Garve
Forres
Elgin
Strathpeffer
Nairn
Peterhead
Muir of Ord
Culloden Moor
Archiestown
Craigellachie
Inverness
Dufftown
Huntly
Rothienorman
Cruden Bay
Ellon
Glen Urquhart
Brackla
Grantown-on-Spey
Oldmeldrum
9
Drumnadrochit
Dulnain Bridge
Kildrummy
Inverurie
Loch Ness
Carrbridge
Nethy Bridge
Strathdon
Boat of Garten
Aviemore
Aberdeen
Fort Augustus
Kincraig
Tarland
10
Newtonmore
Kingussie
Ballater
Banchory
Laggan Bridge
Braemar
Laggan
Stonehaven
11
Dalwhinnie
Laurencekirk
5
Glenshee
Edzell
Blair Atholl
Montrose
Killiecrankie
Glenisla
6

MAP 5

MAP 5
8
Car ferries and terminals:
Brodick
Ardrossan
Scale 1:1 300 000
0   10   20 miles
© Collins Bartholomew Ltd 2006
These maps show locations of establishments appearing in the Main Advertising Section of this guide. For route planning and touring please use a current road atlas.
8
UNST
Gutcher
Belmont
YELL
Oddsta
FETLAR
Ulsta
Toft
OUT SKERRIES
SHETLAND
Laxo
WHALSAY
Symbister
BRESSAY
Lerwick
To Norway
(summer only)
To Faroes & Iceland
(summer only)
FOULA
FAIR ISLE
To Aberdeen
North Ronaldsay
WESTRAY
Papa Westray
NORTH RONALDSAY
Westray
SANDAY
ROUSAY
EDAY
8
STRONSAY
Evie
Dounby
Shapinsay
SHAPINSAY
Stenness
Kirkwall
Stromness
ORKNEY
Scapa Flow
To Aberdeen

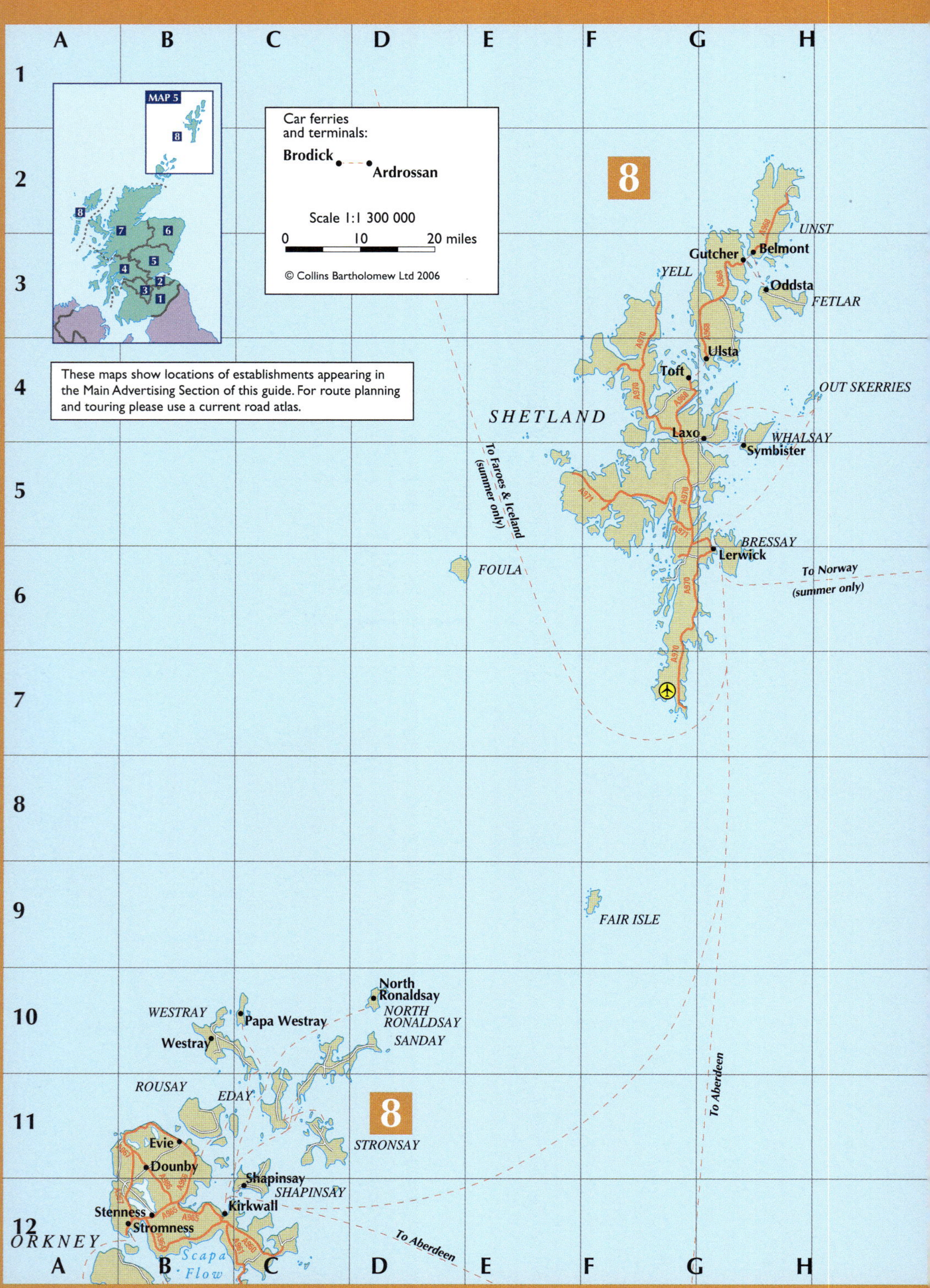

Where to Stay
Hotels and Guest Houses Guide

The Culloden House Hotel, Highlands

Accommodation Listings

Published by VisitScotland 2007 | Photography Paul Tomkins /
VisitScotland / Scottish Viewpoint | www.visitscotland.com | 0845 22 55 121

Main image: Scott's View, Scottish Borders **Bottom left:** Sweetheart Abbey, Dumfries & Galloway
Bottom middle: Walkers in Glen Trool, Dumfries & Galloway **Bottom right:** Corrie, Isle of Arran

SOUTH OF SCOTLAND

Ayrshire and Arran,
Dumfries and Galloway,
Scottish Borders

Anyone who has ever taken the time to explore Scotland's southern parts will know that there's so much to discover in the Scottish Borders, Ayrshire and Arran and Dumfries and Galloway that you could holiday here until the end of time and still never see it all.

Though you could be forgiven for missing the line where England stops and Scotland begins, the cultural identity is a lot more clearly defined. While the border itself has not been contested for many, many years, Scotland is unmistakably Scottish as soon as you arrive.

The people of the South have their own proud heritage and distinct traditions and their history is rich and intense. You may be surprised to discover that the great leaders William Wallace and Robert the Bruce were apparently southerners. Though precise

Sunset at Fairlie, Ayrshire

From the cliffs of St Abbs to the Mull of Galloway and the beautiful Isle of Arran, the South of Scotland is a land of rugged coastlines and rolling hills.

locations have been lost in the mist of time, many historians now believe that both were born in Ayrshire.

Across the South, the trail of an often bloody and turbulent history is easily followed from stout castles to ruined abbeys. Each has a tale or two to tell. The border reivers may be long gone but their stories remain – just peer over the precipitous edge of the Devil's Beeftub (on the Moffat to Edinburgh road) and you'll almost hear the thundering hooves!

If you're around many a Border town in the summer months, you'll hear just that sound when you experience the Common Ridings. Many hundreds of riders on horseback commemorate the times when their ancestors risked their lives patrolling town boundaries and neighbouring villages, protecting them from raiders. These days they're a colourful and spectacular pageant.

The South is alive with history. Traquair House, near Innerleithen, has been continuously inhabited since the 12th Century and it's as

fascinating to visit today as it ever has been. 2007 also celebrates the 700th anniversary of the Battle of Glentrool, one of the first flurries of Robert the Bruce's campaign on the road to Bannockburn and Scottish independence. In Selkirk the whole town seems transformed in early December as locals step back to the days when Sir Walter Scott presided over the local courtroom.

Scott is one of a handful of literary giants who have left their mark in this part of the world. Hugh McDiarmid (arguably the most important Scots poet of the 20th Century) started life as Christopher Murray Grieve in Langholm in 1911 while the most famous Scots poet of all, Robert Burns, was born in Alloway, South Ayrshire in 1759. You can visit his birthplace and trace his life at the Burns National Heritage Park. So many places you'll see as you travel through the beautiful countryside are as inspiring today as they were to the Bard in his prime.

Though it's easy to picture rolling hills and lush farmland when you think of southern Scotland,

You'll find world-class mountain biking and some of the country's finest angling as well as sandy beaches, quaint villages and ruined abbeys.

the sea also figures prominently in local culture. To the east we have the rocky cliffs at St Abbs Head while over on the west, there are the beautiful Ayrshire beaches and more than 200 miles of the lovely Solway Coast to explore.

And off the Ayrshire coast is the Isle of Arran. Just jump on the ferry and head for an enchanted world that seems to pack everything that makes Scotland great into a space that's just 19 miles from top to bottom and 10 miles across its widest point. There's a castle, rugged mountains to the north, gentle hills to the south, pretty towns and villages, beaches, wildlife, fishing and golf – 7 courses in all to test your game to the limit!

In many ways Arran, which is known as 'Scotland in miniature', sums up the south. It's easy to get to and whatever you like to do, you'll find it here. If you love fishing, there's world-class salmon fishing on the Tweed. If golf's your game, Turnberry, Prestwick and Royal Troon are up with the best. If you're a mountain biker, you won't find better than Glentress, one of the 7stanes mountain bike routes. Enjoy reading? Head for Wigtown, Scotland's National Book Town and home to more than 20 bookshops. Ice cream? Who can resist Cream o' Galloway at Gatehouse of Fleet? If you're a gardener, you'll be inspired all year round by the flourishing collection of rare plants at the Logan Botanic Garden near Stranraer and Dawyck Botanic Garden near Peebles.

That's the South of Scotland. Bursting with brilliant places to visit and to stay. From cosy little guesthouses to five star resort hotels, a hearty Scottish welcome awaits and a holiday experience that you will never forget is guaranteed.

Common Riding, Ettrick River, Scottish Borders

Tourist Information Centres

Please refer to the maps on pages xii - xviii for the locations of establishments appearing in the main advertising section of this guide. Only year-round Tourist Information Centres are indicated.

Loch Ken, Dumfries and Galloway

For practical advice, ideas and information about exploring Scotland and to book your accommodation:

Tel: 0845 22 55 121* or if calling from outside the UK: + 44 (0) 1506 832121 In Ireland call: 1800 932 510.

*** A £3 booking fee applies to telephone bookings of accommodation.**

info@visitscotland.com
www.visitscotland.com

SOUTH OF SCOTLAND

Blackwaterfoot, Isle of Arran   Map Ref: 1E7

Blackwaterfoot Lodge
Isle of Arran, KA27 8EU
Tel:01770 860202 Fax:01770 860570
Email:mail@blackwaterfoot-lodge.co.uk
Web:www.blackwaterfoot-lodge.co.uk

Situated 50 yards from the picturesque Blackwaterfoot Harbour, this family run hotel provides creature comforts on Arran's windswept West Coast. The warm, small, bistro style restaurant serves home cooked meals and traditional ale from Arran Breweries is featured in the fully licensed bar.

8 rooms, most en-suite, Open Easter-Oct, B&B per person, single from £24.00, double from £30.00.

Brodick, Isle of Arran   Map Ref: 1F7

Dunvegan House
Shore Road, Brodick, Isle of Arran, KA27 8AJ
Tel/Fax:01770 302811
Email:dunveganhouse1@hotmail.com
Web:www.dunveganhouse.co.uk

Superb sea and mountain views, conveniently situated for ferry terminal. Licensed. Dinner using fresh local produce when available. Private parking. Ground floor bedrooms available.

11 rooms, some en-suite, Open Jan-Dec, B&B per person, single from £35.00, double from £35.00. Evening meal £18.00.

Glencloy Farm Guest House
Glen Cloy Road, Brodick, Isle of Arran, KA27 8DA
Tel:01770 302351
Email:glencloyfarm@aol.com
Web:www.SmoothHound.co.uk/hotels/glencloy

A Farmhouse full of character set in a peaceful glen with views of hills and sea. A good base for exploring all that Arran has to offer. You will receive a very warm family welcome from Neil, Ashleigh and Shelley and their chicks, a real home from home. Our 5 rooms are comfortable and individual with TV/Video and access to a video library. Breakfast is served in our cosy drawing room with some of the freshest eggs you will have eaten.

5 rooms, some en-suite, Open Jan-Dec, B&B pppn, single £30.00-50.00, double £27.50-50.00.

Ormidale Hotel
Brodick, Isle of Arran, KA27 8BY
Tel:01770 302293 Fax:01770 302098
Email:reception@ormidale-hotel.co.uk
Web:www.ormidale-hotel.co.uk

Family run Victorian Hotel built in the 1800s, set in mature woodland by the golf course. Home cooked meals for the family served in the conservatory. CAMRA approved. Good pub atmosphere.

7 rooms, all en-suite, Open Apr-Sep, B&B per person, single from £35.00, double from £35.00.

Kildonan, Isle of Arran   Map Ref: 1F7

Breadalbane Hotel
Kildonan, Isle of Arran, KA27 8SE
Tel:01770 820284
Email:yvonne@breadalbanehotel.co.uk
Web:www.breadalbanehotel.co.uk

Situated on the Shore Road in the quiet village of Kildonan. The Breadalbane Hotel enjoys superb views to the islands of Pladda and the famous Ailsa Craig. A warm and friendly atmosphere in this personally run establishment offering freshly prepared food.

5 rooms, all en-suite, Open Jan-Dec, B&B per person, single from £25.00, double from £25.00.

VAT is shown at 17.5%: changes in this rate may affect prices.   *Key to symbols is on back flap.*

Lochranza, Isle of Arran | Map Ref: 1E6

GUEST HOUSE

Apple Lodge
Lochranza, Isle of Arran, KA27 8HJ
Tel/Fax:01770 830229

A charming intimate country house set amidst spectacular scenery where deer and eagles are often sighted. Taste of Scotland.

4 rooms, Open Jan-Dec, B&B per person single from £50.00, double from £36.00.

Ayr | Map Ref: 1G7

GUEST HOUSE

Belmont Guest House
15 Park Circus, Ayr, KA7 2DJ
Tel:01292 265588   Fax:01292 290303
Email:belmontguesthouse@btinternet.com
Web:www.belmontguesthouse.co.uk

Victorian townhouse in a quiet tree lined conservation area, within easy walking distance of town centre. Ground-floor bedrooms, all with ensuite facilities. Guest lounge with extensive book collection. On street and private car parking. Credit/Debit cards are accepted.

5 rooms, all en-suite, Open Jan-Dec excl Xmas/New Year, B&B per person, single from £28.00, double /twin from £26.00, family from £26.00.

Miller House Guest House
36 Miller Road, Ayr, KA7 2AY
Tel:01292 282016 Fax:01292 611903
Email:millerhouseayr@hotmail.com
Web:www.millerhouseayr.co.uk

GUEST HOUSE

Conveniently situated for beach and town centre, which has a vast range of restaurants. Personal attention assured at all times in this family run guest house. Ample private parking to the rear of the house.

7 rooms, en-suite, Open Jan-Dec, B&B per person, single from £25.00, double from £22.50.

The Richmond
38 Park Circus, Ayr, KA7 2DL
Tel:01292 265153   Fax:01292 288816
Email:Richmond38@btopenworld.com
Web:www.richmond-guest-house.co.uk

GUEST HOUSE

Traditional stone built town house with many period features. Easy walking distance to sea front and town centre with all its amenities including a variety of eating establishments. Credit Cards accepted.

6 rooms, 5 en-suite, 1 priv.facilities, Open Jan-Dec, B&B per person, single from £35.00, double from £27.00.

AWAITING GRADING

St Andrews Hotel
7 Prestwick Road, Ayr, KA8 8LD
Tel:01292 263211   Fax:01292 290738
Email:st-andrewshotel@btconnect.com

St Andrews is a family run hotel. The hotel has a lounge bar, public bar, games room and a newly fitted dining room. The hotel is close to Ayr town centre, railway station and Prestwick Airport. Private parking. Golf packages available, member of South Ayrshire Golf.

7 rooms, some en-suite, Open Jan-Dec, B&B per person, single from £30.00, double from £25.00, family from £30.00, BB & Eve.Meal from £35.00.

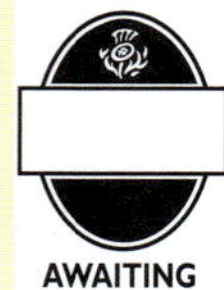

Important: Prices stated are estimates and may be subject to amendments

Ayr	Map Ref: 1G7

★★★

SMALL HOTEL

Savoy Park Hotel
16 Racecourse Road, Ayr, KA7 2UT
Tel:01292 266112 Fax:01292 611488
Email:mail@savoypark.com
Web:www.savoypark.com

15 rooms, all en-suite. Open Jan-Dec, B&B per room, single from £75.00, double from £105.00.

A contemporary, classic Scottish home, recently refurbished to today's quality standards. Ideally located in Ayr's premier residential area. Relax in homely surroundings and experience friendly service. Comfortable, inviting and excellent value.

Castle Douglas, Kirkcudbrightshire	Map Ref: 2A10

Balcary Bay Hotel
**Auchencairn, near Castle Douglas,
Dumfries & Galloway DG7 1QZ
Telephone: 01556 640217/640311
Fax: 01556 640272
e.mail: reservations@balcary-bay-hotel.co.uk
Web: www.balcary-bay-hotel.co.uk**
Family-run country house in three acres of garden. A magnificent and peaceful setting on the shores of the bay. Ideal base for all leisure facilities or a relaxing holiday with warm hospitality, good food and wine.
AA ★★★ ⊛⊛.
One of Scotland's Hotels of Distinction.
★★★★ HOTEL

13881

★★★★

HOTEL

Balcary Bay Hotel
Shore Road, Auchencairn, by Castle Douglas
Kirkcudbrightshire, DG7 1QZ
Tel:01556 640217 Fax:01556 640272
Email:reservations@balcary-bay-hotel.co.uk
Web:www.balcary-bay-hotel.co.uk

20 rooms, all en-suite. Open Feb-Dec, B&B per person, single from £63.00, double from £56.00, BB & Eve.Meal from £85.00.

A lovely country house hotel, with past smuggling associations dating back to 1625. Stands in over 3 acres of garden in a secluded and enchanting situation on the shores of the bay. Cuisine based on local delicacies: Galloway beef, lamb, lobster and of course, Balcary Bay salmon.

★★★

SMALL HOTEL

The Imperial Hotel
35 King Street, Castle Douglas, DG7 1AA
Tel:01556 502086 Fax:01556 503009
Email:david@thegolfhotel.co.uk
Web:www.thegolfhotel.co.uk

12 rooms, all en-suite. Open Jan-Dec excl Xmas/New Year, B&B per person, single £44.00-56.00, double £35.00-37.00.

Privately owned hotel in market town, close to local leisure facilities. Ideal base for touring Galloway. Individual and group golfing holidays arranged. Private secure parking.

VAT is shown at 17.5%: changes in this rate may affect prices.   *Key to symbols is on back flap.*

Colvend, Kirkcudbrightshire — Map Ref: 2A10

★★ SMALL HOTEL

Clonyard House Hotel
Colvend, Dalbeattie, Kircudbrightshire, DG5 4QW
Tel:01556 630372 Fax:01556 630422
Email:info.clonyard@virgin.net
Web:www.clonyardhotel.co.uk

Situated in 7 acres of mature gardens and woodlands, in a secluded position on the Solway Coast between Rockcliffe and Kippford. Choice of modern or traditional rooms, many on the ground floor, with their own private patio.

14 rooms, all en-suite, Open Jan-Dec, B&B per person, single from £40.00, double from £34.00, BB & Eve.Meal from £46.00.

Creetown, Wigtownshire — Map Ref: 1H10

★★ SMALL HOTEL

Ellangowan Hotel
St John Street, Creetown, Dumfries & Galloway, DG8 7JF
Tel:01671 820201 Fax:01671 820226
Email:enquiries@ellangowan.co.uk
Web:www.ellangowan.co.uk

Impressive granite built hotel on the edge of the village Square. Personally run, with emphasis on cuisine using fresh local produce. Adjacent public parking area. Ideally situated for golf, walking, cycling and birdwatching breaks. Special rates for group bookings. Storage and drying facilities.

8 rooms, Open Jan-Dec, B&B per person, single from £36.00, double from £28.00, BB & Eve.Meal from £36.00.

Dalrymple, Ayrshire — Map Ref: 1G7

★★ INN

The Kirkton Inn
1 Main Street, Dalrymple, Ayrshire, KA6 6DF
Tel:01292 560241 Fax:01292 560835
Email:kirkton@cqm.co.uk
Web:www.kirktoninn.co.uk

We organise the PERFECT BREAK for golf, fishing, touring, walking and any other outdoor pursuit. Outstanding Scottish and International food is served in our restaurant and a true Scottish evening may be enjoyed in our Malt Room and bars. Trained and qualified staff ensure the best of Scottish hospitality at all times. Living up to our motto 'There are no strangers here only friends who have never met!' we are sure to exceed your expectations.

11 rooms, all en-suite, Open Jan-Dec. Room only with breakfast, single £45.00, twin £80.00, triple £90.00, family £100.00. Eve.Meal from £16.95.

Dumfries — Map Ref: 2B9

★★★ HOTEL

Cairndale Hotel & Leisure Club
English Street, Dumfries, DG1 2DF
Tel:01387 254111   Fax:01387 250555
Email:info@cairndalehotel.co.uk
Web:www.cairndalehotel.co.uk

Family run hotel in town centre. 91 bedrooms & suites. Extensive leisure facilities. Range of dining options, free parking, WiFi.

91 rooms, all en suite.

★★★ HOTEL

Hetland Hall Hotel
Carrutherstown, Dumfries, DG1 4JX
Tel:01387 840201 Fax:01387 840211
Email:info@hetlandhallhotel.co.uk
Web:www.hetlandhallhotel.co.uk

Elegant 19c country mansion set in 18 acres of sweeping landscaped grounds with fine views over the Solway Firth. Wide range of leisure facilities including indoor pool, sauna and gym. Horse-riding, shooting, golf etc can be arranged nearby. Conference and wedding package facilities available.

32 rooms, all en-suite, Open Jan-Dec, B&B per person, single from £66.00, double from £56.50. Evening meal from £7.50.

Important: Prices stated are estimates and may be subject to amendments

Dumfries

Map Ref: 2B9

Moreig Hotel
67 Annan Road, Dumfries, DG1 3EG
Tel:01387 255524 Fax:01387 267105
Email:enquiries@moreighotel.co.uk
Web:www.moreighotel.co.uk

Originally built as a private residence, this family-run hotel is close to the town centre and has been sympathetically modernised for the comfort of both the Business and Leisure Traveller. Non-residents very welcome. Often used as a base by golf parties.

10 rooms, all en-suite, Open Jan-Dec, B&B per person, single from £45.00, double from £32.50, BB & Eve.Meal from £55.00.

Galashiels, Selkirkshire

Map Ref: 2D6

Kingsknowes Hotel
Selkirk Road, Galashiels, Selkirkshire, TD1 3HY
Tel:01896 758375   Fax:001896 750377
Email:enquiries@kingsknowes.co.uk
Web:www.kingsknowes.co.uk

Family owned and run hotel, built in 1869 overlooking the River Tweed and Eildon Hills. 'A' listed former mansion house with original conservatory and set in its own well tended gardens. Ample parking. Sporting activities can be arranged nearby, golf, fishing, riding, walking, shooting, etc.

12 rooms, all en-suite, Open Jan-Dec, B&B per person, single from £65.00, double from £47.50.

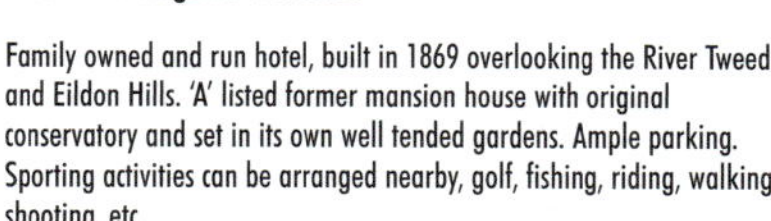

Gatehouse of Fleet, Kirkcudbrightshire

Map Ref: 1H10

Cally Palace Hotel
Gatehouse of Fleet, Kirkcudbrightshire, DG7 2DL
Tel:01557 814341 Fax:01557 814522
Email:info@callypalace.co.uk
Web:www.callypalace.co.uk

Georgian mansion dating from 1763 retaining many original features including moulded ceilings, in 100 acres of forest and parkland. Extensive leisure facilities including swimming pool, private golf course, tennis court and putting green.

55 rooms, all en-suite, Open Feb-Dec, BB & Eve.Meal from £86.00.

Murray Arms Hotel & Restaurant
High Street, Gatehouse of Fleet, Castle Douglas, DG7 2HY
Tel:01557 814207
Email:info@murrayarmshotel.co.uk
Web:www.murrayarmshotel.co.uk

Our Focus is You. A warm, friendly welcome and attentive service awaits all our guests. We serve locally sourced, freshly prepared food all day, every day. At the heart of the Fleet Valley National Scenic Area we are ideally located for walking, mountain biking, bird watching and can offer free fishing and tennis and discounted golf.

12 rooms, all en-suite, Open Jan-Dec, B&B per person £55.00. BB & Eve.Meal from £70.00 per person.

Gretna Green, Dumfriesshire

Map Ref: 2C10

Hunters Lodge Hotel
Annan Road, Gretna, Dumfriesshire, DG16 5DL
Tel:01461 338214
Email:Reception@HuntersLodgeHotel.co.uk
Web:www.HuntersLodgeHotel.co.uk

Closest hotel to the famous Gretna Registration Office. Cross the border into Scotland. Hunters Lodge Hotel is close to major routes. The chef proprietor creates freshly prepared dishes in attractive dining room with its tartan carpet giving a real flavour of Scotland. Staff are warm and welcoming as are the many different malt whiskies in the well stocked bar. Rooms are ensuite and well appointed. Full disabled facilities available.

11 rooms, all en-suite, Open Jan-Dec excl Xmas, B&B per person, single from £50.00, double from £35.00.

VAT is shown at 17.5%: changes in this rate may affect prices.

Key to symbols is on back flap.

Gretna Green, Dumfriesshire — Map Ref: 2C10

LODGE

The Mill
★★★

Grahamshill, Kirkpatrick Fleming, Lockerbie, DG11 3BQ
Tel:01461 800344 Fax:01461 800255
Email:info@themill.co.uk
Web:www.themill.co.uk

Converted farm steading and mill with stone built chalet style, en-suite accommodation. Just off the M74 near Gretna Green. Fully licensed bar/restaurant and function room. Purpose built, churchlike Forge building for marriage ceremonies in attractive grounds.

32 rooms, all en-suite, Open Jan-Dec, B&B per person, single from £55.00, double from £40.00.

by Hawick, Roxburghshire — Map Ref: 2D7

SMALL
HOTEL

Glenteviot Park Hotel
★★★★

Hassendeanburn, by Hawick, Roxburghshire, TD9 8RU
Tel:01450 870660 Fax:01450 870154
Email:enquiries@glenteviotpark.com
Web:www.glenteviotpark.com

Traditional country house hotel located in a rural estate between Hawick and Jedburgh with stunning views across the River Teviot. Luxurious accommodation, excellent cuisine and genuine hospitality are just some of the reasons why discerning guests return time and time again. Available to adult residents only, tranquillity and a sense of calm relaxation is ensured. Golf, walking, horse riding, fishing, cycling and other pursuits.

5 rooms, all en-suite, Open Jan-Dec, B&B per person, single £75.00, double from £48.00, BB & Eve.Meal from £76.00.

nr Irvine, Ayrshire — Map Ref: 1G6

HOTEL

Montgreenan Mansion House Hotel
★★★

Montgreenan Estate, Kilwinning, Ayrshire, KA13 7QZ
Tel:01294 850005 Fax:01294 850397
Email:info@montgreenanhotel.com
Web:www.montgreenanhotel.com

A listed country mansion in 50 acres of garden. Near championship golf courses - Royal Troon, Old Prestwick and Turnberry. Hotel has 3 hole practice golf course, tennis courts, billiard room, bar & restaurant. Ideal base for touring Burns Country, Arran and the Isles.

21 rooms, all en-suite, Open Jan-Dec, B&B per person, single from £65.00, double from £40.00, BB & Eve.Meal from £65.00.

Isle of Whithorn, Wigtownshire — Map Ref: 1H11

INN

Steam Packet Inn
★★

Harbour Row, Isle of Whithorn, Wigtownshire, DG8 8LL
Tel:01988 500334 Fax:01988 500627
Email:steampacketinn@btconnect.com
Web:www.steampacketinn.com

Personally run, on harbour front. Sea fishing. Access to walks, birdwatching and archaeological sites. Children and dogs welcome. Excellent value food with the emphasis on fresh local seafood, meat and game. Separate children's menu. Extensive wine list and range of malt whiskies. Real ales. Traditional Sunday lunches and buffet. Lunches served 12-2pm. Bar meals and restaurant. Conservatory and beer garden. No smoking areas. Open fires.

7 rooms, all en-suite, Open Jan-Dec excl Xmas, B&B per person, single from £30.00, double from £30.00. Evening meals 6.30-9pm.

Jedburgh, Roxburghshire — Map Ref: 2E7

SMALL
HOTEL

Jedforest Hotel
★★★★

Camptown, Jedburgh, Roxburghshire, TD8 6PJ
Tel:01835 840222 Fax:01835 840226
Email:info@jedforesthotel.com
Web:www.jedforesthotel.com

First hotel in Scotland on A68 route. High quality accommodation. All rooms en-suite. Taste of Scotland restaurant. Country setting, in 35 acres of grounds with 1 mile of trout fishing on the Jed Water. Scottish hospitality with a Continental flavour. 2 Red rosettes for cuisine.

12 rooms, all en-suite, Open Jan-Dec, B&B per person, single from £60.00. Dinner B&B from £70.00 per person.

Important: Prices stated are estimates and may be subject to amendments

Kelso, Roxburghshire

Map Ref: 2E6

GUEST HOUSE

Bellevue House
Bowmont Street, Kelso, TD5 7DZ
Tel:01573 224588
Email:bellevuekelso@aol.com
Web:www.bellevuehouse.co.uk

House of character in residential part of the historic town of Kelso. Minutes to the Tweed, town square and Floors Castle. Convenient for a good selection of restaurants, close to race course, ideally situated for local golf course and fishing. Private parking. Non smoking. All rooms ensuite.

6 rooms, all en-suite, Open Jan-Dec excl Xmas/New Year, B&B per person, single from £37.50, double from £30.00.

Largs, Ayrshire

Map Ref: 1F5

HOTEL

Willowbank Hotel
96 Greenock Road, Largs, North Ayrshire, KA30 8PG
Tel:01475 672311 Fax:01475 689027
Email:iaincsmith@btconnect.com

Modern hotel offering bedrooms on ground floor and 1st floor only, in tree-lined location on edge of town. Mid week and weekend entertainment. Bar meals, high teas and dinner available daily.

30 rooms, all en-suite, Open Jan-Dec, B&B per person, single from £60.00, double from £45.00, BB & Eve.Meal from £56.00.

Lauder, Berwickshire

Map Ref: 2D6

SMALL HOTEL

The Lodge, Carfraemill
Lauder, Berwickshire, TD2 6RA
Tel:01578 750750   Fax:01578 750751
Email:enquiries@carfraemill.co.uk
Web:www.carfraemill.co.uk

A former coaching Inn offering friendly hospitality and bistro/restaurant meals. Situated in rural Lauderdale at the junction of the A697/A68. Ideally situated for both Edinburgh and the Borders. Experienced in weddings, business meetings and corporate hospitality.

10 rooms, all en-suite, Open Jan-Dec, B&B per person, single from £60.00, double £40.00-45.00 per person.

Lockerbie, Dumfriesshire

Map Ref: 2C9

SMALL HOTEL

Ravenshill House Hotel
12 Dumfries Road, Lockerbie, Dumfriesshire, DG11 2EF
Tel/Fax:01576 202882
Email:reservations@RavenshillHotelLockerbie.co.uk
Web:www.RavenshillHotelLockerbie.co.uk

A family run hotel set in 2.5 acres of garden in a quiet residential area, yet convenient for town centre and M6/M74. With a chef proprietor the hotel enjoys a reputation for good food, comfortable accommodation and friendly service. Weekend, short and golfing breaks.

8 rooms, most en-suite, Open Jan-Dec, B&B per person, single from £48.00, double from £37.50, BB & Eve.Meal from £50.00.

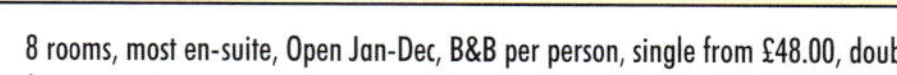

Melrose, Roxburghshire

Map Ref: 2D6

SMALL HOTEL

Burts Hotel
Market Square, Melrose, Roxburghshire, TD6 9PL
Tel:01896 822285   Fax:01896 822870
Email:burtshotel@aol.com
Web:www.burtshotel.co.uk

Family owned and run town house hotel - great bistro food and fine dining. 2 AA Rosette restaurant. AA Pub of the Year for Scotland 2005.

20 rooms, all en-suite, Open Jan-Dec, B&B per person, single from £55.00, double from £53.00, BB & Eve.Meal from £60.00-90.00.

VAT is shown at 17.5%: changes in this rate may affect prices.

Key to symbols is on back flap.

Melrose, Roxburghshire   Map Ref: 2D6

★★★

**SMALL
HOTEL**

The Townhouse Hotel

Market Square, Melrose, Roxburghshire, TD6 9PQ
Tel:01896 822645   Fax:01896 823474
Email:enquiries@thetownhousemelrose.co.uk
Web:www.thetownhousemelrose.co.uk

Situated in the heart of historic Borders town, this delightful family run hotel offers excellent food and wines and best local produce. Eleven well appointed bedrooms. Ideally located for fishers, walkers and cyclists (facilities available). Direct access to St Cuthberts and Southern Upland Ways.

11 rooms, all en-suite, Open Jan-Dec, B&B per person, single from £65.00, double from £48.00, BB & Eve.Meal from £60.00.

★★★

HOTEL

Waverley Castle Hotel

Skirmish Hill, Waverley Road, Melrose, TD6 9AA
Tel:01942 824824
Email:reservations@WAshearings.com
Web:www.WAshearingsholidays.com

Entertainment every night.

81 rooms, all en-suite, Open Feb-Dec, B&B per person, double from £35.00.

---

by Melrose, Roxburghshire   Map Ref: 2D6

★★★★

HOTEL

Dryburgh Abbey Hotel

St Boswells, Melrose, Scottish Borders, TD6 0RQ
Tel:01835 822261   Fax:01835 823945
Email:enquiries@dryburgh.co.uk
Web:www.dryburgh.co.uk

Country house hotel on banks of River Tweed overlooked by 12c Dryburgh Abbey. Ideal base for fishing, shooting or exploring this historic area. Indoor pool, putting green and mountain bikes, trout rights on the Tweed.

38 rooms, all en-suite, Open Jan-Dec, B&B per person, single from £60.00, BB & Eve.Meal from £72.00 Single.

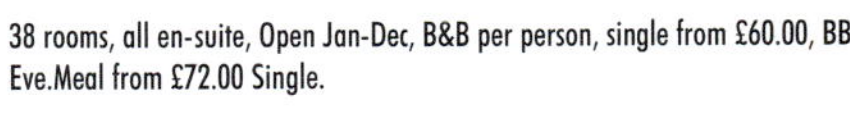

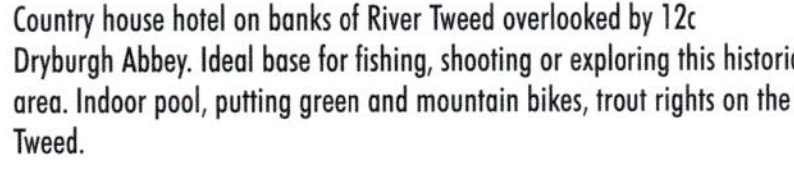

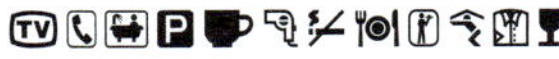

★★★★

B&B

Fauhope House

Gattonside, Melrose, Roxburghshire, TD6 9LU
Tel:01896 823184
Email:fauhope@bordernet.co.uk

Elegant Edwardian house in extensive grounds overlooking River Tweed, Melrose Abbey and the Eildon Hills - ten minutes walk to Melrose over Georgian footbridge.

3 rooms, all en-suite, Open Jan-Dec excl Xmas/New Year, B&B per person, single from £55.00, double from £40.00.

★★★★★

B&B

Whitehouse

St Boswells, Roxburghshire, TD6 OED
Tel:01573 460343
Email:tyrer.whitehouse@lineone.net
Web:www.aboutscotland.com/south/whitehouse.html

Large country house decorated to a high standard, luxurious bedrooms and spacious bathrooms. Full of character, relaxed atmosphere, log fires. Delicious dinners using much of our own or local produce. Kelso, Melrose and Scott's View are all within 10 minutes drive.

3 rooms, all en-suite, Open Jan-Dec, B&B per person, double from £42.00, BB & Eve.Meal from £66.00.

Important: Prices stated are estimates and may be subject to amendments

SOUTH OF SCOTLAND

Moffat, Dumfriesshire

Map Ref: 2B8

★★★

SMALL HOTEL

Annandale Arms Hotel
High Street, Moffat, Dumfriesshire, DG10 9HF
Tel:01683 220013 Fax:01683 221395
Email:vs@annandalearmshotel.co.uk
Web:www.annandalearmshotel.co.uk

Imposing Georgian hotel (1760) set on the tree lined High Street of Moffat. Renowned for good food, hospitality and relaxed atmosphere. Bar and restaurant. Lounge. Private car park. Pets welcome, no extra charge.

11 rooms, all en-suite, Open Jan-Dec excl Christmas & Boxing Day, B&B per person, single from £50.00, double from £40.00.

★★

GUEST HOUSE

Barnhill Springs Country Guest House
Moffat, Dumfries & Galloway, DG10 9QS
Tel:01683 220580
Email:graybarnhill@bushinternet.com

Barnhill Springs is an early Victorian country house standing in its own grounds overlooking upper Annandale. It is a quiet family run guest house situated ½ a mile from the A74/M at the Moffat junction no.15. Barnhill Springs is ideally situated as a centre for touring Southern Scotland, for walking and cycling on the Southern Upland Way or for a relaxing overnight stop for holiday makers heading North or South. AA 3 Diamonds.

5 rooms, Open Jan-Dec, B&B per person, single from £26.00, double from £26.00, BB & Eve.Meal from £45.00.

★★★

SMALL HOTEL

Black Bull Hotel
Churchgate, Moffat, Dumfriesshire, DG10 9EG
Tel:01683 220206 Fax:01683 220483
Email:hotel@blackbullmoffat.co.uk
Web:www.blackbullmoffat.co.uk

An historic Coaching Inn. Dating from 1560, steeped in 'Rabbie Burns' history, and refurbished to modern standards. All bedrooms en-suite and ground floor and annexe rooms available. Retaining much of its character it offers traditional Scottish Hospitality with friendly staff, and a warm informal atmosphere.

13 rooms, all en-suite, Open Jan-Dec, B&B per person, single from £45.00, double from £33.50.

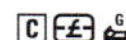

★★★

SMALL HOTEL

Buccleuch Arms Hotel
High Street, Moffat, Dumfriesshire, DG10 9ET
Tel:01683 220003 Fax:01683 221291
Email:enquiries@buccleucharmshotel.com
Web:www.buccleucharmshotel.com

Picturesque Coaching Inn with award winning restaurants. One traditional with a harpist playing on weekends. The other cosy with a real fire. Centrally situated, an excellent base for exploring the Borders. Glasgow/Edinburgh 1 hours drive.

14 rooms, all en-suite, Open Jan-Dec, B&B per person, single from £50.00, double from £40.00, BB & Eve.Meal from £53.00.

★★★

GUEST HOUSE

Buchan Guest House
Beechgrove, Moffat, Dumfriesshire, DG10 9RS
Tel:01683 220378
Email:mailto:buchanguesthouse@moffatbroadband.net
Web:www.buchanguesthouse.co.uk

Victorian house in quiet residential area, close to centre of Moffat. Ideal base for touring.

8 rooms, most en-suite, Open Jan-Dec excl Xmas, B&B per person, single from £30.00, double from £25.00.

VAT is shown at 17.5%: changes in this rate may affect prices.

Key to symbols is on back flap.

Moffat, Dumfriesshire | Map Ref: 2B8

★★

SMALL HOTEL

The Famous Star Hotel

44 High Street, Moffat, DG10 9EF
Tel:01683 220156 Fax:01683 221524
Email:info@famousstarhotel.co.uk
Web:www.famousstarhotel.com

Family run hotel of 21 years. Warm welcome with great homecooking. Restaurant and two bars. Real Ales. Very central for Glasgow/Edinburgh. Great for walking. Only 2 miles from motorway. The hotel only 20ft wide as mentioned in the 'Guiness Book of Records'.

8 rooms, all ensuite, Open Jan-Dec, B&B per room, single en-suite £50.00, twin/double en-suite £60.00, family room from £70.00.

★★★★

GUEST HOUSE

Hartfell House

Hartfell Crescent, Moffat, Dumfriesshire, DG10 9AL
Tel:01683 220153
Email:enquiries@hartfellhouse.co.uk
Web:www.hartfellhouse.co.uk

An elegant Victorian family run guest house with spacious, comfortable rooms in a quiet location only four minutes walk from High Street.

8 rooms, all en-suite, Open Mar-Dec excl Xmas, B&B per person, single from £35.00, double from £30.00.

★★★

SMALL HOTEL

Moffat House Hotel

High Street, Moffat, DG10 9HL
Tel:01683 220039 Fax:01683 221288
Email:moffat@talk21.com
Web:www.moffathouse.co.uk

18c Adam mansion with magnificent staircase, set in own grounds with country views to rear, yet in the centre of the award winning 'Scotland in Bloom' village of Moffat. All rooms en suite, ground floor rooms available including a self contained cottage. Lounge food plus fine dining in Hopetoun Restaurant.

20 ensuite rooms, Open Jan-Dec, B&B per person, single £65.00-70.00, double £50.00-58.00.

★★★★

RESTAURANT WITH ROOMS

Well View Hotel

Ballplay Road, Moffat, Dumfriesshire, DG10 9JU
Tel:01683 220184
Email:info@wellview.co.uk
Web:www.wellview.co.uk

Mid Victorian house converted to comfortable, family run hotel. Overlooking town and surrounding hills, with its own large garden. Innovative and original use of fresh local ingredients, in our attractive award winning restaurant.

3 rooms, all en-suite, Open Jan-Dec, B&B per person, single from £70.00, double from £55.00, BB & Eve.Meal from £85.00.

Newton Stewart, Wigtownshire | Map Ref: 1G10

★★★★

SMALL HOTEL

Kirroughtree House

Newton Stewart, Wigtownshire, DG8 6AN
Tel:01671 402141 Fax:01671 402425
Email:info@kirroughtreehouse.co.uk
Web:www.kirroughtreehouse.co.uk

Georgian mansion (1719c) in 8 acres of landscaped gardens. Attentive personal service coupled with excellent standards of cuisine are the hallmark of this hotel. Golf available locally and at sister hotel at Gatehouse-Of-Fleet.

17 rooms, all en-suite, Open Feb-Dec, BB & Eve.Meal from £85.00.

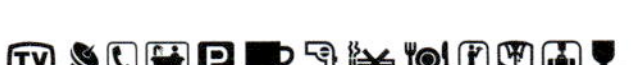

Important: Prices stated are estimates and may be subject to amendments

Peebles

Map Ref: 2C6

★★★
HOTEL

Park Hotel
Innerleithen Road, Peebles, EH45 8BA
Tel:01721 720451   Fax:01721 723510
Email:reserve@parkpeebles.co.uk
Web:www.parkpeebles.co.uk

Quiet and comfortable, with extensive gardens and fine hill views. Ideal touring centre, and only 22 miles (35kms) from Edinburgh.

24 rooms, all en-suite, Open Jan-Dec, B&B per person, single from £59.50, double from £53.50.

Portpatrick, Wigtownshire

Map Ref: 1F10

★★★★
HOTEL

Fernhill Hotel
Heugh Road, Portpatrick, Wigtownshire, DG9 8TD
Tel:01776 810220 Fax:01776 810596
Email:info@fernhillhotel.co.uk
Web:www.fernhillhotel.co.uk

Family run hotel in elevated position with panoramic views over picturesque Portpatrick Harbour. Seafood restaurant with local lobster a speciality. AA Rosette for food. Golf course only 400 yards from hotel. Accommodation available in main hotel, garden house and stables house.

33 rooms, all en-suite, Open Feb-Dec, BB & Eve.Meal from £57.00.

★★★
SMALL
HOTEL

The Waterfront Hotel & Bistro
North Crescent, Portpatrick, DG9 8SX
Tel:01776 810800 Fax:01776 810850
Email:waterfronthotel@aol.com
Web:www.waterfronthotel.co.uk

Dating originally from the 18th Century, this small hotel with popular bar and bistro, has been updated to give a contemporary style. Overlooking the picturesque harbour of Portpatrick, the bedrooms and ensuites are restricted in size but most are sea-facing. Ample free, street parking supplements the small private car park.

8 rooms, all en-suite, Open Jan-Dec, B&B per person, single from £63.00, double from £35.00, BB & Eve.Meal from £55.00.

Prestwick, Ayrshire

Map Ref: 1G7

★★★
GUEST
HOUSE

Fernbank Guest House
213 Main Street, Prestwick, Ayrshire, KA9 1LH
Tel:01292 475027   Fax:01292 678944
Email:stay@fernbank.co.uk
Web:www.fernbank.co.uk

Modernised Edwardian villa near beach and local sports facilities. 0.5 mile (1km) from Glasgow Prestwick Airport and Prestwick town rail station.

7 rooms, all en-suite, Open Jan-Dec excl Xmas/New Year, B&B per person, single from £25.00, double from £25.00.

★★★
HOTEL

Parkstone Hotel
Central Esplanade, Prestwick, Ayrshire, KA9 1QN
Tel:01292 477286 Fax:01292 477671
Email:info@parkstonehotel.co.uk
Web:www.parkstonehotel.co.uk

On the seafront overlooking a sandy beach on the Firth of Clyde. Close to many good golf courses and local amenities, and the town centre. Ideally situated for railway station and Prestwick airport.

30 rooms, all en-suite, Open Jan-Dec, B&B per person, single from £49.00, double from £43.00.

VAT is shown at 17.5%: changes in this rate may affect prices.   *Key to symbols is on back flap.*

Stranraer, Wigtownshire — Map Ref: 1F10

HOTEL

North West Castle Hotel
Stranraer, Wigtownshire, DG9 8EH
Tel:01776 704413 Fax:01776 702646
Email:info@northwestcastle.co.uk
Web:www.northwestcastle.com

North West Castle is the former home of Sir John Ross, the Arctic explorer and for 41 years has been a family owned and run hotel. Many bedrooms have views over Loch Ryan. Many facilities available including a curling rink (October - April), leisure centre including swimming pool and games room, conference and function rooms. A warm Scottish welcome guaranteed. The hotel is licenced as a venue for a civil wedding ceremony.

72 rooms, all en-suite, Open Jan-Dec, B&B per person, double £49.00-59.00, BB & Eve.Meal from £59.00 pppn double.

Swinton, Berwickshire — Map Ref: 2E6

**RESTAURANT
WITH ROOMS**

The Wheatsheaf
Swinton, Berwickshire, TD11 3JJ
Tel:01890 860257 Fax:01890 860688
Email:reception@wheatsheaf-swinton.co.uk
Web:www.wheatsheaf-swinton.co.uk

Award winning restaurant with rooms, personally run by owners. Emphasis on hospitality and customer care and high class cuisine using local produce creatively. Convenient location for touring the Borders. All rooms en-suite. Open 7 days for lunch and dinner. View all rooms and facilities on web site virtual tours.

10 rooms, (6 dbl, 4 superior kings), all en-suite, Open Jan-Dec, B&B per person, single occupancy from £69.00, double occupancy from £53.00.

Troon, Ayrshire — Map Ref: 1G7

HOTEL

Piersland House Hotel
Craigend Road, Troon, Ayrshire, KA10 6HD
Tel:01292 314747 Fax:01292 315613
Email:reservations@piersland.co.uk
Web:www.piersland.co.uk

Unique and historic house built for Sir Alexander Walker with 15 cottage suites set in beautifully landscaped grounds and situated on the Southwest Coast - a haven for golfers. Family owned hotel. Many historic attractions including Robert Burns Cottage and Culzean Castle nearby.

30 rooms, all en-suite, Open Jan-Dec, B&B per person, single from £67.50, double from £62.00, BB & Eve.Meal from £87.50.

Turnberry, Ayrshire — Map Ref: 1G8

**INTERNATIONAL
RESORT HOTEL**

The Westin Turnberry Resort
Turnberry, Ayrshire, KA26 9LT
Tel:01655 331000 Fax:01655 331706
Email:turnberry@westin.com
Web:www.westin.com/turnberry

Located just 50 minutes from Glasgow, this world famous resort offers Open Championship golf, award winning spa facilities and exhilarating outdoor pursuits.

219 rooms, all en-suite, Open Jan-Dec excl Xmas, B&B per room, single from £135.00, double from £159.00.

Important: Prices stated are estimates and may be subject to amendments

Main image: View from Calton Hill **Bottom left:** Royal Mile
Bottom middle: Rosslyn Chapel **Bottom right:** Linlithgow Palace

EDINBURGH AND LOTHIANS

Each year, more than four million visitors make their way to Scotland's capital city. Why? Well, to put it simply, it is one of the world's finest cities.

From the first celebratory drink at the biggest New Year street party in the world to counting down the seconds to midnight a busy 365 days later, Edinburgh is alive with activity.

Take a look up from Princes Street to Edinburgh Castle any day of the week (in any month of the year) and you'll see hundreds of happy faces peering over the ramparts, looking down on the bustle below. Well over a million tourists a year call into the Castle to explore one of the most famous landmarks on Earth.

Roof terrace at Oloroso, Edinburgh

Edinburgh is a thriving modern capital. With streets steeped in history and a myriad of festivals, events and attractions to keep you entertained, it is sure to leave you longing for more.

Many then set off down the Esplanade and into the Royal Mile touching history with every step they take on the cobbled streets that lead to the Palace of Holyroodhouse and the bold architectural statement that is the new Scottish Parliament building at Holyrood. If you're walking the Mile in Festival season, you'll find the streets thronging with revellers as hundreds of performers try to entice audiences with scenes from their shows staged right there in the street.

Although the excitement of modern life is never far away in the shops, cafés and bars, the Old Town's fascinating history is impossible to ignore. Every one of the tightly packed buildings has earned its place in history. Edinburgh's ghosts whisper in the closes: grave robbers and thieves rubbing shoulders with poets, philosophers, kings and queens – each conjured up and colourfully interpreted in the museums, exhibitions and visitor attractions you'll pass along the way. Tragedy, comedy, horror, intrigue. Plots, schemes, enterprise, despair – Edinburgh has known it all. So it is perhaps fitting that these days the city is home

to the biggest Arts festival on the planet, itself a fusion of festivals; The International Festival, The Fringe, Film, Jazz and Book Festivals (not to mention the Military Tattoo) all bumping into each other in four or so hectic weeks in August and early September each year.

But the show never stops in Edinburgh. Its theatres, cinemas, clubs, museums and galleries always have something interesting going on and you'll wish you had more time to do it all.

Though a visit to Edinburgh can be a hectic whirlwind of arts and culture, it doesn't have to be that way. That's the beauty of this special place. You could spend a quiet sunny day in the Royal Botanic Garden marvelling at thousands of species of plants exquisitely arranged and cared for. Or you could climb Arthur's Seat and survey the city and the Lothians beyond. It's incredible really - a great, 650 acre wildscape of extinct volcano, lochs and crags sitting right in the middle of town like a sleeping lion with a Palace and a Parliament at its feet.

What's On?

Ceilidh Culture
24 March - 15 April 2007
A vibrant celebration of
traditional Scottish arts.
www.ceilidhculture.co.uk

**Edinburgh International
Science Festival**
2 - 15 April 2007
Quell the curiosity of inquiring
minds.
www.sciencefestival.co.uk

Mary King's Ghost Fest
11 - 20 May 2007
Explore Edinburgh's haunted
places.
www.edinburghghostfest.com

Edinburgh Festival Fringe
5 - 27 August 2007
The largest arts festival on the
planet.
www.edfringe.com

**Edinburgh International
Festival**
10 August - 2 September 2007
The very best of opera, theatre,
music and dance.
www.eif.co.uk

**East Lothian Food &
Drink Festival**
27 - 30 September 2007
Food and entertainment for all
ages.
www.foodanddrink
eastlothian.com

Edinburgh's Christmas
23 November -
24 December 2007
Edinburgh becomes a winter
wonderland.
www.edinburghs
christmas.com

Edinburgh's Hogmanay
29 December 2007 -
1 January 2008
The world's favourite place to
celebrate Hogmanay.
www.edinburghs
hogmanay.com

Escape to the sandy beaches and seaside resorts of the Lothians, where you can soothe the soul and blow away the cobwebs.

What you will see from the top is that Edinburgh is a very green city with wonderful parks and gardens. You'll also see the boats on the Forth bringing their wares, as they have done for many centuries, to the busy port of Leith which these days is as vibrant as ever and renowned for its wonderful selection of bars and restaurants. You'll see the cityscapes that make for perfect picture postcards, you'll see the church spires, the monuments, the hills that shape the city, the Pentlands to the south, the Forth Bridges to the west and, to the east, The Bass Rock and North Berwick Law.

While the city itself could keep you fascinated forever, it is well worth getting out and about in the Lothians. Take a trip down the coast to places like Aberlady, Gullane, Longniddry, Dirleton, North Berwick and Dunbar. Play golf on courses that date back to the days when the game was being invented, watch the waders scuttle along the shore on a beautiful sandy beach. Or you could go on a boat trip round the Bass Rock to spot gannets and puffins, jump on a bike and cycle for miles along the Union Canal towpath, visit Roslin Glen and take in the mysterious chapel, head for Linlithgow and its ruined Palace or bet on a thrilling day out at the Musselburgh races.

So what is it you'd like to do on your visit to Edinburgh and the Lothians? And where would you like to stay? From five star opulence at the Balmoral, Sheraton or Caledonian to the ultra-stylish new boutique hotels around the New Town, to seaside guesthouses, family-run country houses and lots of special places throughout the city and beyond, there's so much to choose from in an area that will continually delight and inspire you, it will leave you longing for more.

The Glen Golf Club, North Berwick

Tourist Information Centres

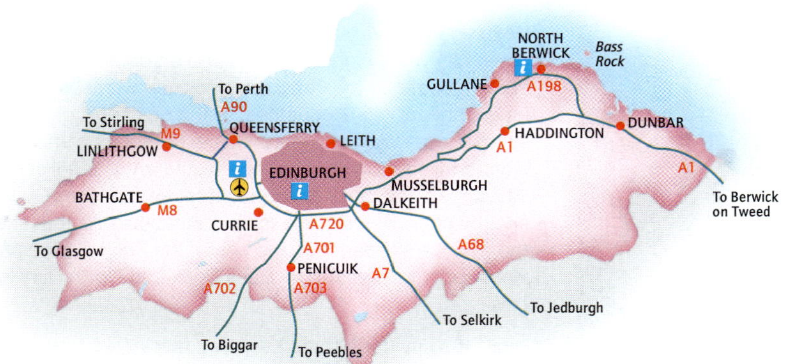

Please refer to the maps on pages xii-xviii for the locations of establishments appearing in the main advertising section of this guide.
Only year-round Tourist Information Centres are indicated.

The Royal Mile during the Festival, Edinburgh

Dunbar	143A High Street	0845 22 55 121	Apr-Oct
Edinburgh	Edinburgh & Scotland Information Centre, 3 Princes Street	0845 22 55 121	Jan-Dec
Edinburgh Airport	Main concourse	0845 22 55 121	Jan-Dec
Linlithgow	Burgh Halls, The Cross	0845 22 55 121	Apr-Oct
Newtongrange	Scottish Mining Museum	0845 22 55 121	Easter-Oct
North Berwick	Quality Street	0845 22 55 121	Jan-Dec
Old Craighall	Old Craighall Service Area (A1)	0845 22 55 121	Apr-Oct

For practical advice, ideas and information about exploring Scotland and to book your accommodation:

Tel: 0845 22 55 121* or if calling from outside the UK: + 44 (0) 1506 832121. In Ireland call: 1800 932 510.

* A £3 booking fee applies to telephone bookings of accommodation.

info@visitscotland.com
www.visitscotland.com

Broxburn, West Lothian — Map Ref: 2B5

★★★★

GUEST HOUSE

Bankhead Farm
Dechmont, Broxburn, West Lothian, EH52 6NB
Tel:01506 811209 Fax:01506 811815
Email:bankheadbb@aol.com
Web:www.bankheadfarm.com

Perfectly placed for Edinburgh and airport. Stay in a traditional farmhouse with modern en-suite bedrooms. Panoramic views of Scottish countryside.

7 rooms, all en-suite, Open Jan-Dec excl Xmas, B&B per person, single from £40.00, double from £35.00.

Dunbar, East Lothian — Map Ref: 2E4

★★

GUEST HOUSE

Springfield Guest House
Belhaven Road, Dunbar, East Lothian, EH42 1NH
Tel:01368 862502
Email:smeed@tesco.net

An elegant 19c villa with attractive garden. Family run with home-cooking. Ground floor room with private bathrooms available. Ideal base for golfing and touring East Lothian, Edinburgh and the Borders.

5 rooms, Open Jan-Nov excl Xmas/New Year, B&B per person, single from £25.00, double from £25.00.

Edinburgh — Map Ref: 2C5

★★★

GUEST HOUSE

Aaron Guest House
16 Hartington Gardens, Edinburgh, EH10 4LD
Tel:0131 229 6459 Fax:0131 228 5807
Email:info@aaronguesthouse.co.uk
Web:www.aaronguesthouse.co.uk

Quiet 18th Century home with private car parking within walking distance of Edinburgh City Centre. Come and enjoy our hospitality.

8 rooms, all en-suite, Open Jan-Dec, B&B per person, single from £30.00, double from £20.00.

Important: Prices stated are estimates and may be subject to amendments

AARON LODGE GUEST HOUSE

128 Old Dalkeith Road, Edinburgh, EH16 4SD
Telephone: 0131 664 2755 Fax: 0131 672 2236
e.mail: dot@baigan.freeserve.co.uk
Web: www.aaronlodgeedinburgh.com

The **Aaron Lodge** is a warm, friendly, family run guest house located on the south side of the city with easy access to the city centre and all its amenities, approximately 5 minutes away by bus or car. **Aaron Lodge** is the nearest guest house to the Edinburgh Royal Infirmary which is a few minutes walk away. All rooms are furnished to a very high standard, with en-suite facilities, hospitality trays and Sky TV. We also have a large private car park.

**Aaron Lodge –
high quality at low prices**

34321

★★★

**GUEST
HOUSE**

Aaron Lodge Guest House
128 Old Dalkeith Road, Edinburgh, EH16 4SD
Tel:0131 664 2755 Fax:0131 672 2236
Email:dot@baigan.freeserve.co.uk
Web:www.aaronlodgeedinburgh.com

Ideal base for sightseeing many of this city's historic attractions. Some ground floor en suite annexe accommodation. On main bus route to city centre. Close to Craigmillar Castle. Within walking distance of Royal Edinburgh Infirmary.

9 rooms, all ensuite, Open Jan-Dec, B&B per person single from £35.00, double from £22.50, Family room available.

★★★

**GUEST
HOUSE**

Adria House
11-12 Royal Terrace, Edinburgh, EH7 5AB
Tel:0131 556 7875   Fax:0131 558 7782
Email:manager@adriahouse.co.uk
Web:www.adriahouse.co.uk

Friendly, family-run guest house in peaceful and historical Georgian terrace. Relaxed and informal, walking distance from all major attractions.

23 rooms, some en-suite, Open Feb-Nov, B&B per person, single from £35.00, double from £27.50.

★★★

**GUEST
HOUSE**

Afton Guest House
1 Hartington Gardens, Edinburgh, EH10 4LD
Tel/Fax:0131 229 1019
Email:info@aftonguesthouse.co.uk
Web:www.aftonguesthouse.co.uk

Newly refurbished end terraced Victorian house in residential area but near main bus route to city centre. Variety of restaurants nearby. Ensuite and private facilities throughout.

7 rooms, some en-suite, Open Jan-Dec, B&B per person, single from £25.00, double from £25.00.

VAT is shown at 17.5%: changes in this rate may affect prices.   Key to symbols is on back flap.

| **Edinburgh** | **Map Ref: 2C5** |

★★★

SMALL HOTEL

A Haven Townhouse
180 Ferry Road, Edinburgh, EH6 4NS
Tel:0131 554 6559 Fax:0131 554 5252
Email:reservations@a-haven.co.uk
Web:www.a-haven.co.uk

Privately owned Townhouse Hotel. Near city centre and on main bus route. Scottish welcome and hospitality including a hearty Highland breakfast. Variety of restaurants nearby or dinner by prior arrangement. 2 new high quality bedrooms in garden annexe.

14 rooms, all en-suite, Open Jan-Dec excl Xmas, B&B per person, single from £30.00, double from £30.00.

★★★★

GUEST HOUSE

Allison House
17 Mayfield Gardens, Edinburgh, EH9 2AX
Tel:0131 667 8049 Fax:0131 667 5001
Email:info@allisonhousehotel.com
Web:www.allisonhousehotel.com

On main route into the city, convenient for all attractions, private parking and regular bus service. All rooms double glazed. One room has private bathroom.

11 rooms, 10 en-suite, Open Jan-Dec, B&B per person, single from £40.00, double/twin from £30.00.

★★★

GUEST HOUSE

Alloway Guest House
96 Pilrig Street, Edinburgh, EH6 5AY
Tel:0131 554 1786
Email:alloway@eh65ay.fsnet.co.uk
Web:www.allowayguesthouse.co.uk

Family run Victorian guest house, within easy reach of the city centre. Unrestricted street parking. Short stroll to Leith Walk with its many restaurants, theatres etc. Frequent bus service to city centre.

6 rooms, some en-suite, 1 room with priv.facilites (twin). Open Jan-Dec, B&B per person, single from £25.00, double/twin from £28.00.

★★

GUEST HOUSE

Alness Guest House
27 Pilrig Street, Edinburgh, EH6 5AN
Tel:0131 554 1187
Email:jenny@ness.wanadoo.co.uk
Web:www.alness.blueyonder.co.uk

Friendly family run guest house. On main bus route, 1 mile (2kms) from Princes Street and all its attractions. Close to Port of Leith and Royal Yacht Britannia.

6 rooms, some en-suite, Open Jan-Dec excl Xmas, B&B per person, single from £23.00, double from £20.00.

★★★★ UP TO
★★★★★

SERVICED APARTMENTS

Apartments Royal
50/35 North Bridge, Edinburgh, EH1 1QN
Tel:0131 554 1301 Fax:0131 553 2942
Email:reservations@apartmentsroyal.com
Web:www.apartmentsroyal.com

The finest selection of quality luxury apartments in the historic Royal Mile of Edinburgh. All within walking distance to Princes Street and all attractions. Make your short break to Edinburgh memorable whilst enjoying the luxury, privacy and comfort these lovely apartments provide.

4 Luxury apartments in central Edinburgh. Open Jan-Dec. Sleeps 4-8, 1-4 bedrooms. Minimum let 1 night. Price per night: from £80.00-£275.00.

Important: Prices stated are estimates and may be subject to amendments

Apex Hotels, Edinburgh

31-35 Grassmarket, Edinburgh EH1 2HS
Telephone: 0845 365 0000   Fax: 0131 666 5128
e.mail: edinburgh.reservations@apexhotels.co.uk
Web: www.apexhotels.co.uk

Apex International Hotel overlooking Edinburgh Castle and the historic Old Town. Contemporary chic bedrooms, many with views of the Castle. Heights Rooftop Restaurant for the best Castle and skyline views. Metro Brasserie for relaxed dining. Yu Spa leisure facilities with pool, gym and tropicarium, available to residents of Apex Hotels.
Apex City Hotel, next to the Apex International, chic bedrooms equipped with widescreen TV's and CD/DVD players. Agua Restaurant offering uplifting cuisine. **Apex European Hotel**, perfectly located at the West End, Metro West End Bar offering classic and contemporary dishes.

65838

★★★★

HOTEL

Apex International Hotel

31/35 Grassmarket, Edinburgh, EH1 2HS
Tel:0845 365 0000 Fax:0131 666 5128
Email:edinburgh.reservations@apexhotels.co.uk
Web:www.apexhotels.co.uk

Modern hotel in city centre with views towards Edinburgh Castle. Roof top restaurant with spectacular views of the castle. Private car parking. Ideal location for visitors to city without a car.

171 rooms, all en-suite, Open Jan-Dec, B&B per person, single from £89.00, double from £49.00, BB & Eve.Meal from £66.00 pppn.

Ardenlee Guest House

9 Eyre Place, Edinburgh EH3 5ES. Telephone: 0131 556 2838
e.mail: info@ardenlee.co.uk Web: www.ardenlee.co.uk

Beautiful Grade 'B' listed Victorian town house in the very centre of Edinburgh (off Dundas Street). Only half a mile from Princes Street and within easy walking distance of all main attractions, train and bus stations. Family run offering a warm welcome, spacious comfortable rooms and a fully cooked breakfast.

12535

★★★

GUEST HOUSE

Ardenlee Guest House

9 Eyre Place, Edinburgh, EH3 5ES
Tel:0131 556 2838 Fax:0131 557 0937
Email:info@ardenlee.co.uk
Web:www.ardenlee.co.uk

Personally run terraced guest house, in New Town approximately 0.5 mile (1km) from Princes Street and city centre. Ideal touring base. Non-smoking house. Variety of shops and restaurants nearby. Most rooms en-suite.

9 rooms, some en-suite, Open Jan-Dec, B&B per person, single from £27.50, double from £27.50.

VAT is shown at 17.5%: changes in this rate may affect prices.

Key to symbols is on back flap.

Edinburgh

Map Ref: 2C5

GUEST HOUSE

Ardgarth Guest House

1 St Mary's Place, Portobello, Edinburgh, EH15 2QF
Tel:0131 669 3021   Fax:0131 468 1221
Email:stay@ardgarth.com
Web:www.ardgarth.com

Comfortable accommodation in friendly guest house. Close to sea. Special diets catered for, full ensuite disabled facilities, with roll-in showers. French spoken. On street parking available.

9 rooms, some en-suite, Open Jan-Dec excl Xmas, B&B per person, single from £17.00, double from £17.00.

GUEST HOUSE

Ardleigh Guest House

260 Ferry Road, Edinburgh, EH5 3AN
Tel:0131 552 1833   Fax:0131 552 4951
Email:info@ardleighhouse.com
Web:www.ardleighhouse.com

Panoramic views of the city and the castle, on the bus routes to the centre - 1.5 miles. Free parking.

7 rooms, 5 en-suite, Open all year, B&B per person, single from £25.00, double/twin from £22.50.

SMALL HOTEL

Ardmillan Hotel

9-10 Ardmillan Terrace, Edinburgh, EH11 2JW
Tel:0131 337 9588   Fax:0131 346 1895
Email:hotelardmillan@hotmail.com
Web:www.ardmillanhotel.com

Small family run hotel, with recently refurbished popular bar restaurant. Located on bus route to city centre and a short walk to Princes Street. Murrayfield Leisure and Tynecastle Stadium are close-by.

10 rooms, mostly en-suite, Open all year, B&B single from £39.00, double room from £59.00. Eve.meal 3 course from £10.00.

GUEST HOUSE

Ashgrove House

12 Osborne Terrace, Edinburgh, EH12 5HG
Tel:0131 337 5014   Fax:0131 313 5043
Email:info@theashgrovehouse.com
Web:www.theashgrovehouse.com

Family run guest house on main road leading into Edinburgh City, from the airport. Non smoking house, private parking, within easy walking distance to Princes Street and E.I. Conference Centre. Also close to Haymarket railway station.

7 rooms, some en-suite, Open Jan-Dec, B&B per person, single £35.00-60.00, double £33.00-50.00.

GUEST HOUSE

Ashlyn Guest House

42 Inverleith Row, Edinburgh, EH3 5PY
Tel/Fax:0131 552 2954
Email:reservations@ashlyn-edinburgh.com
Web:www.ashlyn-edinburgh.com

Semi-detached Georgian family home, only 5 minutes walk from the beautiful Botanical Gardens. This listed building retains many original features with ornate cornicing and period fire places. 20 minute walk to Princes Street and the Castle with frequent bus service on the door step. Unrestricted free street parking nearby.

8 rooms, most en-suite/private bathrooms. Open Jan-Dec excl Xmas, B&B single from £30.00, double from £60.00.

Important: Prices stated are estimates and may be subject to amendments

Map Ref: 2C5

ROCCO FORTE'S THE BALMORAL

1 Princes Street, Edinburgh EH2 2EQ.
Telephone: 0870 460 7040 Fax: 0131 557 8740
e.mail: reservations.balmoral@roccofortehotels.com
Web: www.roccofortehotels.com
Enjoy an outstanding experience in luxurious surroundings at Edinburgh's landmark five-star hotel. Facilities include 188 stunning bedrooms, Michelin-starred number one restaurant, Hadrian's Brasserie, The Bollinger Bar at Palm Court and The Balmoral Spa - an exclusive retreat in the heart of the city.

58132

HOTEL

The Balmoral
1 Princes Street, Edinburgh, EH2 2EQ
Tel:0870 460 7040 Fax:0131 557 8740
Email:reservations.balmoral@roccofortehotels.com
Web:www.roccofortehotels.com

Edinburgh's landmark hotel at Edinburgh's most prestigious address.

188 rooms, all en-suite, Open Jan-Dec. Room rate: single from £270.00, classic double from £320.00.

GUEST HOUSE

Barossa Guest House
21 Pilrig Street, Edinburgh, EH6 5AN
Tel:0131 554 3700

Family run Georgian house only a short walk from city centre on main bus routes. Ensuite rooms available. Unrestricted street parking.

6 rooms, some en-suite, Open Jan-Dec, B&B per person, double £27.00-45.00.

GUEST HOUSE

Belford Guest House
13 Blacket Avenue, Edinburgh, EH9 1RR
Tel:0131 667 2422   Fax:0131 667 7508
Email:mailbox@belfordguesthouse.com
Web:www.belfordguesthouse.com

Family run guest house in quiet road just off main A7/A701. Conveniently situated for main tourist attraction and city centre, buses run to the city centre from either end of the avenue. Variety of eating establishments locally.

7 rooms, some en-suite, Open Jan-Dec, B&B per person, single from £25.00, double from £20.00.

GUEST HOUSE

Beresford Hotel
32 Coates Gardens, Edinburgh, EH12 5LE
Tel:0131 337 0850
Email:bookings@beresford-edinburgh.com
Web:www.beresford-edinburgh.com

Family run establishment close to city centre and Haymarket station. Most rooms en-suite. Children very welcome.

12 rooms, 10 en-suite, Open Jan-Dec, B&B per person, single from £30.00, double from £22.50.

VAT is shown at 17.5%: changes in this rate may affect prices.

Key to symbols is on back flap.

Edinburgh

Map Ref: 2C5

HOTEL

Best Western Bruntsfield Hotel

69 Bruntsfield Place, Edinburgh, EH10 4HH
Tel:0131 229 1393   Fax:0131 229 5634
Email:reservations@thebruntsfield.co.uk
Web:www.thebruntsfield.co.uk

Overlooking a park close to the city centre, the Best Western Bruntsfield Hotel is a well appointed townhouse hotel with friendly & professional service. The 71 comfortably furnished bedrooms offer all facilities & services required by both business & leisure travellers.The Cardoon Restaurant serves modern Scottish cuisine in an elegant but informal atmosphere. A relaxing lounge & stylish bar add to the distinctive character of The Bruntsfield.

71 rooms, all en-suite, Open Jan-Dec excl Xmas, B&B per person, single from £75.00, double from £60.00 per person per night.

HOTEL

Best Western Kings Manor Hotel

100 Milton Road East, Edinburgh, EH15 2NP
Tel:0131 468 8003   Fax:0131 669 6650
Email:reservations@kingsmanor.com
Web:www.kingsmanor.com

Family run hotel 4 miles (6kms) east of city centre, handy for beach and all major road routes. Extensive modern leisure facilities.

93 rooms, all en-suite, Open Jan-Dec, B&B per person, single from £60.00, double from £45.00, BB & Eve.Meal from £60.00.

GUEST HOUSE

The Beverley

40 Murrayfield Avenue, Edinburgh, EH12 6AY
Tel:0131 337 1128   Fax:0131 313 3275
Email:enquiries@thebeverley.com
Web:www.thebeverley.com

An elegant Victorian terraced house, situated in a quiet tree-lined avenue offering ample free parking. Only minutes from Edinburgh's historic city centre and within fifteen minutes of all main coach, rail and air terminals. Non-smoking throughout. TV/DVD's in all bedrooms. Wireless Broadband Network with free Internet Access.

8 rooms, all en-suite, Open Jan-Dec, B&B per person, single £35.00-50.00, double £30.00-50.00.

GUEST HOUSE

Boisdale Hotel

9 Coates Gardens, Edinburgh, EH12 5LG
Tel:0131 337 1134   Fax:0131 313 0048

Victorian terraced house, close to Haymarket station. All rooms have full private facilities.

10 rooms, all en-suite, Open Jan-Dec, B&B per person, single £30.00-45.00, double £30.00-45.00.

HOTEL

The Bonham

35 Drumsheugh Gardens, Edinburgh, EH3 7RN
Tel:0131 274 7400   Fax:0131 274 7405
Email:reserve@thebonham.com
Web:www.thebonham.com

The Bonham is the coolest hotel in Edinburgh, where you'll enjoy an uplifting contemporary ambience within the classic atmosphere of a Victorian town house. During your stay, experience Edinburgh's most timeless contemporary restaurant - Restaurant at the Bonham. You'll be tempted by distinct European-inspired food and enticed by provocative wines.

48 rooms, all en suite, Open Jan-Dec, Room only rates, double from £73.00, single from £108.00.

Important: Prices stated are estimates and may be subject to amendments

Briggend Guest House

19 Old Dalkeith Road, Edinburgh, EH16 4TE
Tel: 0131 258 0810 Fax: 0131 620 2873
e.mail: reservations@briggend.com Web: www.briggend.com

The Briggend is a small family run guest house. All rooms are ground level, en-suite with cable TV, hairdryers, hospitality tray and private parking. We are minutes away from the city centre and all tourist attractions. We are also a short walk from the new E.R.I.
A warm welcome awaits.

16323

GUEST HOUSE
★★★

Briggend Guest House
19 Old Dalkeith Road, Edinburgh, EH16 4TE
Tel:0131 258 0810 Fax:0131 620 2873
Email:reservations@briggend.com
Web:www.briggend.com

Recently extended traditional cottage, now providing 4 ensuite bedrooms, all on ground level, on south side of city with very easy access to main routes, the new Edinburgh Royal Infirmary, Universities and many of the city's attractions. Also on main bus route.

4 rooms, all ensuite, Open Jan-Dec, B&B per person, single from £35.00, double from £22.50. Family room available.

GUEST HOUSE
★★

Caravel Guest House
30 London Street, Edinburgh, EH3 6NA
Tel:0131 556 4444   Fax:0131 557 3615
Email:caravelguest@hotmail.com
Web:www.caravelhouse.co.uk

A warm welcome at this guest house with spacious, en-suite bedrooms. This Georgian house is situated in the heart of Edinburgh's New Town only a short distance from Princes Street and close to Waverley Station and the bus station.

11 rooms, some en-suite, Open Jan-Dec, B&B per person, single from £30.00, double from £25.00.

GUEST HOUSE
★★★

Carrington Guest House
38 Pilrig Street, Edinburgh, EH6 5AL
Tel:0131 554 4769

Large family run guest house convenient for all city centre attractions. On street parking. Open for holiday guests and business people only.

7 rooms, some en-suite, Open Feb-Nov, B&B per person, double £27.00-45.00.

HOTEL
★★★★

Channings
12-16 South Learmonth Gardens, Edinburgh, EH4 1EZ
Tel:0131 274 7401 Fax:0131 274 7402
Email:reserve@channings.co.uk
Web:www.channings.co.uk

Channings is the friendliest hotel in Edinburgh, where you'll enjoy country-style tranquillity in a city setting and be charmed by our people. During your stay, experience great food and flavoursome wine in Channings Restaurant, where you'll enjoy distinctive food in a warm and welcoming ambience.

41 rooms, all en suite, Open Jan-Dec, Room only rates double from £65.50 pppn, single from £101.00.

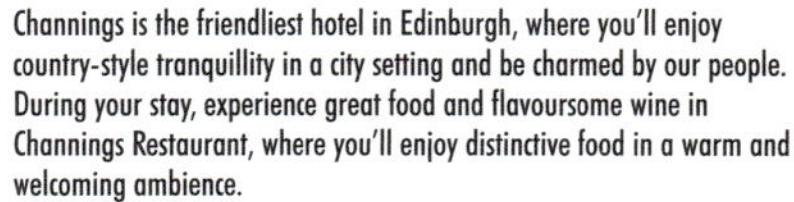

VAT is shown at 17.5%: changes in this rate may affect prices.   *Key to symbols is on back flap.*

Edinburgh	Map Ref: 2C5

SMALL HOTEL

Clan Campbell Hotel
11 Brunswick Street, Edinburgh, EH7 5JB
Tel:0131 557 6910 Fax:0131 557 6929
Email:clan.campbell@virgin.net
Web:www.clancampbellhotel.co.uk

Former Black Watch Club, now a small hotel set in central Georgian town house. On street parking with no charge. French and Spanish spoken. Dinner is not available but there are many restaurants within walking distance.

8 rooms, all en-suite, Open Mar-Nov, B&B per person, single from £25.00, double from £25.00.

GUEST HOUSE

Clan Walker Guest House
96 Dalkeith Road, Edinburgh, EH16 5AF
Tel:0131 667 1244
Email:enquiries@clanwalkerguesthouse.com
Web:www.clanwalkerguesthouse.com

Traditional Victorian built house, family run business, centrally located. Good quality and value for money accommodation with 3 parking spaces. A non-smoking establishment, with good service and a high standard of cleanliness. All rooms are ensuite.

6 rooms, all en-suite. B&B per person, £25.00-£50.00 twin/double, £20.00-£35.00 triple/family, Open Jan-Dec.

CLARENDON HOTEL
25 Shandwick Place, Edinburgh EH2 4RG
Tel: 0131 229 1467 Fax: 0131 229 7549
e.mail: res@clarendonhoteledi.co.uk Web: www.clarendonhoteledi.co.uk
Tastefully refurbished city centre hotel 20 yards from Princes Street. Ideally situated for tourist attractions, financial district, International Conference Centre (EICC), theatres and restaurants. All easy walking distance. Waverley and Haymarket train stations within easy walk. Airport bus stop two minute walk. Car parking nearby. Meeting room available. Free wi-fi internet access. 19507

HOTEL

Clarendon Hotel
25-33 Shandwick Place, Edinburgh, EH2 4RG
Tel:0131 229 1467 Fax:0131 229 7549
Email:res@clarendonhoteledi.co.uk
Web:www.clarendonhoteledi.co.uk

Situated in the heart of the city, approximately 20 yards from Edinburgh's famous Princes Street. Ideally situated for the city's financial district, tourist attractions, theatres, restaurants and the International Conference Centre (EICC), all within minutes walking distance. If arriving at Edinburgh International Airport, the Airport bus drops off and picks up opposite the hotel. Located between Waverley and Haymarket Railway stations, both within easy walking distance.

66 rooms, all en-suite, Open all year, B&B per person, single from £30.00, double from £25.00.

GUEST HOUSE

Crioch Guest House
23 East Hermitage Place, Leith Links, Edinburgh EH6 8AD
Tel/Fax:0131 554 5494
Email:welcome@crioch.com
Web:www.crioch.com

Set on a frequent bus route to the city centre, Crioch overlooks the leafy park of Leith Links. All rooms have ensuite shower or private bathroom, TV, radio alarm and welcome tray. You can choose from continental or full cooked breakfast. Free parking and the frequent bus service leaves you to enjoy Edinburgh's sights on foot, and a short stroll takes you to Leith's fine cafes, bars and restaurants.

6 rooms, 5 en-suite, Open Jan-Dec, B&B per person, single from £25.00, double from £24.50.

Important: Prices stated are estimates and may be subject to amendments

Edinburgh

Map Ref: 2C5

Cumberland Hotel

1-2a West Coates, Edinburgh EH12 5JQ
Tel: 0131 337 1198 Fax: 0131 337 1022
e.mail: cumblhotel@aol.com Web: www.corstorphinehotels.co.uk

Cumberland Hotel, housed in two superb Victorian buildings of great architectural interest, offers excellent accommodation at budget prices. The hotel lies in its own extensive grounds and is within a short walk to the city centre. Fully licensed and offering a choice of breakfast, guests can relax in its residents' lounge or enjoy a drink in the cocktail bar.

21722

★★★

SMALL HOTEL

Cumberland Hotel

1-2 West Coates, Edinburgh, EH12 5JQ
Tel:0131 337 1198 Fax:0131 337 1022
Email:cumblhotel@aol.com
Web:www.corstorphinehotels.co.uk

Family run property in listed Victorian building. A short walk from the West End of the city centre. 10 - 15 min drive to the airport and Ingliston Highland Showground. Murrayfield Stadium within walking distance. The Cumberland offers a choice of continental, traditional or vegetarian breakfasts. There are several restaurants providing a variety of cuisine within easy walking distance of the property.

17 rooms, all en-suite, Open Jan-Dec, B&B per person, single £39.00-99.00, double £25.00-69.00 pppn.

★★★

GUEST HOUSE

Dene Guest House

7 Eyre Place, off Dundas Street, Edinburgh EH3 5ES
Tel:0131 556 2700   Fax:0131 557 9876
Email:deneguesthouse@yahoo.co.uk
Web:www.deneguesthouse.com

Charming Georgian townhouse, situated in the famous 'New Town' of Edinburgh's city centre, providing you with the perfect location to experience the capital's culture, history, shops, restaurants and bars. Enjoy a comfortable stay in a relaxed and informal atmosphere from only £19.50-40.00 pppn, including a hearty breakfast.

11 rooms, some en-suite, Open Jan-Dec, B&B per person, single from £19.50, double from £19.50.

★★

B&B

Doocote House

15 Moat Street, Edinburgh, EH14 1PE
Tel:0131 443 5455

Well established traditional B&B. Approx 2 miles (3kms) from city centre. Unrestricted street parking. Kitchen available for guests.

3 rooms, Open Mar-Oct, B&B from £22.00 per person.

VAT is shown at 17.5%: changes in this rate may affect prices.

Key to symbols is on back flap.

DUNSTANE HOUSE HOTEL
4 West Coates, Haymarket, Edinburgh EH12 5JQ
Tel: 0131 337 6169 Fax: 0131 337 6060
e.mail: reservations@dunstanehousehotel.co.uk
Web: www.dunstane-hotel-edinburgh.co.uk
Impressive Victorian mansion dating 1850's retaining spectacular original features. All rooms luxuriously refurbished. Four poster deluxe rooms available. Unique bar and restaurant themed on the Scottish islands. Excellent range of malt whiskies stocked. Located in the heart of the city, only minutes from Princes Street, the Castle, conference centre and Edinburgh Airport. Private car park.   23861

★★★★

SMALL HOTEL

Dunstane House Hotel
4 West Coates, Haymarket, Edinburgh, EH12 5JQ
Tel:0131 337 6169 Fax:0131 337 6060
Email:reservations@dunstanehousehotel.co.uk
Web:www.dunstane-hotel-edinburgh.co.uk

Impressive Listed Victorian mansion retaining many original features enjoying imposing position within large grounds on the A8 airport road (major bus route). 10 mins walk from city centre. Close to Edinburgh Conference Centre, Murrayfield and Edinburgh Zoo. Private secluded car park. Unique lounge bar and restaurant themed on the Scottish Islands.

16 rooms, all en-suite, Open Jan-Dec, B&B per person, single from £59.00, double from £49.00, BB & Eve.Meal from £69.00.

DUTHUS LODGE
5 West Coates, Edinburgh EH12 5JG
Tel: 0131 337 6876 Fax: 0131 313 2264
e.mail: duthus.lodge@ukgateway.net
Web: www.duthuslodge.com
Splendid detached family run Victorian establishment offering accommodation in tastefully decorated and comfortable surroundings. A perfect base to explore Edinburgh. All bedrooms are ensuite. Private parking, close to the city centre, conference centre and Murrayfield stadium.   23918

★★★

GUEST HOUSE

Duthus Lodge
5 West Coates, Edinburgh, EH12 5JG
Tel:0131 337 6876 Fax:0131 313 2264
Email:duthus.lodge@ukgateway.net
Web:www.duthuslodge.com

Magnificent detached sandstone building with attractive walled gardens. Ideal base for exploring Edinburgh. Close to the city centre, conference centre, zoo and Murrayfield stadium.

8 rooms, all en-suite, Open Jan-Dec, B&B per person, single £35.00-55.00, double £25.00-50.00.

★★★

GUEST HOUSE

Edinburgh House
11 McDonald Road, Edinburgh, EH7 4LX
Tel/Fax:0131 556 3434
Email:salucmirel@aol.com
Web:www.edinburgh-house.co.uk

Small personally run guest house in a traditional tenement building approx 0.5 ml from Princes Street. Good bus service to city centre with all its amenities. Variety of restaurants nearby. Non-smoking house.

4 rooms, all en-suite, Open Jan-Dec, B&B per person, double £27.00-45.00.

Important: Prices stated are estimates and may be subject to amendments

Edinburgh

Map Ref: 2C5

HOTEL

The Edinburgh Residence
7 Rothesay Terrace, Edinburgh, EH3 7RY
Tel:0131 274 7403 Fax:0131 274 7405
Email:reserve@theedinburghresidence.com
Web:www.theedinburghresidence.com

The Edinburgh Residence is the most distinguished collection of luxury townhouse suites in Edinburgh, offering a refreshing alternative to a five star hotel where you will enjoy an experience to remember. Comprising three beautiful architectural Georgian townhouses and situated in Edinburgh's West End, close to both the city's financial district and main shopping area, The Edinburgh Residence enjoys a peaceful yet central location only 5 minutes walk from Edinburgh's main tourist attractions.

29 rooms, all en suite, Open Jan-Dec, Room only rate, double from £85.00, single from £135.00.

GUEST HOUSE

Ellesmere Guest House
11 Glengyle Terrace, Edinburgh, EH3 9LN
Tel:0131 229 4823
Email:celia@edinburghbandb.co.uk
Web:www.edinburghbandb.co.uk

City centre Victorian terraced house in quiet location overlooking Bruntsfield Links. Kings Theatre, Conference Centre and all amenities within walking distance. All rooms en suite. Full Scottish Breakfast is served and a warm welcome is extended to all guests.

4 rooms, all en-suite, Open Jan-Dec, B&B per person, single from £35.00, double from £35.00.

GUEST HOUSE

Falcon Crest Guest House
70 South Trinity Road, Edinburgh, EH5 3NX
Tel/Fax:0131 552 5294
Email:manager@falconcrest.co.uk
Web:www.falconcrest.co.uk

Victorian terraced family home in attractive residential area, near main bus route to city centre. Free on street parking.

6 rooms, some en-suite, (1 single, 2 twin, 2 double, 1 family), from £18.00 Single, double from £18.00.

Frederick House Hotel
42 Frederick St, Edinburgh, EH2 1EX
Tel: 0131 226 1999   Fax: 0131 624 7064
e.mail: frederickhouse@ednet.co.uk   Web: www.townhousehotels.co.uk

Offering an atmosphere of comfort and tradition. Situated in the very heart of Edinburgh's city centre with Princes Street practically on our door step. All 45 rooms have en-suite, satellite TV, telephone/modem, refrigerators, tea/coffee, trouser press and hairdryers.
Free wi-fi internet access. We aim to make your stay as comfortable as possible.   26805

LODGE

Frederick House Hotel
42 Frederick Street, Edinburgh, EH2 1EX
Tel:0131 226 1999 Fax:0131 624 7064
Email:frederickhouse@ednet.co.uk
Web:www.townhousehotels.co.uk

Situated in the heart of Edinburgh close to all city centre amenities and with a wide variety of restaurants and bars in the immediate vicinity. Georgian building with all rooms to a high standard with en-suite facilities, fridges and modem points. Princes Street just 150 yards away. Breakfast available across the road at the award winning Rick's Bar/Restaurant. Street parking.

45 rooms, all en-suite, Open Jan-Dec, B&B per person, single from £35.00, double from £25.00 per person subject to availability and season.

VAT is shown at 17.5%: changes in this rate may affect prices.

Key to symbols is on back flap.

Edinburgh

Map Ref: 2C5

GUEST HOUSE

Gifford House

103 Dalkeith Road, Edinburgh, EH16 5AJ
Tel/Fax:0131 667 4688
Email:giffordhouse@btinternet.com
Web:www.giffordhousehotel.co.uk

A well appointed Victorian stone built house situated on one of the main routes into Edinburgh. Close to Holyrood Park and Arthur's Seat and only 300 metres from Royal Commonwealth Swimming Pool. Regular bus services to all city amenities. Well positioned for conference centre.

7 rooms, all en-suite, Open Jan-Dec excl Xmas, B&B per person, single £35.00-75.00, double from £30.00-55.00.

GUEST HOUSE

Gildun Guest House

9 Spence Street, Edinburgh, EH16 5AG
Tel:0131 667 1368   Fax:0131 668 4989
Email:gildun.edin@btinternet.com
Web:www.gildun.co.uk

A warm and friendly run guest house recently refurbished to an excellent standard situated in cul de sac with private parking. Close to Commonwealth Pool and bus route to city centre. Cameron Toll Shopping Centre nearby and situated near University Halls of Residence. A variety of eating establishments within walking distance.

8 rooms, some en-suite, Open Jan-Dec, B&B per person, single from £24.00, double from £24.00.

GUEST HOUSE

Glenora Hotel

14 Rosebery Crescent, Edinburgh, EH12 5JY
Tel:0131 337 1186   Fax:0131 337 1119
Email:glenorahotel@aol.com
Web:www.glenorahotel.co.uk

Victorian terraced town house a short walk to city centre and within easy reach of city's tourist attractions. Airport bus stops next to hotel.

11 rooms, single from £40.00, double from £35.00. Telephones and modem points in rooms. Buffet & full cooked breakfasts, all entirely organic.

SMALL HOTEL

Greenside Hotel

9 Royal Terrace, Edinburgh, EH7 5AB
Tel:0131 557 0121/0022 Fax:0131 557 0022
Email:greensidehotel@ednet.co.uk
Web:www.townhousehotels.co.uk

Personally run hotel in traditional Georgian terraced house. Quiet location, close to Princes Street and all amenities. 10 minutes walk from Waverley Station and Princes Street. Excellent selection of restaurants in immediate vicinity. Building of architectural interest.

16 rooms, all en-suite, Open Jan-Dec, B&B per person, single from £35.00, double from £25.00.

GUEST HOUSE

Grosvenor Gardens Hotel

1 Grosvenor Gardens, Edinburgh, EH12 5JU
Tel:0131 313 3415 Fax:0131 346 8732
Email:info@stayinedinburgh.com
Web:www.stayinedinburgh.com

Comfortable accommodation at this family run guest house. All rooms are ensuite. Within walking distance of city centre and only two minutes to Haymarket railway station. Very close to airport and bus route. Many restaurants nearby.

8 rooms, all en-suite. B&B per person, single from £49.00-75.00, double from £35.00-75.00.

Important: Prices stated are estimates and may be subject to amendments

Edinburgh

Map Ref: 2C5

SMALL
HOTEL

The Howard

34 Great King Street, Edinburgh, EH3 6QH
Tel:0131 274 7402 Fax:0131 274 7405
Email:reserve@thehoward.com
Web:www.thehoward.com

The Howard is the most discreet 5-star hotel in Edinburgh - attention to detail together with the personal touch will ensure you feel special. 'Dining at The Atholl' is an experience full of decadent pleasures. You'll enjoy dinner, which will be meticulously prepared by our dedicated team of chefs, in this warm and exclusive Georgian setting. Alternatively, you can be served dinner in the comfort of your room.

17 rooms, all en-suite, Room only rates from £108.00 single, double from £90.00 pppn.

GUEST
HOUSE

Ivy Guest House

7 Mayfield Gardens, Edinburgh, EH9 2AX
Tel:0131 667 3411 Fax:0131 620 1422
Email:dolly@ivyguesthouse.com
Web:www.ivyguesthouse.com

Warm and friendly welcome assured at this established Victorian listed town house. With rear parking. Centrally situated on bus route to Edinburgh's many cultural attractions, parks and restaurants.

8 rooms, some en-suite, B&B per person, single from £30.00, double from £25.00.

HOTEL

Jurys Inn Edinburgh

43 Jeffrey Street, Edinburgh, Lothian, EH1 1DH
Tel:0131 200 3300 Fax:0131 200 0400
Email:brenda_kirkland@jurysdoyle.com
Web:www.bookajurysinn.com

Jury's Inn's superb city centre location (adjacent to Royal Mile, Princes Street and Waverley Station) is combined with incredible value for money. For a fixed rate your room can accommodate up to 3 adults or 2 adults and 2 children. All rooms are ensuite and have direct dial phone, satellite TV, hairdryer, modem and tea and coffee making facilities. Warm welcome and friendly prices in the Inn Pub and Arches restaurant.

186 rooms, all en-suite, Open Jan-Dec excl Xmas, B&B per person, single from £60.00, double from £35.00 per person.

GUEST
HOUSE

Kariba Guest House

10 Granville Terrace, Edinburgh, EH10 4PQ
Tel:0131 229 3773   Fax:0131 229 4968
Email:karibaguesthouse@hotmail.com
Web:www.karibaguesthouse.co.uk

A Victorian house on major bus route to city centre about 10 minutes away. Restaurants, theatres and International Conference Centre all within easy reach. Private car parking.

9 rooms, 8 en-suite, Open Jan-Dec, B&B per person, single from £35.00, double £25.00-45.00.

GUEST
HOUSE

Kew House

1 Kew Terrace, Murrayfield, Edinburgh, EH12 5JE
Tel:0131 313 0700 Fax:0131 313 0747
Email:info@kewhouse.com
Web:www.kewhouse.com

We offer comfort in a contemporary style and cater for both business and tourist customers alike. Our immaculately decorated ensuite rooms have all the essentials you require for a comfortable stay. We are just a short walk or brief bus trip from the city centre and on the main road from the airport. We have a residents drinks license and serve light meals. Hot breakfast is included in the tariff. Free broadband internet with Wi-Fi.

6 rooms, all en-suite, Open Jan-Dec, B&B per person, single from £70.00, double from £42.50 pppn.

VAT is shown at 17.5%: changes in this rate may affect prices.

Key to symbols is on back flap.

Edinburgh | Map Ref: 2C5

KENVIE GUEST HOUSE
16 Kilmaurs Road, Edinburgh EH16 5DA
Tel: 0131 668 1964 Fax: 0131 668 1926
e.mail: dorothy@kenvie.co.uk Web: www.kenvie.co.uk

Quiet and comfortable house situated in a residential area with easy access to City Centre on an excellent bus route. All rooms have tea and coffee-making facilities and TVs. Central heating throughout. *A warm and friendly welcome is guaranteed.*

33610

★★★

GUEST HOUSE

Kenvie Guest House
16 Kilmaurs Road, Edinburgh, EH16 5DA
Tel:0131 668 1964   Fax:0131 668 1926
Email:dorothy@kenvie.co.uk
Web:www.kenvie.co.uk

A charming, comfortable, warm, friendly family run Victorian town house in a quiet residential street. Very close to bus routes and the city by-pass. We offer for your comfort, lots of caring touches including complimentary tea / coffee, colour TV, hairdryers and no-smoking rooms. En-suite available and vegetarians catered for. You are guaranteed a warm welcome from Richard and Dorothy.

5 rooms, some en-suite, Open Jan-Dec, B&B per person, single from £27.00, double from £25.00.

Kingsview Guest House
28 Gilmore Place, Edinburgh EH3 9NQ
Tel: 0131 229 8004   Fax: 0131 229 8004
e.mail: kingsviewguesthouse@talk21.com   Web: www.kingsviewguesthouse.com

Warm, friendly, family-run guest house in the city centre within walking distance to major attractions. Tours arranged with pick-ups from Kingsview. Secure parking arranged. Renowned breakfast with fine local produce. All guest rooms ensuite. Complimentary tray, Multi-Channel TV, safe and radio alarm. Children and pets welcome. 24 hour entry. Credit cards accepted. A warm welcome awaits. B&B from £22.50-£40 per person per night.

34095

★★

GUEST HOUSE

Kingsview Guest House
28 Gilmore Place, Edinburgh, EH3 9NQ
Tel/Fax:0131 229 8004
Email:kingsviewguesthouse@talk21.com
Web:www.kingsviewguesthouse.com

Family run, city centre guest house conveniently situated near the Kings Theatre. Close to all main bus routes.

9 rooms, all en-suite, Open Jan-Dec, B&B per person, double from £22.50.

Important: Prices stated are estimates and may be subject to amendments

| Edinburgh | Map Ref: 2C5 |

McDonald Guest House

5 McDonald Road, Edinburgh, EH7 4LX
Tel/Fax:0131 557 5935
Email:white@5mcdonaldroad.co.uk
Web:www.5mcdonaldroad.co.uk

Comfortable accommodation a short walk from Princes Street. Adjacent to main bus routes. Many good restaurants locally. Playhouse Theatre nearby. Free on street parking. French and German spoken.

4 rooms, some en-suite, Open Mar-Dec incl New/Year, B&B per person, single from £28.00, double from £25.00.

Menzies Belford Hotel

69 Belford Road, Edinburgh, EH4 3DG
Tel:0131 332 2545 Fax:0131 332 3805
Email:belford@menzies-hotels.co.uk
Web:www.bookmenzies.com

On the banks of the Water of Leith in a quiet secluded area, and only a 10 minute stroll to Princes Street, the hotel offers the best of both worlds. The Forth Road Bridge and both of Edinburgh's main railway stations are only a short drive away and many of the city's local attractions, including the Dean Gallery and Princes Street are just a short walk from the hotel. Extensive private parking, which is free for all residents.

146 rooms, all en-suite, Open Jan-Dec, B&B per person, single from £72.50, double from £42.50 pppn.

Menzies Guest House

33 Leamington Terrace, Edinburgh, EH10 4JS
Tel/Fax:0131 229 4629
Email:menzies33@blueyonder.co.uk
Web:www.menzies-guesthouse.co.uk

Situated in residential area near Bruntsfield Links and close to main bus route to city centre. Private parking. Princes Street and West End with theatres and restaurants approx. 0.75 mile.

7 rooms, some en-suite, Open Jan-Dec, B&B per person, single from £15.00, double from £15.00.

Parliament House Hotel

15 Calton Hill, Edinburgh, EH1 3BJ
Tel:0131 478 4000 Fax:0131 478 4001
Email:info@parliamenthouse-hotel.co.uk
Web:www.parliamenthouse-hotel.co.uk

Town house hotel in city centre location and situated on historic Calton Hill a few minutes walk from Princes Street and the Playhouse Theatre. 3 minutes walk from Waverley Train Station. Discount Parking at nearby Greenside Multi-storey. 'MP's' Bistro available for dinner and non-residents welcome.

53 rooms, all en-suite, B&B per person, single from £60.00, double from £35.00.

Priestville Guest House

10 Priestfield Road, Edinburgh, EH16 5HJ
Tel/Fax:0131 667 2435
Email:bookings@priestville.com
Web:www.priestville.com

Friendly Scottish Hospitality in Victorian Townhouse, quiet residential area. 20 minute walk to city centre. Excellent bus service. Full fry, Smoked Salmon or Haggis for breakfast. Close to Commonwealth Pool, Holyrood Park and Golf Course. Broadband and wireless Internet access and Parking Available.

6 rooms, some en-suite, Open Jan-Dec, B&B per person, single from £25.00, double from £22.00.

VAT is shown at 17.5%: changes in this rate may affect prices. | *Key to symbols is on back flap.*

Edinburgh

Map Ref: 2C5

HOTEL

Radisson SAS Hotel, Edinburgh
80 High Street, The Royal Mile, Edinburgh, EH1 1TH
Tel:0131 473 6590 Fax:0131 557 9789
Email:reservations.edinburgh@radissonsas.com
Web:www.radissonsas.com

This modern, contemporary, city centre hotel offers first class facilities including 238 en-suite bedrooms, restaurant, lounge, bar, onsite parking for 135 cars, Leisure club with indoor pool, fitness room, saunas, solarium and treatment room. 'Itchycoo Bar and Kitchen' open from 7am till late.

238 air-conditioned rooms, all en-suite (fully refurbished May 2005), Open Jan-Dec incl Xmas/New Year, B&B per person, single from £120.00, double from £65.00.

HOTEL

Ritz Hotel
14-18 Grosvenor Street, Edinburgh, EH12 5EG
Tel:0131 337 4315   Fax:0131 346 0597
Email:ritzhoteledin@aol.com

On five floors, each room of individual character, some featuring four poster beds. Within easy walking distance of Haymarket railway station and West End of Princes Street. There is a wide range of restaurants available in the city centre.

36 rooms, all en-suite, Open Jan-Dec, B&B per person, single £50.00-61.00, double £35.00-50.00.

SMALL HOTEL

Rosehall Hotel
101 Dalkeith Road, Newington, Edinburgh, EH16 5AJ
Tel/Fax:0131 667 9372
Email:info@rosehallhotel.co.uk
Web:www.rosehallhotel.co.uk

This small, recently refurbished hotel retains many fine period features restored to their original Victorian splendour. One room has a 4-Poster bed. Free on-street parking is available nearby. The hotel is located around 1.5 miles from Princes Street.

8 rooms, 7 en-suite, Open Jan-Dec, B&B per person, single £30.00-65.00, double £25.00-50.00.

The St Valery
36 Coates Gardens, Haymarket, Edinburgh EH12 5LE
Tel: +44 (0)131 337 1893 Fax: +44 (0)131 346 8529
e.mail: info@stvalery.co.uk Web: www.stvalery.com

*The St Valery is situated in the heart of Edinburgh's West End. Refurbished to a high standard, but still retaining the charm, friendliness of small hotel.
St Valery is within walking distance of Princes Street, Edinburgh Castle, main shopping and sight-seeing areas, including Royal Mile. Good links to Airport and Railway nearby. Free broadband internet access.*

56103

GUEST HOUSE

The St Valery
36 Coates Gardens, Edinburgh, EH12 5LE
Tel:0131 337 1893 Fax:0131 346 8529
Email:info@stvalery.co.uk
Web:www.stvalery.com

Traditional guest house, centrally situated in West End of Edinburgh. 1 mile from Princes Street. 3 minutes walk from Haymarket Station. Evening meal on request. Internet facilities now available.

11 rooms, some en-suite, Open Jan-Dec, B&B per person, single from £28.00-52.00, double from £28.00-52.00.

Important: Prices stated are estimates and may be subject to amendments

Edinburgh

Map Ref: 2C5

Sakura House

18 West Preston Street, Edinburgh, EH8 9PU
Tel/Fax:0131 668 1204

6 rooms, some en-suite, Open Jan-Dec, B&B per person, single from £18.00, double from £18.00.

Victorian house in central location, close to castle and shopping centre. Numerous good restaurants and pubs in immediate vicinity. On main bus route. Video recorders in bedroom and a selection of videos for guests use. Sky TV. Single guests welcome.

Sandaig Guest House

5 East Hermitage Place, Leith Links, Edinburgh EH6 8AA
Tel:0131 554 7357   Fax:0131 467 6389
Email:info@sandaigguesthouse.co.uk
Web:www.sandaigguesthouse.co.uk

8 rooms, all en-suite, Open Jan-Dec, B&B per person, single from £39.00, double from £34.00.

Marina and Derek personally welcome you to their delightful Victorian terraced villa overlooking historic Leith Links. Unrestricted street parking. Variety of restaurants nearby or frequent bus service to Princes Street with all its amenities. Totally non-smoking house.

Sheridan Guest House

1 Bonnington Terrace, Edinburgh, EH6 4BP
Tel:0131 554 4107 Fax:0131 554 8494
Email:info@sheridanedinburgh.co.uk
Web:www.sheridanedinburgh.co.uk

8 rooms, Open Jan-Dec, B&B per person single from £35.00, double from £30.00, family from £28.00.

Contemporary furnished, sensitively restored, elegant Georgian townhouse with 8 en-suite bedrooms. Good food, warm welcome. Unrestricted street parking. On excellent bus route. Strictly non-smoking.

St Bernards Guest House

22 St Bernards Crescent, Edinburgh, EH4 1NS
Tel:0131 332 2339 Fax:0131 332 8842
Email:alexstbernards@aol.com

8 rooms, some en-suite, Open Jan-Dec, B&B per person, single from £30.00, double from £25.00.

Elegant terrace house in Georgian New Town area of the city. Convenient for Princes Street. Many excellent restaurants within walking distance. A warm and friendly welcome.

Tania Guest House

19 Minto Street, Edinburgh, EH9 1RQ
Tel:0131 667 4144

6 rooms, some en-suite, Open Jan-Dec excl Xmas, B&B per person, single from £20.00, double from £20.00.

Traditional Guest House, welcoming families, conveniently situated on main bus route from city centre. Limited private parking. Choice of restaurants available locally. Non-smoking house.

VAT is shown at 17.5%: changes in this rate may affect prices.

Key to symbols is on back flap.

Edinburgh | Map Ref: 2C5

AWAITING GRADING

Ten Hill Place Hotel

10 Hill Place, Edinburgh, EH8 9DS
Tel:0131 662 2080 Fax:0131 662 2082
Email:reservations@tenhillplace.com
Web:www.tenhillplace.com

Situated in the Old Town and sitting on the edge of Holyrood Park, this newly opened hotel has been designed with all the comforts and conveniences for the discerning traveller. Located within easy walking distance to all major tourist attractions, theatres, restaurants and Princes Street.

78 rooms, all en-suite, Open all year, B&B per person, single from £69.00, double from £55.00 per person.

★★★

HOTEL

Thistle Edinburgh

107 Leith Street, Edinburgh, EH1 3SW
Tel:0870 333 9153 Fax:0870 3339253
Email:edinburgh@thistle.co.uk
Web:www.thistlehotels.com

Modern hotel in city centre location with friendly and efficient staff. Craigs restaurant, Boston Bean cocktail bar.

139 rooms, all en-suite, Open Jan-Dec, B&B per person, single from £65.00, double from £65.00, BB & Eve.Meal from £85.00.

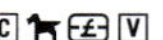

★★★★

GUEST HOUSE

The Town House

65 Gilmore Place, Edinburgh, EH3 9NU
Tel:0131 229 1985
Email:Susan@thetownhouse.com
Web:www.thetownhouse.com

An elegant Victorian town house c1876, situated in the city centre. Easy walking distance of West End, Princes Street and Kings Theatre. A skilful mix of modern and period furnishings enhanced by stylish decor makes for a very warm and comfortable stay.

5 rooms, all en-suite, Open Jan-Dec, single & double rooms from £35.00-50.00 per person per night.

★★★★

GUEST HOUSE

The Walton

79 Dundas Street, Edinburgh, EH3 6SD
Tel:0131 556 1137 Fax:0131 557 8367
Email:enquiries@waltonhotel.com
Web:www.waltonhotel.com

The Walton, in the heart of Edinburgh City Centre, is a small Guest House within a heritage listed building. Located only a short walk from Princes Street and within Georgian New Town, the Walton is convenient for tourists and business travellers alike. Off-street parking available.

10 rooms, all en-suite, Open Jan-Dec, B&B per person, single from £45.00, double from £39.50.

---

nr Edinburgh | Map Ref: 2C5

★★

INN

The Laird & Dog Hotel

5 High Street, Lasswade, Midlothian, EH18 1NA
Tel:0131 663 9219
Web:www.lairdanddog.btinternet.co.uk

Old Coaching Inn (Est 1740) ½ mile from city by-pass with excellent bus service to Edinburgh. New conservatory restaurant, a la carte and bar meals, large car park, Olde World Bar and newly discovered historical well. All bedrooms ensuite.

10 rooms, all en-suite, Open Jan-Dec, B&B per person, single from £45.00, double from £32.50.

Important: Prices stated are estimates and may be subject to amendments

Gullane, East Lothian — Map Ref: 2D4

Greywalls

Muirfield, Gullane, East Lothian, EH31 2EG
Tel:01620 842144 Fax:01620 842241
Email:hotel@greywalls.co.uk
Web:www.greywalls.co.uk

Renowned family owned Lutyens house with friendly atmosphere, gardens by Gertrude Jekyll. Adjacent to Muirfield Golf Course. Views over Forth. Award winning cuisine also attracts a strong following locally.

23 rooms, all en-suite, B&B per person, single from £140.00, double from £150.00.

Haddington, East Lothian — Map Ref: 2D4

Maitlandfield House Hotel

24 Sidegate, Haddington, East Lothian, EH41 4BZ
Tel:01620 826513 Fax:01620 826713
Email:info@maitlandfieldhouse.co.uk
Web:www.maitlandfieldhouse.co.uk

A country house hotel at the edge of town. Ideally located to visit Edinburgh and the Lothian's. A mecca for golf and walking. Splendid facilities for weddings and conferences.

25 rooms, all en-suite, Open Jan-Dec, B&B per person, single from £60.00, double from £55.00 pp, BB & Eve.Meal from £48.50.

North Berwick, East Lothian — Map Ref: 2D4

Nether Abbey Hotel

20 Dirleton Avenue, North Berwick, EH39 4BQ
Tel:01620 892802 Fax:01620 895298
Email:bookings@netherabbey.co.uk
Web:www.netherabbey.co.uk

Stone built hotel with character, situated in attractive grounds. 2 minutes walk to sandy beach and west links. 19 golf courses within 10 mile radius. 30 minute train service to Edinburgh.

13 rooms, all en-suite, Open Jan-Dec, B&B per person, single £55.00-70.00, double £30.00-45.00, BB & Eve.Meal from £50.00.

North Middleton, Midlothian — Map Ref: 2C5

Borthwick Castle Hotel

North Middleton, Gorebridge, Midlothian, EH23 4QY
Tel:01875 820514 Fax:01875 821702
Email:enquiries@borthwickcastle.com
Web:www.borthwickcastle.com

Unique twin tower fortified keep c.1430 with great hall and state room retaining medieval atmosphere. Dine by log fires and candlelight. Only 12 miles South of Edinburgh in a pastoral valley, this romantic Castle stands on the summit of a knoll.

10 rooms, all en-suite, Open Mar-Jan excl Xmas/New Year, B&B per person, single from £80.00, double from £85.00.

South Queensferry, West Lothian — Map Ref: 2B4

Priory Lodge

8 The Loan, South Queensferry, West Lothian EH30 9NS
Tel:0131 331 4345 Fax:0131 331 4345
Email:calmyn@aol.com
Web:www.queensferry.com

Traditional Scottish hospitality in this friendly family run guest house located in the picturesque village of South Queensferry. Edinburgh city centre 7 miles: Airport / Royal Highland Exhibition grounds 3 miles. Priory Lodge is within walking distance of the village shops, variety of eating establishments, Forth Bridges and Dalmeny train station. Internet access available. Non-smoking establishment.

5 rooms, all en-suite, Open Jan-Dec excl Xmas, B&B per person, single from £50.00, double from £30.00.

VAT is shown at 17.5%: changes in this rate may affect prices.   *Key to symbols is on back flap.*

Main image: Kelvingrove Art Gallery and Museum **Bottom left:** The Thinker, Burrell Collection
Bottom middle: Princes Square **Bottom right:** Gourock Golf Club, Inverclyde

GREATER GLASGOW AND CLYDE VALLEY

Every day in a corridor at the incredible Burrell Collection, Rodin's The Thinker sits solemnly contemplating his troubles.

Though this casting of the world-famous statue has been here for quite some time, you can tell he isn't thinking about Glasgow. If he was, he'd have a smile on his face and he wouldn't be sitting around too long either, because there are just too many wonderful things to do in Scotland's largest city.

Glasgow is a great place. It's stylish and flamboyant, confident and imaginative. Glaswegians are irresistibly friendly and it's difficult not to be overwhelmed by their welcome whether you're visiting a bar or a

   THE NO.1 BOOKING AND INFORMATION SERVICE FOR SCOTLAND   0845 22 55 121   visitscotland.com

The Clyde Auditorium, Glasgow

In a single trip to Glasgow you can uncover the Mackintosh legacy, lose yourself in some of Britain's finest museums and galleries, and reward yourself with some first rate retail therapy.

restaurant or just enquiring at a bus stop when the next bus is due.

As a visitor, it's easy to get caught up in its fast-moving social whirl. Glasgow buzzes from dawn until dusk and well beyond. All day long, its streets swarm with shoppers enjoying a retail experience that is second only to London in scale, and second to none for quality and diversity.

Even the most seasoned exponents of retail therapy will appreciate the elegance of Princes Square, the size and variety in the Buchanan Galleries and the classy opulence of the Italian Centre in the chic Merchant City. Glasgow is easily Scotland's most fashion-conscious city and this passion for all things stylish brings an exciting edge to its boutiques and malls.

That passion spills over into the cafés and bars, the boutique hotels, the restaurants, nightclubs, theatres and music venues. Glasgow nightlife is always exhilarating and exciting. Whether you're checking out the next hit band at King Tut's Wah Wah Hut, watching ground-breaking theatre at Oran Mor, taking in

a big European game at Ibrox or Celtic Park or just sipping your pint in a bar in Ashton Lane.

Foodies love Glasgow too. From traditional afternoon tea in the Hotel du Vin at One Devonshire Gardens or the Willow Tearooms to every major culinary style in the world, the city's restaurateurs serve their wares with a degree of enthusiasm and panache that will have you counting the minutes until dinner. And to celebrate the city's culinary talents they even set the month of August aside for Gourmet Glasgow giving the opportunity to more than 60 restaurants and many of the world's top chefs to celebrate their creativity in style.

It is after all, a very creative place. You can't visit Glasgow and fail to appreciate the legacy of its eminent architectural sons, Charles Rennie Mackintosh and Alexander 'Greek' Thomson. The great masters of the visual arts are also well represented amongst one of the biggest collections of publicly owned art in Europe and displayed at so many wonderful venues including the recently restored Kelvingrove Art Gallery and Museum.

When you are in the bustling city centre of Glasgow it is hard to believe that the countryside is just a short journey away.

But you don't have to spend all your time in Glasgow caught up in the whirl. Peace and tranquillity are never far away in the 'dear green place'. With over 70 parks and gardens in the city it's easy to find a quiet place to escape for a while. Equally, if you look beyond the city limits, there's so much more to discover.

Trace the Clyde back to its source and you'll find yourself at the picturesque Falls of Clyde in Lanarkshire, just beside the immaculately preserved village of New Lanark. Now a World Heritage site, New Lanark was founded in 1786 and managed by a social visionary, Robert Owen. His ideas for social reform and social inclusion were so far ahead of their time they are revolutionary even today.

New Lanark is one of many exceptional places that are well worth a day trip from the city. On the Clyde coast you can take a trip 'doon the watter' in the Waverley, the world's last sea-going paddle steamer. At Strathclyde Park near Hamilton and Mugdock Country Park near Milngavie you'll enjoy a wide range of activities including walking, cycling and sailing.

Glasgow's maritime history can be explored at Braehead – where you may also want to check out the recently opened indoor adventure centre Xscape. Paisley is just a short journey away and its impressive Abbey dates back to 1163.

As you'd expect in a city renowned for style, there are some great boutique hotels in Glasgow, many of which are an attraction in themselves and certainly more than just a place to rest your head. In the surrounding areas as well you will find a wide choice and something to suit every need and budget. Whatever you choose, Glasgow and the Clyde Valley will be a revelation and you'll never be disappointed.

New Lanark World Heritage Site

Tourist Information Centres

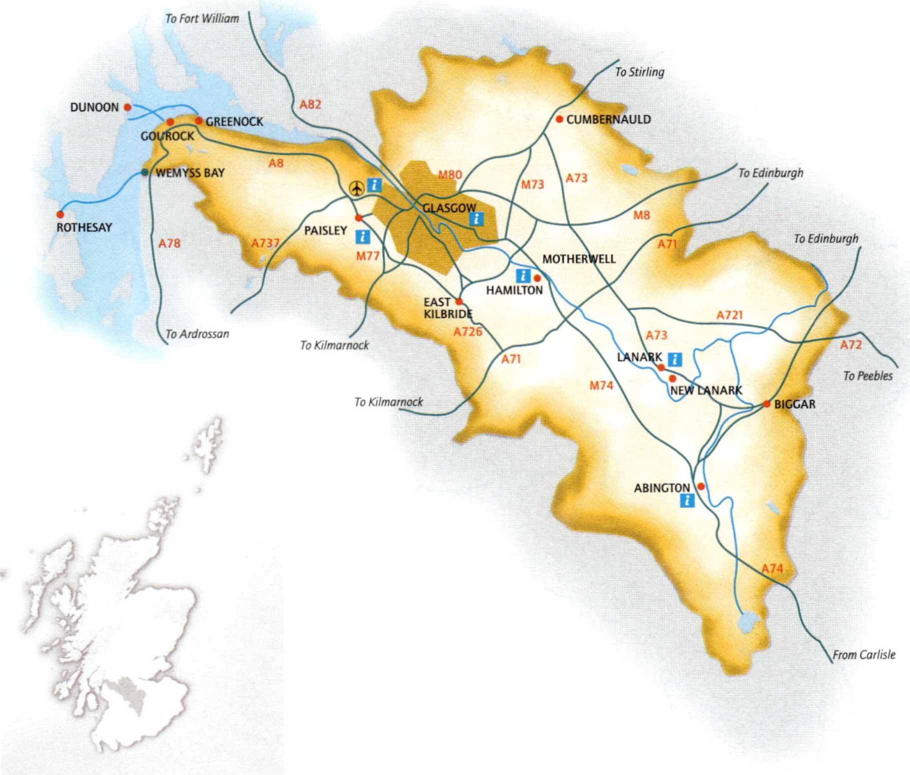

Please refer to the maps on pages xii-xviii for the locations of establishments appearing in the main advertising section of this guide. Only year-round Tourist Information Centres are indicated.

Abington	Welcome Break Service Area, Junction 13, M74	01864 502436	Jan-Dec
Biggar	155 High Street	01899 221066	Easter-Sept
Glasgow	11 George Square	0141 204 4400	Jan-Dec
Glasgow Airport	Tourist Information Desk	0141 848 4440	Jan-Dec
Hamilton	Road Chef Services, M74 northbound	01698 285590	Jan-Dec
Lanark	Horsemarket, Ladyacre Road	01555 661661	Jan-Dec
Paisley	9a Gilmour Street	0141 889 0711	Jan-Dec

For practical advice, ideas and information about exploring Scotland and to book your accommodation:

Tel: 0845 22 55 121* or if calling from outside the UK: + 44 (0) 1506 832121 In Ireland call: 1800 932 510

* A £3 booking fee applies to telephone bookings of accommodation.

info@visitscotland.com
www.visitscotland.com

Biggar, Lanarkshire
Map Ref: 2B6

★★★

SMALL HOTEL

Cornhill House Hotel
Cornhill Road, Coulter, Biggar, Clyde Valley ML12 6QE
Tel:01899 220001 Fax:01899 220112
Email:enquiries@cornhillhousehotel.com
Web:www.cornhillhousehotel.com

William Lieper's French Renaissance period chateau offering comfortable accommodation and excellent food. A new purpose built ballroom wing presently viewing.

7 rooms, all en-suite, Open Jan-Dec, B&B per person, single from £58.00, double from £40.00.

Coatbridge, Lanarkshire
Map Ref: 2A5

★★

SMALL HOTEL

The Georgian Hotel
26 Lefroy Street, Coatbridge, ML5 1LZ
Tel:01236 421888 Fax:01236 421173
Email:thegeorgian@btconnect.com
Web:www.georgianhotel.net

Family run hotel in quiet residential area near the Time Capsule. Easy access to motorway network. Ideal venue for weddings and conferences.

11 rooms, some en-suite, Open Jan-Dec excl Xmas/New Year, B&B per person, single from £25.00, double from £20.00.

Glasgow
Map Ref: 1H5

★★★

SMALL HOTEL

Albion Hotel
405 North Woodside Road, Glasgow, G20 6NN
Tel:0141 339 8620   Fax:0141 334 8159
Email:albion@glasgowhotelsandapartments.co.uk
Web:www.glasgowhotelsandapartments.co.uk

Conveniently located in the heart of Glasgow's highly desirable West End, yet only 1 mile from the City Centre. Ideal for public transport, museums and art galleries. All rooms ensuite.

17 rooms, all en-suite, Open Jan-Dec, B&B per person, single from £48.00, double from £61.00.

★★

GUEST HOUSE

Belgrave Guest House
2 Belgrave Terrace, Hillhead, Glasgow, G12 8JD
Tel:0141 337 1850   Fax:0141 337 1741
Email:belgraveglasgow@aol.com
Web:www.belgraveglasgow.com

Refurbished guest house, in the West End. Convenient for Botanic Gardens, other local attractions and amenities. 5 minute walk from two tube stations. Many restaurants, cafes and bus a few minutes walk away. Small private car-park to rear. Ensuite rooms available.

11 rooms, Open Jan-Dec, B&B per person, single from £25.00, double from £20.00.

VAT is shown at 17.5%: changes in this rate may affect prices. | *Key to symbols is on back flap.*

Glasgow

Map Ref: 1H5

Bothwell Bridge Hotel

89 Main Street, Bothwell, Glasgow, G71 8EU
Tel:01698 852246 Fax:01698 854686
Email:enquiries@bothwellbridge-hotel.com
Web:www.bothwellbridge-hotel.com

Family run hotel, 9 miles (14kms) from Glasgow city centre and
convenient for motorway. Business meeting rooms. Ample parking.
Wireless broadband available for conferences and guest rooms.

90 rooms, all en-suite, Open Jan-Dec, B&B per room, single from £60.00, double
from £70.00.

Campanile Hotel Glasgow

Tunnel Street, Glasgow, G3 8HL
Tel:0141 287 7700 Fax:0141 287 7701
Email:glasgow@campanile-hotels.com
Web:www.campanile.com

The Campanile is Glasgows newest waterside hotel and suitable for both
corporate and leisure visitors. All rooms are ensuite with power shower
and have working space with desk, modem, direct dial telephone and
satellite TV. Our cafe' bistro restaurant offers a wide selection of finest
seasonal products designed to bring you quality and freshness all year
round.

106 rooms, all en-suite, Open Jan-Dec, B&B per person, double from £33.45.

The Heritage Hotel

4-5 Alfred Terrace, Glasgow, G12 8RF
Tel/Fax:0141 339 6955
Email:bookings@heritagehotel.fsbusiness.co.uk
Web:www.visitscotland.com

Privately owned hotel, close to Botanic Garden, University, SECC and the
major hospitals. Short walk to Underground.

27 rooms, all en-suite, Open Jan-Dec excl Xmas, B&B per person, single from
£36.00, double from £28.00, family from £25.00.

Holiday Inn Glasgow City West

Bothwell Street, Glasgow, G2 7EN
Tel:0870 4009032 Fax:0141 221 8986
Email:glasgowcity-reservations@ichotelsgroup.com
Web:www.holiday-inn.co.uk

City centre location with easy access from M8. Choice of dining in the Grill
Room or 'Jules' themed restaurant and bar.

275 rooms, all en-suite, Open Jan-Dec, B&B per person, single from £76.00, double
from £76.00, Eve.Meal from £12.95.

Lomond Hotel

6 Buckingham Terrace, Great Western Road, Glasgow G12 8EB
Tel:0141 339 2339 Fax:0141 339 0477
Email:info@lomondhotel.co.uk
Web:www.lomondhotel.co.uk

Victorian terraced house in the West End. Close to the BBC, Botanical
Gardens and Glasgow University. On main bus routes to city centre and
five minutes walk from underground, restaurants and shops.

17 rooms, some en-suite, Open Jan-Dec, B&B per person, single from £24.00,
double from £21.00.

Important: Prices stated are estimates and may be subject to amendments

Glasgow
Map Ref: 1H5

The Sandyford Hotel
904 Sauchiehall Street, Glasgow, G3 7TF
Tel:0141 334 0000 Fax:0141 337 1812
Email:info@sandyfordhotelglasgow.com
Web:www.sandyfordhotelglasgow.com

Recently refurbished hotel, enjoying a convenient location in the West End, close to museums, Kelvingrove Park and SECC. On main bus route to city centre, and within walking distance of a host of Glasgow's major attractions.

55 rooms, all en-suite, Open Jan-Dec excl Xmas, B&B per person, single from £32.00, double from £26.00.

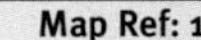

Sherbrooke Castle Hotel
11 Sherbrooke Avenue, Glasgow, G41 4PG
Tel:0141 427 4227 Fax:0141 427 5685
Email:mail@sherbrooke.co.uk
Web:www.sherbrooke.co.uk

The Sherbrooke Castle is situated in Glasgow's most prestigious of residential areas, Pollockshields. This magnificent baronial building crafted in rich red sandstone, combines traditional grace with modern efficiency. The fully air conditioned restaurant serves fresh local produce, prepared by award winning chefs, complimented with an interesting wine cellar. Some annexe accommodation.

21 rooms, all en-suite, Open Jan-Dec, B&B per person, single from £68.00, double from £44.00.

Glasgow Airport, Renfrewshire
Map Ref: 1H5

Ramada Glasgow Airport
Marchburn Drive, Glasgow Airport Business Park, Paisley, PA3 2SJ
Tel:0141 840 2200 Fax:0141 889 6830
Email:sales.glasgowairport@ramadajarvis.co.uk
Web:www.ramadaglasgowairport.co.uk

A chic, contemporary hotel opened in 2002. Free parking during your stay and just 500m from the airport. The hotel has Bagio's, an Italian style cafe bar serving pizzas from the wood burning oven.

108 rooms, all en-suite, Open Jan-Dec, B&B per person, double from £26.50.

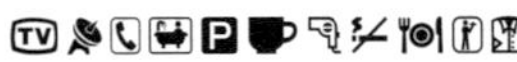

---

nr Glasgow
Map Ref: 1H5

Uplawmoor Hotel
Neilston Road, Uplawmoor, Glasgow, G78 4AF
Tel:01505 850565 Fax:01505 850689
Email:info@uplawmoor.co.uk
Web:www.uplawmoor.co.uk

Quality eighteenth century Coaching Inn situated in quiet picturesque village just thirty minutes from Glasgow City Centre and airport, gateway to Burns Country.

14 rooms, all en-suite, Open Jan-Dec excl Xmas/New Year, B&B per person, single from £42.00, double from £29.50.

Wallace Hotel
1 Yieldshields Road, Carluke, Lanarkshire, ML8 4QG
Tel:01555 773000
Email:info@wallacehotel.co.uk
Web:www.wallacehotel.co.uk

A new purpose built and spacious family run restaurant with rooms. Easy access to major road network (M74, M8, A73) with Edinburgh, Glasgow, Stirling, Ayrshire and the Scottish Borders all within easy reach. 5 golf courses within 5 miles.

10 rooms, all en-suite, Open Jan-Dec, from £40.00 Room Only.

VAT is shown at 17.5%: changes in this rate may affect prices.

Key to symbols is on back flap.

Harthill, by Shotts, Lanarkshire | Map Ref: 2A5

Blairmains Guest House
Harthill, Shotts, Lanarkshire, ML7 5TJ
Tel:01501 751278   Fax:01501 753383
Email:Heather@blairmains.freeserve.co.uk
Web:www.blairmains.co.uk

GUEST HOUSE

5 rooms, some en-suite, Open Jan-Dec, B&B per person, single from £20.00, double from £18.00, BB & Eve.Meal from £25.50.

Comfortable accommodation in separate unit adjacent to farmhouse. Conveniently situated directly beside M8 making it an ideal base for visiting Edinburgh, Glasgow and Stirling (all within 30 mins drive). Ensuite rooms available. Ample private parking. Well behaved pets welcome. Evening meals by prior arrangement.

Inverkip, Renfrewshire | Map Ref: 1F5

Inverkip Hotel
Main Street, Inverkip, Renfrewshire, PA16 OAS
Tel:01475 521478   Fax:01475 522065
Email:enquiries@inverkip.co.uk
Web:www.inverkip.co.uk

SMALL HOTEL

5 rooms, all en-suite, Open Jan-Dec, B&B per person, single from £45.00, double from £34.00.

Family run hotel, on main tourist route adjacent to Scotland's No 1 yachting marina. Reputation for good food. Sports can be arranged. Busy restaurant. Ideally positioned for the Clyde ferries to Dunoon and beyond or trips to Loch Lomond, Stirling and the Trossachs. 45 mins drive to Royal Troon.

by Larkhall, Lanarkshire | Map Ref: 2A6

Shawlands Hotel
Ayr Road, Canderside Toll, by Larkhall
Lanarkshire, ML9 2TZ
Tel/Fax:01698 791111
Email:reception@shawlandshotel.co.uk
Web:www.shawlandshotel.co.uk

LODGE

21 rooms, all en-suite, Open Jan-Dec. From £50.00 per night. Opened in October 2006, the addition of 32 luxury executive rooms, 4 luxury suites and 2 luxury family suites.

Privately owned and family run travel lodge with emphasis on quality food and drink at affordable prices. In central Scotland just off M74, 20 mins from Glasgow and 40 mins travel to Edinburgh.

Motherwell, Lanarkshire | Map Ref: 2A5

Motherwell College - Stewart Halls of Residence
Dalzell Drive, Motherwell, Lanarkshire, ML1 2DD
Tel:01698 261890   Fax:01698 232527/232600
Email:m.coll@motherwell.co.uk
Web:www.motherwell.ac.uk

CAMPUS ACCOMMODATION

41 rooms, Open Jan-Dec excl Xmas/New Year, B&B per person, single from £23.00.

On college campus and all on one level. Close to Strathclyde Park and M8/M74 motorway link for Glasgow and Edinburgh.

Paisley, Renfrewshire | Map Ref: 1H5

Dryesdale Guest House
37 Inchinnan Road, Paisley, Renfrewshire, PA3 2PR
Tel:0141 889 7178
Email:dd@paisley2001.freeserve.co.uk
Web:www.ga-taxis.co.uk/dryesdale.html

GUEST HOUSE

7 rooms, Open Jan-Dec, B&B per person, single from £25.00, double from £22.50.

Personally run guest house 0.5 mile (1km) from Glasgow Airport and M8 access. Close to Paisley with its station for the 15 minute journey to Glasgow city centre. Ideal for touring Loch Lomond, Oban and Edinburgh. Some ground floor rooms.

Important: Prices stated are estimates and may be subject to amendments

Uddingston, Lanarkshire

Map Ref: 2A5

★★★

**SMALL
HOTEL**

Redstones Hotel
8-10 Glasgow Road, Uddingston, Glasgow, G71 7AS
Tel:01698 813744 Fax:01698 815319
Email:info@redstoneshotel.com
Web:www.redstoneshotel.com

Linked Victorian villas retaining original features and with modern
facilities. Situated within easy access to M74, within 10mins of Glasgow.

12 rooms, all en-suite, Open Jan-Dec excl Xmas/New Year, B&B per person, single
from £50.00, double from £60.00.

VAT is shown at 17.5%: changes in this rate may affect prices.

Key to symbols is on back flap.

Main image: Loch Lomond **Bottom left:** Tobermory, Isle of Mull
Bottom middle: Loch Awe and Kilchurn Castle **Bottom right:** The Falkirk Wheel

WEST HIGHLANDS AND ISLANDS, LOCH LOMOND, STIRLING AND TROSSACHS

Stretching across Scotland from the shores of the Forth in the east to the very tip of Tiree in the west, the Highlands and the Lowlands come together in a land of incredible contrasts.

It's a world with a rich and dramatic history but at the same time it embraces some of the best qualities of modern Scottish life.

Starting your journey on the east side of the country, any visitor's itinerary should include a trip to The Falkirk Wheel. Built to celebrate the new Millennium, the Wheel is a triumph of engineering. It's the world's only rotating boat lift and it reconnected the Forth & Clyde Canal with the Union Canal when it was opened in 2002. At 24 metres high (the equivalent of an 8 story building) it's an impressive sight and

 THE NO.1 BOOKING AND INFORMATION SERVICE FOR SCOTLAND   0845 22 55 121   visitscotland.com

Stirling Castle

you'll get a real thrill if you experience the wheel in action from the deck of a boat.

While you're in the area, you can also explore Scotland's industrial heritage. The Bo'ness and Kinneil Steam Railway, Birkhill Fireclay Mine and Callendar House all make for fascinating days out, while you can trace the history of Scotland's woollen industry on the opposite shores of the Forth in Clackmannan. Take the old Mill Trail to Alva and discover how Scotland's woollen mills, powered by the rivers pouring down from the Ochils, fuelled fashion through the ages.

Scotland's newest city, Stirling, is the next stop on the way west. Strategically, placed as it is between the Highlands and the Lowlands, there was a time in days gone by when those in control of Stirling, controlled all of Scotland. That made the town, with its impressive castle, the capital for the Stewart Kings. Mary, Queen of Scots, celebrated her coronation here and you can retrace her early years at Stirling Castle.

Some of the most famous battles in Scottish history were also won and lost around the city. No fewer than seven battle sites can be seen from the Castle ramparts – including Stirling Bridge, a scene of triumph for William Wallace and Bannockburn where Robert the Bruce led the Scots to victory in 1314.

Heading further west, all roads lead to the bonnie banks of Loch Lomond. Now a National Park spanning some 720 square miles, Loch Lomond and the Trossachs is one of the most beautiful places in all the world. There are 20 Munros (mountains over 3000ft) to climb, 50 rivers to fish, 22 lochs to sail and thousands of miles of road and track to cycle. And when you've had your fill of activities, head for Loch Lomond Shores for an unforgettable retail experience.

Travelling ever westwards, you'll come to the Cowal Peninsula with its sea lochs and deep forests. You can jump aboard the ferry at Gourock and sail for Dunoon where the nearby Benmore Botanic Gardens are a wonderfully relaxing place to spend the day. You could

What's On?

Big in Falkirk
28 - 29 April 2007
Scotland's National Street Arts Festival.
www.biginfalkirk.com

Lomond and Clyde Springfest, Helensburgh
28 April – 4 May 2007
A springtime festival with a touch of Japanese culture.

Isle of Bute Jazz Festival
3 - 7 May 2007
A host of well-known names in Bute's annual jazz-fest.
www.butejazz.com

Scottish Pipeband Championships, Dumbarton
19 May 2007
See world-class pipe bands as they battle for top place.
www.rspba.org

Mull of Kintyre Music Festival
16 - 19 August 2007
A musical extravaganza in Campbeltown and the Mull of Kintyre.

Cowal Highland Gathering, Dunoon
23 - 25 August 2007
Experience Scottish tradition and culture in three days.
www.cowalgathering.com

Loch Lomond Food & Drink Festival
14 - 16 September 2007
Enjoy fine food and drink from all over the region.

Cowalfest
5 - 14 October 2007
Scotland's largest combined walking and arts festival.
www.cowalfest.org

Tunnocks Tour of Mull Rally
12 - 14 October 2007
Enjoy the atmosphere at this annual car rally.
www.2300club.org

Aberfoyle Mushroom Festival
19 - 22 October 2007
A long weekend of fantasy, fungi, food and fun.
www.visitaberfoyle.com

Jump aboard a ferry headed for the Isles or cycle round the National Park - there's always plenty to keep you amused.

also head for lovely Lochgilphead and beyond to Kilmartin where you can trace the very roots of the Scots nation. In the 6th Century, the Scots arrived here from Ireland and set up the Kingdom of Dalriada. Hundreds of prehistoric sites and ancient monuments chronicle the former importance of the birthplace of Scots history.

Further down the Kintyre Peninsula things feel more like island than mainland and the beaches are a delight. But for the genuine island experience, you're spoiled for choice. Gigha, Jura, Islay and Colonsay can all be accessed from Kennacraig and from Oban, the gateway to the Isles, you can escape to Coll, Tiree, Mull and Iona.

If island exploring is your thing, you'll be in your element. Each is different with its own attractions. Islay is unmissable for its wonderful whiskies - there are eight distilleries on the island! Iona is deeply spiritual. Mull, thanks in part to the colourful Tobermory, (who wouldn't want to visit the real 'Balamory'?) is always a big hit with families.

Choosing a holiday destination in an area as varied as this will always be difficult but the diversity of the numerous hotels and guesthouses offering high-quality accommodation will help. There's a tantalising array of guesthouses, historical inns, grand hotels and even restaurants with rooms so you're sure to find somewhere that will tempt you to come back for more.

View of Loch Lomond from Duncryne

Tourist Information Centres

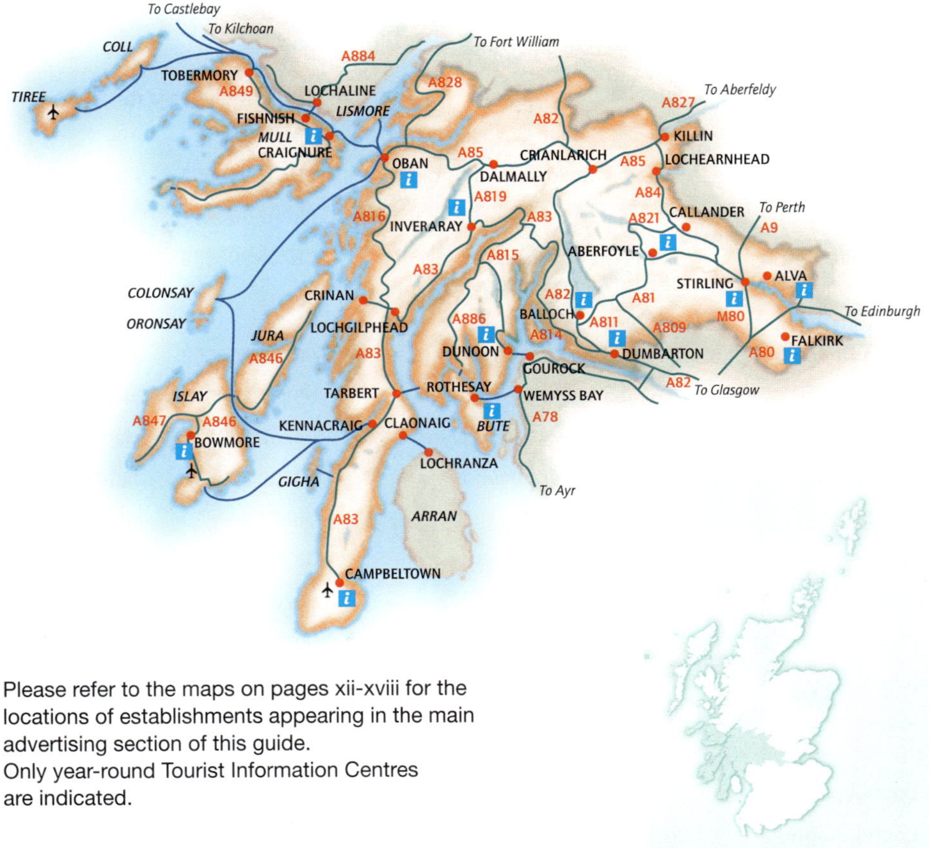

Please refer to the maps on pages xii-xviii for the
locations of establishments appearing in the main
advertising section of this guide.
Only year-round Tourist Information Centres
are indicated.

For practical advice, ideas and information about exploring Scotland and to book your accommodation:

Tel: 0845 22 55 121* or if calling from
outside the UK: + 44 (0) 1506 832121
In Ireland call: 1800 932 510

* A £3 booking fee applies to telephone bookings of accommodation.

info@visitscotland.com
www.visitscotland.com

Aberfoyle	Trossachs Discovery Centre, Main St	08707 200604	Jan-Dec
Alva	Mill Trail Visitor Centre	08707 200605	Jan-Dec
Ardgartan	Arrochar	08707 200606	Apr-Oct
Balloch	The Old Station Building	08707 200607	Apr-Oct
Bo'ness	Bo'ness Station, Union Street	08707 200608	May-Sept
Bowmore	Isle of Islay	08707 200617	Jan-Dec
Callander	Rob Roy and Trossachs Visitor Centre, Ancaster Square	08707 200628	Mar-Dec (Jan and Feb w/ends only)
Campbeltown	Mackinnon House, The Pier	08707 200609	Jan-Dec
Craignure	The Pier, Isle of Mull	08707 200610	Jan-Dec
Drymen	Drymen Library, The Square	08707 200611	May-Sept
Dumbarton	Milton, A82 northbound	08707 200612	Jan-Dec
Dunblane	Stirling Road	08707 200613	May-Sept
Dunoon	7 Alexandra Parade	08707 200629	Jan-Dec
Falkirk	2-4 Glebe Street	08707 200614	Jan-Dec
Helensburgh	The Clock Tower	08707 200615	Apr-Oct
Inveraray	Front Street	08707 200616	Jan-Dec
Killin	Breadalbane Folklore Centre	08707 200627	Mar-Oct (Feb w/ends only)
Lochgilphead	Lochnell Street	08707 200618	Apr-Oct
Loch Lomond	Loch Lomond Gateway Centre, Loch Lomond Shores, Balloch	08707 200631	Jan-Dec
Oban	Argyll Square	08707 200630	Jan-Dec
Rothesay	Discovery Centre, Winter Gardens, Isle of Bute	08707 200619	Jan-Dec
Stirling	41 Dumbarton Road	08707 200620	Jan-Dec
Stirling	Pirnhall Motorway Service Area Junction 9, M9	08707 200624	Apr-Oct
Tarbert, Loch Fyne	Harbour Street	08707 200624	Apr-Oct
Tarbet, Loch Lomond	Main Street	08707 200623	Apr-Oct
Tobermory	The Pier, Isle of Mull	08707 200625	Apr-Oct
Tyndrum	Main Street	08707 200626	Apr-Oct

Aberfoyle, Stirlingshire

Map Ref: 1H3

GUEST HOUSE

Creag-Ard House
Aberfoyle, Stirling, FK8 3TQ
Tel/Fax:01877 382 297
Email:cara@creag-ardhouse.co.uk
Web:www.creag-ardhouse.co.uk

Welcoming Guest House with superb views over Loch Ard 3kms from the centre of Aberfoyle Village in the heart of the Trossachs. A haven of peace and tranquility. Delicious breakfast with homebaking.

6 rooms, all en-suite, Open Mar-Oct, B&B per person, single from £45.00, double from £35.00.

Rob Roy Hotel
Aberfoyle, Trossach National Park, Stirlingshire FK8 3UX
Tel: 01877 382245 Fax: 01877 382262
e.mail: info@robroyhotel.co.uk Web: www.robroyhotel.co.uk
Situated 40 minutes drive from Glasgow/Edinburgh, this excellent value hotel is located at the Gateway to Scotland's First National Park and the entrance to Aberfoyle. Restaurant, beer garden, food served all day. Catering for all functions, weddings/Saturday night dinner dances. Public coaches welcome. Free car and coach parking.

34694

HOTEL

Rob Roy Hotel
Aberfoyle, Stirlingshire, FK8 3UX
Tel:01877 382245 Fax:01877 382262
Email:info@robroyhotel.co.uk
Web:www.robroyhotel.co.uk

Fully refurbished public areas, bar meals plus restaurant and accommodation. Ideal base for touring and playing golf.

104 rooms, all en-suite, Open Jan-Dec, B&B per person, single from £30.00, double from £25.00, BB & Eve.Meal from £30.00.

Ardlui, Argyll

Map Ref: 1G3

SMALL HOTEL

Ardlui Hotel
Ardlui, Loch Lomond, Argyll, G83 7EB
Tel:01301 704269/243 Fax:01301 704268
Email:info@ardlui.co.uk
Web:www.ardlui.co.uk

Former shooting lodge on A82 and on the banks of Loch Lomond with private gardens to shore. Caravan site adjacent. Moorings available. 1 hour from Glasgow or Oban & ½ hours from Fort William via Glencoe.

10 rooms, all en-suite, Open Jan-Dec excl Xmas, B&B per person, single from £50.00, double from £37.50.

Ardrishaig, by Lochgilphead, Argyll

Map Ref: 1E4

SMALL HOTEL

Allt-Na-Craig House
Tarbert Road, Ardrishaig, Argyll, PA30 8EP
Tel:01546 603245
Email:information@allt-na-craig.co.uk
Web:www.allt-na-craig.co.uk

A Victorian Mansion set in picturesque grounds, with magnificent views across Loch Fyne. Entrance to Crinan Canal nearby. Home cooking. Hill-walking, bird-watching, fishing, golf, riding, diving, wind-surfing and many other outdoor activities are available in the area.

5 rooms, all en-suite, Open Jan-Dec excl Xmas/New Year, B&B per person, single from £40.00, double from £40.00.

VAT is shown at 17.5%: changes in this rate may affect prices.

Key to symbols is on back flap.

Balloch, Dunbartonshire | Map Ref: 1G4

GUEST HOUSE

Anchorage Guest House
31 Balloch Road, Balloch, Loch Lomond, G83 8SS
Tel:01389 753336
Email:anchorage_gh@hotmail.com
Web:www.anchorage-guesthouse-balloch.com

Extended cottage in centre of village, near river. Railway station and all other amenities nearby. Ideal touring base. All rooms ground floor.

5 rooms, all en-suite, Open Jan-Dec, B&B per person, single from £25.00, double from £25.00.

Kilchattan Bay, Isle of Bute | Map Ref: 1F6

SMALL HOTEL

St Blane's Hotel
Kilchattan Bay, Isle of Bute, PA20 9NW
Tel:01700 831224 Fax:01700 831381
Email:info@stblaneshotel.com
Web:www.stblaneshotel.com

Family run seafront hotel (1881) secluded location, recently refurbished, views to Ayrshire and Cumbrae coast. Four Poster rooms. Fine selection of malt whiskies, home cooking. Free mooring for visiting yachts. Picnic garden and private parking.

10 rooms, all en-suite, Open Jan-Dec, B&B per person, single from £35.00, double from £30.00.

Rothesay, Isle of Bute | Map Ref: 1F5

SMALL HOTEL

The Ardyne Hotel
38 Mount Stuart Road, Rothesay, Isle of Bute, PA20 9EB
Tel:01700 502052 Fax:01700 505129
Email:ardyne.hotel@virgin.net
Web:www.rothesay-scotland.com

Elegant, licensed Victorian hotel, with spectacular seafront views. All bedrooms en-suite. Reputation for comfortable accommodation and excellent restaurant.

10 rooms, all en-suite, Open Jan-Dec, B&B per person, single from £32.50, double from £29.50, BB & Eve.Meal from £47.00.

HOTEL

Glenburn Hotel
Mount Stuart Road, Rothesay, Isle of Bute, PA20 9JB
Tel:01942 824824
Email:reservations@WAshearings.com
Web:www.WAshearingsholidays.com

Fine Victorian building in an outstanding position above its own terraced gardens overlooking the sea. Entertainment every night.

127 rooms, all en-suite, Open Feb-Dec, B&B per person, double from £25.00.

GUEST HOUSE

The Regent Hotel
23 Battery Place, Rothesay, Isle of Bute, PA20 9DU
Tel:01700 502006
Web:www.theregent.co.uk

A warm welcome awaits you at this small hotel situated a short walk from the town centre. Comfortable rooms are complemented by an a' la carte restaurant, with a choice of Scottish Fayre and Mediterranean-style cuisine. Enjoy a drink on the sea-facing deck or in Dizzy's Bar which has live Saturday night entertainment.

8 rooms, some en-suite, Open Jan-Dec, B&B per person, single from £25.00, double from £37.50.

Important: Prices stated are estimates and may be subject to amendments

Callander, Perthshire

Map Ref: 1H3

★★★

GUEST HOUSE

Annfield Guest House
18 North Church Street, Callander, Perthshire, FK17 8EG
Tel:01877 330204   Fax:01877 330674
Email:reservations@annfieldguesthouse.co.uk
Web:www.annfieldguesthouse.co.uk

A lovely Victorian villa quietly situated just 2 minutes walk from Callanders bustling main street. A superb base to explore Loch Lomond and the Trossachs.

7 rooms, some en-suite, Open Jan-Dec, B&B per person, single from £25.00, double from £24.00.

Callander, Perthshire

Map Ref: 1H3

★★

INN

Coppice Hotel
Leny Road, Callander, Perthshire, FK17 8AL
Tel:01877 330188
Email:coppicehotel@tinyworld.co.uk

Personally run hotel with emphasis on cuisine using fresh local produce when available. Ideal base for touring the Trossachs or day trips to Stirling with its Castle and the Wallace Monument.

5 rooms, all en-suite, Open Jan-Dec, B&B per person, double from £26.00.

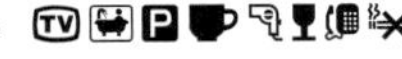

★★★

GUEST HOUSE

The Crags Hotel
101 Main Street, Callander, Perthshire, FK17 8BQ
Tel:01877 330257   Fax:01877 339997
Email:nieto@btinternet.com
Web:www.cragshotel.co.uk

A warm Scottish welcome guaranteed in this personally run small family fully licensed hotel situated on Callander's main street. An ideal base for exploring the Trossachs an area of outstanding natural beauty. Hearty meals using fresh local produce wherever possible.

7 rooms, all en-suite, Open Jan-Dec, B&B per person, single from £32.50, double from £25.00.

Riverview Guest House
Leny Road, Callander, Perthshire, FK17 8AL
Tel:01877 330635   Fax:01877 339386
Email:drew@visitcallander.co.uk
Web:www.visitcallander.co.uk

Detached stone built Victorian house set in its own garden with private parking. Close to town centre, leisure complex and local amenities. Within easy walking distance of pleasant riverside park and cycle track. Ideal base for exploring the beautiful Trossachs.

★★★

GUEST HOUSE

5 rooms, all en-suite, Open Mar-Nov, B&B per person, single from £27.50, double from £25.00.

---

by Campbeltown, Argyll

Map Ref: 1D7

★★★★★

GUEST HOUSE

Dalnaspidal Guest House
Tangy, Kilkenzie, by Campbeltown, Argyll, PA28 6QD
Tel:01586 820466
Email:relax@dalnaspidal-guesthouse.com
Web:www.dalnaspidal-guesthouse.com

4 rooms, all en-suite, Open all year. B&B per person, single £35.00-55.00, double/twin £35.00-55.00. Dinner per person £15.00-25.00.

VAT is shown at 17.5%: changes in this rate may affect prices. | Key to symbols is on back flap.

Carradale, Argyll

Map Ref: 1E6

Carradale Hotel

Carradale, Nr. Campbeltown, Argyll PA28 6RY
Tel: 01583 431223
e.mail: noriffraff@carradalehotel.com
Web: www.carradalehotel.com

Idyllic situation overlooking Arran. An ideal base for golfing at Machrihanish or on the local course, walking or cycling the Kintyre Way, game fishing on the river or hill lochs. We offer modern Scottish food imaginatively prepared with fine wines, local malts, cosy bars and log fires.

18252

Carradale Hotel
Carradale, Argyll, PA28 6RY
Tel:01583 431223
Email:noriffraff@carradalehotel.com
Web:www.carradalehotel.com

SMALL
HOTEL

Family run hotel, overlooking Arran. Beautiful scenery, golf, fishing, beaches, mountain bikes, hillwalking and sauna. Taste of Scotland recommended.

9 rooms, all en-suite, Open Jan-Dec, B&B per person, single from £25.00, double from £25.00, BB & Eve.Meal from £44.00.

Kiloran Guest House
Carradale, Argyll, Mull of Kintyre, PA28 6QG
Tel:01583 431795

GUEST
HOUSE

Traditional Scottish hospitality awaits at this Victorian villa on the outskirts of the village. Evening meal by arrangement. Fishing and golfing are available locally. There are also many established forest trails and local beaches. Non smoking in dining room only.

5 rooms, some en-suite, Open Jan-Dec, B&B per person, single £25.00-30.00, double £25.00-28.00, BB & Eve.Meal £35.00-38.00.

Colintraive, Argyll

Map Ref: 1F5

Colintraive Hotel
Colintraive, Argyll, PA22 3AS
Tel:01700 841207
Email:enquiries@colintraivehotel.com
Web:www.colintraivehotel.com

SMALL
HOTEL

A former hunting lodge, fully refurbished to a high standard with stunning views over the Kyles of Bute. Cosy bar with log fire and excellent bar meals. Elegant a' la carte restaurant using local produce & vegetables from our own garden. Period furniture & big leather chairs in coffee lounge. Beautiful spacious ensuite bedrooms. This family run hotel offers very high standards in relaxed informal surroundings. A great base for walking, sailing, cycling and fishing. Close to Bute ferry and adjoining village shop.

4 rooms, all en-suite, Open Jan-Dec, B&B per person, single from £45.00, double from £30.00.

Coll, Isle of, Argyll

Map Ref: 1B1

Coll Hotel
Arinagour, Isle of Coll, Argyll, PA78 6SZ
Tel:01879 230334   Fax:01879 230317
Email:info@collhotel.com
Web:www.collhotel.com

INN

17c building with panoramic sea views across Mull and the Treshnish Isles. Under 1 mile (2kms) from the ferry terminal. Bar and restaurant meals available, specialising in seafood and using the best of fresh local produce. All rooms furnished to a high standard. Taste of Scotland recommended. Winner of Thistle Award 2003 Flavour of Scotland.

6 rooms, all en-suite, Open Jan-Dec excl Xmas/New Year, B&B per person, single from £35.00, double from £35.00.

Important: Prices stated are estimates and may be subject to amendments

Connel, Argyll

Map Ref: 1E2

GUEST HOUSE ★★★★

Ronebhal Guest House
Connel, by Oban, Argyll, PA37 1PJ
Tel/Fax:01631 710310
Email:ronebhal@btinternet.com
Web:www.ronebhal.co.uk

Victorian Villa set in beautiful gardens with magnificent views of Loch Etive and the mountains beyond. Superior standard of hospitality and comfort with a hearty breakfast served at individual tables. Within walking distance of two restaurants. Ideal touring base. Private parking. Oban 5 miles (8kms).

5 rooms, some en-suite, Open Mar-Oct, B&B per person, single £27.50-50.00, double £22.50-35.00.

Crianlarich, Perthshire

Map Ref: 1G2

INN ★★

Ben More Lodge Hotel & Restaurant
Crianlarich, Perthshire, FK20 8QS
Tel:01838 300210 Fax:01838 300218
Email:info@ben-more.co.uk
Web:www.ben-more.co.uk

Pine lodges of a high standard with restaurant and bar adjacent. Ideal base for touring, hillwalking and fishing. Cash machine on site.

11 rooms, all en-suite, Open Feb-Dec excl Xmas, B&B per person, single from £45.00, double from £26.00.

SMALL HOTEL ★★

Suie Lodge Hotel
Luib, Glen Dochart, Crianlarich, Perthshire, FK20 8QT
Tel:01567 820417 Fax:01567 820040
Email:suielodge@btinternet.com
Web:www.suielodge.co.uk

Family run hotel in former Shooting Lodge, in scenic Glendochart. Offering a relaxed atmosphere, comfortable bedrooms. Many en-suite. Good Scottish food. Excellent centre for touring.

10 rooms, some en-suite, Open Jan-Dec, B&B per person, single from £25.00, double from £27.50.

Dunoon, Argyll

Map Ref: 1F5

GUEST HOUSE ★★★

The Ardtully Hotel
297 Marine Parade, Hunters Quay, Dunoon, Argyll, PA23 8HN
Tel:01369 702478

Friendly run guest house set in its own grounds in an elevated position offering guests outstanding views of the Clyde Estuary, and the hills and mountains of Scotlands first Natural Park. Visit Dunoon's award winning Castle Museum, explore the many coastal, hill and forest walks. Relax over dinner in comfortable surroundings. Meals prepared using fresh produce. Some chalet bedrooms.

7 rooms, all en-suite, Open Jan-Dec, B&B per person, low season £30.00, high season £35.00. BB & Eve.Meal £54.00-59.00.

VAT is shown at 17.5%: changes in this rate may affect prices.

Key to symbols is on back flap.

Dunoon, Argyll

Map Ref: 1F5

ENMORE HOTEL
Marine Parade, Dunoon, Argyll PA23 8HH
Tel: 01369 702230   Fax: 01369 702148
Email: enmorehotel@btinternet.com
Web: www.enmorehotel.co.uk
Small, stylish, family run hotel with a spectacular waterside location and set in well maintained and beautiful gardens. For any occasion or simply just pampering yourself and your loved one, the Enmore will delight in making the occasion very special. Romantic bedrooms, some with four poster beds and double spa baths complete with underwater lighting.   24981

★★★★

SMALL
HOTEL

Enmore Hotel
Marine Parade, Kirn, Dunoon, Argyll, PA23 8HH
Tel:01369 702230   Fax:01369 702148
Email:enmorehotel@btinternet.com
Web:www.enmorehotel.co.uk

Beautifully situated with open sea views. Small, comfortable hotel offering the very best in accommodation, cuisine and hospitality.

10 rooms, all ensuite, Open Jan-Dec, B&B per person, single from £65.00, double from £45.00, family from £60.00. Room Only rates per night, single from £65.00, double from £90.00, family from £120.00.

Fintry, Stirlingshire

Map Ref: 1H4

Culcreuch Castle Hotel and Country Park

Culcreuch Castle, Fintry, Stirlingshire G63 0LW
Tel: 01360 860555 Fax: 01360 860556
e.mail: info@culcreuch.com Web: www.culcreuch.com
Magnificent 1600-acre parkland estate in breathtaking scenery. 700-year-old Culcreuch is a unique opportunity to sample the historic atmosphere of Central Scotland's oldest inhabited castle. Comfortable accommodation, cosy bar, licensed restaurant, free fishing, adjacent squash courts, log fires, warm welcome. Central for all Scotland's attractions, including Edinburgh (55 minutes by road). For free accommodation brochure, free fishing and golf brochures:–

Contact: Laird of Culcreuch, Culcreuch Castle Hotel, Fintry, Stirlingshire G63 0LW.
Tel: (01360) 860555 Fax: (01360) 860556   21662

★★★

SMALL
HOTEL

Culcreuch Castle Hotel
Fintry, Glasgow, G63 0LW
Tel:01360 860555   Fax:01360 860556
Email:info@culcreuch.com
Web:www.culcreuch.com

14c castle with Dungeon Bar set in 1600 acre estate, with impressive views of Campsie Hills. Good base for touring central Scotland. Golfing, walking and fishing all available locally. Specialising in traditional Scottish Weddings.

14 rooms, all en-suite, Open Jan-Dec, B&B per person, single £76.00-115.00, double/twin £51.00-90.00, BB & Eve.Meal from £105.00-132.00.

Important: Prices stated are estimates and may be subject to amendments

Gigha, Isle of, Argyll   Map Ref: 1D6

GIGHA HOTEL & COTTAGES

Isle of Gigha, Argyll PA41 7AA
Tel: 01583 505254 Fax: 01583 505244
e.mail: hotel@gigha.org.uk Web: www.gigha.org.uk

The community-owned Isle of Gigha (Gaelic: God's Island) is known as *The Jewel of the Inner Hebrides*. The Atlantic's crystal clear waters surround this six mile long magical isle, and lap gently on to its white sandy beaches – creating an aura of peace and tranquillity.

The Gigha Hotel caters admirably for the discerning holidaymaker, with comfortable accommodation and first class cuisine, including fresh local seafood. There are also holiday cottages available.

A must for any visitor is a wander around the famous sub-tropical Achamore Gardens, where palm trees and many other exotic plants flourish in Gigha's mild climatic conditions.

Special breaks available all year.   27610

★★★

SMALL HOTEL

Gigha Hotel & Cottages
Isle of Gigha, Argyll, PA41 7AA
Tel:01583 505254 Fax:01583 505244
Email:hotel@gigha.org.uk
Web:www.gigha.org.uk

Originally an old Inn, the hotel has been thoughtfully and tastefully modernised. Scottish fare, using local produce and seafood.

12 rooms, all en-suite, Open Jan-Dec, B&B per person, single from £48.50, double from £48.50, BB & Eve.Meal from £68.50 per person.

Bowmore, Isle of Islay, Argyll   Map Ref: 1C6

★★★★

INN

The Harbour Inn and Restaurant
Bowmore, Isle of Islay, Argyll, PA43 7JR
Tel:01496 810330 Fax:01496 810990
Email:info@harbour-inn.com
Web:www.harbour-inn.com

High quality refurbished accommodation compliments our award winning restaurant. AA 2 Red Rosettes/Egon Ronay. We use the best of Islay produce. New this year .... Oyster Bar .... informal setting with emphasis on seafood.

7 rooms, all en-suite, Open Jan-Dec, B&B per person, single from £65.00, double from £52.50.

Port Charlotte, Isle of Islay, Argyll   Map Ref: 1B6

★★★★

SMALL HOTEL

The Port Charlotte Hotel
Main Street, Port Charlotte, Isle of Islay, PA48 7TU
Tel:01496 850360 Fax:01496 850361
Email:info@portcharlottehotel.co.uk
Web:www.portcharlottehotel.co.uk

Restored Victorian hotel offering all modern facilities in an informal, relaxed atmosphere, situated in this picturesque conservation village on the west shore of Loch Indaal. Fresh local seafood, lamb and beef. Distillery visits, fishing and golfing can be arranged.

10 rooms, all en-suite, Open Jan-Dec, B&B per person, single from £75.00, double from £60.00.

VAT is shown at 17.5%: changes in this rate may affect prices. | *Key to symbols is on back flap.*

Port Ellen, Isle of Islay, Argyll — Map Ref: 1C6

★★★

SMALL
HOTEL

Machrie Hotel & Golf Links
Port Ellen, Isle of Islay, PA42 7AN
Tel:01496 302310   Fax:01496 302404
Email:machrie@machrie.com
Web:www.machrie.com

Built over 250 years ago as a farmhouse, the Machrie combines the relaxed traditonal atmosphere of that period with modern service and comfort. It is an ideal place to relax and unwind from the stresses of the everyday world, be it sitting in front of a peat fire or playing golf, snooker or carpet bowls. The hotel also boasts a hairdressing salon.

16 rooms, all en-suite, Open Jan-Dec, B&B per room, single from £45.00, double from £114.00, BB & Eve.Meal from £70.00.

Jura, Isle of, Argyll — Map Ref: 1D4

★★

SMALL
HOTEL

Jura Hotel
Isle of Jura, Argyll, PA60 7XU
Tel:01496 820243   Fax:01496 820249
Email:jurahotel@aol.com
Web:www.jurahotel.co.uk

Family run hotel with gardens, overlooking Small Isles Bay and close to famous distillery. Showers, drying room and laundry facilities for sailors and walkers.

17 rooms, 8 ensuite, Open Jan-Dec, B&B per person single from £40.00, double from £70.00 (room rate).

Killin, Perthshire — Map Ref: 1H2

★★★★

GUEST
HOUSE

Dall Lodge Country House
Main Street, Killin, Perthshire, FK21 8TN
Tel:01567 820217   Fax:01567 820726
Email:connor@dalllodge.co.uk
Web:www.dalllodge.co.uk

Country house recently modernised with old world charm retained. On outskirts of picturesque village of Killin overlooking River Lochay with own moorings and spectacular views of mountains. Perfect base for outdoor activities, walking and fishing.

9 rooms, all en-suite, Open Mar-Oct, B&B per person, single from £30.00, double from £25.00.

Lochearnhead, Perthshire — Map Ref: 1H2

★★

SMALL
HOTEL

Lochearnhead Hotel
Lochside, Lochearnhead, FK19 8PU
Tel:01567 830229 Fax:01567 830364
Email:info@lochearnhead-hotel.com
Web:www.lochearnhead-hotel.com

The Lochearnhead hotel sits in an elevated position overlooking Loch Earn. Water sports centre and sailing facilities adjacent. Ideal centre for touring, golfing, fishing and hillwalking. Off-season special breaks available.

10 rooms, all en-suite, Open Jan-Dec, B&B per person, single from £45.00, double from £35.00.

Bunessan, Isle of Mull, Argyll — Map Ref: 1C3

★★★

SMALL
HOTEL

Ardachy House Hotel
Uisken, by Bunessan, Isle of Mull, Argyll, PA67 6DS
Tel:01681 700505 Fax:01681 700797
Email:info@ardachy.co.uk
Web:www.ardachy.co.uk

Small, secluded, personally-run hotel, 7 miles (11 kms) from Iona. Safe access to white sands of Ardalanish Beach. Spectacular views to Colonsay, Jura and Islay. 1 room without ensuite. Non-resident dinner available by prior arrangement.

8 rooms, all en-suite, Open Apr-Oct, B&B per person, single from £45.00, double from £45.00, BB & Eve.Meal from £65.00.

Important: Prices stated are estimates and may be subject to amendments

Dervaig, Isle of Mull, Argyll

Map Ref: 1C1

SMALL HOTEL

★★★

Druimnacroish Hotel
Dervaig, Isle of Mull, PA75 6QW
Tel:01688 400274
Web:www.druimnacroish.co.uk

Converted water mill set on a tranquil and secluded hillside offering a relaxed, friendly atmosphere, spacious accommodation, extensive gardens, good food, home made bread, superb views from every room. Put your feet up by the fire or enjoy the view from the conservatory. Well situated for Mull's many attractions including boat trips, wildlife and walking. Taste of Scotland Award.

6 rooms, all en-suite, Open Apr-Oct, B&B per person, single from £60.00, double from £39.00, BB & Eve.Meal from £59.00.

by Dervaig, Isle of Mull, Argyll

Map Ref: 1C1

SMALL HOTEL

★★★

The Calgary Hotel
by Dervaig, Isle of Mull, Argyll, PA75 6QW
Tel:01688 400256
Email:calgary.hotel@virgin.net
Web:www.calgary.co.uk

Converted farm buildings, close to the beautiful white sands of Calgary beach, Cozy, and tastefully decorated friendly small hotel, with much quality local & Scottish produce to be enjoyed in our 'Dovecote Restaurant'. Newly created woodland walk with sculpture combines peace with nature.

9 rooms, all en-suite, Open Easter-Oct (weekends only in Feb, Mar & Nov), B&B from £31.00-48.00. Dinner from £22.00-30.00 for 3x courses a la'carte.

Tobermory, Isle of Mull, Argyll

Map Ref: 1C1

Highland Cottage
Breadalbane Street, Tobermory, Isle of Mull PA75 6PD
Tel: 01688 302030
e.mail: davidandjo@highlandcottage.co.uk
Web: www.highlandcottage.co.uk

Intimate friendly family run hotel in quiet location in Upper Tobermory with reputation for hospitality and good food. 4-poster beds, satellite TV and books galore. Plentiful parking and only minutes from bustling main street and fisherman's pier. Come and relax. Colour brochure from David and Josephine Currie – resident owners. RAC Gold Ribbon. AA Top 200.

AA ⊛⊛
30309

SMALL HOTEL

★★★★

Highland Cottage
Breadalbane Street, Tobermory, Isle of Mull, PA75 6PD
Tel:01688 302030
Email:davidandjo@highlandcottage.co.uk
Web:www.highlandcottage.co.uk

Family-run 'country house in the town' hotel located in the heart of upper Tobermory in conservation area. Well appointed bedrooms themed after local islands and including 2 with 4 poster beds. Imaginative award-winning cuisine using fresh, local ingredients served in our attractive, homely, dining room. High level of personal attention from resident owners. AA Top 200, AA 2 Rosette, RAC Gold Ribbon.

6 rooms, all en-suite, Open Mar-Nov, B&B per person, double from £67.50, BB & Eve.Meal from £105.00.

SMALL HOTEL

★★★

Tobermory Hotel
Main Street, Tobermory, Isle of Mull, PA75 6NT
Tel:01688 302091   Fax:01688 302254
Email:tobhotel@tinyworld.co.uk
Web:www.thetobermoryhotel.com

This small family-run hotel is superbly sited on the waterfront overlooking the bay. The restaurant (1 AA Rosette) promotes the best of local produce superbly cooked. There are sixteen bedrooms, fifteen of which are en suite, and two are on the ground floor. Ample street parking is available.

16 rooms, 15 en-suite, Open Jan-Dec excl Xmas, B&B per person, single from £36.00, double from £36.00.

VAT is shown at 17.5%: changes in this rate may affect prices.

Key to symbols is on back flap.

Oban, Argyll

Map Ref: 1E2

★★★★

GUEST HOUSE

Corriemar House

6 Corran Esplanade, Oban, Argyll, PA34 5AQ
Tel:01631 562476 Fax:01631 564339
Email:info@corriemarhouse.co.uk
Web:www.corriemarhouse.co.uk

Situated on the seafront, this large Victorian family run Guest House is only 10 minutes walk along the prom to the town centre. Spectacular Oban sunsets looking from the lounge and seaview bedroom over to Kerrara with the hills of Mull beyond. Queen size deluxe rooms and four poster rooms available. One suite room with sea views.

14 rooms, 13 en-suite, 1 priv.facilities, Open Jan-Dec, B&B per person, double £30.00-48.00. Queen sized deluxe rooms and 4 poster room available.

★★★★

GUEST HOUSE

Don-Muir Guest House

Pulpit Hill, Oban, Argyll, PA34 4LX
Tel:01631 564536
Email:dina.donmuir@tesco.net

Set in quiet residential area, high up on Pulpit Hill and close to public transport terminals. A short walk away are 360 degree views of Oban, the bay and its ferries. Parking available.

4 rooms, all en-suite, Open all year, B&B per person, double £25.00-35.00.

Foxholes Country Hotel

Cologin, Lerags, Oban, Argyll PA34 4SE
Tel: 01631 564982 Fax: 01631 570890
e.mail: shirley.foxholes@tesco.net
Web: www.foxholeshotel.co.uk

Enjoy peace and tranquility at Foxholes, situated in its own grounds in a quiet glen 3 miles south of Oban, with magnificent views of the surrounding countryside. An ideal spot for those who wish to "get away from it all". Enjoy our superb five-course table d'hote menu and large selection of wines and spirits. All bedrooms ensuite, colour TV and tea/coffee-making facilities. NON-SMOKING HOTEL.
Send for colour brochure and tariff to Mrs S Dowson-Park at the above address.
DB&B from £67 per person per night. B&B from £45 pp per night. Single supplement £18.00 per room per night.
OPEN MARCH TO OCTOBER.

26700

★★★★

SMALL HOTEL

Foxholes Country Hotel

Cologin, Lerags, Oban, Argyll, PA34 4SE
Tel:01631 564982 Fax:01631 570890
Email:shirley.foxholes@tesco.net
Web:www.foxholeshotel.co.uk

Peacefully situated in a quiet glen with magnificent views yet a mere 3 miles (5kms) south of Oban. Ideally placed for the ferries for day trips to the islands of the inner Hebrides, Mull and Iona in particular. Many scenic drives including Fort William are within an hour of the Hotel and gardens. Fresh local produce used in our Table D'Hote dinners.

7 rooms, all en-suite, Open Mar-Oct, B&B from £45.00 per person per night in double/twin. BB & Eve.Meal from £67.00. Single occupancy £18.00 extra per night.

Important: Prices stated are estimates and may be subject to amendments

| Oban, Argyll | Map Ref: 1E2 |

Glenbervie Guest House
Dalriach Road, Oban, Argyll, PA34 5JD
Tel:01631 564770 Fax:01631 566723

8 rooms, 6 en-suite, Open Feb-Dec excl Xmas/New Year, B&B per person, single from £28.00-35.00, double from £28.00-35.00 pp.

Beautifully situated overlooking Oban Bay, commanding magnificent views. 2 minutes walk from town centre, promenade, harbour and amenities. Evening meal. Ensuite.

Great Western Hotel
Corran Esplanade, Oban, Argyll, PA34 5PP
Tel:01942 824824
Email:reservations@WAshearings.com
Web:www.WAshearingsholidays.com

80 rooms, all en-suite, Open Feb-Dec, B&B per person, double from £25.00.

Situated right on the seafront with fine views over Oban Bay. Entertainment every night.

Greencourt Guest House
Benvoullin Road, Oban, Argyll, PA34 5EF
Tel:01631 563987
Email:relax@greencourt-oban.co.uk
Web:www.greencourt-oban.co.uk

6 rooms, most en-suite, Open Feb-Nov, B&B per person, single £25.00-34.00, double £25.00-34.00.

Spacious family run property in quiet situation overlooking outdoor bowling green, a short stroll to town centre and adjacent to leisure centre. Attractive rooms, wholesome breakfasts, private parking. Ideal touring base.

Kathmore Guest House
Soroba Road, Oban, Argyll, PA34 4JF
Tel:01631 562104 Fax:01631 562104/570067
Email:wkathmore@aol.com
Web:www.kathmore.co.uk

9 rooms, some en-suite, B&B per person, single £25.00-40.00, double/twin £21.50-26.50.

Kathmore guest house is just outside Oban Town Centre. A short walk from the bus, train and ferry terminal. Trouble-free parking is assured with our spacious private car park. All rooms are well-furnished and equipped with colour TV's, Tea/Coffee trays, hairdryer etc. Some are ensuite. Restricted drinks licence for guests.

VAT is shown at 17.5%: changes in this rate may affect prices. | *Key to symbols is on back flap.*

Oban, Argyll   Map Ref: 1E2

Kings Knoll Hotel
Dunollie Road, Oban, PA34 5JH
Tel:01631 562536 Fax:01631 566101
Email:info@kingsknollhotel.co.uk
Web:www.kingsknollhotel.co.uk

Family run hotel overlooking Oban Bay and close to the town centre and sea front. Theme bar and dining room.

15 rooms, some en-suite, Open Feb-Dec, B&B per person, single from £25.00, double from £25.00, Room only double £50.00. BB & Eve.Meal from £38.00.

The Manor House
Gallanoch Road, Oban, Argyll, PA34 4LS
Tel:01631 562087 Fax:01631 563053
Email:info@manorhouseoban.com
Web:www.manorhouseoban.com

Georgian house on the foreshore on the south side of Oban with extensive views across the Bay, close to the town centre. AA Rosette for food. Non residents welcome to book for dinner.

11 rooms, all en-suite, Open Jan-Dec excl Xmas, B&B per person, single from £65.00, double from £47.00 (low season).

by Oban, Argyll   Map Ref: 1E2

Falls of Lora Hotel
Connel Ferry, by Oban, Argyll, PA37 1PB
Tel:01631 710483 Fax:01631 710694
Email:enquiries@fallsoflora.com
Web:www.fallsoflora.com

Oban 5 miles, only 2¢ to 3 hours drive North-West of Glasgow/Edinburgh. Overlooking Loch Etive, this fine owner run Victorian Hotel has a modern extension. 30 rooms from special to inexpensive family. The super cocktail bar has an open log fire and over 100 brands of whisky. There is an attractive and comfortable bistro for evening meals - the menu is extensive and features local produce.

30 rooms, all en-suite, Open Feb-mid Dec, B&B per person, single from £39.50, double from £23.50.

Willowburn Hotel
Clachan Seil, by Oban, Argyll, PA34 4TJ
Tel:01852 300276
Email:willowburn.hotel@virgin.net
Web:www.willowburn.co.uk

Personally run, on the shore, in 2 acres of garden, approx. 0.5 miles from famous Atlantic Bridge, on Seil Island. Taste of Scotland recommended. Two AA rosettes. Peaceful, homely atmosphere.

7 rooms, all en-suite, Open Mar-Nov, BB & Eve.Meal from £70.00.

Stirling   Map Ref: 2A4

Garfield Guesthouse
12 Victoria Square, Stirling, Stirlingshire,
FK8 2QZ
Tel/Fax:01786 473730

Family run guest house in traditional stone built Victorian house overlooking quiet square close to the town centre, castle and all local amenities. Ideal base for exploring historic Stirling, Loch Lomond and the Trossachs. Non smoking.

6 rooms, all en-suite, Open Jan-Dec excl Xmas/New Year, B&B per person, double from £28.00.

Important: Prices stated are estimates and may be subject to amendments

Stirling	Map Ref: 2A4

Harviestoun Country Hotel & Restaurant
Dollar Road, Tillicoultry, Clackmannanshire FK13 6PQ
Tel:01259 752522   Fax:01259 752523
Email:harviestounhotel@aol.com
Web:www.harviestouncountryhotel.com

A stunningly converted listed steading. Privately owned and managed, our rooms are ensuite with some on the ground floor. Lounge with open fire, coffees, and homebaking. Restaurant serving A-La-Carte lunches, dinners and high teas. Non-resident breakfast daily. Suitable for conferences or small, intimate weddings. Ideally situated for touring, golfing or business.

11 rooms, all en-suite, Open Jan-Dec, B&B per person, single from £55.00, double from £37.50.

King Robert Hotel
Glasgow Road, Bannockburn, Stirling, FK7 0LJ
Tel:01786 811666   Fax:01786 811507
Email:info@kingroberthotel.co.uk
Web:www.ladyglen.co.uk

Modern hotel situated next to Bannockburn Heritage Centre. About 2 miles (3kms) from Stirling town centre. Regular Scottish entertainment. Extensive conference facilities. Banqueting Suite available for dinner dances, weddings etc.

52 rooms, all ensuite, B&B per room, single from £49.00, double/twin from £59.00.

Paramount Stirling Highland Hotel
Spittal Street, Stirling, FK8 1DU
Tel:01786 272727   Fax:01786 272829
Email:stirling@paramount-hotels.co.uk
Web:www.paramount-hotels.co.uk

Restored, Listed, former High School, converted into very comfortable hotel with full leisure facilities. Friendly, attentive service. In the old town, within walking distance of the castle and other historic attractions. Stirling, an ancient capital of Scotland is now one of its most recent new cities.

96 rooms, all en-suite, Open Jan-Dec.

The Park Lodge Country House Hotel
32 Park Terrace, Stirling, FK8 2JS
Tel:01786 474862   Fax:01786 449748
Email:info@parklodge.net
Web:www.parklodge.net

Part Victorian, part Georgian mansion overlooking the park and castle, set amidst landscaped gardens. Antique furnishings including a four poster bed.

10 rooms, all en-suite, Open Jan-Dec excl Xmas/New Year, B&B per person, single from £55.00, double from £47.50.

The Royal Hotel and Royal Lodge Conference Centre
55 & 103 Henderson Street, Bridge of Allan, Stirlingshire, FK9 4HG
Tel:01786 832284   Fax:01786 834377
Email:stay@royal-stirling.co.uk
Web:www.royal-stirling.co.uk

The Royal Hotel offers 32 rooms, all en-suite. The Royal Lodge, 11 en-suite. Both offer unique conference and banqueting facilities. We are ideally located in the centre of Scotland just off the M9 Motorway. Edinburgh and Glasgow are both within 40 minutes drive. Ideal as a touring base, the whole spectrum of Scotland's rich heritage and magnificent scenery is available within 1 hours drive of Bridge of Allan.

Open Jan-Dec, B&B per person, single from £85.00, double from £65.00, BB & Eve.Meal from £95.00.

VAT is shown at 17.5%: changes in this rate may affect prices.   Key to symbols is on back flap.

Strathyre, Perthshire

Map Ref: 1H3

**RESTAURANT
WITH ROOMS**

Creagan House Restaurant with Accommodation
Strathyre, Callander, Perthshire, FK18 8ND
Tel:01877 384638   Fax:01877 384319
Email:eatandstay@creaganhouse.co.uk
Web:www.creaganhouse.co.uk

A peaceful little gem of comfort surrounded by beautiful scenery. Five charming
bedrooms with many thoughtful extras and a growing collection of antiques,
friendly perfection is our aim. The baronial dining hall helps make each evening
a special occasion, using meat from Perthshire, fruits and vegetables grown
locally, herbs from our garden, all complemented by fine wines. Awarded two AA
Rosettes and Red Star, which have been retained for 9 years.

5 rooms, all en-suite, Open Mar-Jan, B&B per person, single from £65.00, double
from £55.00, BB & Eve.Meal from £83.50.

Tarbert, Loch Fyne, Argyll

Map Ref: 1E5

**SMALL
HOTEL**

Balinakill Country House Hotel
Clachan, by Tarbet, Kintyre, PA29 6XL
Tel:01880 740206   Fax:01880 740298
Email:info@balinakill.com
Web:www.balinakill.com

Located on the edge of the small hamlet of Clachan, 10 miles south of
Tarbrt, Balinakill is a fine family-run country home set within its own
grounds offering its guests an excellent home for enjoying the delights of
this beautiful and peaceful part of Scotland. Ferries to Ireland, Islay,
Jura, Gigha, Arran and Cowal. 'Eat Scotland' and '1 AA Rosette'.

10 rooms, Open Jan-Dec, B&B per person single from £50.00, double from £45.00,
family from £45.00.

Tarbet, by Arrochar, Dunbartonshire

Map Ref: 1G3

HOTEL

Tarbet Hotel
Tarbert, Arrochar, Loch Lomond, Argyll & Bute, G83 7DE
Tel:01942 824824
Email:reservations@WAshearings.com
Web:www.WAshearingsholidays.com

Large touring hotel on the banks of Loch Lomond, central for visiting the
Trossachs, the West Coast and West Highlands. Fishing available.
Entertainment every night.

73 rooms, all en-suite, Open Feb-Dec, B&B per person, double from £25.00.

Important: Prices stated are estimates and may be subject to amendments

Main image: Glen Doll and Glen Cova, Angus **Bottom left:** Elie, Fife
Bottom middle: City Centre, Dundee **Bottom right:** Rafting, Perthshire

PERTHSHIRE, ANGUS AND DUNDEE AND THE KINGDOM OF FIFE

It's hard to believe just how accessible a holiday in these parts can be, and how distanced you can feel from the hustle and bustle of city life.

Finding your own little oasis of calm is easy. It could be one of the great international resort hotels in St Andrews or at Gleneagles where the rich and famous relax. Or you could choose a charming hotel in a holiday town like Pitlochry or a contemporary hotel on Dundee's lively quayside.

The choice is yours but certainly, wherever you decide, getting there won't be a problem. The real challenge will be fitting in the startling array of activities and opportunities on offer in Scotland's heartlands.

The Old Course, St. Andrews, Fife

Relax and enjoy a holiday that's as active as you want it to be in an area renowned for glorious golf, pretty towns and villages, and outstanding beauty.

If you're a golfer, the ancient Kingdom of Fife will be a powerful draw. Every serious golfer wants to play the Old Course at St Andrews at least once in a lifetime and, as it's managed by a Trust and there is a public allocation of rounds each day, you can. There are also 45 other fabulous courses in Fife to put your game to the test.

Fife also has its fishing connections. Once the North Sea herring fleet landed its catch in the East Neuk's ports. The harbour's still busy at Anstruther but the halcyon days of deep sea fishing have been consigned to the fascinating exhibitions in the Scottish Fisheries Museum in the town.

For keen walkers, one of the great ways to explore Fife is on foot. The Fife Coastal Path will take you through some truly delightful places and you'll get to relax on some of the best beaches in the country – there are seven 'blue flag' beaches in Scotland and five of them are in Fife.

The Angus and Dundee area has the other two so if you're a beach lover, you're in the right part of the world. These are real beaches too – unspoiled and interesting no matter what the season. At times windswept and stormy with the waves crashing in from the North Sea, other times warm and inviting, with the peace only occasionally shattered by the cries of seabirds.

Dundee's connections with maritime history can't be overlooked either. Captain Scott's polar research ship the RRS Discovery has returned to the city that built it and it's now a top tourist attraction. These days, Dundee is a lively, modern city but its history is worth exploring. Visit Verdant Works (a former winner of Europe's Top Industrial Museum award) to learn about the jute trade that was once a mainstay of the city's economy.

For a complete contrast to city life, you should explore the Angus Glens. There are five: Glen Isla, Glen Prosen, Glen Lethnot, Glen Clova and Glen Esk. Each has its own unique features but all of the Glens are exceptionally

  THE NO.1 BOOKING AND INFORMATION SERVICE FOR SCOTLAND   0845 22 55 121   visitscotland.com

Enjoy miles of coastline, rich farmland and mountainous peaks in Scotland's heartlands.

beautiful. They're remarkably peaceful places too and feel much more remote than they actually are. In a way, you can get away from it all in the Glens without really getting too far away.

The same can be said for Perthshire. It's one of the most strikingly picturesque parts of all of Scotland. It ranges from the wild and mountainous to sophisticated and cultured. One day, you could be out in the wilderness of Rannoch Moor, the next you could be getting pampered in the lap of luxury at the 5-star Gleneagles Hotel.

There's a spectacular range of activities available in the area from traditional activities like golf, fishing and other field sports to more recent innovations like sphereing and white water rafting. There's even skiing and snowboarding in the winter at Glenshee and all of these activities are done against a backdrop of spectacular scenery; high mountains, deep forests, sparkling lochs and wide rivers.

You don't have to spend the day pushing yourself to the limits, a walk through the forests of Big Tree Country will suffice. Or you could take a romantic stroll through the Birks o' Aberfeldy, visit one of 11 great gardens, marvel at a reconstructed Iron Age Crannog on Loch Tay, go shopping in Perth or just take in the Queen's View near Pitlochry. Whatever you decide to do, you'll always want to come back for more.

The Queen's View, Perthshire

Tourist Information Centres

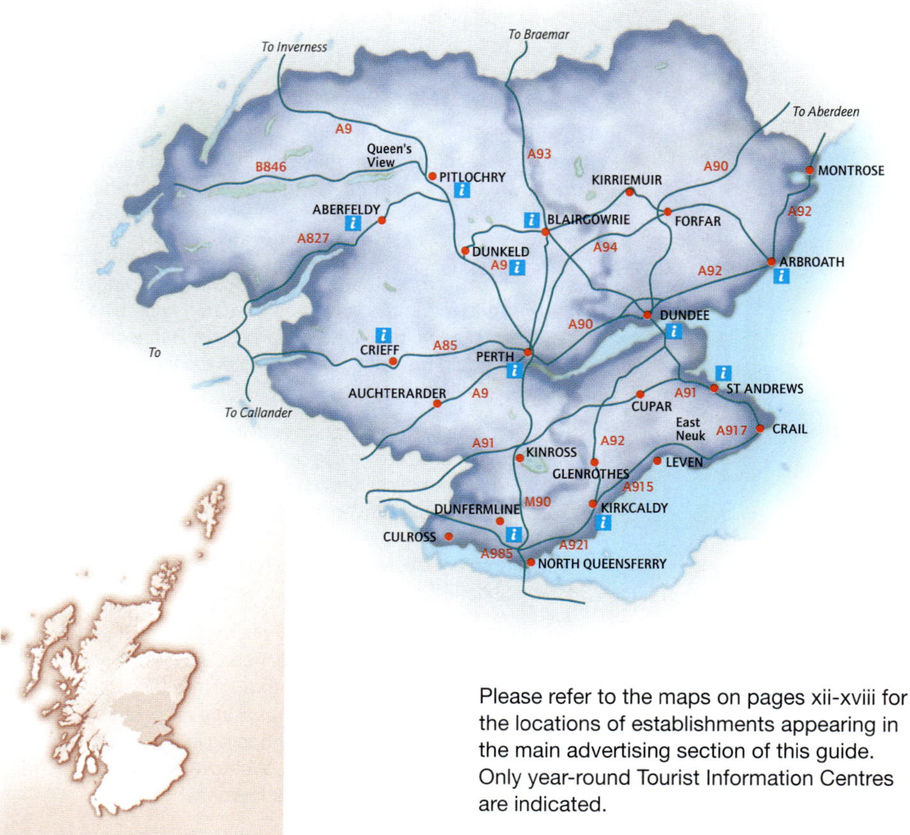

Please refer to the maps on pages xii-xviii for the locations of establishments appearing in the main advertising section of this guide. Only year-round Tourist Information Centres are indicated.

For practical advice, ideas and information about exploring Scotland and to book your accommodation:

Tel: 0845 22 55 121* or if calling from outside the UK: + 44 (0) 1506 832121 In Ireland call:1 800 932 510

* A £3 booking fee applies to telephone bookings of accommodation.

info@visitscotland.com
www.visitscotland.com

Arbroath	Market Place	01241 872609	Jan-Dec
Brechin	Pictavia Centre, Haughmuir	01356 623050	Easter-Sept
Carnoustie	1b High Street	01241 852258	Easter-Sept
Dundee	21 Castle Street	01382 527527	Jan-Dec
Forfar	45 East High Street	01307 467876	Easter-Sept
Kirriemuir	Cumberland Close	01575 574097	Easter-Sept
Montrose	Bridge Street	01674 672000	Easter-Sept

Kingdom of Fife

Anstruther	Scottish Fisheries Museum	01333 311073	Apr-Oct
Crail	Crail Museum and Heritage Centre, Marketgate	01333 450859	Apr-Oct
Dunfermline	1 High Street	01383 720999	Jan-Dec
Kirkcaldy	19 Whytescauseway	01592 267775	Jan-Dec
St Andrews	70 Market Street	01334 472021	Jan-Dec

Perthshire

Aberfeldy	The Square	01887 820276	Jan-Dec
Blairgowrie	26 Wellmeadow	01250 872960	Jan-Dec
Crieff	Town Hall, High Street	01764 652578	Jan-Dec
Dunkeld	The Cross	01350 727688	Jan-Dec
Kinross	Heart of Scotland Visitor Centre, Junction 6, M90	01577 863680	Apr-Oct
Perth	Lower City Mills, West Mill Street	01738 450600	Jan-Dec
Pitlochry	22 Atholl Road	01796 472215/ 472751	Jan-Dec

Aberdour, Fife

Map Ref: 2C4

★★★

SMALL
HOTEL

Aberdour Hotel

38 High Street, Aberdour, Fife, KY3 0SW
Tel:01383 860325 Fax:01383 860808
Email:reception@aberdourhotel.co.uk
Web:www.aberdourhotel.co.uk

Personally run hotel specialising in traditional cooking and real ales on Fife coast in Conservation village 6 miles (10kms) from Forth Bridges. Convenient for touring and golf. Recently converted stables annexe furnished to a high standard. Non residents welcome.

16 rooms, Open Jan-Dec, B&B per person, single from £40.00, double from £30.00, family from £30.00.

★★

INN

The Cedar Inn

20 Shore Road, Aberdour, Fife, KY3 0TR
Tel:01383 860310 Fax:01383 860004
Email:enquiries@cedarinn.co.uk
Web:www.cedarinn.co.uk

Family run, attractive old Inn, CAMRA listed with 'friendly locals' bar and amiable lounges. Close to golf course, shops and beach. Golfing holidays arranged.

9 rooms, some en-suite, Open Jan-Dec, B&B rates, single from £39.00, double £56.00-80.00, BB & Eve.Meal from £40.00 pp.

Aberfeldy, Perthshire

Map Ref: 2A1

Moness House Hotel & Country Club

Crieff Road, Aberfeldy, Perthshire, PH15 2DY
Tel: 0870 443 1460 Fax: 0870 443 1461
Email: info@moness.com
Web: www.worldwide-rentals.co.uk

Set in 35 acres of woodland overlooking the town of Aberfeldy, Moness offers comfortable, quaint rooms, each with its own ensuite. Meals and snacks available daily in our on-site restaurant. Guests receive membership of the onsite leisure club, which includes an indoor heated pool.

38837

★★★

SMALL
HOTEL

The Moness House Hotel & Country Club

Crieff Road, Aberfeldy, Perthshire, PH15 2DY
Tel:0870 4431460 Fax:0870 4431461
Email:info@moness.com
Web:www.moness.com

Former hunting lodge dating from 1758, situated in thirty five acres, on the south side of Aberfeldy. Includes self catering cottages and onsite leisure centre.

12 rooms, all en-suite, Open Jan-Dec, B&B per person, single £41.00-65.00, double £26.00-50.00, BB & Eve.Meal from £41.00-65.00.

Important: Prices stated are estimates and may be subject to amendments

Fortingall Hotel
Fortingall, Aberfeldy, Perthshire, PH15 2NQ
Tel/Fax: 01887 830367
e.mail: hotel@fortingallhotel.com Web: www.fortingallhotel.com

Boutique country house hotel sitting in historic Perthshire village at the foot of Glen Lyon. Eleven comfortable en-suite bedrooms uniquely decorated using Estate Tweeds. Excellent food served using the best local produce. The area is a walkers' paradise and offers a wide variety of sporting activities.
Prices B&B from £85-£170.

26626

★★★★

SMALL HOTEL

Fortingall Hotel
Fortingall, Aberfeldy, Perthshire, PH15 2NG
Te/Fax:01887 830367
Email:hotel@fortingallhotel.com
Web:www.fortingallhotel.com

Independent country hotel offering comfortable ensuite rooms with excellent locally sourced cuisine. Located in the beautiful conservation village of Fortingall, the hotel is a superb centre for touring, walking and fishing.

11 rooms. B&B from £85.00-£170.00.

LANDS OF LOYAL HOTEL
Loyal Road, Alyth, Blairgowrie, Perthshire PH11 8JQ
Tel: 01828 633151 Fax: 01828 633313
e.mail: info@landsofloyal.com Web: www.landsofloyal.com

Set on a hillside overlooking the Vale of Strathmore, the "Lands of Loyal" offers the perfect base for exploring the beautiful and historic county of Perthshire. Superb food and wines, the unique ambience, golden oak panelling and log fires create a captivating combination that our guests cherish for many years.

34851

★★★★

SMALL HOTEL

Lands of Loyal Hotel
Loyal Road, Alyth, Blairgowrie, PH11 8JQ
Tel:01828 633151 Fax:01828 633313
Email:info@landsofloyal.com
Web:www.landsofloyal.com

Country house with magnificent views of surrounding countryside. Central for many sports: walking, fishing, golf. Delicious food, fresh ingredients.

14 rooms, all en-suite, Open Jan-Dec, B&B per person, single from £79.00, double from £58.00 pp. BB & Eve.Meal from £85.00.

Auchterarder, Perthshire   Map Ref: 2B3

Cairn Lodge Hotel
Orchil Road, Auchterarder, PH3 1LX
Tel: 01764 662634/662431 Fax: 01764 664866
e.mail: email@cairnlodge.co.uk & info@cairnlodge.co.uk Web: www.cairnlodge.co.uk

Sitting proudly in beautiful gardens and fronted by Queen Victoria's Commemorative Jubilee Cairn, the Cairn Lodge neighbours the world famous Gleneagles complex on the edge of Auchterarder. Beautiful and luxuriously appointed en-suite accommodation, the elegant 'Capercaille' à la carte restaurant and the new Jubilee Lounge, all add up to Perthshire's premier country house hotel and restaurant. B&B from £60 pppn.
Short breaks: 3 nights for the price of 2 subject to availability.   17405

**SMALL
HOTEL**

Cairn Lodge Hotel
Orchil Road, Auchterarder, Perthshire, PH3 1LX
Tel:01764 662634   Fax:01764 664866
Email:email@cairnlodge.co.uk
Web:www.cairnlodge.co.uk

Personally run country house hotel, with large garden on outskirts of Auchterarder. Fine dining, prepared from fresh local produce.

10 rooms, all en-suite, B&B per person, single from £75.00, double from £60.00.

**INTERNATIONAL
RESORT HOTEL**

The Gleneagles Hotel
Auchterarder, Perthshire, PH3 1NF
Tel:01764 662231 Fax:01764 662134
Email:resort.sales@gleneagles.com
Web:www.gleneagles.com

A traditional hotel in the grand style with a wide range of world class sporting and leisure facilities; situated amidst the beautiful countryside of southern Perthshire. Choice of several dining venues with different styles.

266 rooms, all en-suite, Open Jan-Dec, B&B per room, double from £370.00.

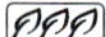

Blair Atholl, Perthshire   Map Ref: 4C12

Atholl Arms Hotel
Old North Road, Blair Atholl, PH18 5SG
Tel: 01796 481205 Fax: 01796 481550
e.mail: hotel@athollarms.co.uk Web: www.athollarms.co.uk

The Atholl Arms Hotel is a traditional Highland hotel situated at the gates of Blair Castle, which has built up its reputation on good food, comfort and friendly service over more than 160 years.

• 31 rooms – each with private facilities • Enjoy the Atholl experience all year round
• An idyllic setting for weddings and functions • Private parties catered for to individual requirements
• Full back up conference facilities available • Open all year.   13304

HOTEL

Atholl Arms Hotel
Old North Road, Blair Atholl, by Pitlochry,
Perthshire, PH18 5SG
Tel:01796 481205
Email:hotel@athollarms.co.uk
Web:www.athollarms.co.uk

Scottish Baronial style Highland Hotel, in centre of Blair Atholl, close to castle. Offering traditional Scottish Hospitality and good base to tour the central highlands. Enjoy the Atholl experience all year around.

31 rooms, all en-suite. B&B per person, single from £35.00-£65.00, double/twin from £25.00-£40.00.

Important: Prices stated are estimates and may be subject to amendments

Blairgowrie, Perthshire

Map Ref: 2B1

Broadmyre Motel

★★ GUEST HOUSE

Carsie, Blairgowrie, Perthshire, PH10 6QW
Tel/Fax:01250 873262
Email:Broadmyreroom@aol.com

Friendly welcome at this motel style accommodation with compact bedrooms, conveniently situated 1½ miles (2½kms) south of Blairgowrie. Ample parking. Evening meals on request. Ensuite available. Ideal base for all activity groups including golfers, fishers, shooters and walkers.

5 rooms, some en-suite, Open Jan-Dec, B&B per person, single from £17.00, double from £18.00, BB & Eve.Meal from £28.00.

Duncraggan

★★★★ GUEST HOUSE

Perth Road, Blairgowrie, Perthshire, PH10 6EJ
Tel:01250 872082
Email:duncraggan@hotmail.com

Comfortable lovely furnished house with off road parking. An ideal location for tourists, hillwalkers, skiers and golfers alike or relax in our acre gardens with small 9 hole putting green.

3 rooms, all en-suite, Open Jun-Oct, B&B per person, double from £22.00.

The Laurels

★★★ GUEST HOUSE

Golf Course Road, Blairgowrie, Perthshire PH10 6LH
Tel/Fax:01250 874920
Email:laurels-blairgowrie@talk21.com
Web:http://member.visitscotland.com/laurelsguesthouse

Originally a farmhouse dating from 1873, set back from main road, on outskirts of Blairgowrie with own large garden and ample parking. Rosemount Golf Course is a short walk away with a selection of 20 golf courses nearby. Ideal base for touring the beautiful Perthshire countryside. Fishing, shooting, mountaineering, ski-ing, pony trekking all in the local area.

6 rooms, some en-suite, Open mid Jan-mid Nov, B&B per person, single from £22.00, double from £22.00, BB & Eve.Meal from £35.00.

Comrie, Perthshire

Map Ref: 2A2

The Royal Hotel

★★★★ SMALL HOTEL

Melville Square, Comrie, Perthshire, PH6 2DN
Tel:01764 679200   Fax:01764 679219
Email:reception@royalhotel.co.uk
Web:www.royalhotel.co.uk

Friendly, family run hotel, offering award winning cuisine and luxurious charming ambience set amidst the stunning Perthshire Highlands.

11 rooms, all en-suite, Open Jan-Dec, B&B per person, single from £80.00, double from £65.00, BB & Eve.Meal from £85.00.

Coupar Angus, Perthshire

Map Ref: 2C1

Red House Hotel

★★★ INN

Station Road, Coupar Angus, Blairgowrie, PH13 9AL
Tel:01828 628500   Fax:01828 628574
Email:stay@red-house-hotel.co.uk
Web:www.red-house-hotel.co.uk

Dating back to Victorian times the building was originally the Railway Hotel. Trains have long ceased to run through Coupar Angus and in its place is the vibrant Red House, a magnet for locals, visitors and business traveller. Family owned and managed you can be sure of a friendly team and genuine hospitality. The accommodation has a separate entrance.

20 rooms, all en-suite, Open Jan-Dec excl Xmas/New Year, B&B per person, single from £42.50, double from £75.00 (2 people).

VAT is shown at 17.5%: changes in this rate may affect prices.

Key to symbols is on back flap.

Cowdenbeath, Fife | Map Ref: 2B4

Struan Bank Hotel
74 Perth Road, Cowdenbeath, Fife, KY4 9BG
Tel/Fax:01383 511057
Email:struanbankhotel@yahoo.co.uk

9 rooms, some en-suite, Open Jan-Dec, B&B per person, single from £25.00, double from £22.50, BB & Eve.Meal from £31.00 pp.

Family run hotel situated in the town centre and convenient for the railway station. Ideal centre for touring. En-suite accommodation available.

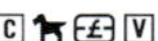

Crail, Fife | Map Ref: 2D3

Balcomie Links Hotel
Balcomie Road, Crail, Anstruther, Fife, KY10 3TN
Tel:01333 450237 Fax:01333 450540
Email:mikekadir@balcomie.fsnet.co.uk
Web:www.balcomie.co.uk

14 rooms, all en-suite, Open Jan-Dec, B&B per person, single from £55.00, twin from £35.00 pp.

A family run hotel only a few minues walk from the picturesque harbour village. 9 miles (14kms) from St Andrews - an ideal golfing base. Families and groups welcome. A varied menu of home-made dishes featuring local Scottish produce is available in either the lounge or modern non-smoking dining room.

Caiplie House
53 High Street, Crail, Fife, KY10 3RA
Tel:01333 450564
Email:mail@caipliehouse.com
Web:www.caipliehouse.com

6 rooms, en-suite, Open Mar-Nov, B&B per person, single from £30.00, double from £25.00, BB & Eve.Meal from £35.00.

Very comfortable and friendly guest house renowned for its home cooking, with restricted table licence. On main street of fishing village near coastal path and picturesque harbour. Some rooms with sea views.

Crieff, Perthshire | Map Ref: 2A2

Fendoch Guest House
Sma' Glen, Crieff, Perthshire, PH7 3LW
Tel:01764 653446/655619 Fax:01764 653446
Email:bookings@fendoch.co.uk
Web:www.fendoch.co.uk

4 rooms, all en-suite, Open Jan-Dec, B&B per person, single from £23.00, double from £23.00, BB & Eve.Meal from £35.00.

Large modern bungalow with all bedrooms ensuite. Open all year. Evening meals available. Lovely countryside with mountains and hills. Crieff 5 miles. Family run with traditional Highland hospitality. Disabled facilities.

Galvelbeg House
Perth Road, Crieff, Perthshire, PH7 3EQ
Tel:01764 655061 Fax:01764 650363
Email:bookings@galvelbeghouse.co.uk
Web:www.galvelbeghouse.co.uk

4 rooms ensuite, 1 priv.facilities, Open Jan-Dec, B&B per person, single from £30.00, double from £23.00.

A warm welcome awaits you at this detached stonebuilt villa, conveniently situated near the town centre with all its amenities. A good base for touring, horseriding and golf, with many local courses. Ample car parking at the rear.

Important: Prices stated are estimates and may be subject to amendments

Crieff, Perthshire

Map Ref: 2A2

KINGARTH
Perth Road, Crieff PH7 3EQ
Tel: 01764 652060 Fax: 01764 655302
e.mail: info@kingarthguesthouse.com Web: www.kingarthguesthouse.com

Set in the heart of Scotland, in the bustling market town of Crieff, Kingarth is a comfortable and friendly guest house with 6 ensuite bedrooms, guest lounge and sunny conservatory. Surrounded by mature gardens and superb views over Strathearn to the Ochil Hills. Ample parking available on site.

33408

GUEST
HOUSE

Kingarth
Perth Road, Crieff, Perthshire, PH7 3EQ
Tel:01764 652060 Fax:01764 655302
Email:info@kingarthguesthouse.com
Web:www.kingarthguesthouse.com

Set in the heart of Scotland, in the bustling town of Crieff, Kingarth is a homely Victorian guest house set in mature gardens, with stunning views overlooking the Strathearn Vale and Ochil Hills. The house has a relaxed, comfortable atmosphere with a cosy residents' lounge, sunny conservatory and dining room. The letting rooms are in the garden wing of the house, and are all ground floor, ensuite and non-smoking. There is ample parking.

6 rooms, all en-suite, Open Jan-Dec, B&B per person, single from £30.00-35.00, double from £25.00.

SMALL
HOTEL

Leven House Hotel
Comrie Road, Crieff, PH7 4BA
Tel:01764 652529

Small family run hotel near town centre serving Scottish high teas. Ideally situated for touring and golf. Spacious car park.

10 rooms, Open Feb-Nov, B&B per person single from £25.00, double from £25.00.

Dundee, Angus

Map Ref: 2C2

Apex City Quay Hotel & Spa
1 West Victoria Dock Road, Dundee, DD1 3JP
Tel: 0845 365 0000 Fax: 0131 666 5128
e.mail: reservations@apexhotels.co.uk Web:www.apexhotels.co.uk

This contemporary hotel sits on Dundee's quayside, ideally situated for St Andrews and Carnoustie. Fantastic chic bedrooms with wide screen TVs, CD/DVD players, two stunning restaurants with award winning chefs, Yu spa with Japanese hot tubs, sauna, steam room, Elemis treatment rooms and gym with the latest Technogym equipment.

12301

HOTEL

Apex City Quay Hotel & Spa
1 West Victoria Dock Road, Dundee, DD1 3JP
Tel:0845 365 0000 Fax:0131 666 5128
Email:reservations@apexhotels.co.uk
Web:www.apexhotels.co.uk

Modern hotel in contemporary style situated on Quayside in centre of Dundee. Excellent location for historic attractions. Full conference and leisure facilities.

153 rooms, all en-suite, Open Jan-Dec, B&B per person, single from £80.00, double from £45.00, BB & Eve.Meal from £58.95 pppn.

VAT is shown at 17.5%: changes in this rate may affect prices.

Key to symbols is on back flap.

Dundee, Angus

Map Ref: 2C2

Hilton Dundee
Earl Grey Place, Dundee, DD1 4DE
Tel:01382 229271 Fax:01382 200072
Email:reservations_dundee@hilton.com
Web:www.hilton.com

HOTEL

Modern hotel with leisure facilities situated on the banks of the River Tay
with views of the Kingdom of Fife. Easy access by road, rail and air.
Conference facilities. Riverside Caffe Cino facility and restaurant and bar
with views of the river. 24 hour room service. 90 Car Parking spaces.

129 rooms, all en-suite, Open Jan-Dec, B&B per person, single from £78.00, double
from £44.00, BB & Eve.Meal from £59.00 sharing twin/double. Single £95.00.

Dunfermline, Fife

Map Ref: 2B4

Best Western Keavil House Hotel
Crossford, Fife, KY12 8QW
Tel:01383 736258 Fax:01383 621600
Email:sales@keavilhouse.co.uk
Web:www.keavilhouse.co.uk

HOTEL

Historic country house, including extensive leisure facilities, is set in 12
acres of grounds and gardens, making it an ideal location for relaxing.
The hotel offers an award winning restaurant. Within easy reach of
Edinburgh - only 25 minutes by train.

47 rooms, B&B per person single from £55.00, double from £55.00, family rooms
from £65.00 per adult. Four poster rooms from £75.00 per person.

Clarke Cottage Guest House
139 Halbeath Road, Dunfermline, Fife, KY11 4LA
Tel:01383 735935 Fax:01383 623767
Email:clarkecottage@ukonline.co.uk
Web:www.clarkecottageguesthouse.co.uk

GUEST
HOUSE

Situated 1 mile West of Junction 3 (M90) and only a 2 minute walk to
Queen Margaret Railway Station, this 19th century Victorian house has
been tastefully extended to provide comfortable en-suite accommodation
with independent access. Ample off-street parking. Ideally situated for
visiting Edinburgh and surrounding areas in Fife.

9 rooms, all en-suite, Open Jan-Dec, B&B per person, single £30.00, double/twin
£24.00.

Davaar House Hotel
126 Grieve Street, Dunfermline, Fife, KY12 8DW
Tel:01383 721886 Fax:01383 623633
Email:enquiries@davaar-house-hotel.com
Web:www.davaar-house-hotel.com

SMALL
HOTEL

Jim and Doreen extend a warm welcome. Experience Davaar's special
atmosphere and enjoy the hospitality comfortable rooms and excellent
food. Central location for golfing, walking, touring and enjoying a
relaxing break.

10 rooms, all en-suite, Open Jan-Dec excl Xmas/New Year, B&B per person, single
from £45.00, double/twin from £40.00.

Garvock House Hotel
St Johns Drive, Dunfermline, KY12 7TU
Tel:01383 621067 Fax:01383 621168
Email:sales@garvock.co.uk
Web:www.garvock.co.uk

SMALL
HOTEL

Peacefully located near the heart of Dunfermline, Scotland's ancient
capital, lies Garvock House. 26 beautifully furnished and comfortable
bedrooms equipped with all the 'little extras', elegant dining room with
taste tempting menus. Within easy distance of Edinburgh, Perth and St
Andrews. Golf arranged locally.

12 rooms, all en-suite, Open Jan-Dec, B&B per person, single from £70.00, double
from £47.50.

Important: Prices stated are estimates and may be subject to amendments

Dunfermline, Fife | Map Ref: 2B4

Pitbauchlie House Hotel
Aberdour Road, Dunfermline, KY11 4PB
Tel:01383 722282 Fax:01383 620738
Email:info@pitbauchlie.com
Web:www.pitbauchlie.com

Nestled in wooded and landscaped gardens, this popular hotel is situated 4 miles from the Forth Bridges. 50 En-Suite Bedrooms, an A La Carte Restaurant plus Bar/Bistro Dining areas. An ideal location for discovering Scotland's Ancient and Modern Capitals.

50 rooms, all en-suite, Open Jan-Dec, B&B per person, single from £85.00, double from £51.50.

Queensferry Hotel
St Margarets Head, North Queensferry, Fife KY11 1HP
Tel:01383 410000 Fax:01383 419708
Email:edinburghnorth@corushotels.com
Web:www.corushotels.com/edinburghnorth

Built in 1989 among landscaped hillside gardens on North shore of Firth of Forth overlooking famous bridges. 77 contemporary style bedrooms designed for the travelling executive with modern communication facilities. Extensive conference and banqueting facilities.

77 rooms, all en-suite, Open Jan-Dec excl Xmas/New Year, B&B per person, single from £40.00, double from £25.00.

Dunkeld, Perthshire | Map Ref: 2B1

Atholl Arms Hotel
Bridgehead, Dunkeld, Perthshire, PH8 0AQ
Tel:01350 727219 Fax:01350 727991
Email:enquiries@athollarmshotel.com
Web:www.athollarmshotel.com

Situated on the banks of the silvery Tay and at the Gateway to the Highlands. 17 ensuite rooms, bar meals, a la carte dinner served daily, weekend entertainment. Open to non-residents. Children welcome.

17 rooms, all en-suite, Open Jan-Dec, B&B per person, single from £49.00, double from £34.00, BB & Eve.Meal from £45.00.

Royal Dunkeld Hotel
Atholl Street, Dunkeld, PH8 0AR
Tel:01350 727322 Fax:01350 728989
Email:reservations@royaldunkeld.co.uk
Web:www.royaldunkeld.co.uk

Personally run, early 19c coaching inn, situated in centre of historic town of Dunkeld. Golfing breaks and fishing packages a speciality. Some annexe bedrooms.

34 rooms, all en-suite, Open Jan-Dec, B&B per person, single from £45.00, double from £34.00, BB & Eve.Meal from £50.00.

Edzell, Angus | Map Ref: 4F12

Panmure Arms Hotel
52 High Street, Edzell, Angus, DD9 7TA
Tel:01356 648950 Fax:01356 648000
Email:david@panmurearmshotel.co.uk
Web:www.panmurearmshotel.co.uk

A recently refurbished family run hotel with the emphasis on quality and service. Set in the picturesque village of Edzell with very easy access for golfing, shooting and fishing. A perfect holiday destination for exploring the beautiful Angus glens.

16 rooms, all en-suite, Open Jan-Dec excl Xmas. New Year, B&B per person, single from £47.50, double from £35.00.

VAT is shown at 17.5%: changes in this rate may affect prices.

Key to symbols is on back flap.

Freuchie, Fife — Map Ref: 2C3

Lomond Hills Hotel and Leisure Centre
Parliament Square, Freuchie, Cupar, Fife, KY15 7EY
Tel:01337 857329 Fax:01337 858180
Email:reception@lomondhillshotel.com
Web:www.lomondhillshotel.com

Situated at the foot of the Lomond Hills in rolling countryside, The Lomond Hills Hotel has 52 golf courses within 25 miles. With swimming pool, gym, spa and sauna this is the ideal base for golf, leisure or business. Our candlelit restaurant serves fresh local produce. St Andrews 25 mins, Edinburgh Airport 30 mins.

24 rooms, all en-suite, Open Jan-Dec, B&B per person, single from £55.00, double from £35.00.

Glenshee, Perthshire — Map Ref: 4D12

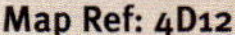

Dalmunzie

Glenshee, Perthshire, PH10 7QG
Tel: 01250 885224 Fax: 01250 885225
e.mail: reservations@dalmunzie.com
Web: www.dalmunzie.com

Dalmunzie is a stunning quintessential Lairds mansion turreted in the Scots Baronial style. Situated on a 6500 acre estate, Dalmunzie enjoys magnificent scenery in a hidden glen, yet is less than 2 hours from Edinburgh airport. Peace and tranquility define Dalmunzie with fires and comfy lounges contributing to a relaxing haven from the outside world.

For the more active, the first tee of Dalmunzie golf course is 30 yards away, with tennis, mountain bikes, fishing, hiking and stalking available.

We are especially proud of the attentive yet relaxed service where guests are made to feel truly at home in this historic setting.

64913

Dalmunzie
Spittal of Glenshee, Blairgowrie, Perthshire PH10 7QG
Tel:01250 885224 Fax:01250 885225
Email:reservations@dalmunzie.com
Web:www.dalmunzie.com

Dalmunzie is a stunning Highland laird's mansion situated in a gloriously remote location, yet is less than 2 hours from Edinburgh. Golf and tennis on-site.

17 rooms, all en-suite, Open Dec 30-Nov 30, B&B per person, single from £65.00, double from £50.00, Dinner £36.00.

Killiecrankie, Perthshire — Map Ref: 4C12

Killiecrankie House Hotel
Pass of Killiecrankie, by Pitlochry, PH16 5LG
Tel:01796 473220 Fax:01796 472451
Email:enquiries@killiecrankiehotel.co.uk
Web:www.killiecrankiehotel.co.uk

Personally run country hotel with warm and friendly atmosphere set in 4 acres of grounds, overlooking Pass of Killiecrankie. With strong food and wine reputation.

10 rooms, all en-suite. Dinner Bed & Breakfast from £84.00 per person.

Important: Prices stated are estimates and may be subject to amendments

Kinloch Rannoch, Perthshire

Map Ref: 1H1

Dunalastair Hotel

The Square, Kinloch Rannoch, Perthshire, PH16 5PW
Tel:01882 632323 Fax:01882 632371
Email:stay@dunalastair.co.uk
Web:www.dunalastair.co.uk

Traditional Scottish hotel in picturesque village square. Ideal touring base for the central Highlands.

28 rooms, all en-suite, Open Feb-Dec excl Xmas/New Year, B&B per person, single from £37.50, double from £37.50.

Kinross, Perthshire

Map Ref: 2B3

The Green Hotel

2 The Muirs, Kinross, KY13 8AS
Tel:01577 863467 Fax:01577 863180
Email:reservations@green-hotel.com
Web:www.green-hotel.com

Ideally located in central Scotland. This is one of Scotland's fine independently owned country house hotels. 46 spacious bedrooms equipped to the highest standard. The leisure complex has indoor pool, sauna, exercise facility and squash court plus a four sheet curling rink in season. The hotel has 2 'all weather' tennis courts and 2 '18 hole' golf courses; trout fishing can be arranged on nearby Loch Leven.

46 rooms, all en-suite, Open Jan-Dec, B&B per person, single from £95.00, double/twin from £85.00, BB & Eve.Meal from £75.00 pp sharing twin/double, min 2 night stay.

Kirklands Hotel

20 High Street, Kinross, Perth and Kinross, Scotland KY13 8AN
Tel/Fax: 01577 863313
e.mail: pd.fraser@virgin.net Web: www.thekirklandshotel.com

Friendly, family hotel with restaurant, two bars and beer garden. Excellent food available from our award winning Italian chef. Handy for beautiful Loch Leven and a good five iron from two quality golf courses. Good local fishing facilities. Centrally positioned, twenty minutes from Edinburgh, and at the gateway to the Highlands. Apartment available for families or groups.

34324

Kirklands Hotel

20 High Street, Kinross, Perthshire, KY13 8AN
Tel:01577 863313
Email:pd.fraser@virgin.net
Web:www.thekirklandshotel.com

Friendly service at this former Coaching Inn, all rooms en-suite. Attractively refurbished bar and restaurant with interesting menu choice from award winning Italian chef. Large suite available which is ideal for groups and families.

9 rooms, all en-suite, Open Jan-Dec excl Xmas/New Year, B&B per person, single from £38.00, double/twin from £33.00.

Roxburghe Guest House

126 High Street, Kinross, KY13 8DA
Tel:01577 862498
Email:guests@roxburgheguesthouse.co.uk
Web:www.roxburgheguesthouse.co.uk

The Roxburghe offers unpretentious Scottish Hospitality with traditional cooking including special diets. Breakfast features continental choices and range of fish dishes. Evening meals are cooked to order and the menu includes Highland Beef, Wild Perthshire Venison, Scotch Lamb and Salmon. The Roxburghe is licensed. Lock-up facilities for cycles and drying room for storage of fishing and golf equipment. Listed in The Good Hotel Guide.

4 rooms, Open Jan-Dec, B&B per person, single from £25.00, double from £22.00, BB & Eve.Meal from £34.00. Pre-booking dinner advisable.

VAT is shown at 17.5%: changes in this rate may affect prices.

Key to symbols is on back flap.

Kinross, Perthshire — Map Ref: 2B3

SMALL HOTEL ★★★

The Well Country Inn

Main Street, Scotlandwell, Kinross, KY13 9JA
Tel/Fax:01592 840444
Email:thewellcountryinn@fsbdial.co.uk
Web:www.thewellcountryinn.co.uk

The Well Country Inn is a family run business and is situated in one of the most beautiful areas of Scotland, renowned for its natural beauty and wealth of sporting and leisure interest. Game shooting is popular sport in this area and our annexe bedrooms are fitted with gun safes and we have kennel facilities.

9 rooms, all en-suite, Open Jan-Dec, B&B per person, double from £37.00-£42.00.

Leven, Fife — Map Ref: 2C3

GUEST HOUSE ★★★★

Dunclutha Guest House

16 Victoria Road, Leven, Fife, KY8 4EX
Tel:01333 425515 Fax:01333 422311
Email:pam.leven@blueyonder.co.uk
Web:www.dunclutha.myby.co.uk

Victorian former manse. 2 minutes level walk from centre of Leven. Good base for golfing enthusiasts and New Fife Coastal Walk. 50 minutes drive from Edinburgh and 40 minutes from the airport. 7 miles to the nearest railway station. All bedrooms with either ensuite or private facilities.

4 rooms, three en-suite, Open Jan-Dec, B&B per person, single from £30.00, double from £28.00. Non smoking, private parking.

Loch Earn, Perthshire — Map Ref: 1H2

SMALL HOTEL ★★★

Achray House Hotel

St Fillans, Perthshire, PH6 2NF
Tel:01764 685231 Fax:01764 685320
Email:info@achray-house.co.uk
Web:www.achray-house.co.uk

Small personally run hotel with fresh homemade produce. Bar and restaurant menus. Picturesque village with stunning views over Loch Earn. Also self catering lodges.

10 rooms, all en-suite, Open Jan-Dec, BB & Eve.Meal from £50.00 pp.

The Four Seasons Hotel, Lochside

St Fillans, Perthshire, PH6 2NF
Tel: 01764 685333
e.mail: info@thefourseasonshotel.co.uk www.thefourseasonshotel.co.uk
Food glorious food @ the Four Seasons Hotel. Award Winning Restaurant for Fine Dining, or more informal restaurant for Bar Meals, both offering imaginative modern European cuisine using the best from Scotland's natural larder. Individually decorated bedrooms, and four poster bedrooms, many with superb loch views.

Art/Walking/Wine/Gourmet Breaks

AA ★★★ ◎◎   Which Good Hotel Guide   26668

SMALL HOTEL ★★★

The Four Seasons Hotel

St Fillans, Perthshire, PH6 2NF
Tel:01764 685333
info@thefourseasonshotel.co.uk
www.thefourseasonshotel.co.uk

Food glorious food @ The Four Seasons Hotel. Modern European influenced cuisine, with ingredients from Scotland's natural larder, to produce a truly memorable meal. The Fine Dining restaurant includes hand dived Scabster Scallops; Smoked Duck Breast; Gateau of Scottish Limousin Beef; Rockall Monkfish; Belgian Chocolate Tart; Banana and Data Samosa. Alternatively we can offer freshly prepared Bar Meals.

18 rooms, all en-suite, Open Mar-Jan, B&B per person, single from £40.00, double from £40.00, BB & Eve.Meal from £66.00.

Important: Prices stated are estimates and may be subject to amendments

Montrose, Angus

Map Ref: 4F12

36 The Mall
Montrose, Angus, DD10 8SS
Tel/Fax:01674 673646
Email:enquiries@36themall.co.uk
Web:www.36themall.co.uk

Recently refurbished 19th century manse with spacious bedrooms all ensuite. Situated in centre of Montrose yet in attractive residential area. Excellent breakfast including continental and traditional Scottish fayre.

3 rooms, all en-suite, Open Jan-Dec, B&B per person, single from £35.00, double from £25.00.

Best Western Links Hotel
Mid Links, Montrose, Angus, DD10 8RL
Tel:01674 671000 Fax:01674 672698
Email:reception@linkshotel.com
Web:www.bw-linkshotel.co.uk

A lovely hotel situated on the historic Midlinks. Within easy walking distance of the town centre, beaches and golf courses. Offering an all day 'Koffiehuis' with al-fresco terrace, a restaurant awarded with one AA Rosette and 25 individually designed bedrooms (some with balconies with views of the Midlinks). Enjoy excellent hospitality & a refreshing & relaxing stay.

25 rooms, all en-suite, Open Jan-Dec, B&B £29.00 per person per night sharing.

Perth

Map Ref: 2B2

Achnacarry Guest House
3 Pitcullen Crescent, Perth, PH2 7HT
Tel:01738 621421
Email:info@achnacarry.co.uk
Web:www.achnacarry.co.uk

Victorian dwelling house located a ten minute walk from city centre. We offer warm hospitality in true Scottish tradition, in tastefully decorated surroundings. En-suite rooms, including one on ground floor. Ample off street parking. An ideal base for visiting the many attractions in the area, and exploring the Central & Highland areas of Bonnie Scotland. Golfers welcome, clubs available. See Website for seasonal offers.

4 rooms, all en-suite, Open Jan-Dec excl New Year, B&B per person, single £30.00-40.00, double/twin £25.00-30.00 pp.

Ackinnoull Guest House
5 Pitcullen Crescent, Perth, PH2 7HT
Tel:01738 634165
Web:www.ackinnoull.com

Beautifully decorated Victorian semi-villa on the outskirts of town. Private parking on premises. 'Perth in Bloom' winners, as picturesque inside as out. Special rates for bookings of 3 days or more.

4 rooms, all en-suite, Open Jan-Dec, B&B per person, single from £25.00, double from £22.00.

VAT is shown at 17.5%: changes in this rate may affect prices.

Key to symbols is on back flap.

Perth

Map Ref: 2B2

★★★★

GUEST HOUSE

Arisaig Guest House
4 Pitcullen Crescent, Perth, PH2 7HT
Tel:01738 628240 Fax:01738 638521
Email:mail@arisaigonline.co.uk
Web:www.arisaigonline.co.uk

Well established environmentally friendly guest house, with off street parking. Close to city's many facilities. Local touring base. Ground floor bedroom.

5 rooms, all en-suite, Open Jan-Dec, B&B per person, single from £25.00-30.00, double/twin £25.00-27.50.

★★★

LODGE

Ballathie House Sportsman's Lodge
Kinclaven, Stanley, Perthshire, PH1 4QN
Tel:01250 883268 Fax:01250 883396
Email:email@ballathiehousehotel.com
Web:www.fishing-shooting-scotland.co.uk

Purpose built Lodge accommodation, situated within the grounds of Ballathie House Hotel, and just a short walk from the hotel. Guests have access to the bar and dining facilities within the hotel, as well as the sporting facilities in the area.

12 rooms, all en-suite, Open Jan-Dec, B&B per person per night: single from £55.00, double from £40.00, BB & Eve.Meal from £75.00. Special breaks available.

★★★

INN

Cherrybank Inn
210 Glasgow Road, Perth, PH2 ONA
Tel:01738 624349 Fax:01738 444962
Email:kenscot.findla@btconnect.com
Web:www.cherrybankinn.co.uk

Cherrybank Inn is situated on the outskirts of Perth, 1 mile off the motorway, offering accommodation in twin bedded ensuite rooms. Bar meals available. Continental breakfast only served in rooms and full breakfast available.

7 rooms, all en-suite, Open Jan-Dec, B&B per person, single from £32.00, double from £46.00.

★★★

GUEST HOUSE

Clunie Guest House
12 Pitcullen Crescent, Perth, PH2 7HT
Tel:01738 623625
Email:ann@clunieguesthouse.co.uk
Web:www.clunieguesthouse.co.uk

A warm welcome awaits you at Clunie Guest House. Situated on the A94 and within easy walking distance of the city centre, Perth Concert Hall, leisure amenities and visitor attractions. All rooms en-suite.

7 rooms, all en-suite, Open Jan-Dec, B&B per person, single from £25.00, double from £25.00 ppn, Room Only double from £44.00.

AWAITING GRADING

The Gables
24-26 Dunkeld Road, Perth, PH1 5RW
Tel:01738 624717
Email:gablesguesthouse@btconnect.com
Web:www.thegablesguesthouse.com

Stone built house on main road ½ mile (1km) north of Perth city centre. Close to sports centre, swimming pool and local golf course. Off road parking. Restricted hotel license.

7 rooms, some en-suite, Open Jan-Dec excl Xmas/New Year, B&B per person, single from £25.00, double from £25.00.

Important: Prices stated are estimates and may be subject to amendments

Perth

Map Ref: 2B2

The New County Hotel

22-30 County Place, Perth, PH2 8EE
Tel:01738 623355 Fax:01738 628909
Email:enquiries@newcountyhotel.com
Web:www.newcountyhotel.com

Family run city centre hotel. 23 Ensuite bedrooms. With 3 separate dining areas each with its own style of menu The New County Hotel is a 'must visit' when visiting Perthshire.

23 rooms, all en suite. Open Jan-Dec (closed Xmas Day/Boxing Day). B&B per person from £40.00 double/twin.

Newton House Hotel

Glencarse, Perth, PH2 7LX
Tel:01738 860250 Fax:01738 860717
Email:res@newton-house.co.uk
Web:www.newton-house.co.uk

Five minutes from Perth, this Victorian Country House in the heart of Scotland has spacious bedrooms, good food, and friendly efficient service.

8 rooms, all en-suite, Open Apr-Mar, B&B per person, single from £45.00, double £25.00-37.50.

Ramada Hotel Perth

West Mill Street, Perth, PH1 5QP
Tel:01738 628281 Fax:01738 643423
Email:sales.perth@ramadajarvis.co.uk
Web:www.jarvishotels.com

Attractive stone building with 15th century watermill feature, situated in town centre. Limited resident car parking available. Arts bar and grill and excellent conference facilities.

76 rooms, all en-suite, Open Jan-Dec, B&B per person, single from £47.50, double from £32.50.

Westview Bed & Breakfast

49 Dunkeld Road, Perth, PH1 5RP
Tel:01738 627787 Tel/Fax:01738 447790
Email:angiewestview@aol.com

Welcoming Victorian villa with original features reflecting the Victorian theme throughout. Attractive rooms with private facilities and elegant touches including Period sitting room and relaxing garden. An enjoyable trip back in time. Ample parking. Smoking area. Scottish High Teas served 5-7pm. Dinner served 7-8.30pm.

4 rooms, 3 en-suite, Open Jan-Dec, B&B per person, single from £30.00, double from £25.00, BB & Eve.Meal from £35.00.

VAT is shown at 17.5%: changes in this rate may affect prices.

Key to symbols is on back flap.

by Perth

Map Ref: 2B2

Ballathie House Hotel

Kinclaven, Stanley, Perthshire, PH1 4QN
Tel:01250 883268   Fax:01250 883396
Email:email@ballathiehousehotel.com
Web:www.ballathiehousehotel.com

Victorian Country House within its own grounds overlooking the River Tay. 12 miles from historic city of Perth. New riverside rooms and suites with balconies overlooking the river.

41 rooms, all en-suite, B&B per person, single from £85.00, double from £85.00. DB&B from £119.00 pp. Special breaks available.

Pitlochry, Perthshire

Map Ref: 2A1

Atholl Palace Hotel

Pitlochry, Perthshire, PH16 5LY
Tel:01796 472400   Fax:01796 473036
Email:info@athollpalace.com
Web:www.athollpalace.com

At the very heart, where the River Tummel flows to the Tay, sits the historic town of Pitlochry. The Atholl Palace Hotel, the epitome of Scottish Baronial splendour, stands overlooking wooded parkland grounds and the town to the surrounding highlands. Many features of the traditional large country house property have now been recreated, including the traditional Victorian Spa, whilst bedroom facilities and standards often now exceed expectations and complement spacious, relaxing public areas.

90 rooms, all en-suite, Open Jan-Dec, B&B per person £64.00-92.00 single or double. BB & Eve.Meal £79.00-109.00 single or double.

Balrobin Hotel

Higher Oakfield, Pitlochry, PH16 5HT
Tel:01796 472901   Fax:01796 474200
Email:info@balrobin.co.uk
Web:www.balrobin.co.uk

Situated in residential yet central part of town with most bedrooms (12-4 on ground floor) with superb panoramic views.Traditional home cooked food from a varied choice menu changing daily accompanied by a selection of fine wines. Residents only bar. Our central location affords easy access to 60% of Scotland making it a perfect base for long & short stays. Special short break & advance booking rates.

14 rooms, all en-suite, Open Mar-Oct, B&B per person, single £39.00-49.00, double £35.00-45.00, BB & Eve.Meal from £46.00-56.00.

Bendarroch House

Strathtay, Pitlochry, PH9 0PG
Tel:01887 840420   Fax:01887 840438
Email:bendarrochhouse@netscape.net
Web:www.bendarroch-house.de

Fully refurbished Victorian house set in landscaped grounds with panoramic views of the River Tay which runs past the estate. Situated between Aberfeldy and Pitlochry. Golfing, fishing and canoeing only 2 minutes away, other sports available in the vicinity. Evening meal by prior arrangement, freshly cooked using local produce. Coffee and liqueurs found in the conservatory lounge.

5 rooms, all en-suite, Open Jan-Dec, B&B per person, single from £30.00, double from £25.00.

Dundarach Hotel

Perth Road, Pitlochry, Perthshire, PH16 5DJ
Tel:01796 472862   Fax:01796 473024
Email:stb@dundarach.co.uk
Web:www.dundarach.co.uk

This hotel on the edge of the village is architecturally interesting, inside and out and stands in its own secluded garden but still close to town centre. A warm friendly welcome is assured by the resident owners the Smail family. The hotel offers both traditional and new bedrooms and all are well equipped. The airy comfortable public rooms are attractively decorated in warm colours and give many fine views over the surrounding countryside.

38 rooms, all en-suite, Open Feb-Nov, B&B per person, single from £30.00, double from £30.00.

Important: Prices stated are estimates and may be subject to amendments

Pitlochry, Perthshire | **Map Ref: 2A1**

The Green Park Hotel

Clunie Bridge Road, Pitlochry, Perthshire, PH16 5JY
Tel:01796 473248 Fax:01796 473520
Email:bookings@thegreenpark.co.uk
Web:www.thegreenpark.co.uk

Family run country house hotel enjoying spectacular views over Loch Faskally. Within strolling distance of the shops and a pleasant walk from the Festival Theatre, the hotel has become a well known landmark of the town. The hotel has a Red Rosette for food, reflecting the emphasis placed on the food served at the Green Park.

51 rooms, all en-suite, Open Jan-Dec, B&B per person, single from £48.00, double from £48.00, BB & Eve.Meal from £65.00.

Knockendarroch House Hotel

Higher Oakfield, Pitlochry, Perthshire, PH16 5HT
Tel:01796 473473 Fax:01796 474068
Email:bookings@knockendarroch.co.uk
Web:www.knockendarroch.co.uk

Victorian mansion set in 1.5 acres of gardens, a short stroll from the centre of Pitlochry. Personal attention and good food help to create a comfortable base from which to explore Perthshire and the central Highlands. AA 3 Stars.

12 rooms, all en-suite, Open Mar-Nov, BB & Eve.Meal from £50.00.

Loch Tummel Inn

Queens View, Strathtummel, Pitlochry, Perthshire, PH16 5RP
Tel/Fax:01882 634272
Email:info@lochtummelinn.co.uk
Web:www.lochtummelinn.co.uk

Just past the famous Queens View, 10 miles from Pitlochry, on a stunning scenic road along the banks of Loch Tummel, Loch Tummel Inn presents a quite charming taste of glorious highland hospitality, quintessentially Scottish, in an unmistakeable, unspoilt traditional country inn style.

7 rooms, some en-suite. B&B per person, single £35.00-50.00, double/twin £65.00-95.00, family £70.00-100.00.

Pine Trees Hotel

Strathview Terrace, Pitlochry, Perthshire, PH16 5QR
Tel:01796 472121 Fax:01796 472460
Email:info@pinetreeshotel.co.uk
Web:www.pinetreeshotel.co.uk

Personally run Victorian country house in elevated position, with 10 acres of garden and woodland yet close to town centre. Walking distance to local golf course. Edradour and Blair Atholl distillery close to village and worth visiting.

20 rooms, all en-suite, Open Jan-Dec, B&B per person, single from £38.00, double from £38.00. Dinner from £21.50 per person.

Pitlochry Hydro Hotel

Knockard Road, Pitlochry, Perthshire, PH16 5JH
Tel:01942 824824
Email:reservations@WAshearings.com
Web:www.WAshearingsholidays.com

The hotel and health club stand in their own grounds overlooking the town. Entertainment every night.

60 rooms, all en-suite, Open Feb-Dec, B&B per person, double from £40.00.

VAT is shown at 17.5%: changes in this rate may affect prices.   *Key to symbols is on back flap.*

Pitlochry, Perthshire

Map Ref: 2A1

★★★

HOTEL

Rosemount Hotel

12 Higher Oakfield, Pitlochry, PH16 5HT
Tel:01796 472302   Fax:01796 474216
Email:info@scottishhotels.co.uk
Web:www.scottishhotels.co.uk

Family run fully licensed hotel with friendly atmosphere, situated in
elevated position overlooking Tummel Valley.

25 rooms, all en-suite, Open Jan-Dec, B&B per person, single from £28.00, double
from £28.00, BB & Eve.Meal from £43.00.

★★★★

**GUEST
HOUSE**

Torrdarach House

Golf Course Road, Pitlochry, Perthshire, PH16 5AU
Tel:01796 472136
Email:torrdarach@msn.com
Web:www.smoothhound.co.uk/hotels/torrdarach.html

Listed Edwardian country house set in secluded gardens with gorgeous
views over the Tummel Valley. A highland burn, a family of red squirrels
and a variety of wildlife all within its grounds. Located approximately 5
minutes walk from the picturesque town centre and golf course. Douglas
and June guarantee a friendly and relaxed atmosphere, heartly
breakfasts and a fine selection of wines and malts.

7 rooms, all en-suite or priv.bathrms, Open Jan-Dec, B&B per person, single from
£22.00, double from £22.00.

★★★★

**GUEST
HOUSE**

The Well House

11 Toberargan Road, Pitlochry, Perthshire, PH16 5HG
Tel/Fax:01796 472239
Email:enquiries@wellhouseandarrochar.co.uk
Web:www.wellhouseandarrochar.co.uk

Personally run, centrally situated in residential area. Easy access to
shops, amenities and theatre.

6 rooms, all en-suite, Open Feb-Nov, B&B per person, double from £24.00, BB &
Eve.Meal from £42.00.

St Andrews, Fife

Map Ref: 2D2

★★★

**SMALL
HOTEL**

The Albany Hotel

56 North Street, St Andrews, Fife, KY16 9AH
Tel:01334 477737 Fax:01334 477742
Email:enqu@thealbanystandrews.co.uk
Web:www.thealbanystandrews.co.uk

Peacefully situated in the heart of St Andrews, close to shops, restaurants,
golf courses and historic buildings, this 19 an elegant Georgian town
house, cleverly and sympathetically converted for use as an hotel. With
22 rooms, tastefully decorated, the Albany Hotel is able to maintain high
standards in accommodation and service.

22 rooms, all en-suite, Open Jan-Dec, B&B per person, single from £45.00, double
from £39.00.

Important: Prices stated are estimates and may be subject to amendments

St Andrews, Fife | Map Ref: 2D2

★★★

**GUEST
HOUSE**

Cleveden House
3 Murray Place, St Andrews, Fife, KY16 9AP
Tel/Fax:01334 474212
Email:bookings@clevedenhouse.co.uk
Web:www.clevedenhouse.co.uk

Personally run guest house, five minutes walk from the Old Course,
beaches and town centre.

2 double, 3 twin rooms all en-suite, 1 single with priv.facilities, B&B per person
from £30.00. Single occupancy from £50.00 pn.

★★★★

**GUEST
HOUSE**

Craigmore Guest House
3 Murray Park, St Andrews, Fife, KY16 9AW
Tel:01334 472142 Fax:01334 477963
Email:enquiries@standrewscraigmore.com
Web:www.standrewscraigmore.com

Victorian stone built guest house in centre of St Andrews. Short walk
from town centre, beaches and 'Old Course'. Ground floor room. Non
smoking. Relax in the comfortable lounge/dining room after a days golf
and sightseeing. Free Internet access.

7 rooms, all en-suite, Open Jan-Dec, B&B per person, single from £45.00, double
from £33.00.

★★★★★

**INTERNATIONAL
RESORT HOTEL**

Fairmont St Andrews, Scotland
St Andrews, Fife, KY16 8PN
Tel:01334 837000 Fax:01334 471115
Email:standrews.scotland@fairmont.com
Web:www.fairmont.com

It provides an international standard of service and attention to detail in
the comfort and convenience of a modern world-class resort.The
extensive facilities, including 209 deluxe guest rooms, five restaurants
each with their own individual character and style, 36 holes of great golf,
a reviving spa offering a wide range of luxurious treatments and an 18
metre indoor pool with sauna, steam-room and jacuzzi.

209 rooms, all en-suite, Open Jan-Dec, B&B per person, double from £85.00, BB &
Eve.Meal from £105.00.

★★★★

**GUEST
HOUSE**

Feddinch Mansion Country Guest House
St Andrews, Fife, KY16 8NR
Tel:01334 470888 Fax:01334 477220
Email:enquiries@feddinch-house.com
Web:www.feddinch-house.com

Feddinch House is a Scottish house with a history of 500 years. Recently
refurbished by Ken and Lois Wood. Views overlook St Andrews and the
Links golf courses. Grass tennis court, outdoor heated swimming pool,
billiard room. Private parking.

5 rooms, all en-suite, Open Jan-Dec, B&B per person, double from £30.00.

★★★★

HOTEL

Macdonald Rusacks Hotel
Pilmour Links, St Andrews, Fife, KY16 9JQ
Tel:0870 4008128 Fax:01334 477896
Email:general.rusacks@macdonald-hotels.co.uk
Web:www.macdonald-hotels.co.uk/rusacks

This traditional hotel dating from c1887 has been extensively refurbished
and 20 new bedrooms have recently been created with magnificent views
of West Sands from many bedrooms. The bar and restaurant overlook
the 18th hole of the famous Old Course. Close to town centre and
University. Modern conference facilities available and non-residents also
very welcome.

68 rooms, all en-suite, Open Jan-Dec, B&B per person, single from £60.00, double
from £80.00, Dinner B&B from £90.00.

VAT is shown at 17.5%: changes in this rate may affect prices.

Key to symbols is on back flap.

St Andrews, Fife	Map Ref: 2D2

GUEST HOUSE

Montague Guest House
21 Murray Park, St Andrews, Fife, KY16 9AW
Tel:01334 479 287
Email:info@montaguehouse.com
Web:www.montaguehouse.com

Quality Victorian terraced house with themed rooms, some with hand painted murals, convenient for the town centre, cinema, shops, restaurants and bars. Golf courses, historic buildings, University, seashore all within a few minutes walk. Completely non - smoking house. Secure storage for golf equipment on ground floor.

7 rooms, all en-suite, Open 1 Mar-31 Jan, B&B per person, single from £35.00, double/twin from £35.00. No dogs, golfers welcome.

HOTEL

New Hall, University of St Andrews
North Haugh, St Andrews, Fife, KY16 9XW
Tel:01334 467000 Fax:01334 467001
Email:new.hall@st-andrews.ac.uk
Web:www.escapetotranquillity.com

New Hall offers quality en-suite facilities and excellent standards of food and service in rooms specially upgraded for summer. Within easy walking distance of the beach, golf courses and town centre, it's ideal for golfers, families, short breaks and holidays.

100 rooms, all en-suite, Open Jun-Sep, B&B per person, single from £47.00, double from £35.00. Evening meals available.

Old Course Hotel, Golf Resort & Spa
St Andrews, Fife, KY16 9SP
Telephone: 01334 474371 Fax: 01334 477668
e.mail: reservations@oldcoursehotel.co.uk
web: www.oldcoursehotel.co.uk
This elegant five red-star hotel overlooks the Old Course and is a five-minute stroll from St Andrews and West Sands beach. Offering the stunning new Kohler Waters Spa, the Championship Duke's Course and an outstanding choice of fine restaurants including the Road Hole Grill (3 AA Rosettes) and Sands Restaurant.

48257

INTERNATIONAL RESORT HOTEL

Old Course Hotel, Golf Resort & Spa
St Andrews, Fife, KY16 9SP
Tel:01334 474371 Fax:01334 477668
Email:reservations@oldcoursehotel.co.uk
Web:www.oldcoursehotel.co.uk

Already one of Europe's finest five-star resorts, the Old Course Hotel's recent multi-million pound refurbishment has lifted it to unprecedented new heights in luxury. Everything that could be improved, has been improved - new guest rooms, the striking transformation of the Duke's Course and, perhaps most impressively of all, the stunning new Kohler Waters Spa.

144 rooms, all en-suite, Open Jan-Dec, B&B per person, single from £155.00, double from £85.50, BB & Eve.Meal from £128.00 (sharing).

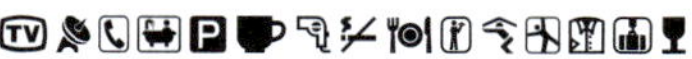

GUEST HOUSE

The Old Station Country Guest House
Stravithie Bridge, St Andrews, KY16 8LR
Tel:01334 880505 Fax:01334 880622
Email:info@theoldstation.co.uk
Web:www.theoldstation.co.uk

Deluxe accommodation in converted Victorian railway station and train carriage, within 2 acres of peaceful gardens only 2 miles from St Andrews. Roaring log fire, candlelight, fresh flowers make this a luxury home from home.

8 rooms, Open Jan-Dec, B&B per person, single from £50.00, room only single from £50.00, double from £80.00, family from £110.00.

Important: Prices stated are estimates and may be subject to amendments

St Andrews, Fife — Map Ref: 2D2

★★★

GUEST
HOUSE

Riverview Guest House
Edenside, St Andrews, Fife, KY16 9SQ
Tel:01334 838009 Fax:01334 839944
Email:admin@riverviewguesthouse.co.uk
Web:www.riverviewguesthouse.co.uk

All rooms ensuite, opening on to courtyard, all extensive views across Eden Estuary. 3 miles (5km) from St Andrews handy for many golf courses. Dining room and 3 bedrooms have level access from car park and are spacious.

7 rooms, Open Jan-Dec, B&B per person single from £45.00, double from £30.00, family from £30.00, room only single from £45.00, double from £60.00, family from £60.00.

★★★★★

HOTEL

Rufflets Country House Hotel
Strathkinness Low Road, St Andrews, Fife, KY16 9TX
Tel:01334 472594 Fax:01334 478703
Email:reservations@rufflets.co.uk
Web:www.rufflets.co.uk

Country house with relaxing ambience, set in 10 acres of beautiful gardens. Fresh seasonal produce served in the restaurant. 1.5 miles (3kms) from golf courses and coast. 'Small Luxury Hotels of the World Member'.

25 rooms, all en-suite, Open Jan-Dec, B&B per person, single from £135.00, double from £105.00, BB & Eve.Meal from £140.00.

★★★★

HOTEL

St Andrews Golf Hotel
40 The Scores, St Andrews, Fife, KY16 9AS
Tel:01334 472611 Fax:01334 472188
Email:reception@standrews-golf.co.uk
Web:www.standrews-golf.co.uk

Privately owned hotel, situated 200 yards from the Old Course, overlooking St Andrews Bay. Imaginative use of local ingredients in award winning restaurant. Highly appointed and furnished bedrooms and bathrooms. This hotel is a superb base for golfers, families or romantic breaks.

21 rooms, all en-suite, Open Jan-Dec, B&B per person, single £130.00, standard £100.00, superior £105.00, junior suite £120.00. BB & Eve.Meal single £160.00, standard £130.00, superior £135.00, junior suite £150.00.

---

by St Andrews, Fife — Map Ref: 2D2

★★★★

INN

The Inn At Lathones
By Largoward, St Andrews, Fife, KY9 1JE
Tel:01334 840494 Fax:01334 840694
Email:Lathones@theinn.co.uk
Web:www.theinn.co.uk

Charming 400 year old Coaching Inn, just 5 miles from St Andrews. Sympathetically restored and enlarged. Offering modern comfort, great food and friendly people to look after your every need. Award winning chef - two AA rosettes - using freshest of local Scottish produce.

13 rooms, all en-suite, B&B per person, single from £110.00, double from £80.00.

VAT is shown at 17.5%: changes in this rate may affect prices.

Key to symbols is on back flap.

Main image: Balmoral Castle and River Dee **Bottom left:** Surfing, Aberdeen
Bottom middle: Craigievar Castle **Bottom right:** Stonehaven

ABERDEEN AND GRAMPIAN HIGHLANDS
Scotland's Castle and Whisky Country

The silvery 'Granite City' of Aberdeen has won more Britain in Bloom titles than any other city – including a gold award last year.

With 45 parks in the city and the celebrated Winter Gardens in Duthie Park, Aberdeen is always in bloom and every season brings further floral flights of fancy.

But then, Aberdeen is a city of acute contrasts. If you were in the Union Street area on a Saturday afternoon you'd probably find it hard to believe that this remarkably busy shopping district is just a short distance away from a brilliant beach.

Strathisla Distillery, Grampian

Steeped in history, with a royal seal of approval and fascinating castle, whisky, coastal and Victorian heritage trails to follow, you'll never struggle to find something exciting to do in Aberdeen and Grampian Highlands.

These days, Aberdeen is more than just an important port with links to the fishing and oil industries, it's a thriving community with a stylish selection of galleries, museums, restaurants, nightclubs and bars. For a further contrast take a wander along the quiet cobbled streets of Old Aberdeen past the charming King's College and over lovely Seaton Park. Go via the beach on the way back to town and you'll encounter Codonas Funfair where you can revisit your childhood on the rollercoaster and have a whale of a time all year round.

Leaving the city behind, the contrasts continue. There are miles of coastline to explore from long, golden, sandy beaches to towering cliffs. The sea (and the fishing, of course) has made such a huge contribution to life in these parts. All along the coast you'll find captivating harbour towns and villages like Stonehaven, Peterhead, Fraserburgh, Banff and Lossiemouth and quaint little places like Pennan, a former smuggler's town and the location for 'Local Hero'.

A great coastline means superb leisure opportunities too. Sailing, scuba-diving, dolphin and bird watching, walking, golf, cycling, fishing – you'll find it all along the North East Coastal Trail.

Another trail you may want to take is the area's Castle Trail. There are over 350 castles in Aberdeen and the Grampian Highlands, testament to a turbulent past and coming in all shapes and sizes from fairytale castles that look like they were designed for a Disney film to crumbling ruins clinging to a cliff face. Many are still occupied to this day – including Balmoral, the Highland holiday home of the Royal Family.

And speaking of royalty, the Deeside towns of Banchory, Ballater and Braemar are privileged to have had many decades of royal patronage. Though the annual highlight in Queen Victoria's 'dear Highland paradise' is the Braemar Gathering in September, there's lots on the go all year round.

If you are looking for an active holiday golf, fishing, horse-riding, sailing, surfing, walking – even skiing in the winter – are all on offer.

You can ski at the Lecht in the winter. You can walk through a last ancient remnant of the Caledonian Pine Forest in Glen Tanar or you could go and explore the beautiful Glenlivet Estate, all part of the Cairngorms National Park.

And while we're mentioning Glenlivet, you may also want to discover the real spirit of this part of the world – malt whisky. The Malt Whisky Trail features 8 famous distilleries and a cooperage in Moray. You may recognise the names: Benromach, Cardhu, Dallas Dhu, The Glenfiddich, Glen Grant, The Glenlivet, Glen Moray and Strathisla. Each has its own unique flavours, each tells the story of 'the water of life' in its own distinctive way. And if you happen to stagger off the trail at any point, there are another 42 distilleries to discover in the Speyside area.

Such a devotion to the art of whisky making deserves a public celebration. The annual Spirit of Speyside Whisky Festival brings together the craftsmen and the people who appreciate their craft for five days of fun in May.

Alongside the whisky, there are other delights that will soon have you raising your glass– music, song and, of course, fine food. Aberdeen and Grampian Highlands is Scotland's natural larder. Beautiful beef, sumptuous seafood, fabulous fruit and vegetables – all come fresh to the table, prepared by the finest chefs. There's even a festival to celebrate the food –Taste of Grampian, held annually in June at Inverurie.

So where would you like to stay in Aberdeen and Grampian Highlands? There's a lot of choice– from historical baronial mansions to Victorian townhouses, elegant country houses, former hunting lodges and coaching inns in some of the best locations in all of Scotland.

Ballater Highland Games

Tourist Information Centres

Please refer to the maps on pages xii-xviii for the locations of establishments appearing in the main advertising section of this guide.
Only year-round Tourist Information Centres are indicated.

The Town House, Aberdeen

Aberdeen	23 Union Street	01224 288828	Jan-Dec
Alford	Railway Museum, Station Yard	01975 562052	Easter-Oct
Ballater	Albert Hall, Station Square	01339 755306	Jan-Dec
Banchory	Bridge Street	01330 822000	Easter-Oct
Banff	Collie Lodge	01261 812419	Easter-Oct
Braemar	The Mews	01339 741600	Jan-Dec
Crathie	Markethill Car Park	01339 742414	Easter-Oct
Dufftown	Clock Tower, The Square	01340 820501	Easter-Oct
Elgin	17 High Street	01343 542666	Jan-Dec
Forres	116 High Street	01309 672938	Easter-Oct
Fraserburgh	3 Saltoun Square	01346 518315	Easter-Oct
Huntly	9a The Square	01466 792255	Easter-Oct
Inverurie	18 High Street	01467 625800	Jan-Dec
Stonehaven	66 Allardice Street	01569 762806	Easter-Oct
Tomintoul	The Square	01807 580285	Easter-Oct

For practical advice, ideas and information about exploring Scotland and to book your accommodation:

Tel: 0845 22 55 121* or if calling from outside the UK: + 44 (0) 1506 832121 In Ireland call:1800 932 510

* A £3 booking fee applies to telephone bookings of accommodation.

info@visitscotland.com
www.visitscotland.com

Aberdeen	Map Ref: 4G10

GUEST HOUSE
★★★

Abbotswell Guest House
28 Abbotswell Crescent, Aberdeen, AB12 5AR
Tel:01224 871788 Fax:01224 891257
Email:gmleith@tiscali.co.uk
Web:www.guesthouse-aberdeen.com

Well established guest house with extensive purpose built accommodation, mostly en-suite. Situated in a quiet residential area with easy access to bus route to city centre. Secure off street private parking close to Deeside tourist route. Ideal for castle and whisky trail routes.

14 rooms, Open Jan-Dec, B&B per person, single from £28.00, double from £20.00.

HOTEL
★★★★

Aberdeen Patio Hotel
Beach Boulevard, Aberdeen, AB24 5EF
Tel:01224 633339 Fax:01224 638833
Email:info@patiohotels.com
Web:www.patiohotels.com

One of Aberdeen's premier hotels located half a mile from the city centre and close to the beach front. Consisting of 90 standard double, 44 deluxe double and 34 premier club double bedrooms, with Atrium bar, full restaurant and conference facilities. In addition, all residents have full use of Breakers Leisure Club, which includes a gymnasium, spa, sauna and swimming pool. Almost 200 car parking spaces available.

168 rooms, all en-suite, B&B per person, single from £60.00, double from £35.00.

GUEST HOUSE
★★★

Aberdeen Springdale Guest House
404 Great Western Road, Aberdeen, AB10 6NR
Tel:01224 316561 Fax:01224 316561
Email:jamesestirling@msn.com
Web:www.aberdeenguesthouse.co.uk

Attractive granite house 2 miles (3kms) from city centre. On main bus routes, 5 miles (8kms) from the airport and on route to Royal Deeside. Private car parking at rear.

6 rooms, some en-suite, Open Jan-Dec excl Xmas/New Year, B&B per person, single from £28.50, double from £27.50.

GUEST HOUSE
★★★★

Allan Guest House
56 Polmuir Road, Aberdeen, AB11 7RT
Tel:01224 584484 Fax:01224 584484
Email:bookings@theallan.co.uk
Web:www.theallan.co.uk

A Victorian terraced house situated on a bus route to the city centre. A free parking area close to Duthie Park and Winter Gardens. Sociable owners who are keen to offer comfortable accommodation and warm hospitality. Wide choice available at breakfast. Special diets can be catered for.

3 rooms, some en-suite, Open Jan-Dec, B&B per person, single £40.00-45.00, king/double £30.00-35.00.

HOTEL
★★★★

Atholl Hotel
54 Kings Gate, Aberdeen, AB15 4YN
Tel:01224 323505 Fax:01224 321555
Email:info@atholl-aberdeen.co.uk
Web:www.atholl-aberdeen.com

Privately owned and managed hotel in the West End of Aberdeen, this distinctive building provides comfortable and well appointed accommodation, along with high standards of service, in a friendly and relaxed atmosphere. Extensive menu, bar, conference and function facilities available. Excellent base for exploring the city, and the countryside beyond.

34 rooms, all en-suite, Open Jan-Dec excl 1 Jan, B&B per person, single from £75.00, double from £60.00.

VAT is shown at 17.5%: changes in this rate may affect prices.

Key to symbols is on back flap.

Aberdeen

Map Ref: 4G10

Beeches Private Hotel

193 Great Western Road, Aberdeen, AB10 6PS
Tel:01224 586413   Fax:01224 596919
Email:beeches.hotel@btconnect.com
Web:www.beeches-hotel.com

Victorian detached granite house in residential area close to city centre. Private car parking. Fitness Suite and solarium.

8 rooms, all en-suite, Open Jan-Dec excl Xmas/New Year, B&B per person, single from £32.00, double from £22.50.

Brentwood Hotel

101 Crown Street, Aberdeen, AB11 6HH
Tel:01224 595440   Fax:01224 571593
Email:reservations@brentwood-hotel.co.uk
Web:www.brentwood-hotel.co.uk

Centrally situated personally run hotel, and within minutes of the city centre. 'Carriages' Brasserie and Bar with a la carte menu.

65 rooms, all en-suite, Open Jan-Dec excl Xmas/New Year, B&B per person, single £41.00-86.00, double £31.00-48.00

Copthorne Hotel Aberdeen

122 Huntly Street, Aberdeen, AB10 1SU
Tel:01224 630404   Fax:01224 640573
Email:reservations.aberdeen@mill-cop.com
Web:www.millenniumhotels.com

Traditional Aberdeen granite facade in the heart of the city. The Copthorne offers guests all the modern comfort, convenience and facilities both business and leisure visitors expect. Poachers Ocean and Steak Grill and Mac's Cocktail lounge bar.

89 rooms, all en-suite, Open Jan-Dec, B&B per person, single from £69.00, double from £44.00, BB & Eve.Meal from £64.00.

Craighaar Hotel

Waterton Road, Bucksburn, Aberdeen, AB21 9HS
Tel:01224 712275   Fax:01224 716362
Email:info@craighaar.co.uk
Web:www.craighaarhotel.com

A charming hotel nestling in pleasant surroundings only 5 minutes from the airport and 15 minutes from the city centre. All 55 bedrooms are well appointed, with satellite TV, CD player and trouser press. The restaurant is renowned for quality cuisine and the hotel atmosphere is informal and relaxed. A courtesy bus to the airport is available by arrangement. 'Wi-Fi' Broadband throughout hotel.

55 rooms, all en-suite, Open Jan-Dec excl Xmas/New Year, B&B per person, single from £45.00, double from £32.50.

Cults Hotel

328 North Deeside Road, Aberdeen, AB15 9SE
Tel:01224 867632 Fax:01224 867699
Email:info@thecultshotel.co.uk
Web:www.thecultshotel.co.uk

One of Aberdeen's oldest hotels refurbished to modern standards. Warm relaxing atmosphere. On the main road to Royal Deeside.

16 rooms, all en-suite, Open Jan-Dec, B&B per person, single from £50.00-75.00, double from £35.00-50.00 pppn. Special rates for long stay.

Important: Prices stated are estimates and may be subject to amendments

Aberdeen	Map Ref: 4G10

Ellenville Guest House
50 Springbank Terrace, Aberdeen, AB11 6LR
Tel/Fax:01224 213334
Email:ellenvillegh@aol.com
Web:www.ellenvilleguesthouse.co.uk

Comfortable and friendly accommodation in the heart of Aberdeen. Convenient for bus/railway station, ferry terminal, theatre and all amenities.

7 rooms, 4 en-suite, Open Jan-Dec, B&B per person, single from £25.00, double from £23.00.

Furain Guest House
92 North Deeside Road, Peterculter, Aberdeen, AB14 0QN
Tel:01224 732189   Fax:01224 739070
Email:furain@btinternet.com

Late Victorian house built of red granite. Family run. Convenient for town, Royal Deeside and the Castle Trail. Private car parking. Dinner available on Wednesday, Friday and Saturday.

8 rooms, all en-suite, Open Jan-Dec excl Xmas/New Year, B&B per person, single from £36.00, double from £24.00.

Greyholme Guest House
35 Springbank Terrace, Aberdeen, AB11 6LR
Tel:01224 587081
Email:info@greyholme-guesthouse.co.uk
Web:www.greyholme-guesthouse.co.uk

Personally run guest house close to city centre and all amenities. Near to main bus routes. Off street parking available.

5 rooms, Open Jan-Dec, B&B per person, single from £27.00, double/twin from £21.00.

Maryculter House Hotel
South Deeside Road, Maryculter, Aberdeenshire, AB12 5GB
Tel:01224 732124   Fax:01224 733510
Email:reservations@maryculterhousehotel.com
Web:www.maryculterhousehotel.com

Step back in time to days of Lairds, Castles and Clans and experience first hand the lifestyle of Scottish Nobility. Home to Knights Templar, set in acres of woodland and landscaped gardens on the banks of the River Dee. Ideally positioned for over forty quality golf courses with Royal Deeside on the doorstep. Explore the Castle and Whisky trails, maybe even take in some fishing. Traditional hospitality and modern comforts await you in this historic setting.

40 rooms, all en-suite, Open Jan-Dec excl Xmas/New Year, B&B per person, single from £45.00, double from £35.00.

Penny Meadow
189 Great Western Road, Aberdeen, AB10 6PS
Tel:01224 588037   Fax:01224 573639
Email:frances@pennymeadow.freeserve.co.uk

A high quality purpose built Guest House with all ensuite bedrooms and off road parking. For the discerning visitor looking for a warm, friendly atmosphere, comfortable accommodation and that little bit extra attention to detail.

3 rooms, all en-suite, Open Jan-Dec, B&B per person, single from £40.00-55.00, double from £30.00-50.00.

VAT is shown at 17.5%: changes in this rate may affect prices.   Key to symbols is on back flap.

Aberdeen

Map Ref: 4G10

HOTEL

Royal Hotel
1-3 Bath Street, Aberdeen, AB11 6BJ
Tel:01224 585152 Fax:01224 583900
Email:info@royalhotel.uk.com
Web:www.royalhotel.uk.com

Located right in the centre of Aberdeen and a short walk from the railway station, the Royal Hotel provides friendly atmosphere and comfortable accommodation, (with food served all day). There is a limited amount of private parking available. Good base for the business traveller, or for weekend breaks, to enjoy the city and all its attractions.

42 rooms, all en-suite, Open Jan-Dec, B&B per person, single from £49.00, double from £27.00.

GUEST HOUSE

St Elmo
64 Hilton Drive, Aberdeen, AB24 4NP
Tel:01224 483065
Email:StElmoBandB@aol.com
Web:http://home.aol.com/StElmoBandB/

A detached bungalow in a residential area, with off-road parking. Totally non-smoking. Most rooms are fully en-suite, and with TV's/Videos; extra facilities in each room, include microwaves and fridges. A full Scottish breakfast is provided. Situated on the main bus route into the city centre.

4 rooms, some en-suite, Open Jan-Dec, B&B per person, single £45.00-60.00, double £30.00-40.00.

SERVICED APARTMENTS

Skene House HotelSuites
96 Rosemount Viaduct, Aberdeen, AB25 1NX
Tel:01224 645971 Fax:01224 626866
Email:rosemount@skene-house.co.uk
Web:www.skene-house.co.uk

A 'home away from home' located in the heart of Aberdeen, Skene House provides a range of 1 to 3 bedrooms. Suites individually furnished and decorated offering comfort and space with independence. Daily maid service and off street parking. Shops and restaurants nearby.

145 suites, en-suite, Open Jan-Dec.

HOTEL

Speedbird Inn
Argyll Road, Aberdeen Airport, Dyce, AB21 0AF
Tel:01224 772883 Fax:01224 772560
Email:reception@speedbirdinns.co.uk
Web:www.speedbirdinns.co.uk

Modern comfortably furnished airport hotel offering facilities expected by todays traveller. 'WiFi' available in public areas and Speedbird Plus rooms. Free 14 channel TV and 4 channel Radio in all rooms. Courtesy transport for surrounding area and airport terminals.

159 rooms, all en-suite, Open Jan-Dec, B&B per person, single from £49.90, double from £27.43.

CAMPUS ACCOMMODATION

University of Aberdeen, Crombie Johnston Hall
University of Aberdeen, Aberdeen, AB24 3TT
Tel:01224 273444 Fax:01224 276246
Email:accommodation@abdn.ac.uk
Web:www.abdn.ac.uk/confevents

Ensuite and standard student accommodation available during summer period. Accommodation is located in historic Old Aberdeen within easy reach of the city centre. Breakfast included.

375 rooms (some en-suite), Open mid Jun-mid Sep, B&B per person from £22.50.

Important: Prices stated are estimates and may be subject to amendments

SCOTLAND'S CASTLE AND WHISKY COUNTRY

6

Aberdeen

Map Ref: 4G10

CAMPUS ACCOMMODATION ★★

University of Aberdeen, King's Hall
College Bounds, Aberdeen, AB24 3TT
Tel:01224 273444 Fax:01224 276246
Email:accommodation@abdn.ac.uk
Web:www.abdn.ac.uk/kingshall

Modern hotel style accommodation located in historic Old Aberdeen. Rooms are available year round, are all ensuite and include a TV, hairdryer, telephone and trouser press. Breakfast is also included within the Zeste restaurant. Guests at King's Hall have access to leisure facilities on the campus during their stay.

65 rooms, all en-suite, Open Jan-Dec excl Xmas/New Year, B&B per room, single from £45.50, twin from £68.50.

nr Aberdeen

Map Ref: 4G10

SMALL HOTEL ★★

The Belvedere Hotel
41 Evan Street, Stonehaven, Aberdeenshire, AB39 2ET
Tel:01569 762672 Fax:01569 767686
Email:gordonflett@aol.com
Web:www.belvederestonehaven.co.uk

The Belvedere is a small hotel a short walk from the town centre, trains and bus station. The hotel offers a comfortable base to explore Dunnatar Castle, the harbour, nearby Aberdeen and Royal Deeside. Beer Garden and full meal service available.

9 rooms, some en-suite, Open Jan-Dec, B&B per person, single from £30.00, double from £25.00. Family rooms available from £70.00 per night B&B.

SMALL HOTEL ★★★

Old Mill Inn
South Deeside Road, Maryculter, Aberdeen, AB12 5FX
Tel:01224 733212   Fax:01224 732884
Email:info@oldmillinn.co.uk
Web:www.oldmillinn.co.uk

A friendly and informal family run country inn under the personal attention of the owners Mr Victor Sang and Mr Michael French. Conveniently located only 5 miles from Aberdeen on the edge of the River Dee and well-known for its wholesome dishes using fresh local produce.

7 rooms, all en-suite, Open Jan-Dec, B&B per person, single from £54.00, double from £32.50.

HOTEL ★★★

Strathburn Hotel
Burghmuir Drive, Inverurie, Aberdeenshire, AB51 4GY
Tel:01467 624422 Fax:01467 625133
Email:strathburn@btconnect.com
Web:www.strathburn-hotel.co.uk

Modern hotel and restaurant with friendly atmosphere, overlooking Strathburn Park in Inverurie. Personally run.

25 rooms, all en-suite, Open 3 Jan-Dec 31, B&B per person, single from £60.00, double from £40.00, BB & Eve.Meal from £60.00.

Ballater, Aberdeenshire

Map Ref: 4E11

SMALL HOTEL ★★★

Cambus O'May Hotel
nr Ballater, Aberdeenshire, AB35 5SE
Tel/Fax:013397 55428
Email:mckechnie@cambusomay.freeserve.co.uk
Web:www.cambusomayhotel.co.uk

Family owned and traditionally run country house hotel dating from the 1870's set amongst its own grounds, 4 miles from Ballater. Very popular with many regular guests. Quality freshly prepared food making use of local produce with the menu changing daily.

12 rooms, all en-suite, Open Jan-Dec, B&B per person, single from £35.00, double from £35.00.

VAT is shown at 17.5%: changes in this rate may affect prices.

Key to symbols is on back flap.

by Ballater, Aberdeenshire

Map Ref: 4E11

★★★

HOTEL

Loch Kinord Hotel

Ballater Road, Dinnet, Royal Deeside, Aberdeenshire, AB34 5JY
Tel:013398 85229 Fax:013398 87007
Email:stay@lochkinord.com
Web:www.lochkinord.com

Under the enthusiastic ownership of Jenny and Andrew Cox the hotel has
undergone public areas refurbishment featuring some 4 poster bedrooms
with all modern facilities. Situated in the centre of this small village it
makes a great base for exploring Royal Deeside, skiing, walking, and
playing golf. The hotel is popular in the area for excellent food from
their AA rosette restaurant. Non-residents very welcome.

21 rooms, all en-suite, Open Jan-Dec, B&B per person, single from £30.00, double
from £30.00, BB & Eve.Meal from £49.50.

Banchory, Aberdeenshire

Map Ref: 4F11

★★★

SMALL
HOTEL

The Burnett Arms Hotel

25 High Street, Banchory, Aberdeenshire, AB31 5TD
Tel:01330 824944 Fax:01330 825553
Email:theburnett@btconnect.com
Web:www.burnettarms.co.uk

Former 19c coaching inn situated at the centre of a small, attractive
gateway town to Royal Deeside. An ideal base for touring numerous local
attractions.

16 rooms, all en-suite, Open Jan-Dec, B&B per person, single £53.00-69.00, double
£38.00-49.00.

Douglas Arms Hotel

22 High Street, Banchory, AB31 5SR
Tel: 01330 822547 Fax: 01330 825989
e.mail: douglasarmshotel@aol.com Web: www.douglasarms.co.uk

Set in the heart of Royal Deeside, the hotel is a mid-Victorian coaching inn offering
comfortable accommodation. Banchory provides an excellent base for exploring the
area with whisky distilleries, castles and golf courses all within the locality. Our
menu offers a mix of traditional meals and dishes with an international flavour, all
made from fresh, and where possible, local produce.   22994

★★

SMALL
HOTEL

Douglas Arms Hotel

22 High Street, Banchory, Aberdeenshire, AB51 5SR
Tel:01330 822547 Fax:01330 825989
Email:douglasarmshotel@aol.com
Web:www.douglasarms.co.uk

Dating from 1816 this former Coaching Inn has been upgraded ensuring
bedrooms offer modern facilities throughout. At centre of this attractive
Deeside Town and Central for all amenities in the area including the
castle and whisky trail, local golf courses, fishing and walking. Popular
venue for bar lunches and suppers. Car parking facilities available.

8 rooms, all ensuite. B&B per room, single £40.00-55.00, double £60.00-80.00,
family £70.00-100.00. Open all year.

Important: Prices stated are estimates and may be subject to amendments

Banchory, Aberdeenshire
Map Ref: 4F11

Raemoir House Hotel
Raemoir, Banchory, Aberdeen AB31 4ED
Tel: 01330 824884   Fax: 01330 822171
e.mail: relax@raemoir.com   Web: www.raemoir.com

Beautiful and timeless, a Scottish Baronial Manor set in 3,500 acres of parkland and forest in Royal Deeside. Filled with a fine collection of antiques. Raemoir is famed and has prestigious awards for its hospitality and food. A host of activities available - including romantic castles and whisky trails. AA ⚘⚘

51007

AWAITING GRADING

Raemoir House Hotel
Banchory, Aberdeenshire, AB31 4ED
Tel:01330 824884   Fax:01330 822171
Email:relax@raemoir.com
Web:www.raemoir.com

Dating from 16c, country house on a 3,500 acre estate. We offer shooting, salmon fishing by prior arrangement, tennis, and golf locally. Outdoor concerts in the summer.

20 rooms, all en-suite, Open Jan-Dec, B&B per person, single from £80.00, double/twin from £55.00 pppn.

Banff
Map Ref: 4F7

★★

SMALL HOTEL

Carmelite House Hotel
Low Street, Banff, AB45 1AY
Tel/Fax:01261 812152
Email:carmelitehoho@aol.com
Web:www.northeastscotlandhotels.com

Small, friendly, family-run hotel in the centre of Banff. Good home cooking, cosy bar with log fire. Private parking. Convenient for golf and all amenities.

9 rooms, most en-suite, Open Jan-Dec, B&B per person, single from £25.00, double/twin from £22.50.

★★★

SMALL HOTEL

Fife Lodge Hotel
Sandyhill Road, Banff, AB45 1BE
Tel:01261 812436 Fax:01261 812636
Email:info@fifelodgehotel.com
Web:www.fifelodgehotel.com

Family run hotel situated 2 acres overlooking the River Deveron and the golf course: a country house yet conveniently located on the edge of Banff. Bar and restaurant meals available; there are function facilities for approximately 250 guests. The area has many interesting attractions and activities available nearby, including Duff House and the Macduff Marine Aquarium.

9 rooms, all en-suite, Open Jan-Dec, B&B per person, single from £45.00, double from £60.00, BB & Eve.Meal from £55.00.

Braemar, Aberdeenshire
Map Ref: 4D11

★★★★

GUEST HOUSE

Callater Lodge Guest House
9 Glenshee Road, Braemar, Aberdeenshire, AB35 5YQ
Tel:013397 41275   Fax:013397 41345
Email:bookings@hotel-braemar.co.uk
Web:www.hotel-braemar.co.uk

A warm welcome awaits you at this pleasant Victorian house in its own spacious grounds. Ideal centre for touring and walking. Close to village centre. 8 miles to Balmoral Castle and Glenshee Ski Centre. Take advantage of our snack menu and enjoy the benefits of our residents lounge.

6 rooms, all en-suite, Open Jan-Oct, B&B per person, single from 30.00, double from £28.00.

VAT is shown at 17.5%: changes in this rate may affect prices.

Key to symbols is on back flap.

Braemar, Aberdeenshire

Map Ref: 4D11

Invercauld Arms

Main Street, Braemar, Aberdeenshire, AB35 5YR
Tel:01942 824824
Email:reservations@WAshearings.com
Web:www.WAshearingsholidays.com

HOTEL

This famous and historic building in Royal Deeside is furnished to
provide traditional Scottish hospitality in sumptuous surroundings.

66 rooms, all en-suite, Open Feb-Dec, B&B per person, single from £35.00, double
from £35.00, BB & Eve.Meal from £45.00.

Schiehallion House

10 Glenshee Road, Braemar, Aberdeenshire, AB35 5YQ
Tel:013397 41679
Email:bookings@schiehallionhouse.com
Web:www.schiehallionhouse.com

GUEST
HOUSE

Comfortable, tastefully decorated, Victorian house with attractive garden
at gateway to Royal Deeside. Offering personal service and log fires. One
ground floor annexe room. All nationalities welcome.

9 rooms, some en-suite, Open Jan-Oct, B&B per person, single from £25.00, double
from £23.00.

Cruden Bay, Aberdeenshire

Map Ref: 4H9

Kilmarnock Arms Hotel

Bridge Street, Cruden Bay, By Peterhead, Aberdeenshire AB42 0HD
Tel: 01779 812213 Fax: 01779 812153
e.mail: reception@kilmarnockarms.com Web: www.kilmarnockarms.com
Situated in the centre of Cruden Bay and only 800m from the world
renowned Cruden Bay Golf Course, the Hotel offers 14 spacious ensuite
single, double/twin or family rooms. Relax and enjoy excellent cuisine and
wines in our Falcon Restaurant or Lounge Bar, or sample one of our
extensive range of Malt Whiskies.
33838

Kilmarnock Arms Hotel

Bridge Street, Cruden Bay, by Peterhead, AB42 0HD
Tel:01779 812213 Fax:01779 812153
Email:reception@kilmarnockarms.com
Web:www.kilmarnockarms.com

SMALL
HOTEL

Traditional Victorian village hotel, providing comfortable and recently
upgraded accommodation for business travellers, golfers and families.
Many activities available in the area - walking, birdwatching, historic
houses and much more.

14 rooms, all en-suite, Open Jan-Dec excl Xmas/New Year, B&B per person, single
from £45.00, double from £35.00.

Elgin, Moray

Map Ref: 4D8

Eight Acres Hotel & Leisure Club

Morriston Road, Elgin, Moray, IV30 6UL
Tel:01343 543077 Fax:01343 540001
Email:enquiries@eightacreshotel.com
Web:www.eightacreshotel.com

HOTEL

Modern hotel set in landscaped grounds on the western approach to
Elgin. Swimming pool, sauna, squash courts, spa bath and games room.

53 rooms, all en-suite, Open Jan-Dec excl Xmas, B&B per person, single from
£49.50, double from £45.00.

Important: Prices stated are estimates and may be subject to amendments

Elgin, Moray

Map Ref: 4D8

The Mansefield Hotel

Mayne Road, Elgin, Moray, IV30 1NY
Tel:01343 540883   Fax:01343 552491
Email:reception@themansefield.com
Web:www.themansefield.com

Recently extended hotel, situated close to the centre of Elgin. Suites and four poster rooms are available, as is a newly built conference and function centre. The hotel provides a choice of dining options, both formal and informal in our A la carte restaurant and Mezzo bar/eaterie. It is an excellent base for the business or leisure traveller.

40 rooms, all en-suite, Open Jan-Dec excl Xmas, B&B per person, single £77.50-87.50, double occupancy £90.00-250.00.

Sunninghill Hotel

Hay Street, Elgin, Moray, IV30 1NH
Tel:01343 547799   Fax:01343 547872
Email:wross@sunninghillhotel.com
Web:www.sunninghillhotel.com

Victorian house, modern extension with annexe accommodation. Near centre of historic Cathedral town. Many golf courses. Sandy beaches 5 miles (8kms).

21 rooms, all en-suite, Open Jan-Dec, B&B per person, single from £45.00, double from £35.00.

West End Guest House

282 High Street, Elgin, IV30 1AG
Tel:01343 549629
Email:westend.house@virgin.net
Web:www.westendguesthouse.co.uk

Traditional Victorian villa with garden, close to A96. 10 minute walk from city centre and all amenities.

6 rooms, some en-suite, Open Jan-Dec, B&B per person, single £25.00-35.00, double £25.00-27.00.

Fordyce, Banffshire

Map Ref: 4F7

Academy House

School Road, Fordyce, nr Portsoy, Banffshire AB45 2SJ
Tel:01261 842743
Email:academy_house@hotmail.com
Web:www.fordyceaccommodation.com

Scottish hospitality in stylish country home set in beautiful conservation village. Quality cooking with local produce. Well located for touring. 2 miles from Portsoy, 11 miles from Banff.

2 rooms, some en-suite, Open Jan-Dec, B&B per person, single from £35.00, double from £30.00, Dinner £18.00.

Forres, Moray

Map Ref: 4C8

Knockomie Hotel

Grantown Road, Forres, Moray, IV36 2SG
Tel:01309 673146 Fax:01309 673290
Email:stay@knockomie.co.uk
Web:www.knockomie.co.uk

A 'B' listed country house c1914, built in an arts and crafts style. Extended and created to a high standard, retaining much warmth and character.

16 rooms, all en-suite, Open Jan-Dec excl Xmas, B&B per person, single £110.00, double £80.00-100.00.

VAT is shown at 17.5%: changes in this rate may affect prices.

Forres, Moray

Map Ref: 4C8

Ramnee Hotel
Victoria Road, Forres, Moray, IV36 3BN
Tel:01309 672410 Fax:01309 673392
Email:info@ramneehotel.com
Web:www.ramneehotel.com

Charming Edwardian Mansion in mature gardens close to town centre and golf course offering delightful accommodation, friendly service and superb cuisine.

19 rooms, all en-suite, Open Jan-Dec excl Xmas/New Year, B&B per person, single from £70.00, double from £47.50.

by Inverurie, Aberdeenshire

Map Ref: 4G9

Pittodrie House Hotel
Chapel of Garioch, by Inverurie, Aberdeen AB51 5HS
Tel:01467 681444 Fax:01467 681648
Email:pittodrie@macdonald-hotels.co.uk
Web:www.macdonaldhotels.com

Country house dating from 1480 on large estate. Mixed arable, forestry and hill land with interesting walks. Open fires, billiards, clay pigeon shooting and 4x4 off road driving.

27 rooms, some en-suite, Open Jan-Dec, B&B per person, single from £75.00, double from £60.00, BB & Eve.Meal from £75.00 pp.

Kildrummy, Aberdeenshire

Map Ref: 4E10

Kildrummy Castle Hotel
Kildrummy, Alford, Aberdeenshire, AB33 8RA
Tel:019755 71288   Fax:019755 71345
Email:bookings@kildrummycastlehotel.co.uk
Web:www.kildrummycastlehotel.co.uk

Traditional Scottish mansion house set amidst acres of gardens and woodland overlooking the original 13th century castle ruins. Tastefully furnished and decorated retaining original features. A la carte restaurant using finest local ingredients.

16 rooms, all en-suite, Open Feb-Dec, B&B per person, single from £80.00, double from £80.00, BB & Eve.Meal from £79.00 (low season rate for a stay of 2 nights or more).

Laurencekirk, Kincardineshire

Map Ref: 4F12

Marykirk Hotel
Main Street, Marykirk, Laurencekirk, Aberdeenshire, AB30 1UT
Tel:01674 840239
Email:marykirkhotel@tesco.net
Web:www.marykirkhotel.com

Small village hotel restaurant/lounge bar, village bar, breakfast room, beer garden, large car park at rear.

4 rooms, all en-suite, Open Jan-Dec excl Xmas/New Year, B&B per person, single from £33.00, double from £30.00.

Oldmeldrum, Aberdeenshire

Map Ref: 4G9

The Redgarth
Kirk Brae, Oldmeldrum, Aberdeenshire, AB51 0DJ
Tel:01651 872353

Quality family run inn enjoying outstanding views of surrounding countryside. Our menu is home cooked using local produce and includes two vegetarian options. A selection of cask conditioned ales available.

3 rooms, all en-suite, Open Jan-Dec excl Xmas/New Year, B&B per person, single from £60.00, double from £37.50.

Important: Prices stated are estimates and may be subject to amendments

Peterhead, Aberdeenshire

Map Ref: 4H8

GUEST HOUSE

Carrick Guest House
16 Merchant Street, Peterhead, Aberdeenshire,
AB42 1DU
Tel:01779 470610
Email:carrickpeterhead@aol.com

Comfortable accommodation, centrally situated for all amenities. Two minutes walk from main shopping centre, harbour and beach. Convenient for maritime museum, lighthouse museum and several nearby golf courses.

6 rooms, all en-suite, Open Jan-Dec excl Xmas/New Year, B&B per person, single from £22.00, double from £22.00.

Portsoy, Banffshire

Map Ref: 4F7

SMALL HOTEL

The Boyne Hotel Portsoy
2 North High Street, Portsoy, Aberdeenshire, AB45 2PA
Tel/Fax:01261 842242
Email:enquiries@boynehotel.co.uk
Web:www.boynehotel.co.uk

Refurbished 18c building on Square in seaside town, close to harbour and sandy seaside. Home cooking. Under personal supervision.

12 rooms, all en-suite, Open Jan-Dec, B&B per person, single £28.00-38.00, double £28.00-38.00, BB & Eve.Meal from £38.00-48.00.

Rothienorman, Aberdeenshire

Map Ref: 4F9

INN

Rothie Inn
Main Street, Rothienorman, Aberdeenshire, AB51 8UD
Tel:01651 821206
Email:rothieinn@accom90.freeserve.co.uk

Family run 19c stone built inn located in the centre of the village, with own garden. 10 miles (16kms) north of Inverurie, situated on Castle Trail. Home cooking in a cosy lounge. Cosy ensuite bedrooms.

2 rooms, all en-suite, Open Jan-Dec excl Xmas/New Year, B&B per person, single from £30.00, double from £25.00.

VAT is shown at 17.5%: changes in this rate may affect prices.

Key to symbols is on back flap.

Main image: Sango Bay, Durness **Bottom left:** Walkers, Glen Finnan
Bottom middle: Rothiemurchus Highland Games **Bottom right:** Mustard Seed, Inverness

THE HIGHLANDS AND SKYE

One thing that is immediately noticeable whenever you holiday in the Highlands is that life moves at a distinctly different pace. Life is more relaxed. Things are, in a way, approached with a much more balanced perspective.

And why not? Who wants to go rushing about chasing shadows when you can sit quietly by a serenely beautiful loch and watch an osprey calmly surveying the crystal clear waters for a flash of silver? Who wouldn't take time out from climbing the career ladder to conquer a real mountain, experiencing a rush of achievement while you survey the breathtaking glen below?

As a visitor to the Highlands, you can hardly fail to be moved by its beauty. Rugged and majestic, the mountainous north provides a backdrop of epic proportions. It's the stuff

 THE NO.1 BOOKING AND INFORMATION SERVICE FOR SCOTLAND   0845 22 55 121   visitscotland.com

Loch Ness, Highlands

For many people the majestic scenery of the Highlands defines their image of Scotland. Indeed, the exhilarating, awe-inspiring beauty of the mountainous north is matched only by its sense of adventure.

of picture postcards and coffee table books, the views that will be etched in your memory forever. There are so many places you have to experience: the eerie silence of Glen Coe; the arctic wilderness of the Cairngorms; the deep mysteries of Loch Ness; the wild flat lands of the Flow Country; the astonishing beauty of Glen Affric; and the golden beaches of the west coast where you can gaze out to the Atlantic and never meet a soul all day.

It is, after all, a very big area and in this great, unspoiled, natural environment, wildlife flourishes. You'll see red squirrels and tiny goldcrests in the trees, otters chasing salmon in fast flowing rivers, deer coming down from the hill to the forest edge, dolphins and whales off the coast, ospreys and eagles soaring overhead and many other birds and animals going about their business as they always have done.

Fortunately, the wildlife happily co-exists alongside a relatively modest human population and they share a great natural playground that is THE ideal place for an active holiday.

Climbers, walkers, mountain bikers, skiers and hunters take to the hills. Surfers, sailors, canoeists and fishermen enjoy the beaches, rivers and lochs. And as if the traditional outdoor pastimes weren't enough, there are lots of increasingly adrenaline-filled activities like sphereing, canyoning, white water rafting and a host of others that will ensure the thrills never stop. Whatever outdoor activity you like to pursue, you'll find it here – and you'll find experienced, professional guides and experts on hand to ensure you enjoy it to the full.

And once you've had enough exercise and fresh air, you can be assured of some fine Highland hospitality. Whether you're staying in a tiny village, a pretty town, a thriving activity centre like Aviemore or in the rapidly expanding city of Inverness, you'll get a great welcome from a lively bunch of people who know how to share good times.

In the pubs and hotels, restaurants and other venues around the community, you'll find music and laughter, perhaps a riotous ceilidh in full fling and unforgettable nights of eating and drinking into the wee small hours.

This year celebrates Highland 2007 and presents a unique opportunity to experience traditional and contemporary Highland culture up close.

There's a spectacular selection of hotels and guesthouses to choose from – many in stunning locations. You can stay in castles and coach houses, stately homes, traditional inns and much more from the historical to the modern.

You'll get a taste of Highland culture too. 2007 is the year Scotland celebrates Highland culture with a wealth of special events and activities going on throughout the Highlands. Go to www.highland2007.com for the latest event updates.

The past is also a draw in the Highlands. You can join the many people every year who come to trace their Scottish roots. Discover the traditional homeland of your clan, learn about their history and walk in your ancestors' footsteps over the battlefields like Culloden where the Jacobite army made its last stand against the English.

You could follow Bonnie Prince Charlie over the sea to Skye whether it's by boat or by bridge. You can even take a glass bottom boat trip around Skye and watch the sea life below.

When you get there you'll see the jagged Cuillins climbing dramatically from the sea, scratching at the sky and you'll find some utterly delightful places to visit. There's Sleat pensinsula – 'the garden of Skye'. There are lovely towns like Portree and Broadford. There's the formidable Dunvegan Castle, home of the MacLeod Clan for over 800 years and the amazing rock formations and pinnacles of the Quiraing.

Wherever you decide to go, the Highlands and Skye will cast a spell on you and it will be a holiday you will remember for as long as you live.

The Mountain Bike World Cup, Nevis Range, Highlands

Tourist Information Centres

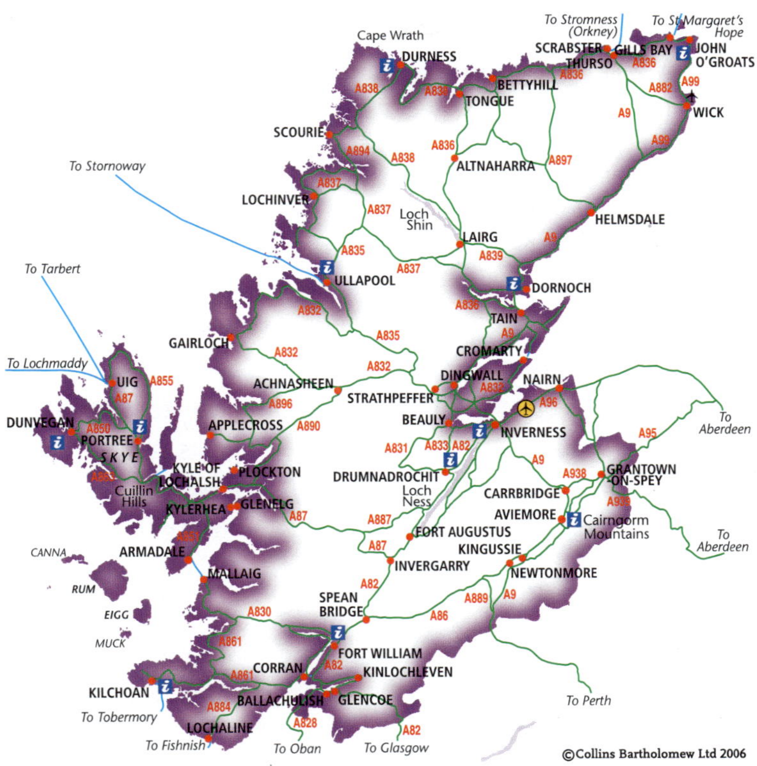

Please refer to the maps on pages xii-xviii for the locations of establishments appearing in the main advertising section of this guide. Only year-round Tourist Information Centres are indicated.

Aviemore	Grampian Road	0845 22 55 121	Jan-Dec
Ballachulish	Albert Road	0845 22 55 121	Jan-Dec
Daviot Wood	Picnic Area, A9	0845 22 55 121	Apr-Oct
Dornoch	The Square	0845 22 55121	Jan-Dec
Drumnadrochit	The car park	0845 22 55 121	Jan-Dec
Dunvegan	2 Lochside	0845 22 55 121	Jan-Dec
Durness	Durine	0845 22 55 121	Jan-Dec
Fort Augustus	Car park	0845 22 55 121	Apr-Oct
Fort William	Cameron Centre	0845 22 55 121	Jan-Dec
Gairloch	Auchtercairn	0845 22 55 121	Jan-Dec
Grantown-on-Spey	54 High Street	0845 22 55 121	Jan-Dec
Inverness	Castle Wynd	0845 22 55 121	Jan-Dec
John O'Groats	County Road	0845 22 55 121	Apr-Oct
Kilchoan	Pier Road	0845 22 55 121	Jan-Dec
Kingussie	Duke Street	0845 22 55 121	Easter-Oct
Lairg	Ferrycroft Centre	0845 22 55 121	April-Oct
Lochinver	Kirk Lane	0845 22 55 121	Apr-Oct
Newtonmore	Main Street	0845 22 55 121	Jan-Dec
North Kessock	Picnic site	0845 22 55 121	Apr-Oct
Portree	Bayfield House	0845 22 55 121	Jan-Dec
Strontian	The Square	0845 22 55 121	Apr-Oct
Thurso	Riverside	0845 22 55 121	Apr-Oct
Ullapool	Argyle Street	0845 22 55 121	Jan-Dec
Wick	High Street	0845 22 55 121	Jan-Dec

For practical advice, ideas and information about exploring Scotland and to book your accommodation:

Tel: 0845 22 55 121*
or if calling from outside the UK: + 44 (0) 1506 832121
In Ireland call:1800 932 510

* A £3 booking fee applies to telephone bookings of accommodation.
info@visitscotland.com www.visitscotland.com

Aultbea, Ross-shire   Map Ref: 3F6

SMALL HOTEL ★★★

Aultbea Hotel
Aultbea, Ross-shire, IV22 2HX
Tel:01445 731201
Email:aultbeahotel@btconnect.com
Web:www.aultbeahotel.co.uk

Comfortable hotel situated on the shore of Loch Ewe with magnificent views. Fishing available. Inverewe Gardens, 5 miles (9kms). Food served in our Waterside Bistro, lounge bar & Zetland Restaurant.

8 rooms, all en-suite, Open Jan-Dec, B&B per person, single from £33.00, double from £33.00.

Aviemore, Inverness-shire   Map Ref: 4C10

GUEST HOUSE ★★★

Cairngorm Guest House
Grampian Road, Aviemore, Inverness-shire, PH22 1RP
Tel:01479 810630
Email:conns@lineone.net
Web:www.cairngormguesthouse.com

Peter and Gail welcome you to our lovely Victorian House, 5 min walk from Aviemore centre. Relax by the open fire in the guest lounge and enjoy homemade cake. Hearty breakfasts with vegetarian option. En-suite rooms some on ground floor. King sized beds with TV and VCR also available. Drying/storage facilities and private parking. Wi-Fi enabled.

12 rooms, all en-suite, Open Jan-Dec, B&B per person, single from £30.00, double from £25.00.

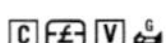

HOTEL ★★★

Cairngorm Hotel
Grampian Road, Aviemore, PH22 1PE
Tel:01479 810233 Fax:01479 810791
Email:reception@cairngorm.com
Web:www.cairngorm.com

Independent hotel providing 3 star accommodation with that friendly, caring service only a privately run hotel can offer.

31 rooms, all en-suite, Open Jan-Dec, B&B per person, single from £47.50, double from £37.50.

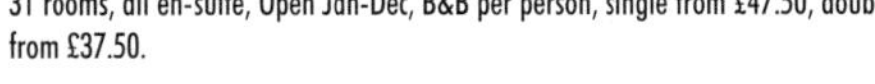

GUEST HOUSE ★★★

Ravenscraig Guest House
Grampian Road, Aviemore, Inverness-shire, PH22 1RP
Tel:01479 810278   Fax:01479 810210
Email:info@aviemoreonline.com
Web:www.aviemoreonline.com

Ravenscraig is centrally located in the village and an ideal base for touring the Highlands. Popular with birdwatchers, golfers, walkers & cyclists are our quiet ground floor garden rooms with their own front doors allowing easy access as well as privacy. We also offer family rooms, a comfortable guest lounge with local information, drying facilities, ski/golf locker, plentiful parking and legendary breakfasts!

12 rooms, all en-suite, Open Jan-Dec, B&B per person, single from £25.00, double from £25.00.

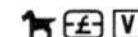

SMALL HOTEL ★★★

The Rowan Tree Country Hotel
Loch Alvie, by Aviemore, Inverness-shire, PH22 1QB
Tel/Fax:01479 810207
Email:enquiries@rowantreehotel.com
Web:www.rowantreehotel.com

The hotel is set amid stunning scenery overlooking peaceful Loch Alvie and offers a calm, relaxing haven, ideally located for the area's many activities. Our 11 characterful, well equipped, bedrooms, cosy lounges with open fires, home cooked 4 course dinners and selection of superb wines all combine with our warm welcome to ensure that you enjoy your stay to the full.

11 rooms, 10 en-suite, Open all year, B&B per person, single from £32.50, double from £35.00.

VAT is shown at 17.5%: changes in this rate may affect prices.

Key to symbols is on back flap.

Ballachulish, Argyll — Map Ref: 1F1

★★★★

GUEST HOUSE

Craiglinnhe House
Lettermore, Ballachulish, Argyll, PH49 4JD
Tel:01855 811270
Email:info@craiglinnhe.co.uk
Web:www.craiglinnhe.co.uk

Lochside Victorian villa amid spectacular mountain scenery offering period charm with modern comfort. Warm, friendly atmosphere, good food and wine. Ideal base for exploring the Western Highlands.

5 rooms, all en-suite, Open Feb-Dec, B&B per person, double from £28.00, BB & Eve.Meal from £45.50.

★★★★

GUEST HOUSE

Lyn Leven Guest House
Ballachulish, Argyll, PH49 4JP
Tel:01855 811392 Fax:01855 811600
Web:www.lynleven.co.uk

A very warm Highland welcome awaits you at this RAC award winning establishment. Situated within attractive, well cared for gardens overlooking Loch Leven in the heart of some of Scotland's most spectacular scenery. Traditional home cooking. Ample parking. Glencoe only 1 mile. Ideal base for skiing, walking, climbing and fishing.

8 rooms, all en-suite, Open Jan-Dec excl Xmas, B&B per person, double from £25.00-30.00.

Boat of Garten, Inverness-shire — Map Ref: 4C10

The Boat

The Boat, Deshar Road, Boat of Garten, Inverness-shire PH24 3BH
Tel: 01479 831258 Fax: 01479 831414
e.mail: info@boathotel.co.uk Web: www.boathotel.co.uk

Relax and enjoy log fires, lovely comfortable individually decorated rooms, superb 2 AA Rosette cuisine, golf, fishing, lochs, mountains and activities in the Cairngorms National Park in this privately owned Victorian country hotel overlooking an 18 hole golf course and the River Spey.

15542

★★★★

HOTEL

The Boat Hotel
Boat of Garten, Inverness-shire, PH24 3BH
Tel:01479 831258 Fax:01479 831414
Email:info@boathotel.co.uk
Web:www.boathotel.co.uk

Privately owned Victorian hotel recently refurbished to a very high standard, overlooking the 18 hole championship golf course. Award winning '2 AA Rosette' cuisine in 'The Capercaillie' restaurant. Individual in style with friendly personalised service. Golf and fishing packages arranged.

26 rooms, all en-suite, Open Feb-5 Jan, B&B per person, single from £84.50, double from £64.50, BB & Eve.Meal from £89.50.

Important: Prices stated are estimates and may be subject to amendments

Boat of Garten, Inverness-shire   Map Ref: 4C10

MOORFIELD HOUSE

Informality is the key to this luxuriously furnished Victorian house.
Ideally suited to those seeking relaxed and peaceful surroundings. A friendly
welcome, comfortable beds and a hearty breakfast await. Fully non smoking.
Evening meal by arrangement. Central for birdwatching, golf, fishing and walking.

Deshar Road, Boat of Garten, Inverness-shire PH24 3BN
Tel: 01479 831646
e.mail: enquiries@moorfieldhouse.com
Web: www.moorfieldhouse.com

38931

★★★★

**GUEST
HOUSE**

Moorfield House

Deshar Road, Boat of Garten, Inverness-shire, PH24 3BN
Tel:01479 831646
Email:enquiries@moorfieldhouse.com
Web:www.moorfieldhouse.com

Informality is the key to this luxuriously furnished Victorian house.
Ideally suited to those seeking relaxed and peaceful surroundings. A
friendly welcome, comfortable beds and a hearty breakfast await. Fully
non smoking. Evening meal by arrangement.

6 rooms, all en-suite, Open Dec-Nov excl Xmas, B&B per person, single from
£40.00, double from £33.00.

Brackla, Loch Ness-side, Inverness-shire   Map Ref: 4A9

LOCH NESS
CLANSMAN HOTEL

BRACKLA, LOCH NESS-SIDE, INVERNESS IV3 8LA
Tel: 01456 450326 Fax: 01456 450845
e.mail: lochnessclansman@aol.com Web: www.lochnessview.com
The ONLY hotel situated on the banks of Loch Ness. Large gift shop/café on site. Our
bedroom facilities now include Deluxe Bedrooms overlooking the Loch at excellent
rates. The 'Observation Lounge Bar' & Restaurant have stunning views over the Loch to
the hills beyond. Wide range of meal options, including local Scottish produce. 31330

★★★

HOTEL

Loch Ness Clansman Hotel

Brackla, Loch Ness Side, Inverness-shire, IV3 8LA
Tel:01456 450326 Fax:01456 450845
Email:lochnessclansman@aol.com
Web:www.lochnessview.com

Family run hotel situated on the west shores of Loch Ness. 9 miles from
Inverness, and 4 miles from Drumnadrochit. Wheelchair access to all
public areas. Many attractions within 90 minutes drive, including the Isle
of Skye and the Whisky Trail. Historic Sites such as Culloden Battlefield
and Cawdor Castle, plus numerous Golf courses. Short break packages
available, whether you are travelling by plane, train or by car.

25 rooms, all en-suite, Open Jan-Dec excl Xmas/New Year, B&B per person, single
from £49.00, double from £34.50.

Brora, Sutherland   Map Ref: 4C6

★★★★

HOTEL

Royal Marine Hotel

Golf Road, Brora, Sutherland, KW9 6GS
Tel:01408 621252 Fax:01408 621181
Email:info@highlandescape.com
Web:www.highlandescapehotels.com

Traditional country house hotel, offering excellent facilities and access to
golfing, fishing and countryside. Leisure complex with indoor pool,
sauna, steam room, jacuzzi and curling rink. Easily accessible from
Inverness, approximately one hours drive away, with its rail and airport
links to the south.

22 rooms, all en-suite, Open Jan-Dec, B&B per person, single from £75.00, double
from £60.00.

VAT is shown at 17.5%: changes in this rate may affect prices.   Key to symbols is on back flap.

Carrbridge, Inverness-shire　　　　　Map Ref: 4C9

★★★

INN

The Cairn Hotel

Main Road, Carrbridge, Inverness-shire, PH23 3AS
Tel:01479 841212　Fax:01479 841362
Email:info@cairnhotel.co.uk
Web:www.cairnhotel.co.uk

Enjoy the country pub atmosphere, log fire, malt whiskies, real ales and affordable food in this family owned village centre hotel. Close to the historic bridge. A perfect base for touring the Cairngorms, Whisky Trail and Loch Ness.

7 rooms, most en-suite, Open Jan-Dec, B&B per person from £26.00.

Dalrachney Lodge Hotel

CARRBRIDGE, INVERNESS-SHIRE PH23 3AT
Tel: 01479 841252　Fax: 01479 841383
e.mail: dalrachney@aol.com　Web: www.dalrachney.co.uk
A lovingly refurbished Victorian Sporting Lodge in the heart of the Scottish Highlands, Dalrachney is an ideal base for a memorable holiday. Enjoy the breathtaking scenery, abundant wildlife and numerous outdoor activities of the Cairngorm National Park. Spacious well-appointed rooms. Emphasis on good food and wines served in a relaxed and friendly setting.　22083

★★★★

SMALL
HOTEL

Dalrachney Lodge Hotel

Carrbridge, Inverness-shire, PH23 3AT
Tel: 01479 841252　Fax: 01479 841383
Email: dalrachney@aol.com
Web: www.dalrachney.co.uk

Victorian former hunting lodge, with many antique and period furnishings, set in 16 acres of peaceful surroundings. Cuisine using local produce.

10 rooms, 9 en-suite, 1 priv.facilities, Open Jan-Dec, B&B per person, single from £50.00, double from £35.00, BB & Eve.Meal from £45.00.

Cromarty, Ross-shire　　　　　Map Ref: 4B7

★★★

SMALL
HOTEL

Royal Hotel

Marine Terrace, Cromarty, Ross-shire, IV11 8YN
Tel:01381 600217　Fax:01381 600813
Email:info@royalcromartyhotel.co.uk
Web:www.royalcromartyhotel.co.uk

Family run hotel overlooking harbour and beach with fine views over Cromarty Firth. Specialising in food using good local produce. Situated in the historic conservation village of Cromarty. Dolphin watching, museums, good walks or just quiet relaxation.

10 rooms, some en-suite, Open Jan-Dec, B&B per person, single from £35.00, double from £30.00, BB & Eve.Meal from £45.00.

Dornie, by Kyle of Lochalsh, Ross-shire　　　　　Map Ref: 3G9

★★★

SMALL
HOTEL

Dornie Hotel

Francis Street, Dornie, Ross-shire, IV40 8DT
Tel:01599 555205　Fax:01599 555429
Email:dornie@madasafish.com
Web:www.dornie-hotel.co.uk

Occupying one of the most scenic areas in Scotland, this family run 13 bedroom hotel is situated in the village of Dornie & is only a short walk from the magnificent Eilean Donan Castle. Rooms are well equipped & the hotel offers an excellent selection of modern cuisine specialising in local seafood. Castle weddings attractively catered for. We look forward to welcoming you to a relaxing & peaceful stay.

13 rooms, some en-suite, Open Jan-Dec, B&B per person, single £25.00-35.00, double £25.00-35.00.

Important: Prices stated are estimates and may be subject to amendments

Dornie, by Kyle of Lochalsh, Ross-shire
Map Ref: 3G9

Eilean A-Cheo
Dornie, by Kyle of Lochalsh, Ross-shire, IV40 8DY
Tel:01599 555485
Email:stay@scothighland.com
Web:www.scothighland.com

Situated on a quiet side road just a few minutes walk from the picturesque Eilean Donan Castle and overlooking the loch. Easy access to the Isle of Skye, Plockton with its famous palm trees and the wonderful countryside round about. Excellent hospitality and a true Gaelic welcome.

5 rooms, some en-suite, Open Jan-Dec, B&B per person, single from £26.00, double from £18.00.

Dornoch, Sutherland
Map Ref: 4B6

Dornoch Hotel
Grange Road, Dornoch, IV25 3LD
Tel:01942 824824
Email:reservations@WAshearings.com
Web:www.WAshearingsholidays.com

Close to famous golf course and overlooking Dornoch Firth, this hotel offers comfortable accommodation and entertainment every night, and a pitch and putt on front lawn.

110 rooms, all en-suite, Open Feb-Dec, B&B per person, double from £25.00.

The Eagle Hotel & Bank House
Castle Street, Dornoch, Sutherland, IV25 3SR
Tel:01862 810008   Fax:01862 811355
Email:irene@eagledornoch.co.uk
Web:www.eagledornoch.co.uk

Paul and Irene welcome you to the Eagle Hotel where personal attention is guaranteed. 'Every customer is a new friend'. Meals - all day, every day in a friendly pub atmosphere where families are welcome. Three new bedrooms are located in the nearby Bank House and are furnished to an excellent standard.

12 rooms, all en-suite, Open Jan-Dec, B&B per person, double from £35.00.

Fort Augustus, Inverness-shire
Map Ref: 4A10

Caledonian Hotel
Fort Augustus, Inverness-shire, PH32 4BQ
Tel:01320 366256   Fax:08701 602708
Email:hotel@thecaledonianhotel.com
Web:www.thecaledonianhotel.com

Small lodge hotel situated 300 mtrs from village centre, Caledonian Canal/Loch Ness. Cruises, fishing and tourist attractions within walking distance. Peaceful and spacious reception room and lounge. Ideal rates for half board short breaks. In addition to the hotel facilities there is golfing, boat cruises, exhibitions and fishing available within the village area. Fort Augustus's central position is suitable for exploring the rest of the Highlands.

11 rooms, 10 en-suite, 1 priv.facilities, Open Easter-Nov, B&B per person, single from £45.00, double from £33.00, BB & Eve.Meal from £44.50.

Fort William, Inverness-shire
Map Ref: 3H12

Caledonian Hotel
Achintore Road, Fort William, Inverness-shire, PH33 6RW
Tel:01942 824824
Email:reservations@WAshearings.com
Web:www.WAshearingsholidays.com

Modern hotel situated on the edge of the town with extensive views across Loch Linnhe.

68 rooms, all en-suite, Open Feb-Dec, B&B per person, single from £30.00, double from £30.00, BB & Eve.Meal from £40.00.

VAT is shown at 17.5%: changes in this rate may affect prices.

Key to symbols is on back flap.

Fort William, Inverness-shire | Map Ref: 3H12

Clan MacDuff Hotel

Achintore Road, Fort William, Inverness-shire PH33 6RW
Tel: 01397 702341 Fax: 01397 706174
e.mail: reception@clanmacduff.co.uk Web: www.clanmacduff.co.uk

Situated overlooking Loch Linnhe, with outstanding views of magnificent Highland scenery. Well-appointed en-suite bedrooms with colour television, hospitality tray etc. Large choice dinner menu. Delicious bar suppers. Fine selection of malt whiskies. Large car-park. This friendly family-run hotel is dedicated to providing good quality and value hospitality.

19453

★★★

HOTEL

Clan MacDuff Hotel

Achintore Road, Fort William, Inverness-shire, PH33 6RW
Tel:01397 702341   Fax:01397 706174
Email:reception@clanmacduff.co.uk
Web:www.clanmacduff.co.uk

This family run hotel overlooks Loch Linnhe, 2 miles south of Fort William. The hotel is situated in its own grounds with large car park. Enjoy the highland scenery from the conservatory or patio. All public rooms have magnificent views of the Loch and the mountains beyond. Dinner is a traditional menu with varied choice. We offer the comfort and freedom of a hotel at economic prices. Brochure on request.

42 rooms, all en-suite, Open Apr-Nov, B&B per person, single from £34.00, double from £25.50, BB & Eve.Meal from £39.50.

★★

HOTEL

Cruachan Hotel

Achintore Road, Fort William, Inverness-shire, PH33 6RQ
Tel:01397 702022   Fax:01397 702239
Email:reservations@cruachan-hotel.co.uk
Web:www.cruachan-hotel.co.uk

Victorian villa, modern wing attached, standing in own grounds overlooking Loch Linnhe and only 400 yards from Fort William's main shopping street.

57 rooms, Open Jan-Dec, B&B per person, single from £25.00, double from £22.00 per person.

Distillery Guest House

Nevis Bridge, North Road, Fort William PH33 6LR
Tel: 01397 700103 Fax: 01397 702980
e.mail: disthouse@aol.com
Web: www.stayinfortwilliam.co.uk

Situated at the entrance to Glen Nevis just 5 minutes from the Town Centre. *Distillery House* has been upgraded to high standards. Set in the extensive grounds of the *Glenlochy Distillery* with views over the River Nevis, all bedrooms are ensuite. As recommended in the Daily Mail feature article on 'The Great Glen Way'. *Bed & Breakfast from £22.50 per person.* Complimentary Whisky or Sherry upon arrival.

22781

★★★★

GUEST HOUSE

Distillery Guest House

Nevis Bridge, Fort William, Inverness-shire, PH33 6LR
Tel:01397 700103   Fax:01397 702980
Email:disthouse@aol.com
Web:www.stayinfortwilliam.co.uk

Distillery house at old Glenlochy Distillery in Fort William beside A82, Road to the Isles. Situated at the entrance to Glen Nevis short distance from the town centre. Distillery House has been upgraded to high standards. Set in the extensive grounds of the Glenlochy Distillery with views over the River Nevis. All bedrooms are ensuite with TV, and hospitality tray. Non smoking establishment. Complimentary whisky upon arrival.

8 rooms, all en-suite, Open Jan-Dec, B&B per person, single from £22.50, double from £22.50.

Important: Prices stated are estimates and may be subject to amendments

★★★

GUEST HOUSE

Glenlochy Guest House

Nevis Bridge, Fort William, Inverness-shire, PH33 6LP
Tel:01397 702909
Email:glenlochy1@aol.com
Web:www.glenlochy.co.uk

Detached house with garden situated at Nevis Bridge, midway between Ben Nevis and the town centre. 0.5 miles (1km) to railway station. 2 annexe rooms.

10 rooms, all en-suite, Open Jan-Dec, B&B per person, single £25.00-50.00, double £25.00-38.00.

★★★

HOTEL

Grand Hotel

Gordon Square, Fort William, Inverness-shire, PH33 6DX
Tel/Fax:01397 702928
Email:grandhotel.scotland@virgin.net
Web:www.grandhotel-scotland.co.uk

Conveniently located in the town centre, our family run hotel offers good food and accommodation at competitive prices. Excellent base from which to explore the scenic West Highlands by car or by foot. Children welcome. Baby listening service as well as highchairs and cots. Our chef is happy to assist with all your dietary requests.

30 rooms, all en-suite, Open Feb-Dec excl Xmas/New Year, B&B per person, single from £39.50, double from £29.50.

★★★

GUEST HOUSE

Mansefield Guest House

Corpach, Fort William, Inverness-shire, PH33 7LT
Tel:01397 772262
Email:mansefield@btinternet.com
Web:www.fortwilliamaccommodation.com

This traditional Scottish guest house is situated on the 'Road to the Isles' and set in mature gardens with views of the surrounding mountains. We specialise in relaxation, comfort and home cuisine. Being small and select the ambience is special and attention personal and friendly. Sorry we are unable to accommodate children under 12 years of age.

6 rooms, all en-suite, Open Jan-Dec, B&B per person, single from £21.00, double from £21.00, BB & Eve.Meal from £34.00.

VAT is shown at 17.5%: changes in this rate may affect prices.

Key to symbols is on back flap.

Fort William, Inverness-shire   Map Ref: 3H12

West End Hotel

Achintore Road, Fort William PH33 6ED
Tel: 01397 702614 Fax: 01397 706279
e.mail: welcome@westend-hotel.co.uk
Web: www.westend-hotel.co.uk

Family run hotel overlooking Loch Linnhe on main road into town,
3 minutes walk from shops. All rooms ensuite with colour television,
telephone and tea-making facilities. Table d'hôte menu/bar meals.
Entertainment 2 nights during summer season. Enjoys breathtaking views of
Loch Linnhe and the Ardgour mountains.   63632

★★★

HOTEL

West End Hotel

Achintore Road, Fort William, PH33 6ED
Tel:01397 702614   Fax:01397 706279
Email:welcome@westend-hotel.co.uk
Web:www.westend-hotel.co.uk

Family run hotel in the centre of Fort William overlooking Loch Linnhe.
Ideal base for touring the West Highlands.

51 rooms, all en-suite, Open Feb-Dec excl Xmas/New Year, B&B per person, single
from £35.00, double from £25.00.

---

by Fort William, Inverness-shire   Map Ref: 3H12

★★★★

B&B

Dailanna Guest House

Kinlocheil, Fort William, Inverness-shire PH33 7NP
Tel/Fax:01397 722253
Email:flo@dailanna.co.uk
Web:www.dailanna.co.uk

Detached bungalow with large garden in elevated, peaceful position with
fine views southwards over Loch Eil to the hills of Ardgour. Enjoy the
colourful sunset skies from our spacious lounge. The Isle of Skye, Morvan
and Moidart are all easily accessible along the 'Road to the Isles'.

3 rooms, all en-suite, Open Apr-Oct, B&B per person, double £25.00-30.00.
Children 12 years and over.

★★★★

**SMALL
HOTEL**

Old Pines Hotel & Restaurant

Spean Bridge, by Fort William, PH34 4EG
Tel:01397 712324
Email:enquiries@oldpines.co.uk
Web:www.oldpines.co.uk

A unique blend of relaxed informality and excellent food. All rooms
ensuite with T.V. Light lunches and five course evening meals. Children
welcome.

8 rooms, all en-suite, Open Jan-Dec.

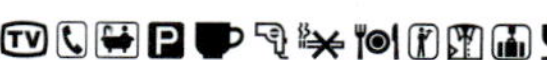

---

nr Fort William, Inverness-shire   Map Ref: 3H12

★★★

INN

The Tailrace Inn

Riverside Road, Kinlochleven, Argyll, PH50 4QH
Tel:01855 831777   Fax:01855 831291
Email:tailrace@btconnect.com
Web:www.tailraceinn.co.uk

The Tailrace Inn is situated in the centre of the scenic village of
Kinlochleven. Surrounded by the Mamore Mountains midway between
Glencoe and Ben-Nevis. An ideal stopover for walkers, climbers or those
who enjoy the outdoors. Excellent drying room facilities. Lively,
atmospheric bar with wide-screen satellite TV. All rooms comfortably
furnished with TV's, DVD players and tea trays.

6 rooms, all en-suite, Open Jan-Dec, B&B per person, single from £40.00, double
from £30.00 pp.

Important: Prices stated are estimates and may be subject to amendments

Gairloch, Ross-shire | Map Ref: **3F7**

HOTEL

Gairloch Hotel
Gairloch, Highland Region, IV21 2BL
Tel:01942 824824
Email:reservations@WAshearings.com
Web:www.WAshearingsholidays.com

Victorian hotel overlooking the Gair Loch. Recently refurbished throughout. Ideal centre for touring west coast. Golf and sailing nearby.

72 rooms, all en-suite, Open Mar-Nov, B&B per person, double from £25.00.

THE OLD INN
FLOWERDALE GLEN, GAIRLOCH, ROSS-SHIRE IV21 2BD
TEL: 01445 712006 FAX: 01445 712044
E.MAIL: info@theoldinn.net WEB: www.theoldinn.net

AA PUB OF THE YEAR FOR SCOTLAND & N.I. 2003

AA BEST SEAFOOD PUB OF THE YEAR FOR SCOTLAND 2005/6
CAMRA SCOTTISH HIGHLAND PUB OF THE YEAR 2004/5

ABBOT ALE PERFECT PUB FOR SCOTLAND AWARD 2005/2006

A must visit for seafood lovers (langoustine, scallops, mussels). Renowned for the range and quality of real ales, fine malts and wines. 14 well-appointed rooms. Ideal base for outdoor enthusiasts.

59848

INN

The Old Inn
Gairloch, Ross-shire, IV21 2BD
Tel:01445 712006   Fax:01445 712044
Email:info@theoldinn.net
Web:www.theoldinn.net

18c coaching Inn in picturesque harbour location. Renowned for selection of seafood, real ales, and friendly atmosphere. 'AA' Pub of the Year for Scotland and N.I. for 2003. CAMRA Highland Pub of the Year 2004/5. Abbot Ale Perfect Pub for Scotland 2005/6. AA Best Seafood Pub of the Year for Scotland 2005/6.

14 rooms, all en-suite, Open Feb-Dec excl Xmas/New Year, B&B per person, single from £35.00, double from £27.50.

VAT is shown at 17.5%: changes in this rate may affect prices.

Key to symbols is on back flap.

Gairloch, Ross-shire

Map Ref: 3F7

SHIELDAIG LODGE HOTEL
GAIRLOCH, ROSS-SHIRE IV21 2AW
Tel: 01445 741250 Fax: 01445 741305
e.mail: enquiries@shieldaiglodge.com
Web: www.shieldaiglodge.com

Situated just outside Gairloch, the Shieldaig Lodge is a beautiful traditional country house in its own private bay. The lodge has 26,000 acres of fishing and shooting, its own river system and nine major lochs.
Nature cruises and Torridon Mountains nearby.

54538

★★★

SMALL
HOTEL

Shieldaig Lodge Hotel
Gairloch, Ross-shire, IV21 2AW
Tel:01445 741250 Fax:01445 741305
Email:enquiries@shieldaiglodge.com
Web:www.shieldaiglodge.com

12 rooms. 11 ensuite. B&B per person, double/twin from £35.00-55.00.
Open Mar-Oct.

Glencoe, Argyll

Map Ref: 1F1

CLACHAIG INN
Glencoe, Argyll PH49 4HX
Tel: 01855 811252 Fax: 01855 812030
e.mail: inn@clachaig.com
Web: www.clachaig.com

Set in the heart of this awe-inspiring glen with glorious mountain views, the Clachaig has been a source of hospitality to visitors to the glen for over 300 years.
A magnificent Highland setting ideal for your holiday to relax unwind and adjust to a slower pace. A perfect base for touring and sightseeing the beautiful West Coast or local walking and bird watching. Mountain sports, water sports and fishing available locally. Comfortable accommodation in en-suite rooms with TV. Imaginative freshly prepared food. Great range of cask conditioned ales and malt whiskies. Good Beer Guide listed. Luxury chalets also available.
B&B from £34.

19383

★★

INN

Clachaig Inn
Glencoe, Argyll, PH49 4HX
Tel:01855 811252 Fax:01855 812030
Email:inn@clachaig.com
Web:www.clachaig.com

23 en-suite bedrooms, B&B from £34.00-40.00 per person per night.

Located in the heart of Glencoe with stunning mountain views and a great Highland atmosphere. The Inn offers upgraded ensuite accommodation, an imaginative all day menu and an unrivalled selection of cask ales and malt whiskies. Recent winners Best Pub in Scotland. An Outdoor Inn for Outdoor Folk. Open all Year.

Important: Prices stated are estimates and may be subject to amendments

MACDONALD HOTEL

Fort William Road, Kinlochleven, Argyll PH50 4QL
Tel: 01855 831539 Fax: 01855 831416
e.mail: enquiries@macdonaldhotel.co.uk
Web: www.macdonaldhotel.co.uk

A modern hotel in Highland style on the shore of Loch Leven. The Walker's bar provides an informal atmosphere, superb views of the Loch and surrounding mountains. Our kitchen offers quality Highland specialities, which are served in the dining room or bar. The ideal location for a walking holiday. 36849

★★★

SMALL HOTEL

MacDonald Hotel

Fort William Road, Kinlochleven, Argyll, PH50 4QL
Tel:01855 831539   Fax:01855 831416
Email:enquiries@macdonaldhotel.co.uk
Web:www.macdonaldhotel.co.uk

A modern, yet traditional, hotel set beside a tidal creek at the head of Loch Leven. Mid-way between Glen Nevis and Glencoe at the foot of the Mamores, the Macdonald Hotel is the perfect base to enjoy the best of west Highland walking or touring. Personally managed by John, Lynn and team who pride themselves on providing a relaxed, informal, environment and the very best of Highland foods from fresh local produce.

10 rooms, all en-suite, Open Jan-Dec, B&B per person, single from £40.00, double from £28.00, BB & Eve.Meal from £40.00.

★★★

GUEST HOUSE

Scorrybreac Guest House

Glencoe, Argyll, PH49 4HT
Tel:01855 811354 Fax:01855 811024
Email:info@scorrybreac.co.uk
Web:www.scorrybreac.co.uk

Scorrybreac sits on the edge of Glencoe village in an elevated forested location amidst some of the most dramatic scenery Scotland has to offer. The house has 6 well appointed bedrooms all with en-suite or private facilities. The lounge and dining room have excellent views across Loch Leven and to the mountains beyond, where guests talk enthusiastically to one another about their daily activities.

6 rooms, 5 en-suite, Open Jan-Dec, B&B per person, single from £25.00, double/twin from £21.00,

★★★

SMALL HOTEL

The Princes' House Hotel

Glenfinnan, Inverness-shire, PH37 4LT
Tel:01397 722246 Fax:01397 722323
Email:princeshouse@glenfinnan.co.uk
Web:www.glenfinnan.co.uk

Set amidst stunning West Highland scenery, this family run former coaching inn, with its award winning restaurant offers an excellent base for touring historic Bonnie Prince Charlie country along the romantic 'Road to the Isles'. 2 AA Rosettes for dining room.

9 rooms, all en-suite, Open Mar-Dec excl Xmas and 1wk Oct, B&B per person, single from £49.00, double from £37.00.

★★★

SMALL HOTEL

Kintail Lodge Hotel

Glenshiel, Ross-shire, IV40 8HL
Tel:01599 511275 Fax:01599 511226
Email:kintaillodgehotel@btinternet.com
Web:www.kintaillodgehotel.co.uk

Converted well appointed former shooting lodge on the shores of Loch Duich near Eilean Donan Castle and the Five Sisters of Kintail. Ideal touring and hill walking centre. Conservatory Restaurant and Bar open to non-residents.

12 rooms, all en-suite, Open Jan-Dec, B&B per person, single from £38.00, double from £38.00, BB & Eve.Meal from £65.00.

Glen Urquhart, Inverness-shire — Map Ref: 4A9

Glenurquhart House

Glenurquhart, Drumnadrochit, Inverness-shire, IV63 6TJ
Tel:01456 476234 Fax:01456 476286
Email:carol@glenurquhartlodges.co.uk
Web:www.glenurquhart-house-hotel.co.uk

★★★

SMALL
HOTEL

Situated in a scenic location overlooking Loch Meiklie. Attractions nearby include Loch Ness, Glen Affric for hill-walking, loch and river fishing, and pony trekking. Restaurant using freshly prepared produce. At the end of your day relax in our comfortable lounge by the log fires.

6 rooms, some en-suite, Open Mar-Nov, B&B per person, single from £40.00, double from £40.00, BB & Eve.Meal from £55.00.

Grantown-on-Spey, Moray — Map Ref: 4C9

An Cala Guest House

Woodlands Terrace, Grantown on Spey, Moray, PH26 3JU
Tel/Fax:01479 873293
Email:ancala@globalnet.co.uk
Web:www.ancala.info

★★★★

GUEST
HOUSE

AA 5 Diamond rating. A lovely large Victorian house set in ½ an acre with on-site parking, overlooking woods yet within easy walking distance of Grantown centre. Doubles are kingsize, including a magnificent mahogany 4 poster bed from Castle Grant; all rooms en-suite. We aim to make you feel welcome, relaxed and comfortable.

4 rooms, Open Jan-Dec, B&B per person single from £40.00, double from £26.00, family from £25.00. Room rate, single from £40.00, double from £52.00, triple from £75.00.

Garden Park Guest House

Woodside Avenue, Grantown-on-Spey, Moray, PH26 3JN
Tel:01479 873235
Email:gardenpark@waitrose.com
Web:www.garden-park.co.uk

★★★★

GUEST
HOUSE

Victorian, stone built house set in own colourful garden, quietly located a short walk from the centre of Grantown on Spey. Guests' lounge with log-burning stove; home cooked breakfast made with fresh produce served in the dining room with its individual tables. A short selection of malt whiskies are available. Five ensuite rooms, one 4 poster, one on the ground floor. A friendly and relaxing base for exploring the area.

5 rooms, all en-suite, Open Jan-Dec, B&B per person, single from £30.00, double from £26.00.

Rossmor Guest House

Woodlands Terrace, Grantown on Spey, Moray, PH26 3JU
Tel/Fax:01479 872201
Email:rossmorgrantown@yahoo.com
Web:www.rossmor.co.uk

AWAITING
GRADING

Spacious Victorian detached house with original features and large garden. A warm welcome. Parking. Panoramic views. No smoking throughout. Tudor style four poster bed, iron and trouser press facility available.

6 rooms, all en-suite, Open Jan-Dec, B&B per person, single from £26.00, double from £26.00.

Important: Prices stated are estimates and may be subject to amendments

Glengarry Castle Hotel

Invergarry, Inverness-shire PH35 4HW
Tel: 01809 501254 Fax: 01809 501207
e.mail: castle@glengarry.net
Web: www.glengarry.net

Country House Hotel privately owned and personally run by the MacCallum family for over 40 years. Situated in the heart of the Great Glen, this is a perfect centre for touring both the West Coast and Inverness/Loch Ness area. Magnificently situated in 60 acres of wooded grounds overlooking Loch Oich. Recently refurbished, 5 rooms with 4-poster beds, all rooms have ensuite bathrooms, TV, radio and telephone. Private tennis court, trout and pike fishing in Loch Oich. Children and dogs welcome.

For brochure please contact Mr D MacCallum.   28180

★★★★

HOTEL

Glengarry Castle Hotel

Invergarry, Inverness-shire, PH35 4HW
Tel:01809 501254   Fax:01809 501207
Email:castle@glengarry.net
Web:www.glengarry.net

Privately owned country mansion, some rooms with four-poster beds. Extensive wooded grounds to loch with impressive hill and forest views.

26 rooms, some en-suite, Open mid Mar-mid Nov, B&B per person, single from £68.00, double from £50.00.

Kincraig House Hotel

Invergordon, Ross-shire, IV18 0LF
Tel: 01349 852587 Fax: 01349 852193
e.mail: info@kincraig-house-hotel.co.uk
Web: www.kincraig-house-hotel.co.uk

Recently re-furbished Kincraig House Hotel offers a choice of individually designed Premier, Executive and Standard rooms. Excellent fine dining is available in the hotel restaurant or more informally in the bar, both of which overlook the extensive gardens. Twenty minutes drive north of Inverness, the hotel offers easy access to the Scottish Highlands.

33956

★★★★

HOTEL

Kincraig House Hotel

Invergordon, Ross-shire, IV18 0LF
Tel:01349 852587 Fax:01349 852193
Email:info@kincraig-house-hotel.co.uk
Web:www.kincraig-house-hotel.co.uk

Kincraig House Hotel offers 15 en-suite rooms, a number of which are newly created Premier and Executive rooms, A refurbished a'la Carte Restaurant and bar and a spacious oak panelled lounge offer superb character and comfort.

15 rooms, all en-suite, Open Jan-Dec, B&B per person, single from £55.00, double from £45.00, BB & Eve.Meal from £68.00.

VAT is shown at 17.5%: changes in this rate may affect prices.   Key to symbols is on back flap.

Inverness	Map Ref: 4B8

GUEST HOUSE ★★★★

Ballifeary House Hotel
10 Ballifeary Road, Inverness, IV3 5PJ
Tel:01463 235572   Fax:01463 717583
Email:william.gilbert@btconnect.com
Web:www.ballifearyhousehotel.co.uk

Attractive detached Victorian villa situated in quiet residential area, and just a short walk to the Eden Court Theatre, River Ness and many excellent restaurants. The house is tastefully decorated and furnished throughout and has a very relaxed and friendly atmosphere. Lovely sitting room with wealth of tourist information. Large car park in the grounds. Establishment not suitable for families as minimum age is 15 years.

6 rooms, all en-suite, Open Jan-Dec excl Xmas, B&B per person, single from £40.00, double from £30.00.

HOTEL ★★★

Best Western Inverness Palace Hotel & Spa
Ness Walk, Inverness, IV3 5NG
Tel:01463 223243 Fax:01463 236865
Email:palace@miltonhotels.com
Web:www.bw-invernesspalace.co.uk

Modernised Victorian hotel on banks of the River Ness opposite the castle. Many rooms recently refurbished. Milton Leisure Club features 50ft swimming pool. Close to town centre and Eden Court Theatre. Some parking at the hotel, plus valet parking available. Free 'Wi-Fi' internet access.

88 rooms, all en-suite, Open Jan-Dec, B&B per person, single from £69.00, double from £44.95. Evening meal £16.95 pp.

SMALL HOTEL ★★★★

Bunchrew House Hotel
Bunchrew, Inverness, IV3 8TA
Tel:01463 234917 Fax:01463 710620
Email:welcome@bunchrew-inverness.co.uk
Web:www.bunchrew-inverness.co.uk

Bunchrew House is more than just another Country House Hotel. Steeped in history and lovingly restored, the house has an incredibly warm and welcoming atmosphere. It lies in 20 acres of lawns and magnificent woodlands and is rightfully known as 'the hotel on the shore' standing as it does only yards from the sea. Yet this fabulous house is only 3 miles from the Highland Capital - the City of Inverness and right in the heart of some of the most spectacular scenery in the world.

16 rooms, all en-suite, Open Jan-Dec excl Xmas, B&B per person, single from £97.50 pp, double from £72.50 pp.

GUEST HOUSE ★★★

Castle View Guest House
2A Ness Walk, Inverness, IV3 5NE
Tel/Fax:01463 241443
Email:jmunro4161@aol.com
Web:www.castleviewinverness.co.uk

Centrally situated comfortable Guest House on the banks of the River Ness. Easy walking to all Inverness city centre attractions, restaurants and shops. Short distance walk to Eden Court Theatre.

6 rooms, some en-suite, Open Jan-Dec, B&B per person, single from £26.00, double/twin from £24.00.

Important: Prices stated are estimates and may be subject to amendments

Inverness

Map Ref: 4B8

AWAITING GRADING

Dunain Park Hotel
Inverness, IV3 8JN
Tel:01463 230512 Fax:01463 224532
Email:dunainparkhotel@btinternet.com
Web:www.dunainparkhotel.co.uk

13 rooms, 1 four-poster, 1 half tester, all en-suite. Open Jan-Dec. B&B per person, from £69.00.

HOTEL

Inverness Marriott Hotel
Culcabock Road, Inverness, IV2 3LP
Tel:01463 237166   Fax:01463 225208
Email:mhrs.invkm.frontdesk@marriotthotels.com
Web:www.invernessmarriott.co.uk

Original manor house dating back to the 18th century set in 4 acres of gardens. Leisure club with indoor swimming pool, jacuzzi, sauna, steam room, exercise room, hairdresser, beauty treatments. Choice of 2 restaurants. 1 mile (2kms) from city centre, 7 miles (11kms) from airport.

82 rooms, all en-suite, Open Jan-Dec, B&B per person from £55.00.

GUEST HOUSE

Moray Park House
Island Bank Road, Inverness, IV2 4SX
Tel/Fax:01463 233528
Email:info@morayparkhotel.co.uk
Web:www.morayparkhotel.co.uk

Run by owners and pleasantly situated with open outlook over gardens and river, yet close to town centre and all its amenities. Private car park.

8 rooms, all en-suite, Open Jan-Dec excl Xmas, B&B per person, single from £27.00, double from £22.00.

VAT is shown at 17.5%: changes in this rate may affect prices.

Key to symbols is on back flap.

Inverness   Map Ref: 4B8

★★★

GUEST HOUSE

Parkhill Guest House
17 Ardconnel Street, Inverness, IV2 3EU
Tel:01463 223300
Email:cherryparkhill@hotmail.com
Web:www.parkhill-inverness.co.uk

Family run Guest House in quiet street; 2 minutes walk from city centre and within 5 minutes walk from bus and railway station.

7 rooms, Open Jan-Dec, B&B per person, from £20.00.

★★★

GUEST HOUSE

Pitfaranne Guest House
57 Crown Street, Inverness, IV2 3AY
Tel:01463 239338 Fax:01463 240356
Email:jims@pitfaranne.fsnet.co.uk
Web:www.pitfaranne.co.uk

End terraced house in quiet residential area within 10 minutes walk from town centre. Some off-road private parking. Collection from station/airport available by prior arrangement.

7 rooms, some en-suite, B&B per person, single from £24.00, double from £22.00.

★★★

HOTEL

The Priory Hotel
The Square, Beauly, Inverness-shire, IV4 7BX
Tel:01463 782309   Fax:01463 782531
Email:reservations@priory-hotel.com
Web:www.priory-hotel.com

Situated in the attractive village square of Beauly, this privately run hotel offers excellent facilities, coupled with friendly, efficient informal service. Enjoy the flexibility of early check-in's, late check out's, food available all day and best of all - breakfast available till lunchtime.

34 rooms, all en-suite, Open Jan-Dec, B&B per person, single from £42.50, double from £35.00, BB & Eve.Meal from £45.00.

John o'Groats, Caithness   Map Ref: 4E2

★★

GUEST HOUSE

Caber Feidh Guest House
John O'Groats, Wick, Caithness, KW1 4YR
Tel:01955 611219

Centrally situated in John O' Groats and 2 miles (3kms) from Duncansby Head. It is well situated for exploring the north east, including the north coast of Sutherland, the inland Flow Country, and more. Day trips to Orkney are a popular choice and the Castle of Mey 6 miles West.

14 rooms, some en-suite, Open Jan-Dec, B&B per person, single from £18.00, double from £17.00.

★★

SMALL HOTEL

Seaview Hotel
John O'Groats, Caithness, KW1 4YR
Tel/Fax:01955 611220
Email:seaviewhotel@btinternet.com
Web:www.johnogroats-seaviewhotel.co.uk

Comfortable range of accommodation, situated 300 yds from Orkney Passenger Ferry. Secure facilities for bikes/cycles. Internet access available. Off-road parking. John 'O' Groats Visitor/Craft Centre, Stacks of Duncansby, cliff walks and puffins, fine views of the sea and nearby Orkney.

10 rooms, 9 en-suite, Open Jan-Dec, B&B per person, single from £35.00, double from £30.00, BB & Eve.Meal from £40.00.

Important: Prices stated are estimates and may be subject to amendments

Laggan Bridge, by Newtonmore, Inverness-shire — Map Ref: 4B11

Monadhliath Hotel
Laggan Bridge, nr Newtonmore, Inverness-shire PH20 1BT
Tel/Fax:01528 544276
Email:monadhliath@lagganbridge.com
Web:www.lagganbridge.com

Family run hotel in secluded area but close to main Spey Valley tourist resorts and on main road from Newtonmore to Fort William/Isle of Skye.

8 rooms, all en-suite, Open Feb-Dec, B&B per person, single from £20.00, double from £20.00, BB & Eve.Meal from £29.50.

---

by Lairg, Sutherland — Map Ref: 4A6

The Overscaig House Hotel
Loch Shin, Sutherland, IV27 4NY
Tel:01549 431203 Fax:01549 431210
Email:visits@overscaig.com
Web:www.overscaig.com

Located on the banks of Loch Shin, the Overscaig is an ideal base to explore all the attractions of the Northern Highlands. Hill walking, bird watching, fishing available. A warm Highland welcome awaits.

8 rooms, all ensuite, Open Mar-Oct, B&B single/double/twin £36.00-£45.00. DB&B single/double/twin £54.00-£63.00

Lochinver, Sutherland — Map Ref: 3G5

Inver Lodge Hotel
Lochinver, Sutherland, IV27 4LU
Tel:01571 844496 Fax:01571 844395
Email:stay@inverlodge.com
Web:www.inverlodge.com

Modern hotel with accent on comfort and friendliness. Restaurant and all bedrooms can enjoy sea-scape and setting sun over Lochinver harbour.

20 rooms, all en-suite, Open Apr-Oct, B&B per person, single from £80.00, double from £75.00, BB & Eve.Meal from £100.00.

Kylesku Hotel
Kylesku, by Lochinver, Sutherland, IV27 4HW
Tel:01971 502231 Fax:01971 502313
Email:info@kyleskuhotel.co.uk
Web:www.kyleskuhotel.co.uk

This former ferry hotel in NW Highlands has stunning views of Loch Glendhu and the mountains beyond from the restaurant, bar and most bedrooms. The chef uses local produce wherever possible and seafood (particularly langoustine) and game are a speciality. Many photo's sample menus and local attractions and activities can be found on our website.

8 rooms, 6 en-suite, Open Mar-Oct, B&B per person, single from £40.00, double from £35.00.

VAT is shown at 17.5%: changes in this rate may affect prices.

Key to symbols is on back flap.

Lochinver, Sutherland — Map Ref: 3G5

Polcraig Guest House
Lochinver, Sutherland, IV27 4LD
Tel/Fax:01571 844429
Email:cathelmac@aol.com
Web:www.smoothhound.co.uk/hotels/polcraig.html

A warm, friendly welcome awaits you here at Polcraig. Ideally situated in a quiet location with views across Lochinver Bay & Harbour. A short walk takes you to a choice of places for eating out. Your hosts Jean and Cathel will provide you with a hearty breakfast before you set out for your day. Explore the Highlands, taking in the spectacular views and an abundance of wildlife.

GUEST HOUSE

6 rooms, all en-suite, Open Jan-Dec, B&B per person, single from £30.00, double from £25.00.

Loch Ness, Inverness-shire — Map Ref: 4A10

Whitebridge Hotel
Whitebridge, Inverness-shire, IV2 6UN
Tel:01456 486226   Fax:01456 486413
Email:info@whitebridgehotel.co.uk
Web:www.whitebridgehotel.co.uk

Personally run hotel nestling in foothills of Monadliath Mountains. Beside the quiet B862 on the East side of Loch Ness and 24 miles South of Inverness.

SMALL HOTEL

12 rooms, all en-suite, Open Jan-Dec, B&B per person, single from £38.00, double from £29.00, BB & Eve.Meal from £42.00.

by Loch Torridon, Ross-shire — Map Ref: 3G9

Tigh an Eilean Hotel
Shieldaig, by Strathcarron, Ross-shire, IV54 8XN
Tel:01520 755251 Fax:01520 755321
Email:tighaneileanhotel@shieldaig.fsnet.co.uk

Personally run, small loch front hotel in charming village. All rooms en suite, most with sea views. Famous for its fresh produce and local seafood.

SMALL HOTEL

11 rooms, Open Mar-Nov, B&B per person, from £68.00 single, £144.00 double, £144.00 family.

Mallaig, Inverness-shire — Map Ref: 3F11

Western Isles
East Bay, Mallaig, Inverness-shire, PH41 4QG
Tel/Fax:01687 462320
Email:westernisles@aol.com

Modern house overlooking the harbour and fishing boats, well situated for ferries to the islands. 4 miles (6kms) from renowned Morar sands 10mins from ferry to Skye, Eigg, Rhum, Canna & the Knoydart Peninsula.

GUEST HOUSE

4 rooms, some ensuite, Open Mar-Oct, B&B per person, single £28.00, double £25.00-30.00.

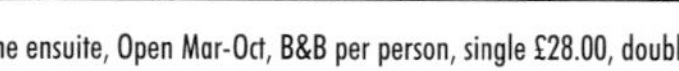

West Highland Hotel
Mallaig, Inverness-shire, PH41 4QZ
Tel:01687 462210   Fax:01687 462130
Email:westhighland.hotel@virgin.net
Web:www.westhighlandhotel.co.uk

Hotel with recent conservatory extension. Stands above the village of Mallaig with views over the harbour to the Isle of Skye beyond. All public areas recently upgraded to high standard. Bar meals served and non-residents welcome. 4 annexe bedrooms.

HOTEL

40 rooms, all en-suite, Open Apr-Nov, B&B per person, single from £40.00, double from £35.00, BB & Eve.Meal from £50.00.

Important: Prices stated are estimates and may be subject to amendments

Muir of Ord, Ross-shire

Map Ref: 4A8

Ord House Hotel

Muir of Ord, Ross-shire, IV6 7UH
Tel/Fax:01463 870492
Email:admin@ord-house.co.uk
Web:www.ord-house.co.uk

SMALL HOTEL

Country house dating from 1637, set in extensive grounds of both formal garden and park and woodland. Taste of Scotland with emphasis on fresh food. Friendly and informal service in comfortable surroundings - a relaxing environment. 'AA' rosette. 'Wi-Fi' internet hotspot.

10 rooms, all en-suite, Open May-Oct, single B&B per person from £40.00, BB & Eve.Meal from £66.00.

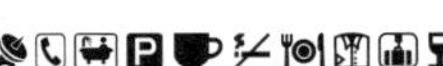

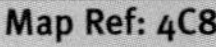

Nairn

Map Ref: 4C8

Claymore House Hotel

Seabank Road, Nairn, IV12 4EY
Tel:01667 453731   Fax:01667 455290
Email:claymorehouse@btconnect.com
Web:www.claymorehousehotel.com

SMALL HOTEL

Family run hotel with the emphasis on friendliness, traditional food and flexibility and customer care.

13 rooms, all en-suite, Open Jan-Dec, B&B per person, single from £47.50, double from £47.50, BB & Eve.Meal from £59.50.

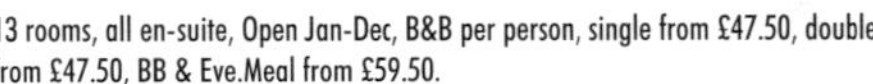

Invernairne Guest House

Thurlow Road, Nairn, Inverness-shire, IV12 4EZ
Tel:01667 452039   Fax:01667 456760
Email:info@invernairne.com
Web:www.invernairne.com

GUEST HOUSE

Elegant, comfortable and family run, the stately Invernairne has magnificent views over the Moray Firth and garden path down to the sandy beach and promenade. The friendly wood-panelled lounge bar serves real ale and malt whiskies. Accommodation all en-suite. Ground floor bedroom available. Nearby restaurants and local amenities. The perfect base for touring, golf, cycling and total relaxation.

9 rooms, all en-suite, Open Jan-Dec, B&B per person, single from £33.00, double from £33.00.

Windsor Hotel

Albert Street, Nairn, IV12 4HP
Tel:01667 453108   Fax:01667 456108
Email:windsornairnscot@btconnect.com
Web:www.windsor-hotel.co.uk

HOTEL

Set within residential area of Nairn and within 3 mins walk of town centre, close to the beach, many sporting activities, including the town's two championship golf courses. It has retained much of its character, whilst being sympathetically refurbished in line with the owners commitment to a continual upgrade. Ideal base for touring the Inverness Highlands. Fort George, Culloden Battlefield, Cawdor and Brodie Castles and Loch Ness.

52 rooms, all en-suite, Open Jan-Dec, B&B per person, single from £45.00, double from £95.00.

Nethy Bridge, Inverness-shire

Map Ref: 4C10

Nethybridge Hotel

Nethybridge, Inverness-shire, PH25 3DP
Tel:01479 821203 Fax:01479 821686
Email:salesnethybridge@strathmorehotels.com
Web:www.strathmorehotels.com

HOTEL

Victorian building of character recently upgraded, situated in Highland village and ideally situated for the amenities of Strathspey.

69 rooms, all en-suite, Open Jan-Dec, B&B per person, single from £45.00, double from £90.00, Evening meal from £19.00.

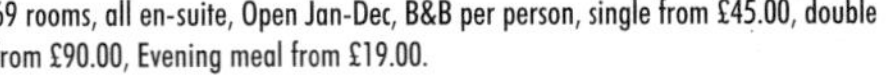

VAT is shown at 17.5%: changes in this rate may affect prices.

Key to symbols is on back flap.

Newtonmore, Inverness-shire

Map Ref: 4B11

★★★

SMALL
HOTEL

Alvey House Hotel

Golf Course Road, Newtonmore, Inverness-shire, PH20 1AT
Tel:01540 673260 Fax:01540 673003
Email:enquiries@alveyhouse.co.uk
Web:www.alveyhouse.co.uk

In the heart of Monarch of the Glen country, a friendly small hotel with
spectacular mountain views. Perfect base for exploring Scotland with
walking, cycling, horse riding, watersports and golf on our doorstep.
Home cooking and a true Scottish welcome make this a memorable place
to stay.

5 rooms, all en-suite, Open Jan-Dec, single from £22.50, double from £22.50, BB &
Eve.Meal from £40.00.

Poolewe, Ross-shire

Map Ref: 3F7

★★★

SMALL
HOTEL

Poolewe Hotel

Main Street, Poolewe, IV22 2JX
Tel:01445 781241
Email:info@poolewehotel.co.uk
Web:www.poolewehotel.co.uk

Former inn dating in part from 18C. Now a family run hotel recently
refurbished. Situated in village and close to Inverewe Gardens. Excellent
restaurant - real ale bar.

9 rooms, all en-suite, Open Jan-Dec, B&B per person, single from £32.50, double
from £30.00, BB & Eve.Meal from £48.00.

Rhiconich, Sutherland

Map Ref: 3H3

★★★

SMALL
HOTEL

Rhiconich Hotel

Rhiconich, Sutherland, IV27 4RN
Tel:01971 521224 Fax:01971 521732
Email:rhiconichhotel@aol.com
Web:www.rhiconichhotel.co.uk

Imagine a place where beauty, peace & tranquility are the order of the day,
where your every need is looked after by the friendliest staff, where you can
Salmon & Trout fish, walk, climb, birdwatch, beachcomb or just amaze at the
finest mountain & Loch scenery in the Highlands, a place specializing in fresh
seafood, vension, beef, lamb, halibut & sole and proud of its malt whisky
selection and open log fire. No need to imagine it any longer.

11 rooms, en-suite, Open Jan-Dec closed Xmas/New Year, B&B per person, single
from £40.00, double from £39.50.

Scourie, Sutherland

Map Ref: 3H4

EDDRACHILLES HOTEL

Badcall Bay, Scourie, Sutherland IV27 4TH
Tel: 01971 502080 Fax: 01971 502477
e.mail: info@eddrachilles.com
Web: www.eddrachilles.com

*Escape to the peace and tranquillity of Eddrachilles Hotel, magnificently situated at the head
of the island studded Badcall Bay. The former manse of Eddrachillis Parish, this 18th
Century building has been completely refurbished, whilst maintaining the character of older
times. The restaurant serves fresh local produce and the menu changes daily.*   24356

★★★

SMALL
HOTEL

Eddrachilles Hotel

Badcall Bay, Scourie, Sutherland, IV27 4TH
Tel:01971 502080 Fax:01971 502477
Email:enq@eddrachilles.com
Web:www.eddrachilles.com

Magnificently situated overlooking the islands of Eddrachilles Bay, this 200 year old
building has been carefully refurbished, providing modern comfortable bedrooms but
retaining the charm and character of older times. Fully licensed with an extensive
wine list, cooking concentrates on traditional style benefiting from high quality local
produce, commended by Taste of Scotland. Close to Handa Island bird sanctuary. Deer,
seals, otters and badgers can be seen in and around the hotel grounds.

11 rooms, all en-suite, Open Mar-Oct.

Important: Prices stated are estimates and may be subject to amendments

Scourie, Sutherland

Map Ref: 3H4

★★★

SMALL HOTEL

Scourie Hotel
Scourie, Sutherland, IV27 4SX
Tel:01971 502396   Fax:01971 502423
Email:patrick@scourie-hotel.co.uk
Web:www.scourie-hotel.co.uk

Personally run, ideally situated for touring this rugged area of North West Scotland. Hotel specialises in fishing for brown trout and salmon. Some boats available. Four course dinner with local produce.

20 rooms, some en-suite, Open Apr-Oct, B&B per person, single from £38.00, double from £33.00 per person.

Portree, Isle of Skye, Inverness-shire

Map Ref: 3E9

★★★★

GUEST HOUSE

Corran House
Kensaleyre, Portree, Isle of Skye,
Inverness-shire, IV51 9XE
Tel:01470 532311

In a small country village overlooking Loch Snizort, 8 miles (10kms) from Portree and from Uig ferry terminal. Extensive gardens with lovely views.

4 rooms, some en-suite, Open Jan-Dec, B&B per person, single £23.00-25.00, double £23.00-25.00.

Cuillin Hills Hotel

Portree, Isle of Skye, IV51 9QU
Tel: 01478 612003 Fax: 01478 613092
e.mail: info@cuillinhills-hotel-skye.co.uk Web:www.cuillinhills-hotel-skye.co.uk
Superbly situated with breathtaking views over Portree Bay towards the grandiose Cuillin Mountain range. A very fine hotel open all-year-round enjoying an excellent location for exploring the island. Excellent award-winning restaurant and bar. Enjoy high standards of comfort, cuisine and service in a warm, friendly atmosphere.
Contact: **Mr Murray Mcphee.**   AA ★★★ ⊛⊛   21631

★★★★

HOTEL

Cuillin Hills Hotel
Portree, Isle of Skye, IV51 9QU
Tel:01478 612003   Fax:01478 613092
Email:info@cuillinhills-hotel-skye.co.uk
Web:www.cuillinhills-hotel-skye.co.uk

19th Century former hunting lodge, set in 15 acres of grounds overlooking Portree Bay, with views towards the Cuillin Hills. Friendly staff, and an emphasis on good food, with a choice of formal or informal dining. Facilities available for conferences, functions and weddings. Open all year.

27 rooms, all en-suite, Open Jan-Dec, B&B per person, single from £55.00, double from £55.00, BB & Eve.Meal from £89.00.

VAT is shown at 17.5%: changes in this rate may affect prices.

Key to symbols is on back flap.

Portree, Isle of Skye, Inverness-shire | Map Ref: 3E9

★★★

HOTEL

Rosedale Hotel

Beaumont Crescent, Portree, Isle of Skye, IV51 9DB
Tel:01478 613131   Fax:01478 612531
Email:rosedalehotelsky@aol.com
Web:www.rosedalehotelskye.co.uk

Very comfortable and unusual hotel imaginatively created from former fishermens houses dating back to the reign of William IV. Award winning cuisine in an outstanding waterside location. Described by leading food critic as 'Portree's best kept secret'. AA Rosette.

18 rooms, all en-suite, Open Mar-Nov, B&B per person, single from £30.00, double from £30.00, BB & Eve.Meal from £56.00.

Sleat, Isle of Skye, Inverness-shire | Map Ref: 3F10

★★★★

**SMALL
HOTEL**

Kinloch Lodge

Sleat, Isle of Skye, IV43 8QY
Tel:01471 833214 Fax:01471 833277
Email:bookings@kinloch-lodge.co.uk
Web:www.claire-macdonald.com

Ancestral home of Lord and Lady Macdonald in secluded lochside setting with panoramic views throughout the year. Unique demonstration cooking residential breaks are presented by Lady Macdonald.

12 rooms, all en-suite, Open Jan-Dec excl Xmas, B&B per person, single from £75.00, double from £75.00.

Important: Prices stated are estimates and may be subject to amendments

Toravaig House Hotel, Restaurant and Daily Sailing on Hotel Yacht

Knock Bay, Sleat, Isle of Skye IV44 8RE
Tel: 01471 833231/0845 055 1117
e.mail: info@skyehotel.co.uk
Web: www.skyehotel.co.uk

Simply stylish...simply unique. "Scottish Island Hotel of the Year 2005". (Hotel Review Scotland) "Most Excellent Service UK 2006" Award - Conde Nast Johansens. VisitScotland's "Tourism Excellence Award" 2006. Charming 9 bedroom Country House Hotel, totally refurbished, beautifully decorated, with open fire in drawing room. Personally run by Ken and Anne. Set in large garden, enjoying fine views over the sea and surrounding countryside. Parking. Beautiful ensuite bedrooms, most having bath and shower, feature beds, Sky TV, direct dial telephones, and delightful restaurant. Exclusive daily sailing available to residents on hotel yacht. **B&B £59.50-£79.00 pppn.**

61518

SMALL HOTEL

Toravaig House Hotel & Iona Restaurant
Knock Bay, Sleat, Isle of Skye, IV44 8RE
Tel:01471 833231/820200
Email:info@skyehotel.co.uk
Web:www.skyehotel.co.uk

Scottish Island Hotel of the Year 2005 - Toravaig is situated on the Sleat Peninsula. Personally-run by the owners Toravaig is enjoying a growing reputation for quality food and a high standard of accommodation and service. New in 2006 - daily yacht trips for residents.

9 rooms, all en-suite, Open Jan-Dec, B&B per person, single from £75.00, double from £59.50.

INN

Stein Inn
**Macleod's Terrace, Waternish
Isle of Skye, Inverness-shire, IV55 8GA**
Tel:01470 592362
Email:angus.teresa@steininn.co.uk
Web:www.steininn.co.uk

Set in a beautiful lochside position, this historic village Inn C1790 offers traditional hospitality. Comfortable rooms, good food and a warm welcome. Excellent base for touring.

7 rooms, all en-suite, Open Jan-Dec excl Xmas/New Year, B&B per person, single from £26.00, double from £26.00.

VAT is shown at 17.5%: changes in this rate may affect prices.   **Key to symbols is on back flap.**

Corriegour Lodge Hotel

LOCH LOCHY, BY SPEAN BRIDGE,
LOCHABER, INVERNESS-SHIRE PH34 4EA
TEL: +44 (0)1397 712685 FAX: +44 (0)1397 712696
E.MAIL: info@corriegour-lodge-hotel.com
WEB: www.corriegour-lodge-hotel.com

"Better food than the top London restaurants, and a view to die for" - THE MIRROR.

This former Victorian hunting lodge enjoys the very finest setting in "The Great Glen". Dine in our Loch View Conservatory, enjoying the very best Scottish cuisine, fresh seafood, Aberdeen Angus, homemade breads and puddings, extensive selection of wines and malt whiskies. Our emphasis is on your total relaxation and comfort. Log fires and big comfy sofas. Come and be cushioned from the stresses of everyday life. Walking, scenery, skiing, history. Private beach and fishing school. Special spring/autumn breaks available.

 BEST LOVED HOTELS  

20535

★★★★

SMALL HOTEL

Corriegour Lodge Hotel
Loch Lochy, by Spean Bridge, Inverness-shire PH34 4EA
Tel:01397 712685 Fax:01397 712696
Email:info@corriegour-lodge-hotel.com
Web:www.corriegour-lodge-hotel.com

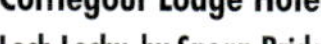

Corriegour Lodge Hotel, a former hunting lodge, is set in nine acres of mature woodland and garden with open views over Loch Lochy. Seventeen miles North of Fort William on the road to Skye, many of Scotland's attractions are in easy reach. Local activities include walking, cycling, climbing, pony trekking or fishing from the hotel jetty.

12 rooms, all en-suite, Open Feb-Nov & New Year, B&B per person, single £59.50-69.50, double £59.50-69.50, BB & Eve.Meal from £79.50-110.00.

★★★
GUEST HOUSE

Inverour Guest House
Roy Bridge Road, Spean Bridge, Inverness-shire PH34 4EU
Tel/Fax:01397 712218
Email:enquiries@inverourguesthouse.co.uk
Web:www.inverourguesthouse.co.uk

Comfortable guest house located centrally in the village of Spean Bridge. Ideal base for touring the West Highlands of Scotland.

8 rooms, some en-suite, Open Jan-Dec, B&B per person, single from £22.50, double from £25.00. Family room from £70.00. Evening meals by pre-order. Packed lunches by arrangement. Drying facilities.

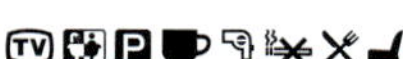

★★★★
GUEST HOUSE

Smiddy House Guest House
Spean Bridge, Inverness-shire, PH34 4EU
Tel:01397 712335 Fax:01397 712043
Email:enquiry@smiddyhouse.co.uk
Web:www.smiddyhouse.co.uk

'Robert and Glen extend a warm welcome to Smiddy House Guest House and Russels Restaurant...The Place to Eat. All rooms tastefully decorated to high standard. Ideal for all local activities including touring, walking, climbing, fishing, horse riding, golf and winter skiing. Dogs Welcome.'

4 rooms, all en-suite, Open Dec-Oct, B&B per person, single from £45.00, double £30.00-37.50, family £75.00-90.00 per room.

Important: Prices stated are estimates and may be subject to amendments

Strathpeffer, Ross-shire
Map Ref: 4A8

★★★

SMALL HOTEL

Brunstane Lodge Hotel
Golf Road, Strathpeffer, Ross-shire, IV14 9AT
Tel:01997 421261 Fax:01997 421272
Email:chris@guichot.freeserve.co.uk
Web:www.brunstanelodge.com

Family run hotel set in its own mature garden in residential area and close to golf course. All rooms with ensuite facilities. Conveniently situated for touring Northern Highlands. Fresh local produce prepared and served by French chef/patron Chris Guichot and Paul Mackay.

6 rooms, all en-suite, Open all year, B&B per person, single from £42.00, double from £36.00. No dogs.

★★★

HOTEL

Highland Hotel
Strathpeffer, Highland Region, IV14 9AN
Tel:01942 824824
Email:reservations@WAshearings.com
Web:www.WAshearingsholidays.com

Large Victorian Hotel with oak panelled public areas. Hotel overlooks village square and pump room. Entertainment every night.

132 rooms, all en-suite, Open Feb-Dec, B&B per person, double from £25.00.

Thurso, Caithness
Map Ref: 4D3

★★★

SMALL HOTEL

Park Hotel
Thurso, KW14 8RE
Tel:01847 893251 Fax:01847 804044
Email:reception@parkhotelthurso.co.uk
Web:www.parkhotelthurso.co.uk

Comfortable and friendly family run hotel fully licenced with 21 well appointed ensuite bedrooms all with TV, hairdryer, tea and coffee etc. All meals served. Conservatory lounge and dining room. Large private car park. Gold Green Tourism Award.

21 rooms, all en-suite, Open Jan-Dec excl New Year, B&B per person, single from £45.00, double from £38.00. Reduced rates off season.

★★★

HOTEL

Station Hotel and Apartments
54-58 Princes Street, Thurso, Caithness, KW14 7DH
Tel:01847 892003   Fax:01847 891820
Email:stationhotel@lineone.net
Web:www.stationthurso.co.uk

Personally run hotel, situated in the centre of Thurso, a short walk from the railway and bus stations. Good friendly base for the business traveller or for the visitor who is coming up to explore the coastline, archaeology and wildlife of the country of Caithness; not to mention a good base for making that trip to Orkney.

30 rooms, all en-suite, Open Jan-Dec, B&B per person, single from £45.00, double from £30.00.

★★★

HOTEL

Weigh Inn Hotel
Burnside, Thurso, KW14 7UG
Tel:01847 893722 Fax:01847 892112
Email:reception@weighinn.co.uk
Web:www.weighinn.co.uk

Recently built sixteen bedroom hotel, situated a short distance from the harbour, and ideal for travellers catching the Orkney ferry. The hotel also makes an excellent base for the business traveller or for the winter visitor wanting to explore the county of Caithness, and the north Sutherland coastline.

16 rooms, all en-suite, Open Jan-Dec excl Xmas/New Year, B&B per person, single from £65.00, double from £42.50.

VAT is shown at 17.5%: changes in this rate may affect prices. | *Key to symbols is on back flap.*

Tongue, Sutherland	Map Ref: 4A3

SMALL HOTEL

Ben Loyal Hotel
Main Street, Tongue, Sutherland, IV27 4XE
Tel:01847 611216 Fax:01847 611212
Email:stay@benloyal.co.uk
Web:www.benloyal.co.uk

Stone built hotel with fine views of Ben Loyal and Kyle of Tongue.
Friendly atmosphere. Fishing available. À la Carte menu.
AA ★★ AA ⊛ .

11 rooms, all en-suite, Open Mar-Nov, B&B per person, single from £35.00, double from £35.00.

Ullapool, Ross-shire	Map Ref: 3G6

GUEST HOUSE

Ardvreck House
North Road, Morefield, Ullapool, IV26 2TH
Tel:01854 612028 Fax:01854 613000
Email:ardvreck@btinternet.com
Web:www.smoothhound.co.uk/hotels/ardvreck.html

Guest house set amidst some of the best hillwalking country and breathtaking scenery in Scotland. Elevated country position overlooking Ullapool and Lochbroom. Spacious, well appointed rooms most with spectacular sea view, all with ensuite shower room, T.V and tea/coffee facility. Residents lounge available at all times. Local facilities include a leisure centre, swimming pool, sauna, golf course, fishing and museum.

10 rooms, all en-suite, Open Mar-Nov, B&B per person, single from £30.00, double from £30.00.

GUEST HOUSE

Dromnan Guest House
Garve Road, Ullapool, Ross-shire, IV26 2SX
Tel:01854 612333
Email:info@dromnan.com
Web:www.dromnan.com

Modern family run guest house overlooking Lochbroom. Ideally situated, excellent facilities and stunning views. Sumptous buffet breakfasts served in our newly built conservatory. "All in All - First Class Accommodation" AA 5 Diamonds.

7 rooms, all en-suite, Open Jan-Dec, B&B per person, single £28.00-£38.00, double £26.00-£29.00.

GUEST HOUSE

Strathmore House
Morefield, Ullapool, Ross-shire, IV26 2TH
Tel:01854 612423 Fax:01854 613752
Email:murdo_urquhart1957@msn.com

Guest house enjoying panoramic views over Loch Broom and Ullapool.
Ideal touring base for north west coast. Comfortable TV lounge and reading room.

5 rooms, all en-suite, Open Easter-Sep, B&B per person, double from £23.00.

Important: Prices stated are estimates and may be subject to amendments

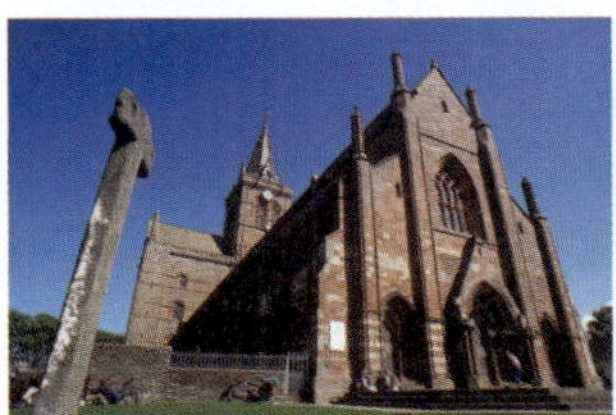  

Main image: Tolsta Beach, Outer Hebrides **Bottom left:** St Magnus Cathedral, Orkney
Bottom middle: Skara Brae, Orkney **Bottom right:** Shetland Ponies

THE OUTER ISLANDS
Outer Hebrides, Orkney, Shetland

For those who love nothing more than a bit of island exploring, Scotland is the place to be. There's something about island life that makes it fascinating.

Perhaps being surrounded by sea allows each to develop its own distinct ways and traditions and getting to know an island and its people is a great way to spend a holiday.

At Scotland's western edge, the Outer Hebrides look out to the Atlantic swell and life moves at a relaxed pace. In this last Gaelic stronghold, a warm welcome awaits.

It's easy to adapt to island life, though you will be constantly surprised and delighted by the awesome splendour of the scenery. There are

Callanish Stones, Outer Hebrides

From unique culture to stunning seascapes, from abundant wildlife to Atlantic surf, a unique holiday experience awaits you in the Outer Islands where life moves at an unhurried pace.

hundreds of miles of coastline – rugged cliffs, sheltered bays and white sandy beaches. There are high mountains, rivers and lochs full of fish, quiet roads to cycle along and there's the machair which is a pretty, floral carpet in the summer months.

You can travel to the Outer Hebrides by ferry from Ullapool, Oban, or Uig on Skye or by plane. Fly to Barra and you'll land on the beach at low tide! Getting around is easy. Some of the islands are connected by road bridges and causeways, others have frequent ferry services.

Lewis is the largest of the islands with a busy town at Stornoway and historical sites like the standing stones at Calanais stretching back over 5000 years. It's distinctly different from the more mountainous Harris. Don't forget to visit the traditional weavers making the wonderful Harris Tweed.

The Uists, Benbecula, Eriskay and Barra all have their own diverse attractions and whichever you choose, you won't be disappointed.

Island life can also be experienced in Scotland's two great northern archipelagos of Orkney and Shetland. Some 70 islands make up the Orkneys with 16 inhabited. Shetland, at the crossroads where the Atlantic meets the North Sea, is home to around 22,000 people and well over a million seabirds.

Each archipelago has its own distinctive culture and history. In Orkney, you can see the oldest houses in northern Europe at Papa Westray, dating back to 3800 BC. You can even see 900 year old examples of Viking graffiti at the Neolithic Ring of Brodgar and Maes Howe.

The influence of the Vikings is everywhere. Orcadians spoke Old Norse until the mid 1700s and you'll hear it in their dialect to this day. That Viking influence is even stronger in Shetland where the ancient Viking Parliament once met at Tingwall.

Both Orkney and Shetland are famous for their long summer days. The sun shines for almost 19 hours at midsummer and the 'Simmer

 THE NO.1 BOOKING AND INFORMATION SERVICE FOR SCOTLAND   0845 22 55 121   visitscotland.com

What's on?

Up Helly Aa Festival
30 January 2007
Britain's biggest fire festival and torchlight procession.
www.up-helly-aa.org.uk

Orkney Ceilidh Weekend
13 - 15 April 2007
A new event with various dance workshops.
www.orkneycommunities.
co.uk/otda

Shetland Folk Festival
3 - 6 May 2007
The UK's most northerly folk festival.
www.shetlandfolkfestival.com

Orkney Folk Festival
24 – 27 May 2007
The 25th festival bringing modern and traditional music.
www.orkneyfolkfestival.com

Johnsmas Foy
15 - 24 June 2007
Shetland's summer festival.
www.johnsmasfoy.co.uk

The St. Magnus Festival
22 – 27 June 2007
Orkney's midsummer celebration of the Arts.
www.stmagnusfestival.com

Ceolas Music School (South Uist)
1 – 6 July 2007
www.ceolas.co.uk

Hebridean Maritime Festival (Stornoway)
9 – 14 July 2007
The 9th annual Sail Hebrides Maritime Festival.
www.sailhebrides.info

Hebridean Celtic Festival (Stornoway)
11 – 14 July 2007
Artists and visitors from around the world come together.
www.hebceltfest.com

Walk Shetland Week
25 August – 1 September 2007
Some of the best walking in Europe.
www.visitshetland.com

Orkney International Science Festival
30 August – 5 September 2007
A kaleidoscopic mix of insights, ideas and activities.
www.oisf.org

A deep sense of history is everywhere and there is so much to explore.

Dim' as they call it in Shetland, means it never really gets dark. You can even play midnight golf in both Orkney and Shetland.

Long summer days, of course, means long winter nights but the islanders have perfected the art of indoor life. Musicians fill the bars and community halls and there always seems to be something to celebrate. Two great unmissable events are the Festival of Up Helly Aa at Lerwick, one of the many winter fire festivals in Shetland. The other is the Ba' in Kirkwall, Orkney where up to 400 players take to the streets of the town for a great rough and tumble that is somewhere between football, rugby and all-out war. Needless to say, the partying is equally wild and visitors are always welcome to join in the fun.

Though these islands enjoy a rich cultural life, the lasting impression on any visitor will be the islands' closeness to nature. Orkney and Shetland are a joy for wildlife watchers. There are millions of birds to observe as well as otters, seals, dolphins and whales. With hundreds of freshwater lochs and miles of coastline, the fishing's great too. Being surrounded by sea, yachting, sea-kayaking, cruising and diving are all possible activities – if you love boats, this is the place for you.

There's a surprisingly good selection of small hotels and guesthouses in the outer islands. Most are small family-run establishments in great locations with wonderful sea views and all provide a comfortable base from which to explore. Island holidays are a popular choice however, especially for the festivals, so make your selection quickly and book well in advance.

Lerwick, Shetland

Tourist Information Centres

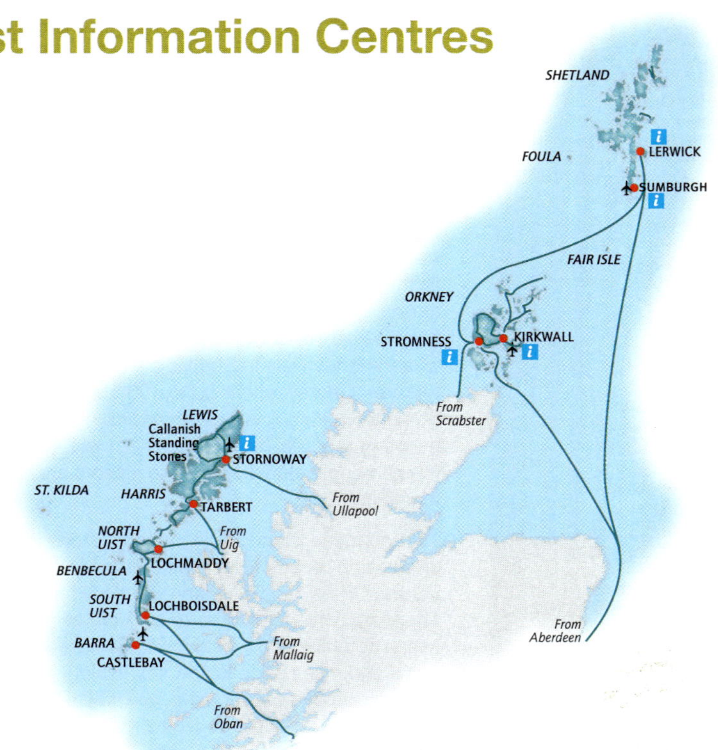

Please refer to the maps on pages xii-xviii for the locations of establishments appearing in the main advertising section of this guide. Only year-round Tourist Information Centres are indicated.

For practical advice, ideas and information about exploring Scotland and to book your accommodation:

Tel: 0845 22 55 121* or if calling from outside the UK: + 44 (0) 1506 832121
In Ireland Call:1800 932 510

*** A £3 booking fee applies to telephone bookings of accommodation.**

info@visitscotland.com
www.visitscotland.com

Castlebay, Isle of Barra, Western Isles — Map Ref: 3A11

Castlebay Hotel
Castlebay, Isle of Barra, HS9 5XD
Tel:01871 810223 Fax:01871 810455
Email:bookings@castlebayhotel.com
Web:www.castlebayhotel.com

SMALL HOTEL

Elevated position, overlooking bay, pier and Kisimul Castle. Central location, easy access to ferry terminal. All rooms ensuite. Some rooms on ground floor level.

10 rooms, all en-suite, Open Jan-Dec excl Xmas/New Year.

Creagorry, Isle of Benbecula, Western Isles — Map Ref: 3B8

The Isle of Benbecula House Hotel
Creagorry, Isle of Benbecula, Western Isles, HS7 5PG
Tel:01870 602024 Fax:01870 603108
Email:reservations@iobhh.co.uk
Web:www.isleshotelgroup.co.uk

HOTEL

Long established hotel (over 100 years) with popular local bar and regular entertainment. Bar lunches and suppers available, non-residents very welcome. Hotel has fishing rights over 16 Lochs and some sea-pools.

20 rooms, all en-suite, B&B single from £60.00, double from £90.00. BB & Eve.meal from £77.00 per person. Sea-fishing boat charters available.

Ardhasaig, Isle of Harris, Western Isles — Map Ref: 3C6

Ardhasaig House
Ardhasaig, Isle of Harris, HS3 3AJ
Tel:0185950 2066/2500 Fax:01859 502077
Email:accommodation@ardhasaig.co.uk
Web:www.ardhasaig.co.uk

SMALL HOTEL

The Good Hotel Guide. Scottish Hotel Breakfast of the Year Runner Up 2005. Scottish Island Hotel of the Year Runner Up 2005.

6 rooms, all en-suite, Open Mar-Nov, B&B per person, single from £55.00, double from £55.00. Evening meals from £36.00.

Tarbert, Isle of Harris, Western Isles — Map Ref: 3C6

MacLeod Motel
Pier Road, Tarbert, Isle of Harris, HS3 3DG
Tel:01859 502364 Fax:01859 502578
Email:angus@macleodmotel.com
Web:www.macleodmotel.com

INN

Friendly welcome, great food (seafood highly recommended) and a lively lounge bar situated directly beside ferry pier.

15 rooms, some en-suite, Open Jan-Dec, B&B per person, single from £30.00, twin from £25.00, double from £35.00.

Stornoway, Isle of Lewis, Western Isles — Map Ref: 3D4

Cabarfeidh Hotel
Manor Park, Stornoway, Isle of Lewis, HS1 2EU
Tel:01851 702604 Fax:01851 705567
Email:donnie@calahotels.com
Web:www.calahotels.com

HOTEL

Set on the outskirts of Stornoway in 8 acres of grounds with an A'la Carte restaurant where the emphasis is on local produce. Popular venue for weddings. Group rates and holiday packages are available.

46 rooms, all en-suite, Open Jan-Dec excl Xmas/New Year, B&B per person, single from £79.00, double from £59.00.

Important: Prices stated are estimates and may be subject to amendments

OUTER ISLANDS

Stornoway, Isle of Lewis, Western Isles

Map Ref: 3D4

★★

HOTEL

Caladh Inn
James Street, Stornoway, Isle of Lewis, HS1 2QN
Tel:01851 702604 Fax:01851 703158
Email:caladhinn@calahotels.com
Web:www.calahotels.com

Modern hotel, the largest on the island, situated in the centre of Stornoway, within walking distance of the ferry terminal. Local leisure and fitness centre is just across the road. The hotel makes an excellent base for exploring Lewis and Harris.

68 rooms, Open all year, Rates from £42.00 room only single, £49.00 B&B single, from £32.50 B&B twin/double pp.

Carinish, Isle of North Uist, Western Isles

Map Ref: 3B8

★★★★

SMALL HOTEL

Temple View Hotel
Carinish, Isle of North Uist, Western Isles, HS6 5EJ
Tel:01876 580676 Fax:01876 580682
Email:templeviewhotel@aol.com
Web:www.templeviewhotel.co.uk

Warm and friendly family run small hotel traditionally furnished to high standards offering comfort and style with contemporary quality facilities.

10 rooms, Open Jan-Dec, room only single from £50.00, double from £90.00, family from £95.00.

Locheport, Isle of North Uist, Western Isles

Map Ref: 3B8

Langass Lodge

NORTH UIST, THE WESTERN ISLES HS6 5HA
Telephone: 01876 580285 Fax: 01876 580385
e.mail: langasslodge@btconnect.com Web: www.langasslodge.co.uk
Commanding scenic views over a sea loch and situated beside a stone circle and neolithic burial chamber. This comfortable small hotel is the ideal base for exploring the Western Isles. All the well-appointed rooms have ensuite facilities and the excellent restaurant specializes in seafood and game.
Prices from £60.00 B&B.

27700

★★★

SMALL HOTEL

Langass Lodge
Locheport, North Uist, Western Isles, HS6 5HA
Tel:01876 580285 Fax:01876 580385
Email:langasslodge@btconnect.com
Web:www.langasslodge.co.uk

Traditional Hotel, set in splendid isolation, overlooking Loch Eport and about 8 miles (13kms) from Lochmaddy ferry terminal. Popular retreat for anglers, ornithologists and lovers of the outdoors. Fishing available on all of the North Uists renowned lochs.

12 rooms, all en-suite, Open Jan-Dec, B&B per room, single from £60.00, double from £90.00.

Kirkwall, Orkney

Map Ref: 5B12

★★★

GUEST HOUSE

Sanderlay Guest House
2 Viewfield Drive, Kirkwall, Orkney, KW15 1RB
Tel:01856 875587 Fax:01856 876350
Email:enquiries@sanderlay.co.uk
Web:www.sanderlay.co.uk

Comfortable modern house in quiet residential area on outskirts of town. Some ensuite and 2 self-contained family units. Private parking available. Credit cards accepted. Ideal base for exploring the Orkney mainland or for visiting the North Isles.

8 rooms, 6 en-suite, Open Jan-Dec excl Xmas, New Year, B&B per person, single £25.00-35.00, double/twin £20.00-28.00, family £20.00-26.00.

VAT is shown at 17.5%: changes in this rate may affect prices.

Key to symbols is on back flap.

North Ronaldsay, Orkney

Map Ref: 5D10

GUEST HOUSE ★★★

The Observatory Guest House
North Ronaldsay, Orkney, KW17 2BE
Tel:01857 633200 Fax:01857 633207
Email:bookings@nrbo.prestel.co.uk
Web:www.nrbo.f2s.com

Unique eco-friendly activity centre offering comfortable accommodation in a crofting environment. Resident specialists in ornithology.

7 rooms, all en-suite, Open Jan-Dec excl Xmas, B&B per person from £26.50.

Stenness, Orkney

Map Ref: 5B12

HOTEL ★★★

Standing Stones Hotel
Stenness, nr Stromness, Orkney, KW16 3JX
Tel:01856 850449   Fax:01856 851262
Email:standingstones@sol.co.uk
Web:www.standingstoneshotel.co.uk

Situated on the shores of the Loch of Stenness, just off the main Kirkwall to Stromness road. This is an excellent central base for exploring Orkney's many historical and archaeological attractions, or for fishing or birdwatching.

17 rooms, all en-suite, Open Jan-Dec excl Xmas/New Year, B&B per person, single from £35.00, double from £35.00.

Daliburgh, Isle of South Uist, Western Isles

Map Ref: 3B10

SMALL HOTEL ★★★

Borrodale Hotel
Daliburgh, South Uist, Western Isles, HS8 5SS
Tel:01878 700444 Fax:01878 700446
Email:reception@borrodalehotel.co.uk
Web:www.isleshotelgroup.co.uk

Family run hotel with all bedrooms recently refurbished in village of Daliburgh. Only 3 miles (5kms) from Lochboisdale ferry terminal. Bar lunches and suppers available, non-residents very welcome.

14 rooms, some en-suite, Open Jan-Dec excl Xmas/New Year, B&B per person, single from £38.00, double from £35.00.

Lochcarnan, Isle of South Uist, Western Isles

Map Ref: 3B9

SMALL HOTEL ★★★

Orasay Inn
Lochcarnan, South Uist, Outer Hebrides, HS8 5PD
Tel:01870 610298 Fax:01870 610267
Email:orasayinn@btinternet.com
Web:www.orasayinn.co.uk

In an area of outstanding natural beauty. The inn offers extensive menus, including local seafood dishes. Conservatory dining area serving evening meals. Non-residents very welcome. Booking essential.

9 rooms, all en-suite, Open Jan-Dec, B&B per person, single from £50.00, double from £35.00, BB & Eve.Meal from £45.00.

Important: Prices stated are estimates and may be subject to amendments

Facilities

For visitors with disabilities

VisitScotland, in conjunction with the English Tourism Council and Wales Tourist Board operates a national accessible scheme that identifies, acknowledges and promotes those accommodation establishments that meet the needs of visitors with disabilities.

The three categories of accessibility, drawn up in close consultation with specialist organisations concerned with the needs of people with disabilities are:

Category 1

Unassisted wheelchair access for residents

Category 2

Assisted wheelchair access for residents

Category 3

Access for residents with mobility difficulties

Category 1

ABERDEEN
Aberdeen Patio Hotel
Beach Boulevard
Aberdeen
Aberdeenshire
AB24 5EF
Tel: 01224 633339

Express by Holiday Inn
Chapel Street
Aberdeen
AB10 1SQ
Tel: 01224 623500

Kings Hall
University of Aberdeen
Aberdeen
AB24 3FX
Tel: 01224 272660

Copthorne Hotel
122 Huntly Street
Aberdeen
AB10 1SU
Tel: 01224 630404

Thistle Aberdeen Airport Hotel
Argyll Road
Aberdeen
Aberdeenshire
AB21 0AF
Tel: 01224 725252

ABERNETHY
Gattaway Farm
Abernethy
Perthshire
PH2 9LQ
Tel: 01738 850746

ABINGTON
Days Inn
Welcome Break M74/A7
Abington
Lanarkshire
ML12 6RG
Tel: 01864 502782

ACHNASHEEN
Loch Torridon Hotel
Torridon
Achnasheen
Ross-shire
IV22 2EY
Tel: 01445 791242

ALEXANDRIA
De Vere Cameron House
Loch Lomond
Alexandria
Dunbartonshire
G83 8QZ
Tel: 01389 755565

ALTENS, ABERDEEN
Thistle Aberdeen Altens
Soutarhead Road
Altens, Aberdeen
Aberdeenshire
AB12 3LF
Tel: 01224 877000

AUCHENCAIRN,
BY CASTLE DOUGLAS
Balcary Bay Hotel
Auchencairn,
By Castle Douglas
Kirkcudbrightshire
DG7 1QZ
Tel: 01556 640217

AUCHTERARDER
The Gleneagles Hotel
Auchterarder
Perthshire
PH3 1NF
Tel: 01764 662231

AULDEARN
Covenanters' Inn
High Street
Auldearn
Nairn
IV12 5TG
Tel: 01667 452456

BALLACHULISH
Isles of Glencoe Hotel &
Leisure Centre
Ballachulish
Argyll
PH49 4HL
Tel: 01855 821582

BALLATER
Glenernan
37 Braemar Road
Ballater
Aberdeenshire
AB35 5RQ
Tel: 013397 53111

ISLE OF BARRA
Northbay House
Balnabodach
Isle of Barra
Outer Hebrides
HS9 5UT
Tel: 01871 890255

BRECHIN
Northern Hotel
2 Clerk Street
Brechin
Angus
DD9 6AE
Tel: 01356 625400

BRODICK
Auchrannie Spa Resort
Brodick
Isle of Arran
KA27 8BZ
Tel: 01770 302234

BROUGHTON, BY BIGGAR
The Glenholm Centre
Broughton,
by Biggar
Lanarkshire
ML12 6JF
Tel: 01899 830408

BROUGHTY FERRY, DUNDEE
The Fishermans Tavern Hotel
10-16 Fort Street
Broughty Ferry, Dundee
Angus
DD5 2AD
Tel: 01382 775941

BURNTISLAND
Kingswood Hotel
Kinghorn Road
Burntisland
Fife
KY3 9LL
Tel: 01592 872329

CARRADALE
Dunvalanree
Portrigh Bay
Carradale
Argyll
PA28 6SE
Tel: 01583 431226

CLYDEBANK
Beardmore Hotel
Beardmore Street
Clydebank
Greater Glasgow
G81 4SA
Tel: 0141 951 6000

CONNEL, BY OBAN
Wide Mouthed Frog
Dunstaffnage Marina
Connel, by Oban
Argyll
PA37 1PX
Tel: 01631 567005

DAVIOT
The Lodge at Daviot Mains
Daviot
By Inverness
IV2 5ER
Tel: 01463 772215

DUMFRIES
Glenlossie Guest House
75 Annan Road
Dumfries
Dumfries-shire
DG1 3EG
Tel: 01387 254305

DUNDEE
West Park Centre
319 Perth Road
Dundee
Angus
DD2 1NN
Tel: 01382 573050

DUNFERMLINE
Express By Holiday Inn
Dunfermline
Halbeath
Dunfermline
Fife
KY11 8DY
Tel: 01383 748222/
Tel: 01383 748220

DUNOON
Dhailling Lodge
155 Alexandra Parade
Dunoon
Argyll
PA23 8AW
Tel: 01369 701253

EDINBURGH
Premier Travel Inn
1 Morrison Link
Edinburgh
EH3 8DN
Tel: 0870 238 3319

Express By Holiday Inn
16-22 Picardy Place
Edinburgh
Lothian
EH1 3JT
Tel: 0131 5582300

Express By Holiday Inn
Britannia Way
Ocean Drive
Edinburgh
Lothian
EH6 6LA
Tel: 0131 5554422

Jurys Inn Edinburgh
43 Jeffrey Street
Edinburgh
Lothian
EH1 1DH
Tel: 0131 200 3300

Ramada Mount Royal Hotel
53 Princes Street
Edinburgh
EH2 2DG
Tel: 0131 225 7161

Thistle Edinburgh
107 Leith Street
Edinburgh
EH1 3SW
Tel: 0141 3323311

Melville Guest House
2 Duddingston Crescent
Edinburgh
Lothian
EH15 3AS
Tel: 0131 6697856

Ardgarth Guest House
1 St Mary's Place
Portobello
Edinburgh
EH15 2QF
Tel: 0131 669 3021

Brae Lodge Guest House
30 Liberton Brae
Edinburgh
Lothian
EH16 6AF
Tel: 0131 6722876

Novotel Edinburgh Centre
80 Lauriston Place
Edinburgh
Lothian
EH3 9DE
Tel: 0131 656 3500

Toby Carvery & Innkeepers
Lodge Edin/Wes
114-116 St Johns Road
Edinburgh
EH12 8AX
Tel: 0131 334 8235

FORGANDENNY
Battledown Bed & Breakfast
Off Station Road
Forgandenny
Perthshire
PH2 9EL
Tel: 01738 812471

GAILES
The Gailes Lodge
Marine Drive
Gailes
Irvine
KA11 5AE
Tel: 01294 204040

GLASGOW
Holiday Inn
161 West Nile Street
Glasgow
G1 2RL
Tel: 0141 352 8300

Glasgow Hilton
1 William Street
Glasgow
G3 8HT
Tel: 0141 204 5555

Carlton George Hotel
44 West George Street
Glasgow
G2 1DH
Tel: 0141 353 6373

Jurys Inn Glasgow
Jamaica Street
Glasgow
G1 4QE
Tel: 0141 314 4800

Tulip Inn Glasgow
80 Ballater Street
Glasgow
G5 0TW
Tel: 0141 429 4233

Glasgow Marriott
500 Argyle Street
Glasgow
G3 8RR
Tel: 0141 226 5577

Holiday Inn Glasgow City West
Bothwell Street
Glasgow
G2 7EN
0870 400 9032

GREENOCK
Express by Holiday Inn
Cartsburn
Greenock
PA15 4RT
Tel: 01475 786666

James Watt College
Waterfront Campus
Customhouse Way
Greenock
Renfrewshire
PA15 1EN
Tel: 01475 731360

GRETNA
The Garden House Hotel
Sarkfoot Road
Gretna
Dumfriesshire
DG16 5EP
Tel: 01461 337621

Hunters Lodge Hotel
Annan Road
Gretna
Dumfriesshire
DG16 5DL
Tel: 01461 338214

GRETNA GREEN
Days Inn
Welcome Break Service Area
M74
Gretna Green
Dumfriesshire
DG16 5HQ
Tel: 01461 337566

HADDINGTON
Maitlandfield House Hotel
24 Sidegate
Haddington
East Lothian
EH41 4BZ
Tel: 01620 826513

INVERGORDON
Delny House
Delny
Invergordon
Ross-shire
IV18 0NP
Tel: 01862 842678

INVERNESS
Inverness Marriott
Culcabock Road
Inverness
Inverness-shire
IV2 3LP
Tel: 01463 237166

IRVINE
Thistle Irvine
46 Annick Road
Irvine
Ayrshire
KA11 4LD
Tel: 0141 332 3311

KILDONAN, ISLE OF ARRAN
Kildonan Hotel
Kildonan
Isle of Arran
KA27 8SE
Tel: 0141 779 9205

KILKENZIE
Dalnaspidal Guest House
Tangy
Kilkenzie
Argyll
PA28 6QD
Tel: 01586 820466

KILMARNOCK
Park Hotel
Rugby Park
Kilmarnock
Ayrshire
KA1 2DP
Tel: 01563 545999

KINLOCHLEVEN
Tigh-Na-Cheo
Garbien Road
Kinlochleven
Argyll
PH50 4SE
Tel: 01855 831434

KIRKWALL
Lav'rockha Guest House
Inganess Road
Kirkwall
Orkney
KW15 1SP
Tel: 01856 876103

LERWICK
Shetland Hotel
Holmsgarth Road
Lerwick
Shetland
ZE1 0PW
Tel: 01595 695515

LEUCHARS, BY ST ANDREWS
Drumoig Hotel & Golf Resort
Drumoig
Leuchars
by St Andrews
Fife
KY16 0BE
Tel: 01382 541800

LEWIS, WESTERN ISLES
Dolly's B & B
33 Aignish Point
Lewis Western Isles
HS2 0PB
Tel: 01851 870755/870724

The Cross Inn
Cross Ness
Lewis Western Isles
HS2 0SN
Tel: 01851 810152

LIVINGSTON
Ramada Jarvis Livingston
Almondview
Livingston
West Lothian EH54 6QB
Tel: 01506 431222

LOCHMABEN
The Crown Hotel
8 Bruce Street
Lochmaben
Dumfriesshire
DG11 1PD
Tel: 01387 811750

LOSSIEMOUTH
Ceilidh B&B
34 Clifton Road
Lossiemouth
Moray
IV31 6DP
Tel: 01343 815848

MELROSE
Dryburgh Abbey Hotel
St Boswells
Melrose
Scottish Borders
TD6 0RQ
Tel: 01835 822261

MOFFAT
Lochhouse Farm Retreat Centre
Beattock
Moffat
Dumfries & Galloway
DG10 9SG
Tel: 01683 300451

MOTHERWELL
Motherwell College Stewart Hall
Dalzell Drive
Motherwell
Lanarkshire
ML1 2DD
Tel: 01698 261890

Express By Holiday Inn
Strathclyde Park M74 Jct 5
Motherwell
Lanarkshire
ML1 3RB
Tel: 01698 858585

NAIRN
Claymore House Hotel
45 Seabank Road
Nairn
Inverness-shire
IV12 4EY
Tel: 01667 453731

Windsor Hotel
16 Albert Street
Nairn
Inverness-shire
IV12 4HP
Tel: 01667 453108

BY NEWTOMORE
Crubenbeg House
Falls of Truim
By Newtonmore
PH20 1BE
Tel: 01540 673300

PAISLEY
Express by Holiday Inn Glasgow
Airport
St Andrews Drive
Paisley
PA3 2TJ
Tel: 0141 8421100

Travelodge Glasgow Airport
Marchburn Drive
Paisley
Glasgow
PA3 2AR
Tel: 0141 848 1359

PEEBLES
Cringletie House Hotel
Edinburgh Road
Peebles
Peeblesshire
EH45 8PL
Tel: 01721 725750

PETERHEAD
Invernettie Guest House
South Road Burnhaven
Peterhead
Aberdeenshire
AB42 0YX
Tel: 01779 473530

PITFODELS, ABERDEEN
Marcliffe at Pitfodels
North Deeside Road
Pitfodels, Aberdeen
AB15 9YA
Tel: 01224 861000

PORTREE, ISLE OF SKYE
Cuillin Hills Hotel
Portree
Isle of Skye
IV51 9QU
Tel: 01478 612003

Viewfield House Hotel
Portree
Isle of Skye
IV51 9EU
Tel: 01478 612217

PRESTWICK
Golf View
17 Links Road
Prestwick
Ayrshire
KA9 1QG
Tel: 01292 671234

SALEN
Ard Mhor House
Pier Road, Salen
Isle of Mull
PA72 6JL
Tel: 01680 300255

BY SPEAN BRIDGE
Old Pines Hotel and Restaurant
Gairlochy Road
By Spean Bridge
Inverness-shire
PH34 4EG
Tel: 01397 712324

SOUTH UIST, WESTERN ISLES
Crossroads
Stoneybridge
South Uist
Western Isles
HS8 5SD
Tel: 01870 620321

ST ANDREWS
The Old Station
Country House
Stratvithie Bridge
St Andrews
Fife
KY16 8LR
Tel: 01334 880505

STIRLING
Express by Holiday Inn - Stirling
Springkerse Business Park
Stirling
Stirlingshire
FK7 7XH
Tel: 01786 449922

Stirling Management Centre
University of Stirling
Stirling
FK9 4LA
Tel: 01786 451666

STONEHOUSE
Thorndale Guest House
Manse Road
Stonehouse
Lanarkshire
ML9 3NX
Tel: 01698 791133

SWINTON
The Wheatsheaf at Swinton
Main Street
Swinton
Berwickshire
TD11 3JJ
Tel: 01890 860257

THURSO
Park Hotel
Oldfield
Thurso
Caithness
KW14 8RE
Tel: 01847 893251

TURNBERRY
The Westin Turnberry Resort
Turnberry
Ayrshire
KA26 9LT
Tel: 01655 331000

TURRIFF
Deveron Lodge B&B Guesthouse
Bridgend Terrace
Turriff
Aberdeenshire
AB53 4ES
Tel: 01888 563613

SHETLAND
Burrastow House
Walls
Shetland
ZE2 9PD
Tel: 01595 809307

Category 2

ABBOTSINCH
Ramada Glasgow Airport
Marchburn Drive
Abbotsinch
Paisley
PA3 2SJ
Tel: 0141 8402200

ABERDEEN
Crombie House
University of Aberdeen
Aberdeen
AB24 3TS
Tel: 01224 272660

ABERFELDY
Tomvale
Tom of Cluny
Aberfeldy
Perthshire
PH15 2JT
Tel: 01887 820171

ABERFOYLE
Crannaig House
Trossachs Road
Aberfoyle
Stirlingshire
FK8 3SR
Tel: 01877 382276

BY ABERFOYLE
Forest Hills Hotel
Kinlochard
By Aberfoyle
Stirlingshire
FK8 3TL
08701 942105

AVIEMORE
MacDonald Academy
Aviemore Highland Resort
Aviemore
Inverness-shire
PH22 1PF
Tel: 01479 815100

AYR
Western House Hotel
2 Whitletts Road
Ayr
Ayrshire
KA9 2TA
0870 8505666

Horizon Hotel
Esplanade
Ayr
Ayrshire
KA7 1DT
Tel: 01292 264384

BY AYR
Alt-Na-Craig
Hollybush
By Ayr
KA6 7EB
Tel: 01292 560555

Facilities

For visitors with disabilities

BALLANTRAE
Glenapp Castle
Ballantrae
Ayrshire
KA26 0NZ
Tel: 01465 831212

BALLACHULISH
The Ballachulish Hotel
Ballachulish
Argyll
PH49 4JY
Tel: 01855 811606

BALTASOUND UNST
The Baltasound Hotel
Baltasound Unst
Shetland
ZE2 9DS
Tel: 01957 711334

BLACK ISLE
Autumn Gold
Blablair
Black Isle
Ross & Cromarty
IV7 8LR
Tel: 01381 610770

BONNYRIGG
The Retreat Castle
Cockpen Road
Bonnyrigg
Midlothian
EH19 3HS
Tel: 0131 660 3200

BRIDGE OF ALLAN
The Queen's Hotel
24 Henderson Street
Bridge of Allan
Stirlingshire
FK9 4HP
Tel: 01786 833268

BRODICK, ISLE OF ARRAN
Auchrannie Country
House Hotel
Brodick
Isle of Arran
KA27 8BZ
Tel: 01770 302234

BRORA
Glenaveron
Golf Road
Brora
Sutherland
KW9 6QS
Tel: 01408 621 601

CARDRONA, BY PEEBLES
Cardrona Hotel Golf &
Country Club
Cardrona
Near Peebles
Peebles-shire
EH45 6LZ
Tel: 01896 831144

CARRUTHERSTOWN
Hetland Hall Hotel
Carrutherstown
Dumfriesshire
DG1 4JX
Tel: 01387 840201

CRIEFF
Comely Bank Guest House
32 Burrell Street
Crieff
Perthshire
PH7 4DT
Tel: 01764 653409

Murraypark Hotel
Connaught Terrace
Crieff
Perthshire PH7 3DJ
Tel: 01764 653731

CUMBERNAULD
Red Deer & Innkeeper's Lodge
1 Auchenkilns Park
Cumbernauld
North Lanarkshire
G68 9AZ
Tel: 01236 795861

DRUMNADROCHIT
Clunebeg Lodge Guest House
Clunebeg Estate
Drumnadrochit
Inverness-shire
IV63 6US
Tel: 01456 450387

Woodlands
East Lewiston
Drumnadrochit
Inverness-shire
IV63 6UW
Tel: 01456 450356

DRYMEN
Winnock Hotel
The Square
Drymen
Stirlingshire
G63 0BL
Tel: 01360 660245

DUMFRIES
Aston Hotel
The Crichton
Bankend Road
Dumfries
Dumfries and Galloway
DG1 4ZZ
Tel: 01325 329600

DUNFERMLINE
Rooms at 29 Bruce Street
29-35 Bruce Street
Dunfermline
Fife
KY12 7AG
Tel: 01383 840041

**Best Western Keavil
House Hotel**
Crossford
Dunfermline
Fife
KY12 8QW
Tel: 01383 736258

Garvock House Hotel
St John's Drive Transy
Dunfermline
Fife
KY12 7TU
Tel: 01383 621067

**DUNFERMLINE
Aberdeen Marriott Hotel**
Riverview Drive
Farburn Dyce
Aberdeenshire
AB21 7AZ
0870 400 7291

Dyce Skean Dhu Hotel
Farburn Terrace
Dyce
Aberdeenshire
AB21 7DW
Tel: 01224 877000

Speedbird Inn
Argyll Road
Dyce
Aberdeen
Aberdeenshire
AB21 0AF
Tel: 01224 772884

**EDINBURGH
Edinburgh First**
Chancellor Court
Pollock Halls
18 Holyrood Park Road
Edinburgh
EH10 5AY
Tel: 0131 651 2011

Salisbury Green Hotel
Conference Centre
University of Edinburgh
Pollock Halls
18 Holyrood Park Road
Edinburgh
EH16 5AY
Tel: 0131 6622000

Caledonian Hilton Hotel
Princes Street
Edinburgh
EH1 2AB
Tel: 0131 222 8888

Hilton Edinburgh Grosvenor
7-21 Grosvenor Street
Edinburgh
EH12 5EF
Tel: 0131 527 1411

Queen Margaret College
36 Clerwood Terrace
Edinburgh
EH12 8TS
Tel: 0131 317 3317/3314

Edinburgh Marriott
111 Glasgow Road
Edinburgh
EH12 8NF
Tel: 0870 400 7293

Holiday Inn Edinburgh
Corstorphine Road
Edinburgh
EH12 6UA
Tel: 0870 400 9026

Holiday Inn Edinburgh-North
107 Queensferry Road
Edinburgh
EH4 3HL
Tel: 0870 400 9025

Hilton Edinburgh Airport
Edinburgh International Airport
Edinburgh
EH28 8LL
Tel: 0131 519 4400

**FORT WILLIAM
Clan MacDuff Hotel**
Achintore Road
Fort William
Inverness-shire
PH33 6RW
Tel: 01397 702341

**GLASGOW
Bewleys Hotel Glasgow**
110 Bath Street
Glasgow
G2 2EN
Tel: 0141 3530800

Campanile Glasgow
Tunnel Street
Glasgow
Scotland
G3 8HL
Tel: 0141 2877700

Crowne Plaza Hotel
Congress Road
Glasgow
G3 8QT
Tel: 0141 306 9988

Ibis Hotel Glasgow
220 West Regent Street
Glasgow
G2 4DQ
Tel: 0141 225 6000

Novotel Glasgow Centre
181 Pitt Street
Glasgow
G2 4DT
Tel: 0141 222 2775

Queen Margaret Hall
55 Bellshaugh Road
Glasgow
G12 0SQ
Tel: 0141 3303110

Wolfson Hall
Kelvin Campus
West Scotland Science Park
Maryhill Road
Glasgow
G20 0TH
Tel: 0141 3303110

GLENCARSE, BY PERTH
Glencarse Hotel
Glencarse
by Perth
Perthshire
PH2 7LX
Tel: 01382 737555

GOREBRIDGE
Ivory House
14 Vogrie Road
Gorebridge
Midlothian
EH23 4HH
Tel: 01875 820755

GRANGEMOUTH
Leapark Hotel
130 Bo'ness Road
Grangemouth
Stirlingshire
FK3 9BX
Tel: 01324 486733

GRANTOWN-ON-SPEY
Muckrach Lodge Hotel
Dulnain Bridge
Grantown-on-spey
Moray
PH26 3LY
Tel: 01479 851257

GRETNA
The Willows
Loanwath Road
Gretna
Dumfriesshire
DG16 5ES
Tel: 01461 337996

HAWICK
Whitchester Guest House
Hawick
Roxburghshire
TD9 7LN
Tel: 01450 377477

Elm House Hotel
17 North Bridge Street
Hawick
Roxburghshire
TD9 9BD
Tel: 01450 372866

HOY, ORKNEY
Stromabank
Hoy
Orkney
KW16 3PA
Tel: 01856 701494

INVERARAY
Loch Fyne Hotel
Newtown
Inveraray
Argyll
PA32 8XJ
Tel: 0131 554 7173

INVERNESS
Ramada Jarvis Inverness
Church Street
Inverness
Inverness-shire
IV1 1DX
Tel: 01463 235181

INVERURIE
Grant Arms Hotel
Monymusk
Inverurie
Aberdeenshire
AB51 7HJ
Tel: 01467 651333

KELSO
Inglestone House
Abbey Row
Kelso, Roxburghshire
TD5 7HQ
Tel: 01573 225800/225315

KILCHRENAN. BY TAYNUILT
Roineabhal Country House
Kilchrenan
by Taynuilt
Argyll
PA35 1HD
Tel: 01866 833207

KINLOCH RANNOCH
Dunalastair Hotel
The Square
Kinloch Rannoch
Perthshire
PH16 5PW
Tel: 01882 632323

KIRKMICHAEL, BLAIRGOWRIE
The Log Cabin Hotel
Glen Derby
Kirkmichael
Blairgowrie
Perthshire
PH10 7NA
Tel: 01250 881288

KIRRIEMUIR
Lochside Lodge & Roundhouse
Restaurant
Bridgend of Lintrathen
Kirriemuir
Angus
DD8 5JJ
Tel: 01575 560340

LARGS
Burnlea Hotel
Burnlea Road
Largs
Ayrshire
KA30 8BX
Tel: 01475 687235

LEDAIG
Isle of Eriska Hotel
Ledaig
Argyll PA37 1SD
Tel: 01631 720371

LOCHCARNAN, SOUTH UIST
Orasay Inn
Lochcarnan
South Uist
Outer Hebrides
HS8 5PD
Tel: 01870 610 298

LOCHGILPHEAD
Empire Travel Lodge
Union Street
Lochgilphead
Argyll PA31 8JS
Tel: 01546 602381

LOCKERBIE
Dryfesdale Country House Hotel
Dryfebridge
Lockerbie
Dumfriesshire
DG11 2SF
Tel: 01576 202427

MARKINCH, BY GLENROTHES
Balbirnie House Hotel
Balbirnie Park
Markinch by Glenrothes
Fife KY7 6NE
Tel: 01592 610066

MILLPORT
The Cathedral of the Isles
The College
Millport
Isle of Cumbrae
KA28 0HE
Tel: 01475 530353

MINARD
Minard Castle
Minard
Argyll PA32 8YB
Tel: 01546 886272

MOTHERWELL
The Alona Hotel
Strathclyde Country Park
Motherwell
North Lanarkshire
ML1 3RT
Tel: 01698 333777

Moorings Hotel
114 Hamilton Road
Motherwell
Lanarkshire
ML1 3DG
Tel: 01698 258131

Nethybridge
Nethybridge Hotel
Nethybridge
Inverness-shire
PH25 3DP
Tel: 01479 821203

New Lanark Mill Hotel
New Lanark
Lanarkshire
ML11 9DB
Tel: 01555 667200

LOCHDON, ISLE OF MULL
Seilisdeir
Lochdon
Isle of Mull
PA64 6AP
Tel: 01680 812465

LOCHMADDY,
ISLE OF NORTH UIST
Tigh Dearg Hotel
Lochmaddy
Isle of North Uist
Western Isles
HS6 5AE
Tel: 01876 500700

ORKNEY
Observatory Guest House
North Ronaldsay
Orkney
KW17 2BE
Tel: 01857 633200

PERTH
Huntingtower Hotel
Crieff Road
Perth
Perthshire
PH1 3JT
Tel: 01738 583771

PITLOCHRY
Cuil -an- Daraich
2 Cuil -an- Daraich
Logierait
Pitlochry
Perthshire
PH9 0LH
Tel: 01796 482750

POLMONT
Inchyra Grange Hotel
Grange Road
Polmont
Stirlingshire
FK2 0YB
Tel: 01324 711911

PORTREE
Auchendinny
Treaslane
Portree
Isle of Skye
Inverness-shire
IV51 9NX
Tel: 01470 532470

Facilities

For visitors with disabilities

PRESTWICK
Parkstone Hotel
Esplanade
Prestwick
Ayrshire
KA9 1QN
Tel: 01292 477286

ROY BRIDGE
The Stronlossit Inn
Roy Bridge
Inverness-shire
PH31 4AG
0800 015 5321

SANQUHAR
Newark
Sanquhar
Dumfriesshire
DG4 6HN
Tel: 01659 50263

STRATHKINNESS
Rufflets Country House Hotel
Strathkinness Low Road
St Andrews
Fife
KY16 9TX
Tel: 01334 472594

TALMINE
Cloisters
Church Holme
Talmine
Sutherland
IV27 4YP
Tel: 01847 601286

TIBBERMORE
The Bield at Blackruthven
Blackruthven House
Tibbermore
Perthshire
PH1 1PY
Tel: 01738 583238

TOBERMORY, ISLE OF MULL
Highland Cottage
Breadalbane Street
Tobermory
Isle of Mull
PA75 6PD
Tel: 01688 302030

TROON
South Beach Hotel
South Beach
Troon
Ayrshire
KA10 6EG
Tel: 01292 312033

TUMMEL
Kynachan Loch Tummel Hotel
Tummel Bridge
Perthshire
PH16 5SB
Tel: 01389 713713

WEST LINTON
Drochil Castle Farm
West Linton
Peeblesshire
EH46 7DD
Tel: 01721 752249

WESTHILL
Copperfield
Culloden Road
Westhill
Inverness
IV2 5BP
Tel: 01463 792251

WHITBURN
Hilcroft Hotel
East Main Street
Whitburn
West Lothian
EH47 0JU
Tel: 01501 740818

Category 3

ABERDEEN
Britannia Hotel
Malcolm Road
Aberdeen
Grampian
AB21 9LN
Tel: 01224 409988

Northern Hotel
1 Great Northern Road
Aberdeen
AB24 3PS
Tel: 01224 483342

ABERDOUR
Aberdour Hotel
38 High Street
Aberdour
Fife
KY3 0SW
Tel: 01383 860325

ABERFOYLE
Rob Roy Hotel
Aberfoyle
Stirlingshire
FK8 3UX
Tel: 01877 382245

ABOYNE
Chesterton House
Formaston Park
Aboyne
Aberdeenshire
AB34 5HF
Tel: 013398 86740

ALLOA
Gean House
Tullibody Road
Alloa
Clackmannanshire
FK10 2EL
Tel: 01259 226400

ANNAN
Rowanbank
20 St Johns Road
Annan
Dumfriesshire
DG12 5AW
Tel: 01461 204200

ARDFERN, BY LOCHGILPHEAD
Galley of Lorne Inn
Main Street
Ardfern, by Lochgilphead
Argyll
PA31 8QN
Tel: 01852 500284

ARROCHAR
Village Inn
Main Street
Arrochar
Dunbartonshire
G83 7AX
Tel: 01301 702279

AUCHTERARDER
Greystanes
Western Road
Auchterarder
Perthshire
PH3 1JJ
Tel: 01764 664239

AVIEMORE
Waverley
35 Strathspey Avenue
Aviemore
Inverness-shire
PH22 1SN
Tel: 01479 811226

Ravenscraig Guest House
141 Grampian Road
Aviemore
Inverness-shire
PH22 1RP
Tel: 01479 810278

AVOCH
Inverleod
Toll Road
Avoch
Ross-shire
IV9 8PR
Tel: 01381 621595

AYR
Fairfield House Hotel
12 Fairfield Road
Ayr
Ayrshire
KA7 2AS
Tel: 01292 267461

BY AYR
Enterkine Country House
Annbank by Ayr
Ayrshire
KA6 5AL
Tel: 01292 520580

BALLATER
Story House
Anderson Road
Ballater
Aberdeenshire
AB35 5QW
Tel: 013397 56333

Moorside Guest House
26 Braemar Road
Ballater
Aberdeenshire
AB35 5RL
Tel: 01339 755492

Darroch Learg Hotel
Braemar Road
Ballater
Aberdeenshire
AB35 5UX
Tel: 01339 755443

BALLOCH
Anchorage Guest House
31 Balloch Road
Balloch
Dunbartonshire
G83 8SS
Tel: 01389 753336

BELLOCHANTUY
by Campbeltown
Argyll Hotel
Bellochantuy
by Campbeltown
Argyll
PA28 6QE
Tel: 01583 421212

BELLSHILL
Hilton Strathclyde
Pheonix Crescent
Bellshill
North Lanarkshire
ML4 3JQ
Tel: 01698 395500

BIGGAR
Cormiston Cottage
Cormiston Road
Biggar
Lanarkshire
ML12 6NS
Tel: 01899 220200

BLACKFORD
Blackford Hotel
Moray Street
Blackford
Perthshire
PH4 1QF
Tel: 01764 682497

BLAIRGOWRIE
Bridge of Cally Hotel
Bridge of Cally
Blairgowrie
Perthshire
PH10 7JJ
Tel: 01250 886231

Facilities

Holmrigg
Wester Essendy
Blairgowrie
Perthshire
PH10 6RD
Tel: 01250 884309

BRIDGE OF ALLAN
Lynedoch
7 Mayne Avenue
Bridge of Allan
Stirlingshire
FK9 4QU
Tel: 01786 832178

BRIDGE OF CALLY
Glen Albyn
Bridge of Cally
Perthshire
PH10 7JL
Tel: 01250 886352

BRODICK, ISLE OF ARRAN
Belvedere Guest House
Alma Road
Brodick
Isle of Arran
KA27 8AZ
Tel: 01770 302397

Strathwhillan House
Strathwhillan Road
Brodick
Isle of Arran
KA27 8BQ
Tel: 01770 3023313

BUCKIE
The Bungalow
81 High Street
Buckie
Banffshire
AB56 1BB
Tel: 01542 832367

BRAEINTRA, BY ACHMORE
Soluis Mu Thuath
Braeintra by Achmore
Lochalsh
IV53 8UP
Tel: 01599 577219

BY FORT WILLIAM
The Inn at Ardgour
Ardgour
by Fort William
Inverness-shire
PH33 7AA
Tel: 01855 841225

KILMARNOCK
Fenwick Hotel
Fenwick by Kilmarnock
Ayrshire
KA3 6AU
Tel: 01560 600 478

LOCH ASSYNT, BY LAIRG
Ruddyglow Park
Loch Assynt, by Lairg
Sutherland
IV27 4HB
Tel: 01571 822216

BY OBAN
Falls of Lora Hotel
Connel Ferry by Oban
Argyll
PA37 1PB
Tel: 01631 710483

BY PETERHEAD
Greenbrae Farmhouse
Longside, by Peterhead
Aberdeenshire
AB42 4JX
Tel: 01779 821051

BY PITLOCHRY
East Haugh House Country Hotel & Residence
East Haugh, by Pitlochry
Perthshire
PH16 5JS
Tel: 01796 473121

BY SPEAN BRIDGE
Dreamweavers
Mucomir By Spean Bridge
Inverness-shire
PH34 4EQ
Tel: 01397 712 548

BY STRANRAER
Corsewall Lighthouse Hotel
Kirkcolm by Stranraer
Wigtownshire
DG9 0QG
Tel: 01776 853220

BY THURSO
Forss House Hotel
Forss, by Thurso
Caithness
KW14 7XY
Tel: 01847 861201

Creag-Na-Mara
East Mey, by Thurso
Caithness
KW14 8XL
Tel: 01847 851850

CALLANDER
The Old Rectory Guest House
Leny Road
Callander
Perthshire
FK17 8AL
Tel: 01877 339215

The Crags Hotel
101 Main Street
Callander
Perthshire
FK17 8BQ
Tel: 01877 330257

Roman Camp Hotel
Main Street
Callander
Perthshire
FK17 8BG
Tel: 01877 330003

The Knowe
Ancaster Road
Callander
Perthshire
FK17 8EL
Tel: 01877 330076

**CANDERSIDE TOLL,
BY LARKHALL**
Shawlands Hotel
Ayr Road
Canderside Toll,
 by Larkhall
Lanarkshire
ML9 2TZ
Tel: 01698 791111

COLDINGHAM
Dunlaverock
Coldingham Bay
Coldingham
Berwickshire
TD14 5PA
Tel: 01890 771450

COLVEND
Clonyard House Hotel
Colvend by Dalbeattie
Kircudbrightshire
DG5 4QW
Tel: 01556 630372

COMRIE
Drumearn Cottage
The Ross
Comrie
Perthshire
PH6 2JU
Tel: 01764 670030

CONTIN
Hideaway
Craigdarroch Drive
Contin
Ross-shire
IV14 9EL
Tel: 01997 421127

COUPAR
Red House Hotel
Station Road
Coupar Angus
Perthshire
PH13 9AL
Tel: 01828 628500

CRIEFF
Achray House Hotel
St Fillans
Crieff
Perthshire
PH6 2NF
Tel: 01764 685 231

Crieff Hydro Hotel
Crieff
Perthshire
PH7 3LQ
Tel: 01764 655555

Fendoch Guest House
Sma' Glen
Crieff
Perthshire
PH7 3LW
Tel: 01764 653446

DALBEATTIE
Bellevue B & B
Port Road
Dalbeattie
DG5 4AZ
Tel: 01556 611833

DALMALLY
Glenorchy Lodge Hotel
Dalmally
Argyll
PA33 1AA
Tel: 018382 00312

DALRYMPLE
Kirkton Inn
1 Main Street
Dalrymple
Ayrshire
KA6 6DF
Tel: 01292 560241

DIRLETON
Station House
Station Road
Dirleton
North Berwick
EH39 5LR
Tel: 01620 890512

DORNOCH
Dornoch Castle Hotel
Castle Street
Dornoch
Sutherland
IV25 3SD
Tel: 01862 810216

DUMFRIES
Wallamhill House
Kirkton
Dumfries
Dumfriesshire
DG1 1SL
Tel: 01387 248249

Hazeldean Guest House
4 Moffat Road
Dumfries
DG1 1NJ
Tel: 01387 266178

Netherfield
Lochanhead
Dumfries
Dumfries & Galloway
DG2 8JE
Tel: 01387 730217

Facilities

For visitors with disabilities

DUNDEE
Hilton Dundee
Earl Grey Place
Dundee
Angus
DD1 4DE
Tel: 01382 229271

DUNFERMLINE
Clarke Cottage Guest House
139 Halbeath Road
Dunfermline
Fife
KY11 4LA
Tel: 01383 735935

Pitbauchlie House Hotel
Aberdour Road
Dunfermline
Fife
KY11 4PB
Tel: 01383 722282

DUNTOCHER
West Park Hotel
Great Western Road
Duntocher
Clydebank
G81 6DB
Tel: 01389 872333

EDINBURGH
Holyrood Hotel
Holyrood Road
Edinburgh
EH8 6AE
Tel: 0131 550 4500

Masson House
18 Holyrood Park Road
Edinburgh
EH16 5AY
Tel: 0131 651 2011

Ben Craig House
3 Craigmillar Park
Edinburgh
EH16 5PG
Tel: 0131 667 2593

Abbey Lodge Hotel
137 Drum Street Gilmerton
Edinburgh
EH17 8RJ
Tel: 0131 6649548

Roxburghe Hotel
38 Charlotte Square
Edinburgh
EH2 4HG
Tel: 0131 240 5500

Kelly's Guest House
3 Hillhouse Road
Edinburgh
Lothian
EH4 3QP
Tel: 0131 332 3894

Lindsay Guest House
108 Polwarth Terrace
Edinburgh
Midlothian
EH11 1NN
Tel: 0131 337 1580

Holland House
18 Holyrood Park Road
Edinburgh
EH16 5AY
Tel: 0131 651 2011

EDZELL
Kelvingrove
Dunlappie Road
Edzell
Angus
DD9 7UB
Tel: 01356 648316

ERSKINE
Erskine Bridge Hotel
Erskine
Renfrewshire
PA8 6AN

ESKBANK
Glenarch House
Melville Road
Eskbank
Dalkeith
EH22 3NJ
Tel: 0131 6631478

FINTRY
Culcreuch Castle
Culcreuch Castle Country Park
Fintry
Stirlingshire
G63 0LW
Tel: 01360 860555

FORT WILLIAM
Lochan Cottage Guest House
Lochyside
Fort William
Inverness-shire
PH33 7NX
Tel: 01397 702695

Craig Nevis West
Belford Road
Fort William
Inverness-shire
PH33 6BU
Tel: 01397 702023

GALASHIELS
Ettrickvale
33 Abbotsford Road
Galashiels
Selkirkshire
TD1 3HW
Tel: 01896 755224

GIRVAN
Garryloop
Penkill Old Dailly
Girvan
South Ayrshire
KA26 9TG
Tel: 01465 871 393
Tel: 0788 443 8425

GOUROCK
Spinnaker Hotel
121 Albert Road
Gourock
Renfrewshire
PA19 1BU
Tel: 01475 633107

GRANTOWN ON SPEY
Willowbank
High Street
Grantown on Spey
Morayshire
PH26 3EN
Tel: 01479 872089

Holmhill House
Woodside Avenue
Grantown on Spey
Morayshire PH26 3JR
Tel: 01479 873977

Kinross Guest House
Woodside Avenue
Grantown-on-Spey
Moray PH26 3JR
Tel: 01479 872042

Dunallan House
Woodside Avenue
Grantown-on-Spey
Moray
PH26 3JN
Tel: 01479 872140

Craiglynne Hotel
Woodlands Terrace
Grantown-on-Spey
Morayshire
PH26 3JX
Tel: 01479 872597

GREENOCK
Tontine Hotel
6 Ardgowan Square
Greenock
Renfrewshire
PA16 8NG
Tel: 01475 723316

GRETNA
The Gables Hotel & Restaurant
1 Annan Road
Gretna
Dumfriesshire
DG16 5DQ
Tel: 01461 338300

GULBERWICK
Virdafjell
Shurton Brae
Gulberwick
Shetland
ZE2 9TX
Tel: 01595 694336

HELENSBURGH
RSR Braeholm
31 East Montrose Street
Helensburgh
Argyll & Bute
G84 7HR
Tel: 01436 671880

HELMSDALE
Kindale House
5 Lilleshall Street
Helmsdale
Sutherland KW8 6JF
Tel: 01431 821415

INVERGOWRIE, DUNDEE
Swallow Hotel
Kingsway West
Invergowrie, Dundee
Angus DD2 5JT
Tel: 01382 641122

INVERNESS
Avalon Guest House
79 Glenurquhart Road
Inverness
Inverness-shire IV3 5PB
Tel: 01463 239075

Drumossie Park Cottage
Drumossie Brae
InvernessInverness-shire
IV2 5BB
Tel: 01463 224127

INVERURIE
Strathburn Hotel
Burghmuir Drive
Inverurie
Aberdeenshire AB51 4GY
Tel: 01467 624422

ISLE OF HARRIS
Carminish House
1A Strond
Isle of Harris
HS5 3UB
Tel: 01859 520400

ISLE OF IONA
Ardhasaig House
9 Ardhasaig
Isle of Harris
HS3 3AJ
Tel: 01859 5020663

Finlay Ross (Iona) Ltd
Martyr's Bay
Isle of Iona
Argyll
PA76 6SP
Tel: 01505 704000

ISLE OF MULL
Birchgrove
Lochdon
Isle of Mull
PA64 4AP
Tel: 01680 812364

ISLE OF NORTH UIST
Redburn House
Lochmaddy
Isle of North Uist
Western Isles
HS6 5AA
Tel: 01671 402554/07860
600925

ISLE OF SOUTH UIST
Caloraidh
Milton
Isle of South Uist
HS8 5RY
Tel: 01878 710365

JEDBURGH
Allerton House
Oxnam Road
Jedburgh
Roxburghshire
TD8 6QQ
Tel: 01835 869633

Crailing Old School
Jedburgh
Roxburghshire
TD8 6TL
Tel: 01835 850382

KELSO
Cross Keys Hotel
36-37 The Square
Kelso
Roxburghshire
TD5 7HL
Tel: 01573 223303

Edenmouth Farm
Kelso
Roxburghshire
TD5 7QB
Tel: 01890 830391

Craignethan House
Jedburgh Road
Kelso
Roxburghshire
TD5 8AZ
Tel: 01573 224818

KINCLAVEN, BY STANLEY
Ballathie House Hotel
Kinclaven
by Stanley
Perthshire
PH1 4QN
Tel: 01250 883268

KINGUSSIE
The Auld Poor House
Kingussie
Inverness-shire
PH21 1LS
Tel: 01540 661558

The Hermitage Guest House
Spey Street
Kingussie
Inverness-shire
PH21 1HN
Tel: 01540 662137

KINTYRE
Hunting Lodge Hotel
Bellochantuy
Kintyre
Argyll
PA28 6QE
Tel: 01583 421323

KYLE OF LOCHALSH
Isle of Raasay Hotel
Raasay
Kyle of Lochalsh
Ross-shire
IV40 8PB
Tel: 01478 660222

LAMLASH
Lilybank
Shore Road
Lamlash
Isle of Arran
KA27 8LS
Tel: 01770 600230

LERWICK
Glen Orchy Guest House
20 Knab Road
Lerwick
Shetland
ZE1 0AX
Tel: 01595 692031

LINLITHGOW
Arden House
Belsyde
Linlithgow
West Lothian
EH49 6QE
Tel: 01506 670172

LOANHEAD
Aaron Glen Guest House
7 Nivensknowe Road
Loanhead
Midlothian
EH20 9AU
Tel: 0131 440 1293

LOCH LOMOND
Culag Lochside Guest House
Luss
Loch Lomond
Argyll and Bute
G83 8PD
Tel: 01436 860248

LOCHMABEN
Ardbeg Cottage
19 Castle Street
Lochmaben
Dumfries-shire
DG11 1NY
Tel: 01387 811855

MELROSE
Easter Cottage
Lilliesleaf
Melrose
Roxburghshire
TD6 9JD
Tel: 01835 870281

MILTON
Milton Inn
Dumbarton Road
Milton
Dunbartonshire
G82 2DT
Tel: 01389 761401

MOFFAT
Black Bull Hotel
Churchgate
Moffat
Dumfriesshire
DG10 9EG
Tel: 01683 220206

Limetree House
Eastgate
Moffat
Dumfriesshire DG10 9AE
Tel: 01683 220001

MONTROSE
Best Western Links Hotel
Mid Links
Montrose
Angus
DD10 8RL
Tel: 01674 671000

MUIR-OF-ORD
Hillview Park
Muir-of-Ord
Ross-shire
IV6 7TU
Tel: 01463 870787

MUSSELBURGH
Carberry Tower
Musselburgh
East Lothian
EH21 8PY
Tel: 0131 665 3135

NEWTON STEWART
East Culkae Farm House
Sorbie
Newton Stewart
Wigtownshire
DG8 8AS
Tel: 01988 850214

NORTHBAY
Airds Guest House
244 Bruernish
Northbay
Isle of Barra
HS9 5UY
Tel: 01871 890720

ORPHIR
Houton Bay Lodge
Houton Bay
Orphir Scapa Flow
Orkney
KW17 2RD
Tel: 01856 811320

PAISLEY
Ardgowan Town House Hotel
92 Renfrew Road
Paisley
Renfrewshire
PA3 4BJ
Tel: 0141 889 4763

PERTH
Petra's B & B
4 Albany Terrace
Perth
Perthshire
PH1 2BD
Tel: 01738 563050

Cherrybank Inn
210 Glasgow Road
Perth
PH2 0NA
Tel: 01738 624349

Arisaig Guest House
4 Pitcullen Crescent
Perth PH2 7HT
Tel: 01738 628240

Sunbank House Hotel
50 Dundee Road
Perth
Perthshire
PH2 7BA
Tel: 01738 624882

PIRNHALL STIRLING
Barn Lodge
Croftside
Pirnhall Stirling
Stirlingshire
FK7 8EX
Tel: 01786 813591

PITLOCHRY
Craigatin House & Courtyard
165 Atholl Road
Pitlochry
Perthshire
PH16 5QL
Tel: 01796 472478

Green Park Hotel
Clunie Bridge Road
Pitlochry
Perthshire
PH16 5JY
Tel: 01796 473248

Craigvrack Hotel
38 West Moulin Road
Pitlochry
Perthshire
PH16 5EQ
Tel: 01796 472399

The Well House
11 Toberargan Road
Pitlochry
Perthshire
PH16 5HG
Tel: 01796 472239

The Poplars
27 Lower Oakfield
Pitlochry
Perthshire
PH16 5DS
Tel: 01796 472129

PORTPATRICK
The Fernhill Hotel
Heugh Road
Portpatrick
Wigtownshire
DG9 8TD
Tel: 01776 810220

Braefield Guest House
Braefield Road
Portpatrick
Wigtownshire
DG9 8TA
Tel: 01776 810255

Portpatrick Hotel
Heugh Road
Portpatrick
Wigtownshire
DG9 8TQ
Tel: 01776 810333

SCONE
Perth Airport Skylodge
Norwell Drive
 Perth Airport
Scone
Perthshire
PH2 6PL
Tel: 01738 555700

SOUTH QUEENSFERRY
Priory Lodge
8 The Loan
South Queensferry
West Lothian
EH30 9NS
Tel: 0131 331 4345

SPEAN BRIDGE
The Heathers
Invergloy Halt
Spean Bridge
Inverness-shire
PH34 4DY
Tel: 01397 712077

ST. ANDREWS
Pitmilly West Lodge
Kingsbarns
St Andrews
Fife
KY16 8QA
Tel: 01334 880581

STIRLING
Cambria Guest House
141 Bannockburn Road
Stirling
FK7 OEP
Tel: 01786 814603

STRATHAVEN
Baxters Country Inn
Darvel Road
Strathaven
Lanarkshire
ML10 6QR
Tel: 01357 440341

Rissons At Springvale
18 Lethame Road
Strathaven
Lanarkshire
ML10 6AD
Tel: 01357 521131

TOBERMORY
Tobermory Hotel
53 Main Street
Tobermory
Isle of Mull
PA75 6NT
Tel: 01688 302091

TROON
Piersland House Hotel
15 Craigend Road
Troon
Ayrshire
KA10 6HD
Tel: 01292 314747

ULLAPOOL
Dromnan Guest House
Garve Road
Ullapool
Ross-shire
IV26 2SX
Tel: 01854 612333

UPPER LARGO
Bayview
Drumeldrie
Upper Largo
Fife
KY8 6JD
Tel: 01333 360454

SOUTH OF SCOTLAND

Ayrshire and Arran, Dumfries & Galloway, Scottish Borders

ALLOWAY

Belleisle Country House Hotel
Belleisle Park, Doonfoot,
Ayr, Ayrshire, KA7 4DU
Tel: 01292 442331
★★ Small Hotel

ANNAN

Rowanbank
20 St Johns Road, Annan,
Dumfriesshire, DG12 5AW
Tel: 01461 204200
★★ Guest House

ANNBANK

Enterkine Country House
Annbank, by Ayr,
Ayrshire, KA6 5AL
Tel: 01292 520580
★★★★★ Hotel

BLACKWATERFOOT

Blackwaterfoot Lodge
Isle of Arran, KA27 8EU
Tel: 01770 860202
★★ Small Hotel

Kinloch Hotel
Blackwaterfoot,
Isle of Arran, KA27 8ET
Tel: 01770 860444
★★★ Hotel

BRODICK

Belvedere Guest House
Alma Road, Brodick,
Isle of Arran, KA27 8AZ
Tel: 01770 302397
★★★ Guest House

Kilmichael Country House Hotel
Brodick,
Isle of Arran, KA27 8BY
Tel: 01770 302219
★★★★★ Small Hotel

Dunvegan House
Shore Road, Brodick,
Isle of Arran, KA27 8AJ
Tel: 01770 302811
★★★★ Guest House

Glenartney Hotel
Mayish Road, Brodick,
Isle of Arran, KA27 8BX
Tel: 01770 302220
★★★ Small Hotel

Glencloy Farm Guest House
Glen Cloy Road, Brodick,
Isle of Arran, KA27 8DA
Tel: 01770 302351
★★★ Guest House

Strathwhillan House
Strathwhillan Road,
Brodick,
Isle of Arran, KA27 8BQ
Tel: 01770 302331
★★ Guest House

Auchrannie Spa Resort
Brodick,
Isle of Arran, KA27 8BZ
Tel: 01770 302234
★★★★ Hotel

Auchrannie Country House Hotel
Brodick,
Isle of Arran, KA27 8BZ
Tel: 01770 302234
★★★★ Hotel

Allandale House
Corriegills Road, Brodick,
Isle of Arran, KA27 8BJ
Tel: 01770 302278
★★★ Guest House

Ormidale Hotel
Brodick, Isle of Arran,
KA27 8BY
Tel: 01770 302293
★★ Small Hotel

Invercloy Hotel
Shore Road, Brodick,
Isle of Arran, KA27 8AJ
Tel: 01770 302225
★★★ Guest House

KILDONAN

Kildonan Hotel
Kildonan, Isle of Arran,
KA27 8SE
Tel: 01770 820207
★★★ Small Hotel

Breadalbane Hotel
Kildonan, Isle of Arran,
KA27 8SE
Tel: 01770 820284
★★★ Inn

Mare
6 The Keys, Kildonan,
Isle Of Arran, KA27 8AS
Tel: 07900 680930
Awaiting Inspection

LAGG

Lagg Hotel
Lagg, Kilmory, Isle of Arran,
KA27 8PQ
Tel: 01770 870255
★★ Small Hotel

LAMLASH

Marine House Hotel
Shore Road, Lamlash,
Isle of Arran, KA27 8JZ
Tel: 01770 600298
★★★ Guest House

Glenisle Hotel
Shore Road, Lamlash,
Isle of Arran, KA27 8LY
Tel: 01770 600559
★★★ Small Hotel

Lilybank
Shore Road, Lamlash,
Isle of Arran, KA27 8LS
Tel: 01770 600230
★★★★ Guest House

LOCHRANZA

Apple Lodge
Lochranza,
Isle of Arran, KA27 8HJ
Tel: 01770 830229
★★★★ Guest House

Lochranza Hotel
Shore Road, Lochranza,
Isle of Arran, KA27 8HL
Tel: 01770 830223
★★★ Small Hotel

SANNOX

Sannox Bay Hotel
Main Road, Sannox,
Isle of Arran, KA27 8JD
Tel: 01770 810225
★★★ Small Hotel

WHITING BAY

Viewbank House
Golf Course Road,
Whiting Bay,
Isle of Arran, KA27 8QT
Tel: 01770 700326
★★★ Guest House

Burlington Hotel
Shore Road, Whiting Bay,
Isle of Arran, KA27 8PZ
Tel: 01770 700255
★★★ Small Hotel

Eden Lodge
Whiting Bay, Isle of Arran,
KA27 8QH
Tel: 01770 700357
★★★ Small Hotel

AULDGIRTH

Friars Carse Hotel
Auldgirth, Dumfriesshire,
DG2 0SA
Tel: 01387 740388
★★ Hotel

AYR

The Cariston Hotel
11 Miller Road, Ayr,
Ayrshire, KA7 2AX
Tel: 01292 262474
★★ Small Hotel

Belmont Guest House
15 Park Circus, Ayr, KA7 2DJ
Tel: 01292 265588
★★★ Guest House

Eglinton Guest House
23 Eglinton Terrace, Ayr,
Ayrshire, KA7 1JJ
Tel: 01292 264623
★★ Guest House

Swallow Station Hotel Ayr
Burns Statue Square, Ayr,
Ayrshire, KA7 3AT
Tel: 01292 263268
★★ Hotel

Burnside Guest House
14 Queens Terrace, Ayr,
Ayrshire, KA7 1DU
Tel: 01292 263912
★★★ Guest House

The Ivy House
2 Alloway, Ayr, Ayrshire,
KA7 4NL
Tel: 01292 442336
Small Hotel

Directory of all VisitScotland Quality Assured Serviced Hotels and Guest Houses

Arrandale Hotel
2-4 Cassillis Street, Ayr,
Ayrshire, KA7 1DW
Tel: 01292 289959
★★★ Small Hotel

Kilkerran Guest House
15 Prestwick Road, Ayr,
Ayrshire, KA8 8LD
Tel: 01292 266477
★★ Guest House

Glenpark Hotel
5 Racecourse Road, Ayr,
Ayrshire, KA7 2DG
Tel: 01292 263891
★★ Small Hotel

Queen's Guest House
10 Queen's Terrace, Ayr,
Ayrshire, KA7 1DU
Tel: 01292 265618
Awaiting Inspection

Daviot House
12 Queen's Terrace, Ayr,
Ayrshire, KA7 1DU
Tel: 01292 269678
Awaiting Inspection

Windsor Hotel
6 Alloway Place, Ayr,
Ayrshire, KA7 2AA
Tel: 01292 264689
★★ Guest House

Elms Court Hotel
21-23 Miller Road, Ayr,
Ayrshire, KA7 2AX
Tel: 01292 264191
★★★ Small Hotel

Abbotsford Hotel
14 Corsehill Road, Ayr,
Ayrshire, KA7 2ST
Tel: 01292 261506
★★★ Small Hotel

Ellisland
19 Racecourse Road, Ayr,
Ayrshire, KA7 2TD
Tel: 01292 260111
Awaiting Inspection

Fairfield House Hotel
12 Fairfield Road, Ayr,
Ayrshire, KA7 2AS
Tel: 01292 267461
★★★★ Hotel

Brig O' Doon Hotel
Alloway, Ayr, Ayrshire,
KA7 4PQ
Tel: 01292 442466
★★★★ Small Hotel

Craigholm
7 Queens Terrace, Ayr,
Ayrshire, KA7 1DU
Tel: 01292 261955
Awaiting Inspection

Craggallan Guest House
8 Queens Terrace, Ayr,
Ayrshire, KA7 1DU
Tel: 0192 264998
★★★★ Guest House

Horizon Hotel
Esplanade, Ayr, Ayrshire,
KA7 1DT
Tel: 01292 264384
★★★ Hotel

Miller House Guest House
36 Miller Road, Ayr, KA7
2AY
Tel: 01292 282016
★★★ Guest House

Langley Bank Guest House
39 Carrick Road, Ayr,
Ayrshire, KA7 2RD
Tel: 01292 264246
★★★★ Guest House

Glenmore Guest House
35 Bellevue Crescent, Ayr,
Ayrshire, KA7 2DP
Tel: 01292 269830
★★★ Guest House

Burnbank Hotel
49 Maybole Road, Ayr,
Ayrshire, KA7 4SF
Tel: 01292 441986
★★ Small Hotel

Carrick Lodge Hotel
Carrick Road, Ayr, Ayrshire,
KA7 2RE
Tel: 01292 262846
★★★ Small Hotel

The Beechwood Guest House
37/39 Prestwick Road, Ayr,
New Prestwick, Ayrshire,
KA8 8LE
Tel: 01292 262093
★★★ Guest House

The Richmond
38 Park Circus, Ayr, KA7
2DL
Tel: 01292 265153
★★★ Guest House

Western House Hotel
2 Whitletts Road, Ayr,
Ayrshire, KA9 2TA
Tel: 0870 8505666
★★★★ Hotel

St Andrews Hotel
7 Prestwick Road, Ayr,
KA8 8LD
Tel: 01292 263211
★ Small Hotel

Savoy Park Hotel
16 Racecourse Road, Ayr,
KA7 2UT
Tel: 01292 266112
★★★ Small Hotel

Ramada Jarvis
Dalblair Road, Ayr,
Ayrshire, KA7 1UG
Tel: 01292 269331
★★★ Hotel

Coila Guest House
10 Holmston Road, Ayr,
Ayrshire, KA7 3BB
Tel: 01292 262642
★★★★ Guest House

Dunlay House
1 Ailsa Place, Ayr, Ayrshire,
KA7 1JG
Tel: 01292 610230
★★★★ Guest House

Ayrshire & Galloway Hotel
1 Killoch Place, Ayr,
Ayrshire, KA7 2EA
Tel: 01292 262626
★★★ Hotel

BALLANTRAE
Glenapp Castle
Ballantrae, Ayrshire, KA26
0NZ
Tel: 01465 831212
★★★★★ Hotel

BEATTOCK
Marchbankwood House
Beattock, Moffat, Dumfries
& Galloway, DG10 9RG
Tel: 01683 300118
★★★★ Guest House

BROUGHTON, BY BIGGAR
Over Tweed
Near Broughton, Biggar,
Lanarkshire, ML12 6QH
Tel: 01899 830455
Awaiting Inspection

The Glenholm Centre
Broughton, by Biggar,
Lanarkshire, ML12 6JF
Tel: 01899 830408
★★★ Guest House

BURNHOUSE, BY BEITH
The Burnhouse Manor Hotel
Burnhouse, by Beith,
Ayrshire, KA15 1LJ
Tel: 01560 484006
★★★ Hotel

CAIRNRYAN
Cairnryan House
Main Street, Cairnryan,
Wigtownshire, DG9 8QX
Tel: 01581 200624
Awaiting Inspection

CANONBIE
Cross Keys Hotel
Canonbie, Dumfriesshire,
DG14 0SY
Tel: 013873 71205
★★★ Small Hotel

CASTLE DOUGLAS
The Urr Valley Hotel
Ernespie Road, Castle
Douglas,
Kirkcudbrightshire,
DG7 3JG
Tel: 01556 502188
★★★ Small Hotel

Balcary Bay Hotel
Shore Road, Auchencairn,
by Castle Douglas,
Kirkcudbrightshire,
DG7 1QZ
Tel: 01556 640217
★★★★ Hotel

Kings Arms Hotel
St Andrew Street, Castle
Douglas,
Kirkcudbrightshire,
DG7 1EL
Tel: 01556 502626
★★ Small Hotel

The Imperial Hotel
35 King Street, Castle
Douglas, DG7 1AA
Tel: 01556 502086
★★★ Small Hotel

Station Hotel
1 Queen Street, Castle
Douglas,
Kirkcudbrightshire,
DG7 1HX
Tel: 01556 502152
★★★ Small Hotel

Market Inn Hotel
6/7 Queen Street, Castle Douglas,
Kirkcudbrightshire,
DG7 1HX
Tel: 01556 502105
★★ Small Hotel

CHIRNSIDE, BY DUNS

Chirnside Hall Hotel
Chirnside, By Duns,
Berwickshire, TD11 3LD
Tel: 01890 818219
★★★★ Small Hotel

COLVEND

Clonyard House Hotel
Colvend, Dalbeattie,
Kircudbrightshire,
DG5 4QW
Tel: 01556 630372
★★ Small Hotel

CREETOWN

Ellangowan Hotel
St John Street, Creetown,
Dumfries & Galloway,
DG8 7JF
Tel: 01671 820201
★★ Small Hotel

CROCKETFORD

Galloway Arms Hotel
Crocketford, By Dumfries,
Kirkcudbrightshire, DG2
8RA
Tel: 01556 690248
★★ Small Hotel

MILLPORT

The Millerston
29 West Bay Road,
Millport, Isle of Cumbrae,
KA28 0HA
Tel: 01475 530480
★★★ Small Hotel

The Cathedral of the Isles
The College, Millport, Isle
of Cumbrae, KA28 0HE
Tel: 01475 530353
★★★ Guest House

DALRY

Blair House
Blair, Dalry, Ayrshire, KA24
4ER
Tel: 01294 833100
★★★★★
Exclusive Use Venue

DALRY, BY CASTLE DOUGLAS

The Lochinvar
3 Main Street, St Johns
Town of Dalry,
Dumfriesshire, DG7 3UP
Tel: 01644 430210
Awaiting Inspection

The Clachan Inn
8-10 High Street,
St John's Town of Dalry,
by Castle Douglas,
DG7 3UW
Tel: 01644 430241
Awaiting Inspection

DALRYMPLE

The Kirkton Inn
1 Main Street, Dalrymple,
Ayrshire, KA6 6DF
Tel: 01292 560241
★★ Inn

DUMFRIES

Torbay Lodge
31 Lovers Walk, Dumfries,
DG1 1LR
Tel: 01387 253922
Awaiting Inspection

Edenbank Hotel
17 Laurieknowe, Dumfries,
DG2 7AH
Tel: 01387 252759
★★★ Small Hotel

Cairndale Hotel & Leisure Club
English Street, Dumfries,
DG1 2DF
Tel: 01387 254111
★★★ Hotel

Aston Hotel
The Crichton, Bankend
Road, Dumfries,
Dumfries and Galloway,
DG1 4ZZ
Tel: 0845 6340205
Awaiting Inspection

Hazeldean Guest House
4 Moffat Road, Dumfries,
DG1 1NJ
Tel: 01387 266178
★★★★ Guest House

Huntingdon House Hotel
18 St Marys Street,
Dumfries, DG1 1LZ
Tel: 01387 254893
★★★ Small Hotel

Hetland Hall Hotel
Carrutherstown, Dumfries,
DG1 4JX
Tel: 01387 840201
★★★ Hotel

Dalston House Hotel
5 Laurieknowe, Dumfries,
Dumfrieshire, DG2 7AH
Tel: 01387 254422
★★★ Small Hotel

Glenlossie Guest House
75 Annan Road, Dumfries,
Dumfries-shire,
DG1 3EG
Tel: 01387 254305
★★★★ Guest House

Woodland House Hotel
Newbridge, Dumfries,
Dumfriesshire, DG2 0HZ
Tel: 01387 720233
★ Small Hotel

Aberdour Hotel
16-20 Newall Terrace,
Dumfries, Dumfries-shire,
DG1 1LW
Tel: 01387 252060
★★★ Small Hotel

Station Hotel
49 Lovers Walk, Dumfries,
Dumfries-shire, DG1 1LT
Tel: 01387 254316
★★★ Hotel

Moreig Hotel
67 Annan Road, Dumfries,
DG1 3EG
Tel: 01387 255524
★★★ Small Hotel

Albyn Hotel
Courance, Near Dumfries,
Dumfries & Galloway,
DG11 1TS
Tel: 01387 830696
Awaiting Inspection

Fulwood Hotel
30 Lovers Walk, Dumfries,
DG1 1LX
Tel: 01387 252262
★★★ Guest House

BY DUMFRIES

Nith Hotel
Glencaple, Dumfriesshire,
DG1 4RE
Tel: 01387 770213
★★ Small Hotel

Comlongon Castle
Clarencefield,
Dumfriesshire, DG1 4NA
Tel: 01387 870283
★★★ Small Hotel

DUNS

Duns Castle
Duns, Berwickshire,
TD11 3NW
Tel: 01361 883211
★★★★ Exclusive Use
Venue

DUNSCORE, BY DUMFRIES

Morrington House
Stepford Road, Dunscore,
Dumfriesshire, DG2 0JN
Tel: 01387 820391
Awaiting Inspection

EARLSTON

Broomfield House
10 Thorn Street, Earlston,
Berwickshire, TD4 6DR
Tel: 01896 848084
★★★ Guest House

ECCLEFECHAN

Cressfield Country House Hotel
Townfoot, Ecclefechan,
Dumfriesshire, DG11 3DR
Tel: 01576 300281
★★★ Small Hotel

ETTRICKBRIDGE, BY SELKIRK

Ettrickshaws Hotel
Ettrick Bridge, by Selkirk,
Selkirkshire, TD7 5HW
Tel: 01750 52229
★★★★ Small Hotel

EYEMOUTH

Ship Hotel
Harbour Road, Eyemouth,
Berwickshire, TD14 5HT
Tel: 018907 50224
Awaiting Inspection

FENWICK, BY KILMARNOCK

Fenwick Hotel
Fenwick, by Kilmarnock,
Ayrshire, KA3 6AU
Tel: 01560 600478
★★★ Hotel

Directory of all VisitScotland Quality Assured Serviced Hotels and Guest Houses

GALASHIELS

Morven Guest House
12 Sime Place,
Galashiels, Selkirkshire,
TD1 1ST
Tel: 01896 756255
★★ Guest House

Monorene
23 Stirling Street,
Galashiels, Selkirkshire,
TD1 1BY
Tel: 01896 753073
★★ Guest House

Kingsknowes Hotel
Selkirk Road, Galashiels,
Selkirkshire,
TD1 3HY
Tel: 01896 758375
★★★ Small Hotel

Kings Hotel
56 Market Street,
Galashiels, Selkirkshire,
TD1 3AN
Tel: 01896 755497
★★ Small Hotel

Watson Lodge Guest House
15/16 Bridge Street,
Galashiels, Selkirkshire,
TD1 1SW
Tel: 01896 750551
★★★ Guest House

Abbotsford Arms Hotel
63 Stirling Street,
Galashiels, Selkirkshire,
TD1 1BY
Tel: 01896 752517
Awaiting Inspection

GATEHOUSE OF FLEET

Cally Palace Hotel
Gatehouse of Fleet,
Kirkcudbrightshire,
DG7 2DL
Tel: 01557 814341
★★★★ Hotel

The Bobbin Guest House
36 High Street,
Gatehouse-of-Fleet,
Kirkcudbrightshire,
DG7 2HP
Tel: 01557 814229
★★★ Guest House

The Bank of Fleet Hotel
47 High Street,
Gatehouse of Fleet,
Kirkcudbrightshire,
DG7 2HR
Tel: 01557 814302
★★★ Small Hotel

Murray Arms Hotel + Restaurant
High Street,
Gatehouse of Fleet,
Castle Douglas, DG7 2HY
Tel: 01557 814207
★★★ Small Hotel

GIRVAN

Hotel Westcliffe
15 Louisa Drive, Girvan,
Ayrshire, KA26 9AH
Tel: 01465 712128
★★ Hotel

GRETNA

The Garden House Hotel
Sarkfoot Road, Gretna,
Dumfriesshire, DG16 5EP
Tel: 01461 337621
★★★ Hotel

Solway Lodge Hotel
97-99 Annan Road,
Gretna Green,
Dumfriesshire, DG16
Tel: 01461 338266
★★★ Small Hotel

The Gables Hotel & Restaurant
1 Annan Road, Gretna,
Dumfriesshire, DG16 5DQ
Tel: 01461 338300
★★★★ Hotel

The Beeches
Loanwath Road, Gretna,
Dumfries-shire,
DG16 5EP
Tel: 01461 337448
Awaiting Inspection

GRETNA GREEN

Hunters Lodge Hotel
Annan Road, Gretna,
Dumfriesshire, DG16 5DL
Tel: 01461 338214
★★★ Small Hotel

Hazeldene Hotel
Gretna Green, Gretna,
Dumfriesshire, DG16 5EA
Tel: 01461 338292
★★ Small Hotel

Smiths @ Gretna Green
Gretna Green,
Dumfries & Galloway,
DG16 5EA
Tel: 0845 3676768
★★★★ Hotel

The Mill
Grahamshill, Kirkpatrick
Fleming, Lockerbie,
DG11 3BQ
Tel: 01461 800344
★★★ Lodge

Gretna Hall Hotel
Gretna Green,
Dumfriesshire, DG16 5DY
Tel: 01461 338257
★★★ Hotel

Kirkcroft
Glasgow Road, Gretna
Green, Dumfriesshire,
DG16 5DU
Tel: 01461 337403
★★ Guest House

HAWICK

Bridge House
Sandbed, Hawick,
Roxburghshire,
TD9 0HE
Tel: 01450 370701
★★ Guest House

Mansfield House Hotel
Weensland Road,
Hawick, Roxburghshire,
TD9 8LB
★★★ Small Hotel

Elm House Hotel
17 North Bridge Street,
Hawick, Roxburghshire,
TD9 9BD
Tel: 01450 372866
★★★ Small Hotel

BY HAWICK

Glenteviot Park Hotel
Hassendeanburn, by
Hawick, Roxburghshire,
TD9 8RU
Tel: 01450 870660
★★★★ Small Hotel

Whitchester Guest House
Hawick, Roxburghshire,
TD9 7LN
Tel: 01450 377477
★★★ Guest House

IRVINE

Annfield House Hotel
6 Castle Street, Irvine,
Ayrshire, KA12 8RJ
Tel: 01294 278903
Awaiting Inspection

Laurelbank Guest House
3 Kilwinning Road, Irvine,
Ayrshire, KA12 8RR
Tel: 01294 277153
★★★ Guest House

Thistle Irvine
46 Annick Road, Irvine,
Ayrshire, KA11 4LD
Tel: 01294 274272
★★★ Hotel

The Gailes Lodge
Marine Drive, Gailes,
Irvine, KA11 5AE
Tel: 01294 204040
★★★ Hotel

The Golf Hotel
18 Kilwinning Road, Irvine,
Ayrshire, KA12 8RU
Tel: 01294 278 633
★★ Small Hotel

NR IRVINE

Montgreenan Mansion House Hotel
Montgreenan Estate,
Kilwinning, Ayrshire,
KA13 7QZ
Tel: 01294 850005
★★★ Hotel

ISLE OF WHITHORN

Steam Packet Inn
Harbour Row, Isle of
Whithorn, Wigtownshire,
DG8 8LL
Tel: 01988 500334
★★ Inn

JEDBURGH

The Spread Eagle Hotel
20 High Street, Jedburgh,
Roxburghshire, TD8 6AG
Tel: 01835 862870
★ Small Hotel

Glenfriars House
The Friars, Jedburgh,
Roxburghshire, TD8 6BN
Tel: 01835 862000
★★ Guest House

Glenbank House Hotel
Castlegate, Jedburgh,
Roxburghshire, TD8 6BD
Tel: 01835 862258

★ Small Hotel

Allerton House
Oxnam Road, Jedburgh,
Roxburghshire, TD8 6QQ
Tel: 01835 869633

★★★★ Guest House

Meadhon House
48 Castlegate, Jedburgh,
Roxburghshire, TD8 6BB
Tel: 01835 862504

★★★ Guest House

BY JEDBURGH
Ferniehirst Mill Lodge
Jedburgh, Roxburghshire,
TD8 6PQ
Tel: 01835 863279

★ Guest House

JOHNSTONE BRIDGE
Dinwoodie Lodge Hotel
Johnstone Bridge, by
Lockerbie, Dumfriesshire,
DG11 2SL
Tel: 01576 470289

★★ Small Hotel

KELSO
Cross Keys Hotel
36-37 The Square,
Kelso, Roxburghshire,
TD5 7HL
Tel: 01573 223303

★★★ Hotel

Bellevue House
Bowmont Street, Kelso,
TD5 7DZ
Tel: 01573 224588

★★★ Guest House

Ednam House Hotel
Bridge Street, Kelso,
Roxburghshire,
TD5 7HT
Tel: 01573 224168

★★★ Hotel

Dispensary House
106 Roxburgh Street,
Kelso, Roxburghshire,
TD5 7DY
Tel: 01573 228738
Awaiting Inspection

Ingleston House
Abbey Row, Kelso,
Roxburghshire,
TD5 7HQ
Tel: 01573 225800

★★★ Guest House

KELSO BY
**Roxburghe Hotel and Golf
Course**
Heiton, Kelso,
Roxburghshire,
TD5 8JZ
Tel: 01573 450331

★★★★ Hotel

KILMARNOCK
Howard Park Hotel
136 Glasgow Road,
Kilmarnock, Ayrshire,
KA3 1UT
Tel: 01563 312111

★★★ Hotel

Dean Park Guest House
27 Wellington Street,
Kilmarnock, Ayrshire,
KA3 1DZ
Tel: 01563 572794

★★★ Guest House

Park Hotel
Rugby Park, Kilmarnock,
Ayrshire, KA1 2DP
Tel: 01563 545999

★★★★ Hotel

KILWINNING
Claremont Hotel
69 Byres Road, Kilwinning,
Ayrshire, KA13 6JU
Tel: 01294 558455
Hotel

KIPPFORD, BY DALBEATTIE
Rosemount
Kippford, Dalbeattie,
Kirkcudbrightshire,
DG5 4LN
Tel: 01556 620214

★★★★ Guest House

KIRKBEAN
Grovewood House
Kirkbean, Dumfries,
Dumfries & Galloway,
DG2 8DW
Tel: 01387 880721
Awaiting Inspection

Cavens
Kirkbean, by Dumfries,
By Dumfries,
DG2 8AA
Tel: 01387 880234

★★★★ Small Hotel

KIRKCOLM
Corsewall Arms Hotel
24 Main Street, Kirkcolm,
Stranraer, Wigtownshire,
DG9 0NN
Tel: 01776 853554
Awaiting Inspection

KIRKCUDBRIGHT
Gladstone House
48 High Street,
Kirkcudbright,
DG6 4JX
Tel: 01557 331734

★★★★ Guest House

Royal Hotel
50 St Cuthbert Street,
Kirkcudbright,
DG6 4DY
Tel: 01557 331213

★★ Small Hotel

Gordon House Hotel
116 High Street,
Kirkcudbright,
Kirkcudbrightshire,
DG6 4JQ
Tel: 01557 330670

★★★ Small Hotel

Selkirk Arms Hotel
High Street, Kirkcudbright,
Kirkcudbrightshire,
DG6 4JG
Tel: 01557 330402

★★★ Small Hotel

LARGS
Haylie Hotel
108 Irvine Road, Largs,
Ayrshire, KA30 8EY
Tel: 01475 673207

★★ Small Hotel

Nixons Hotel
2 Barr Crescent, Largs,
Ayrshire, KA30 8PX
Tel: 01475 673381

★★★ Small Hotel

Burnlea Hotel
Burnlea Road, Largs,
Ayrshire, KA30 8BX
Tel: 01475 687235

★★ Hotel

Tigh-Na-Ligh
104 Brisbane Road, Largs,
Ayrshire, KA30 8NN
Tel: 01475 673975

★★★ Guest House

Tigh An Struan
29 Gogo Street, Largs,
North Ayrshire, KA30 8BU
Tel: 01475 670668

★★★ Guest House

Lea-Mar Guest House
20 Douglas Street, Largs,
Ayrshire, KA30 8PS
Tel: 01475 672447

★★★ Guest House

Lilac Holm Guest House
14 Noddleburn Road,
Largs, Ayrshire,
KA30 8PY
Tel: 01475 672020

★★★ Guest House

LAUDER

LOCKERBIE
Somerton House Hotel
35 Carlisle Road,
Lockerbie, Dumfries-shire,
DG11 2DR
Tel: 01576 202583

★★★ Small Hotel

Lockerbie Manor
Boreland Road, Lockerbie,
Dumfriesshire, DG11 2RG
Tel: 01576 203939

★★ Hotel

Directory of all VisitScotland Quality Assured Serviced Hotels and Guest Houses

South Hayrigg Cottage
Lockerbie, Dumfrieshire,
DG11 1BJ
Tel: 01576 225002
Awaiting Inspection

Queens Hotel
Annan Road, Lockerbie,
Dumfriesshire, DG11 2RB
Tel: 01576 202415
★★★ Hotel

Ravenshill House Hotel
12 Dumfries Road,
Lockerbie, Dumfriesshire,
DG11 2EF
Tel: 01576 202882
★★ Small Hotel

Kings Arms Hotel
29 High Street, Lockerbie,
Dumfriesshire, DG11 2JL
Tel: 01576 202410
★★★ Small Hotel

Dryfesdale Country House Hotel
Dryfebridge, Lockerbie,
Dumfriesshire, DG11 2SF
Tel: 01576 202427
★★★★ Small Hotel

MACMERRY

Adniston Manor
West Adniston Farm,
Macmerry, East Lothian,
EH33 1EA
Tel: 01875 611190
★★★★ Guest House

MAYBOLE

Merrick View
9 Cargill Avenue, Maybole,
Ayrshire, KA19 8AD
Tel: 01655 884329
Awaiting Inspection

MELROSE

Burts Hotel
Market Square, Melrose,
Roxburghshire, TD6 9PL
Tel: 01896 822285
★★★★ Small Hotel

Dryburgh Abbey Hotel
St Boswells, Melrose,
Scottish Borders, TD6 0RQ
Tel: 01835 822261
★★★★ Hotel

George & Abbotsford Hotel
High Street, Melrose,
Roxburghshire, TD6 9PD
Tel: 01896 822308
★★ Hotel

The Townhouse Hotel
Market Square, Melrose,
Roxburghshire, TD6 9PQ
Tel: 01896 822645
★★★ Small Hotel

Waverley Castle Hotel
Skirmish Hill, Waverley
Road, Melrose, TD6 9AA
Tel: 01942 824824
★★★ Hotel

BY MELROSE

Fauhope House
Gattonside, Melrose,
Roxburghshire, TD6 9LU
Tel: 01896 823184
★★★★ Bed & Breakfast

Clint Lodge Country House
Clinthill, St Boswells,
Melrose, Roxburghshire,
TD6 0DZ
Tel: 01835 822027
★★★★ Guest House

Whitehouse
St Boswells,
Roxburghshire, TD6 OED
Tel: 01573 460343
★★★★★ Bed & Breakfast

MOFFAT

Annandale Arms Hotel
High Street, Moffat,
Dumfriesshire, DG10 9HF
Tel: 01683 220013
★★★ Small Hotel

Barnhill Springs Country Guest House
Moffat, Dumfries &
Galloway, DG10 9QS
Tel: 01683 220580
★★ Guest House

Black Bull Hotel
Churchgate, Moffat,
Dumfriesshire, DG10 9EG
Tel: 01683 220206
★★★ Small Hotel

Buccleuch Arms Hotel
High Street, Moffat,
Dumfriesshire,
DG10 9ET
Tel: 01683 220003
★★★ Small Hotel

Buchan Guest House
Beechgrove, Moffat,
Dumfriesshire, DG10 9RS
Tel: 01683 220378
★★★ Guest House

The Famous Star Hotel
44 High Street, Moffat,
DG10 9EF
Tel: 01683 220156
★★ Small Hotel

Rockhill Guest House
14 Beechgrove, Moffat,
Dumfriesshire, DG10 9RS
Tel: 01683 220283
★★ Guest House

Hartfell House
Hartfell Crescent, Moffat,
Dumfriesshire, DG10 9AL
Tel: 01683 220153
★★★ Guest House

Moffat House Hotel
High Street, Moffat,
DG10 9HL
Tel: 01683 220039
★★★ Small Hotel

Bridge House
Well Road, Moffat,
Dumfrieshire, DG10 9JT
Tel: 01683 220558
★★★★ Guest House

Well View Hotel
Ballplay Road, Moffat,
Dumfriesshire, DG10 9JU
Tel: 01683 220184
★★★★ Small Hotel

BY MOFFAT

Auchen Castle Hotel
Beattock, Moffat,
Dumfriesshire, DG10 9SH
Tel: 01683 300407
★★★ Hotel

NEW CUMNOCK NEAR

Lochside House Hotel
New Cumnock, Ayrshire,
KA18 4PN
Tel: 01290 333000
★★★ Small Hotel

NEW GALLOWAY

Leamington Hotel
High Street, New Galloway,
Kirkcudbrightshire,
DG7 3RN
Tel: 01644 420327
★★ Guest House

NEWTON STEWART

Galloway Arms Hotel
Victoria Street, Newton
Stewart, Wigtownshire,
DG8 6DB
Tel: 01671 402653
★★ Small Hotel

Rowallan
Corsbie Road, Newton
Stewart, Wigtownshire,
DG8 6JB
Tel: 01671 402520
★★★ Guest House

Stables Guest House
Corsbie Road, Newton
Stewart, Wigtownshire,
DG8 6JB
Tel: 01671 402157
★★★ Guest House

Crown Hotel
101 Queen Street, Newton
Stewart, Wigtownshire,
DG8 6EF
Tel: 01671 402727
Awaiting Inspection

Kirroughtree House
Newton Stewart,
Wigtownshire, DG8 6AN
Tel: 01671 402141
★★★★ Small Hotel

The Bruce Hotel
88 Queen Street,
Newton Stewart,
Wigtownshire, DG8 6JL
Tel: 01671 402294
★★★ Small Hotel

PEEBLES

Peebles Hotel Hydro
Innerleithen Road, Peebles,
Peebles-shire, EH45 8LX
Tel: 01721 720602
★★★★ Hotel

Cardrona Hotel Golf & Country Club
Cardrona, Near Peebles,
Peebles-shire, EH45 6LZ
Tel: 01896 831144
★★★★ Hotel

Tontine Hotel
High Street, Peebles,
Peeblesshire, EH45 8AJ
Tel: 01721 720892
★★★ Hotel

Park Hotel
Innerleithen Road, Peebles,
EH45 8BA
Tel: 01721 720451
★★★ Hotel

Castle Venlaw Hotel
Edinburgh Road, Peebles,
Peeblesshire, EH45 8QG
Tel: 01721 720384
★★★★ Small Hotel

BY PEEBLES
Glentress Hotel
Innerleithen Road,
Peebles, Peebles-shire,
EH45 8NB
Tel: 01721 720100
★★ Small Hotel

Cringletie House Hotel
Edinburgh Road, Peebles,
Peeblesshire, EH45 8PL
Tel: 01721 725750
★★★★ Small Hotel

PORTPATRICK
The Knowe
1 North Crescent,
Portpatrick,
Wigtownshire, DG9 8SX
Tel: 01776 810441
★★★ Guest House

Dunskey Guest House
Heugh Road, Portpatrick,
Wigtownshire, DG9 8TD
Tel: 01776 810241
★★ Guest House

Torrs Warren Hotel
Stoneykirk,
Stranraer, Dumfries &
Galloway, DG9 9DH
Tel: 1776830204
★★★ Small Hotel

Fernhill Hotel
Heugh Road, Portpatrick,
Wigtownshire, DG9 8TD
Tel: 01776 810220
★★★★ Hotel

Rickwood House Hotel
Heugh Road, Portpatrick,
Wigtownshire, DG9 8TD
Tel: 01776 810270
★★★ Guest House

Knockinaam Lodge
Portpatrick, Wigtownshire,
DG9 9AD
Tel: 01776 810471
★★★★ Small Hotel

Braefield Guest House
Braefield Road,
Portpatrick, Wigtownshire,
DG9 8TA
Tel: 01776 810255
★★ Guest House

Portpatrick Hotel
Heugh Road, Portpatrick,
Wigtownshire, DG9 8TQ
Tel: 01776 810333
★★★ Hotel

The Waterfront Hotel & Bistro
North Crescent,
Portpatrick, DG9 8SX
Tel: 01776 810800
★★★ Small Hotel

POWFOOT, BY ANNAN
Powfoot Golf Hotel
Links Avenue, Powfoot,
Dumfriesshire, DG12 5PN
Tel: 01461 700254
★★ Small Hotel

PRESTWICK
North Beach Hotel
5-7 Link's Road,
Prestwick, Ayrshire,
KA9 1QG
Tel: 01292 479069
★★★ Small Hotel

Fernbank Guest House
213 Main Street, Prestwick,
Ayrshire, KA9 1LH
Tel: 01292 475027
★★★ Guest House

Prestwick Old Course Hotel
13 Links Road, Prestwick,
Ayrshire, KA9 1QG
Tel: 01292 477446
★★★ Small Hotel

Kincraig Private Hotel
39 Ayr Road, Prestwick,
Ayrshire, KA9 1SY
Tel: 01292 479480
★★★ Guest House

Parkstone Hotel
Central Esplanade,
Prestwick, Ayrshire, KA9
1QN
Tel: 01292 477286
★★★ Hotel

Golf View
17 Links Road,
Prestwick, Ayrshire,
KA9 1QG
Tel: 01292 671234
★★★★ Guest House

ROCKCLIFFE, BY DALBEATTIE
Baron's Craig Hotel
Rockcliffe, by Dalbeattie,
Kirkcudbrightshire,
DG5 4QF
Tel: 01556 630225
★★ Hotel

ST ABBS
Castle Rock
Murrayfield, St Abbs,
Berwickshire, TD14 5PP
Tel: 01890 771715
★★★ Guest House

ST BOSWELLS
Buccleuch Arms Hotel
The Green, St Boswells,
Roxburghshire, TD6 0EW
Tel: 01835 822243
★★★ Small Hotel

SANDYHILLS, BY DALBEATTIE
Craigbittern House
Sandyhills, Dalbeattie,
Kirkcudbrightshire,
DG5 4NZ
Tel: 0138778 247
★★★★ Guest House

SANQUHAR
Blackaddie House Hotel
Blackaddie Road,
Sanquhar, Dumfriesshire,
DG4 6JJ
Tel: 01659 50270
★★★ Small Hotel

SEAMILL
Seamill Hydro
39 Ardrossan Road,
Seamill, Ayrshire,
KA23 9NB
Tel: 01294 822217
★★★ Hotel

SELKIRK
Philipburn Country House Hotel and Restaurant
Selkirk, Selkirkshire,
TD7 5LS
Tel: 01750 20747
★★★★ Small Hotel

The County Hotel
Market Square,
3-5 High Street, Selkirk,
TD7 4BZ
Tel: 01750 721233
★★★ Small Hotel

The Glen Hotel
Yarrow Terrace, Selkirk,
Selkirkshire, TD7 5AS
Tel: 01750 20259
★★★ Small Hotel

Heatherlie House Hotel
Heatherlie Park, Selkirk,
Selkirkshire, TD7 5AL
Tel: 01750 721200
★★★ Small Hotel

Tower Street Guest House
29 Tower Street, Selkirk,
Scottsh Borders,
TD7 4LR
Tel: 01750 23222
★★★ Guest House

The Coach House
51 Ettrick Terrace, Selkirk,
TD7 4JS
Tel: 01750 20696
Awaiting Inspection

SKIRLING, BY BIGGAR
Skirling House
Skirling, by Biggar,
Lanarkshire, ML12 6HD
★★★★★ Guest House

STRANRAER
Harbour Lights Guest House
7 Agnew Crescent,
Stranraer, Wigtownshire,
DG9 7JY
Tel: 01776 706261
★★★ Guest House

Neptunes Rest Guest House
25 Agnew Crescent,
Stranraer, Wigtownshire,
DG9
Tel: 01776 704729
★★ Guest House

George Hotel
49 George Street,
Stranraer, Wigtownshire,
DG9 7RJ
Tel: 01776 702487
Awaiting Inspection

North West Castle Hotel
Stranraer, Wigtownshire,
DG9 8EH
Tel: 01776 704413
★★★★ Hotel

Hartforth Guest House
33 London Road,
Stranraer, Wigtownshire,
DG9 8AF
Tel: 01776 704832
★★ Guest House

Harbour Guest House
11 Market Street,
Stranraer, Wigtownshire,
DG9 7RF
Tel: 01776 704626
★★★ Guest House

NR STRANRAER
Corsewall Lighthouse Hotel
Kirkcolm, by Stranraer,
Wigtownshire,
DG9 0QG
Tel: 01776 853220
★★★★ Small Hotel

SWINTON
The Wheatsheaf
Swinton, Berwickshire,
TD11 3JJ
Tel: 01890 860257
★★★★
Restaurant with Rooms

TEVIOTHEAD, BY HAWICK
17 Woodriffe
Newburgh, Fife,
KY14 6DJ
Tel: 0131 331 3089
Awaiting Inspection

THORNHILL
Gillbank House
8 East Morton Street,
Thornhill, Dumfriesshire,
DG3 5LZ
Tel: 01848 330597
★★★★ Guest House

The Thornhill Inn
103-106 Drumlanrig Street,
Thornhill, Dumfriesshire,
DG3 5LU
Tel: 01848 330326
★★★ Small Hotel

Buccleuch & Queensferry Hotel
112 Drumlanrig Street,
Thornhill, Dumfriesshire,
DG3 5LU
Tel: 01848 330215
★★★ Small Hotel

BY THORNHILL
Trigony House Hotel
Closeburn, Thornhill,
Dumfriesshire, DG3 5EZ
Tel: 01848 331211
★★★★ Small Hotel

**TORTHORWALD,
BY DUMFRIES**
**The Manor Country
House Hotel**
Lockerbie Road,
Torthorwald,
Dumfries & Galloway,
DG1 3PT
Tel: 01387 750555
★★ Small Hotel

TROON
Marine Hotel
Crosbie Road, Troon,
Ayrshire, KA10 6HE
Tel: 01292 314444
★★★★ Hotel

Ardneil Hotel
St Meddans Street,
Troon, Ayrshire, KA10 6NU
Tel: 01292 311611
★★ Small Hotel

Lochgreen House
Monktonhill Road, Troon,
Ayrshire, KA10 7EN
Tel: 01292 313343
★★★★★ Hotel

Piersland House Hotel
Craigend Road, Troon,
Ayrshire, KA10 6HD
Tel: 01292 314747
★★★★ Hotel

South Beach Hotel
South Beach, Troon,
Ayrshire, KA10 6EG
Tel: 01292 312033
★★★ Hotel

TURNBERRY
Malin Court
Turnberry, Ayrshire,
KA26 9PB
Tel: 01655 331457
★★★ Hotel

The Westin Turnberry Resort
Turnberry, Ayrshire,
KA26 9LT
Tel: 01655 331000
★★★★★
International Resort

WALKERBURN
The George Hotel
29 Galashiels Road,
Walkerburn,
Peebleshire,
EH43 6AF
Tel: 01896 870336
★★ Small Hotel

WIGTOWN
Hillcrest House
Maidland Place, Station
Road, Wigtown,
Wigtownshire,
DG8 9EU
Tel: 01988 402018
★★★ Guest House

Fordbank Country House Hotel
Potato Mill Road,
Bladnoch,
Dumfries & Galloway,
DG8 9BT
Tel: 01988 402346
★★★ Small Hotel

EDINBURGH AND LOTHIANS

BATHGATE
The Cairn Hotel
Blackburn Road,
Bathgate, West Lothian,
EH48 2EL
Tel: 01506 633366
★★ Hotel

BONNYRIGG
The Retreat Castle
Cockpen Road, Bonnyrigg,
Midlothian, EH19 3HS
Tel: 0131 6603200
★★ Small Hotel

BROXBURN
Bankhead Farm
Dechmont, Broxburn,
West Lothian, EH52 6NB
Tel: 01506 811209
★★★★ Guest House

DALKEITH
The County Hotel
152 High Street, Dalkeith,
Midlothian, EH22
Tel: 0131 663 3495
★★★ Hotel

Glenarch House
Melville Road, Eskbank,
Dalkeith, EH22 3NJ
Tel: 0131 6631478
★★★ Guest House

The Guest House @ Eskbank
45 Eskbank Road,
Rathaonn House,
Midlothian, EH22 3BH
Tel: 0131 663 3291
★★★★ Guest House

DIRLETON
Open Arms Hotel
Dirleton, East Lothian,
EH39 5EG
Tel: 01620 850241
★★★★ Small Hotel

DUNBAR
Broxmouth Park
Dunbar, East Lothian,
EH2 1QW
Tel: 01313 371180
Awaiting Inspection

Barns Ness Hotel
Station Road, Dunbar,
East Lothian, EH42 1JY
Tel: 01386 863231
★★★ Small Hotel

The Rossborough Hotel
Queens Road, Dunbar,
East Lothian, EH42 1LG
Tel: 01368 862356
★★ Small Hotel

Springfield Guest House
Belhaven Road, Dunbar,
East Lothian, EH42 1NH
Tel: 01368 862502

★★ Guest House

EDINBURGH

Aaron Guest House
16 Hartington Gardens,
Edinburgh, EH10 4LD
Tel: 0131 229 6459

★★★ Guest House

Aaron Lodge Guest House
128 Old Dalkeith Road,
Edinburgh, EH16 4SD
Tel: 0131 664 2755

★★★ Guest House

Regent House Hotel
3-5 Forth Street,
Edinburgh, EH1 3JX
Tel: 0131 556 1616
Awaiting Inspection

Adria House
11-12 Royal Terrace,
Edinburgh, EH7 5AB
Tel: 0131 556 7875

★★★ Guest House

Afton Guest House
1 Hartington Gardens,
Edinburgh, EH10 4LD
Tel: 0131 229 1019

★★★ Guest House

A Haven Townhouse
180 Ferry Road,
Edinburgh, EH6 4NS
Tel: 0131 554 6559

★★★ Small Hotel

Capital Guest House
7 Mayfield Road,
Newington, Edinburgh,
EH9 2NG
Tel: 0131 466 0717

★★★ Guest House

Merith House Hotel
2-3 Hermitage Place,
Leith Links, Edinburgh,
EH6 8AF
Tel: 0131 554 5045
Awaiting Inspection

Salisbury Green Hotel Conference Centre
University of Edinburgh,
Pollock Halls,
18 Holyrood Park Road,
Edinburgh, EH16 5AY

★★★ Hotel

Allison House
17 Mayfield Gardens,
Edinburgh, EH9 2AX
Tel: 0131 667 8049

★★★ Guest House

Alloway Guest House
96 Pilrig Street,
Edinburgh, EH6 5AY
Tel: 0131 554 1786

★★★ Guest House

Alness Guest House
27 Pilrig Street,
Edinburgh, EH6 5AN
Tel: 0131 554 1187

★★ Guest House

Murrayfield Park Hotel
89 Corstorphine Road,
Edinburgh, EH12 5QE
Tel: 0131 337 5370

★★★ Guest House

Apartments Royal
50/35 North Bridge,
Edinburgh, EH1 1QN
Tel: 0131 554 1301

★★★★★

Serviced Apartments

Apex International Hotel
31/35 Grassmarket,
Edinburgh, EH1 2HS
Tel: 0845 365 0000

★★★★ Hotel

Ardenlee Guest House
9 Eyre Place, Edinburgh,
EH3 5ES
Tel: 0131 556 2838

★★★ Guest House

Ardgarth Guest House
1 St Mary's Place,
Portobello, Edinburgh,
EH15 2QF
Tel: 0131 669 3021

★★★ Guest House

Ardleigh Guest House
260 Ferry Road,
Edinburgh, EH5 3AN
Tel: 0131 552 1833

★★★ Guest House

Ardmillan Hotel
9-10 Ardmillan Terrace,
Edinburgh, EH11 2JW
Tel: 0131 337 9588

★★ Small Hotel

Ashgrove House
12 Osborne Terrace,
Edinburgh, EH12 5HG
Tel: 0131 337 5014

★★★ Guest House

Ashlyn Guest House
42 Inverleith Row,
Edinburgh, EH3 5PY
Tel: 0131 552 2954

★★★★ Guest House

The Balmoral
1 Princes Street,
Edinburgh, EH2 2EQ
Tel: 0870 460 7040

★★★★★ Hotel

Strathallan Guest House
44 Minto Street,
Edinburgh, Lothian,
EH9 2BR
Tel: 0131 667 6678

★★★ Guest House

Mardale Guest House
11 Hartington Place,
Edinburgh, EH10 4LF
Tel: 0131 229 2693

★★★ Guest House

Barossa Guest House
21 Pilrig Street,
Edinburgh, EH6 5AN
Tel: 0131 554 3700

★★ Guest House

Royal Terrace Hotel
18 Royal Terrace,
Edinburgh, EH7 5AQ
Tel: 0131 557 3222

★★★★ Hotel

Belford Guest House
13 Blacket Avenue,
Edinburgh, EH9 1RR
Tel: 0131 667 2422

★★ Guest House

Beresford Hotel
32 Coates Gardens,
Edinburgh, EH12 5LE
Tel: 0131 337 0850

★★★ Guest House

Barony House
23 Mayfield Gardens,
Edinburgh, EH9 2BX
Tel: 0131 667 5806

★★★★ Guest House

Best Western Bruntsfield Hotel
69 Bruntsfield Place,
Edinburgh, EH10 4HH
Tel: 0131 229 1393

★★★★ Hotel

Best Western Kings Manor Hotel
100 Milton Road East,
Edinburgh, EH15 2NP
Tel: 0131 468 8003

★★★ Hotel

The Beverley
40 Murrayfield Avenue,
Edinburgh, EH12 6AY
Tel: 0131 337 1128

★★★★ Guest House

The Lairg
11 Coates Gardens,
Edinburgh, EH12 5LG
Tel: 0131 3371050

★★★ Guest House

Casa Buzzo Guest House
8 Kilmaurs Road,
Edinburgh, EH16 5DA
Tel: 0131 667 8998

★★★ Guest House

Aonach Mor Guesthouse
14 Kilmaurs Terrace,
Edinburgh, EH16 5DR
Tel: 0131 667 8694

★★★ Guest House

Caledonian Hilton Hotel
Princes Street, Edinburgh,
EH1 2AB
Tel: 0131 222 8888

★★★★★ Hotel

Fairholme
13 Moston Terrace,
Edinburgh, EH9 2DE
Tel: 0131 667 8645

★★★ Guest House

Brae Lodge Guest House
30 Liberton Brae,
Edinburgh, Lothian,
EH16 6AF
Tel: 0131 6722876

★★★ Guest House

Boisdale Hotel
9 Coates Gardens,
Edinburgh, EH12 5LG
Tel: 0131 337 1134

★★★ Guest House

The Bonham
35 Drumsheugh Gardens, Edinburgh, EH3 7RN
Tel: 0131 274 7400
★★★★ Hotel

Briggend Guest House
19 Old Dalkeith Road, Edinburgh, EH16 4TE
Tel: 0131 258 0810
★★★ Guest House

Abbey Lodge Hotel
137 Drum Street, Gilmerton, Edinburgh, EH17 8RJ
Tel: 0131 6649548
★★ Guest House

Tankard Guest House
40 East Claremont Street, Edinburgh, EH7 4JR
Tel: 0131 556 4218
★ Guest House

Edinburgh Capital Hotel
187 Clermiston Road, Edinburgh, EH12 6UG
Tel: 0131 535 9988
★★★ Hotel

St Conan's Guest House
30 Minto Street, Edinburgh, EH9 1SB
Tel: 0131 667 8393
★★★ Guest House

Links Hotel and Bar
4 Alvanley Terrace, Whitehouse Loan, Edinburgh, Lothian, EH9 1DU
Tel: 0131 622 6800
★★ Hotel

Ellersly House Hotel
Ellersly Road, Edinburgh, EH12 6HZ
Tel: 0131 337 6888
★★ Hotel

Murrayfield Hotel
18 Corstorphine Road, Edinburgh, EH12 6HN
Tel: 0131 337 1844
★ Hotel

Orwell Lodge Hotel
29 Polwarth Terrace, Edinburgh, EH11 1NH
Tel: 0131 229 1044
★★ Small Hotel

Appin House
4 Queens Crescent, Edinburgh, Midlothian, EH9 2AZ
Tel: 0131 668 2947
★★ Guest House

Caravel Guest House
30 London Street, Edinburgh, EH3 6NA
Tel: 0131 556 4444
★★ Guest House

Carrington Guest House
38 Pilrig Street, Edinburgh, EH6 5AL
Tel: 0131 554 4769
★★★ Guest House

The Inverleith Hotel
5 Inverleith Terrace, Edinburgh, EH3 5NS
Tel: 0131 556 2745
★★★ Small Hotel

Villa Nina Guest House
39 Leamington Terrace, Edinburgh, EH10 4JS
Tel: 0131 229 2644
★★ Guest House

The Royal Over-Seas League
100 Princes Street, Edinburgh, EH2 3AB
Tel: 0131 225 1501
★★★ Small Hotel

Channings
12-16 South Learmonth Gardens, Edinburgh, EH4 1EZ
Tel: 0131 274 7401
★★★★ Hotel

Judy Guest House
2 St Catherines Gardens, Edinburgh, EH12 7AZ
Tel: 0131 334 6159
★★ Guest House

Failte Guest House
117 Willowbrae Road, Edinburgh, EH8 7HN
Tel: 0131 661 3629
★★★ Guest House

Arden Guest House
126 Old Dalkeith Road, Edinburgh, Lothian, EH16 4SD
Tel: 0131 6643985
★★★ Guest House

Clan Campbell Hotel
11 Brunswick Street, Edinburgh, EH7 5JB
Tel: 0131 557 6910
★★★ Small Hotel

Clan Walker Guest House
96 Dalkeith Road, Edinburgh, EH16 5AF
Tel: 0131 667 1244
★★★ Guest House

Galloway Guest House
22 Dean Park Crescent, Edinburgh, EH4 1PH
Tel: 0131 332 3672
★★★ Guest House

The Broughton Hotel
37 Broughton Place, Edinburgh, Lothian, EH1 3RR
Tel: 0131 558 9792
★★★ Guest House

Amaragua Guest House
10 Kilmaurs Terrace, Edinburgh, Lothian, EH16 5DR
Tel: 0131 667 6775
★★★★ Guest House

Holiday Inn Edinburgh
Corstorphine Road, Edinburgh, EH12 6UA
Tel: 0870 400 9026
★★★★ Hotel

The Royal Scotsman
Edinburgh Waverley Station, Edinburgh
★★★★★ Train

Brodie's Guest House
22 East Claremont Street, Edinburgh, EH7 4JP
Tel: 0131 556 4032
★★★ Guest House

Cluaran House
47 Leamington Terrace, Edinburgh, EH10 4JS
Tel: 0131 2210047
★★★★ Guest House

Crioch Guest House
23 East Hermitage Place, Leith Links, Edinburgh, EH6 8AD
Tel: 0131 554 5494
★★★ Guest House

Mingalar
2 East Claremont Street, Edinburgh, Midlothian, EH7 4JP
Tel: 0131 556 7000
★★★ Guest House

Abbotsford Guest House
36 Pilrig Street, Edinburgh, EH6 5AL
Tel: 0131 554 2706
★★★ Guest House

Hanover House Hotel
26 Windsor Street, Edinburgh, EH7 5JR
Tel: 0131 556 1325
★★★ Guest House

Roxburghe Hotel
38 Charlotte Square, Edinburgh, EH2 4HG
Tel: 0131 2405500
★★★★ Hotel

Ashdene House
23 Fountainhall Road, Edinburgh, EH9 2LN
Tel: 0131 6676026
★★★★ Guest House

The Scotsman Hotel
20 North Bridge, Edinburgh, EH1 1YT
Tel: 0131 556 5565
★★★★★ Hotel

The Morningside Guest House
7 Hermitage Terrace,
Edinburgh, EH10 4RP
Tel: 0131 447 4089
★★★ Guest House

Dene Guest House
7 Eyre Place,
off Dundas Street,
Edinburgh, EH3 5ES
Tel: 0131 556 2700
★★★ Guest House

Castle View
30 Castle Street,
Edinburgh, Lothian,
EH2 3HT
Tel: 0131 226 5784
★★★★ Guest House

Braid Hills Hotel
134 Braid Road, Edinburgh,
EH10 6JD
Tel: 0131 447 8888
★★★ Hotel

The Quality Hotel Edinburgh Airport
Ingliston, by Edinburgh,
Midlothian, EH28 8AU
Tel: 0131 333 4331
★★★ Hotel

Gillis
100 Strathearn Road,
Edinburgh, EH9 1BB
Tel: 0131 623
Awaiting Inspection

Doocote House
15 Moat Street, Edinburgh,
EH14 1PE
Tel: 0131 443 5455
★★ Bed & Breakfast

Edinburgh Marriott
111 Glasgow Road,
Edinburgh, EH12 8NF
Tel: 0870 400 7293
★★★★ Hotel

Hotel Ibis Edinburgh
6 Hunter Square,
Edinburgh, EH1 1QW
Tel: 0131 240 7000
★★ Hotel

Four Twenty Guest House
420 Ferry Road, Edinburgh,
EH5 2AD
Tel: 0131 552 2167
★ Guest House

Parklands Guest House
20 Mayfield Gardens,
Edinburgh, EH9 2BZ
Tel: 0131 667 7184
★★★ Guest House

Dunstane House Hotel
4 West Coates, Haymarket,
Edinburgh, EH12 5JQ
Tel: 0131 337 6169
★★★★ Small Hotel

Duthus Lodge
5 West Coates, Edinburgh,
EH12 5JG
Tel: 0131 337 6876
★★★ Guest House

Edinburgh House
11 McDonald Road,
Edinburgh, EH7 4LX
Tel: 0131 556 3434
★★★ Guest House

The Edinburgh Residence
7 Rothesay Terrace,
Edinburgh, EH3 7RY
Tel: 0131 274 7403
★★★★★ Hotel

Garfield Guest House
264 Ferry Road, Edinburgh,
EH5 3AN
Tel: 0131 552 2369
★ Guest House

The Alexander Guest House
35 Mayfield Gardens,
Edinburgh, EH9 2BX
Tel: 0131 258 4028
★★★★ Guest House

Elas Guest House
10 Claremont Crescent,
Edinburgh, EH7 4HX
Tel: 0131 556 1929
★ Guest House

Ellesmere Guest House
11 Glengyle Terrace,
Edinburgh, EH3 9LN
Tel: 0131 229 4823
★★★★ Guest House

The Point Hotel
34 Bread Street,
Edinburgh, EH3 9AF
Tel: 0131 221 5555
★★★ Hotel

Gilmore Guest House
51 Gilmore Place,
Edinburgh, EH3 9NT
Tel: 0131 229 5008
★★ Guest House

Star Villa
36 Gilmore Place,
Edinburgh, EH3 9NQ
Tel: 0131 229 4991
★★★ Guest House

Falcon Crest Guest House
70 South Trinity Road,
Edinburgh, EH5 3NX,
1 Single
Tel: 0131 552 5294
★ Guest House

Bellerose Guest House
36 Minto Street,
Edinburgh, EH9 2BS
Tel: 0131 667 8933
★★ Guest House

Thistle Hotel
59 Manor Place,
Edinburgh, EH3 7EG
Tel: 0131 225 6144
★★ Small Hotel

Northumberland Hotel
31-33 Craigmillar Park,
Edinburgh, EH16 5PE
Tel: 0131 668 3131
★★★ Small Hotel

Airlie Guest House
29 Minto Street,
Edinburgh, EH9 1SB
Tel: 0131 667 3562
★★★ Guest House

The Corstorphine Lodge
188 St Johns Road,
Edinburgh, Lothians,
EH12 8SG
Tel: 0131 5394237
★★★ Guest House

Cumberland Hotel
1 West Coates, Edinburgh,
EH12 5JQ
Tel: 0131 337 1198
★★★ Small Hotel

Corstorphine Lodge Hotel
186 St Johns Road,
Edinburgh, Lothian,
EH12 8SG
Tel: 0131 476 7116
★★★ Guest House

Glenalmond Guest House
25 Mayfield Gardens,
Edinburgh, EH9 2BX
Tel: 0131 668 2392
★★★ Guest House

Novotel Edinburgh Centre
80 Lauriston Place,
Edinburgh, Lothian,
EH3 9DE
Tel: 0131 656 3500
★★★★ Hotel

Frederick House Hotel
42 Frederick Street,
Edinburgh, EH2 1EX
Tel: 0131 226 1999
★★★ Lodge

Southside
8 Newington Road,
Edinburgh, EH9 1QS
★★★★ Guest House

A'Abide'an'Abode
18 Moat Place, Edinburgh,
EH14 1PP
Tel: 0131 443 5668
★★★ Guest House

Greens Hotel
24 Eglinton Crescent,
Edinburgh, EH12 5BY
Tel: 0131 337 1565
★★★ Hotel

Thistle Court Hotel
5 Hampton Terrace,
Edinburgh, Lothian,
EH12 5JD
Tel: 0131 313 5500
Small Hotel

San Marco
24 Mayfield Gardens,
Edinburgh, EH9 2BZ
Tel: 0131 667 8982
★★★ Guest House

Shalimar Guest House
20 Newington Road,
Edinburgh, EH9 1QS
Tel: 0131 6672827/0789
★★ Guest House

Cruachan Guest House
53 Gilmore Place,
Edinburgh, Midlothian,
EH3 9NT
Tel: 0131 229 6219
★★★ Guest House

Directory of all VisitScotland Quality Assured Serviced Hotels and Guest Houses

Gifford House
103 Dalkeith Road,
Edinburgh, EH16 5AJ
Tel: 0131 667 4688
★★★★ Guest House

Gildun Guest House
9 Spence Street,
Edinburgh, EH16 5AG
Tel: 0131 667 1368
★★★★ Guest House

Davenport House
58 Great King Street,
Edinburgh, Lothian,
EH3 6QY
Tel: 0131 558 8495
★★★★ Guest House

Edinburgh Brunswick Hotel
7 Brunswick Street,
Edinburgh, EH7 5JB
Tel: 0131 556 1238
★★ Guest House

Glenora Hotel
14 Rosebery Crescent,
Edinburgh, EH12 5JY
Tel: 0131 337 1186
★★★★ Small Hotel

One Royal Circus
1 Royal Circus, Edinburgh,
EH3 6TL
Tel: 0131 225 5854
★★★★★★
Exclusive Use Venue

Edinburgh Agenda Hotel
92 St John's Road,
Edinburgh, EH12 8AT
Tel: 0131 316 4466
★★★ Hotel

Greenside Hotel
9 Royal Terrace, Edinburgh,
EH7 5AB
Tel: 0131 557 0121
★★★ Small Hotel

Aynetree Guest House
12 Duddingston Crescent,
Milton Road, Edinburgh,
EH15 3AS
Tel: 0131 258 2821
★★★ Guest House

Sherwood Guest House
42 Minto Street,
Edinburgh, EH9 2BR
Tel: 0131 667 1200
★★★ Guest House

Grosvenor Gardens Hotel
1 Grosvenor Gardens,
Edinburgh, EH12 5JU
Tel: 0131 313 3415 ·
★★★ Guest House

Ben Craig House
3 Craigmillar Park,
Edinburgh, EH16 5PG
Tel: 0131 667 2593
★★★ Guest House

Tigerlily
125 George Street,
Edinburgh, EH7 4GG
★★★★ Hotel

Apex European Hotel
90 Haymarket Terrace,
Edinburgh, EH12 5LQ
Tel: 0131 474 3456
★★★★ Hotel

The Royal Scots Club
30 Abercromby Place,
Edinburgh, Lothian,
EH3 6QE
Tel: 0131 556 4270
★★★ Hotel

Borough
72-80 Causewayside,
Edinburgh, EH9 1PY
Tel: 0131 668 2255
★★★ Small Hotel

Hilton Edinburgh Grosvenor
7-21 Grosvenor Street,
Edinburgh, EH12 5EF
Tel: 0131 226 6001
★★★ Hotel

Swanlake Guest House
106 Ferry Road, Edinburgh,
EH6 4PG
Tel: 0131 5544578
★★ Guest House

Morita
3 Mayfield Gardens,
Edinburgh, Lothian,
EH9 2AX
Tel: 0131 667 1337
Awaiting Inspection

Fraoch House
66 Pilrig Street, Edinburgh,
Midlothian, EH6 5AS
Tel: 0131 554 1353
★★★ Guest House

Ayden Guest House
70 Pilrig Street, Edinburgh,
EH6 5AS
Tel: 0131 554 2187
★★★★ Guest House

The Howard
34 Great King Street,
Edinburgh, EH3 6QH
Tel: 0131 274 7402
★★★★★ Small Hotel

Kingsburgh House
2 Corstorphine Road,
Edinburgh, Midlothian,
EH12 6HN
Tel: 0131 313 1679
★★★★★ Guest House

Heatherlea Guest House
13 Mayfield Gardens,
Edinburgh, EH9 2AX
Tel: 0131 667 3958
★ Guest House

Classic Guest House
50 Mayfield Road,
Edinburgh, EH9 2NH
Tel: 0131 6675847
★★★ Guest House

Ivy Guest House
7 Mayfield Gardens,
Edinburgh, EH9 2AX
Tel: 0131 667 3411
★★★ Guest House

Ardmor House
74 Pilrig Street, Edinburgh,
Lothians, EH6 5AS
Tel: 0131 554 4944
★★★★ Guest House

Ravensdown Guest House
248 Ferry Road, Edinburgh,
Midlothian, EH5 3AN
Tel: 0131 552 5438
★★★ Guest House

Thrums Hotel
14-15 Minto Street,
Edinburgh, EH9 1RQ
Tel: 0131 667 5545
★★ Guest House

Gladstone Guest House
90 Dalkeith Road,
Edinburgh, EH16 5AF
Tel: 0131 6674708
★★★ Guest House

Lindsay Guest House
108 Polwarth Terrace,
Edinburgh, Midlothian,
EH11 1NN
Tel: 0131 337 1580
★★★ Guest House

Jurys Inn Edinburgh
43 Jeffrey Street,
Edinburgh, Lothian,
EH1 1DH
Tel: 0131 200 3300
★★★ Hotel

Kaimes Guest House
12 Granville Terrace,
Edinburgh, EH10 4PQ
Tel: 0131 4782779
★★ Guest House

Kariba Guest House
10 Granville Terrace,
Edinburgh, EH10 4PQ
Tel: 0131 229 3773
★★★ Guest House

Kelly's Guest House
3 Hillhouse Road,
Edinburgh, Lothian,
EH4 3QP
Tel: 0131 3323894
★★★ Guest House

Carlton Hotel
North Bridge, Edinburgh,
EH1 1SD
Tel: 0131 472 3001
★★★★ Hotel

Beechcroft House
46 Murrayfield Avenue,
Edinburgh, Lothian,
EH12 6AY
Tel: 0131 337 4009
★★★★ Guest House

Kenvie Guest House
16 Kilmaurs Road,
Edinburgh, EH16 5DA
Tel: 0131 668 1964
★★★ Guest House

Kew House
1 Kew Terrace, Murrayfield,
Edinburgh, EH12 5JE
Tel: 0131 313 0700
★★★★ Small Hotel

Kirklea Guest House
11 Harrison Road,
Edinburgh, EH11 1EG
Tel: 0131 337 1129
★★★ Guest House

Duke's of Windsor Street
17 Windsor Street, c,
EH7 5LA
Tel: 0131 556 6046
★★★ Small Hotel

Directory of all VisitScotland Quality Assured Serviced Hotels and Guest Houses

Kingsview Guest House
28 Gilmore Place,
Edinburgh, EH3 9NQ
Tel: 0131 229 8004
★★ Guest House

Brig O'Doon Guest House
262 Ferry Road, Edinburgh,
EH5 3AN
Tel: 0131 552 3953
★★★ Guest House

Old Waverley Hotel
43 Princes Street,
Edinburgh, EH2 2BY
Tel: 0131 556 4648
★★★ Hotel

Mayfield Lodge
75 Mayfield Road,
Edinburgh, EH9 3AA
Tel: 0131 6628899
★★★ Guest House

Christopher North House Hotel
6 Gloucester Place,
Edinburgh, EH3 6EF
Tel: 0131 225 2720
★★★ Small Hotel

Ben Doran
11 Mayfield Gardens,
Edinburgh, Lothian,
EH9 2AX
Tel: 0131 667 8488
★★★★ Guest House

Roselea Guest House
4 Kew Terrace, Edinburgh,
EH12 5JE
Tel: 0131 467 4166
★★★ Guest House

Express By Holiday Inn
Britannia Way, Ocean Drive,
Edinburgh, Lothian,
EH6 6LA
Tel: 0131 555 4422
★★★ Hotel

Lochend Serviced Apartments
147/1 Lochend Road,
Edinburgh, EH7 6ET
Tel: 0131 561 4000
Boat

Buchan & Haymarket Hotel
1-3 Coates Gardens,
Edinburgh, Lothian,
EH12 5LG
Tel: 0131 337 1045
★★★ Small Hotel

Ecosse International
15 MacDonald Road,
Edinburgh, EH7 4LX
Tel: 0131 556 4967
★★★ Guest House

Ard-Na-Said
5 Priestfield Road,
Edinburgh, Lothian,
EH16 5HH
Tel: 0131 667 8754
★★★★ Guest House

Kingsway Guest House
5 East Mayfield, Edinburgh,
EH9 1SD
Tel: 0131 667 5029
★★★ Guest House

McDonald Guest House
5 McDonald Road,
Edinburgh, EH7 4LX
Tel: 0131 557 5935
★★★ Guest House

Herald House Hotel
70/72 Grove Street,
Edinburgh, EH3 8AP
Tel: 0131 228 2323
★★ Hotel

The Turret Guest House
8 Kilmaurs Terrace,
Edinburgh, EH16 5DR
Tel: 0131 667 6704
★★★★ Guest House

Clarendon Hotel
25-33 Shandwick Place,
Edinburgh, EH2 4RG
Tel: 0131 229 1467
★★★ Hotel

Terrace Hotel
37 Royal Terrace,
Edinburgh, EH7 5AH
Tel: 0131 556 3423
★★ Guest House

Lauderville House
52 Mayfield Road,
Edinburgh, EH9 2NH
Tel: 0131 667 7788
★★★★ Guest House

Claymore Guest House
68 Pilrig Street, Edinburgh,
EH6 5AS
Tel: 0131 554 2500
★★ Guest House

Staven Guest House
3 Brunstane Road North,
Edinburgh, EH15 2DL
Tel: 0131 669 5580
★★★ Guest House

Fountainhall Guest House
40 Fountainhall Road,
Edinburgh, EH9 2LW
Tel: 0131 667 2544
★ Guest House

Abercorn Guest House
1 Abercorn Terrace,
Edinburgh, East Lothian,
EH15 2DD
Tel: 0131 6696139
★★★★ Guest House

Auld Reekie Guest House
16 Mayfield Gardens,
Edinburgh, EH9 2BZ
Tel: 0131 667 6177
★★★ Guest House

Garlands Guest House
48 Pilrig Street, Edinburgh,
EH6 5AL
Tel: 0131 5544205
★★★ Guest House

Albany Hotel
39/43 Albany Street,
Edinburgh, EH1 3QY
Tel: 0131 556 0397
★★★★ Hotel

Learmonth Hotel
18-20 Learmonth Terrace,
Edinburgh, EH4 1PW
Tel: 0131 343 2671
★ Hotel

Halcyon Hotel
8 Royal Terrace,
Edinburgh, EH7 5AB
Tel: 0131 556 1033
★ Guest House

Melvin House Hotel
3 Rothesay Terrace,
Edinburgh, EH3 7RY
Tel: 0131 225 5084
★★★ Hotel

Kilmaurs House
9 Kilmaurs Road,
Edinburgh, EH16 5DA
Tel: 0131 667 8315
★★★ Guest House

Hampton Hotel
14 Corstorphine Road,
Edinburgh, EH12 6HN
Tel: 0131 337 1130
★★★ Small Hotel

Dean Hotel
10 Clarendon Crescent,
Edinburgh, EH4 1PT
Tel: 0131 332 0308
★ Small Hotel

Airdenair Guest House
29 Kilmaurs Road,
Edinburgh, EH16 5DB
Tel: 0131 668 2336
★★★ Guest House

Ardgowan House
1 Lady Road, Edinburgh,
EH16 5PA
Tel: 0131 667 7774
★★ Guest House

**Best Western
Edinburgh City Hotel**
79 Lauriston Place,
Edinburgh, EH3 9HZ
Tel: 0131 622 7979
★★★★ Hotel

Amaryllis Guest House
21 Upper Gilmore PLace,
Edinburgh, EH3 9NL
Tel: 0131 2293293
★★ Guest House

Melville Guest House
2 Duddingston Crescent,
Edinburgh, Lothian,
EH15 3AS
Tel: 0131 669 7856
★★★ Guest House

Menzies Belford Hotel
69 Belford Road,
Edinburgh, EH4 3DG
Tel: 0131 332 2545
★★★★ Hotel

Menzies Guest House
33 Leamington Terrace,
Edinburgh, EH10 4JS
Tel: 0131 229 4629

★★ Guest House

Holyrood Hotel
Holyrood Road, Edinburgh,
EH8 6AE
Tel: 0131 550 4500

★★★★ Hotel

Botanic House Hotel
27 Inverleith Row,
Edinburgh, Lothians,
EH3 5QH
Tel: 0131 5522563

★★★ Small Hotel

Royal British Hotel
20 Princes Street,
Edinburgh, EH2 2AN
Tel: 0131 556 4901

★★★ Hotel

Brothaigh House
18 Craigmillar Park,
Edinburgh, EH16 5PS
Tel: 0131 667 2202

★★★ Guest House

Valentine Guest House
19 Gilmore Place,
Tollcross, Edinburgh,
EH3 9NE
Tel: 0131 229 5622

★★ Guest House

Braveheart Guest House
26 Gilmore Place,
Edinburgh, EH3 9NQ
Tel: 0131 221 9192

★ Guest House

Sheraton Grand Hotel & Spa, Edinburgh
1 Festival Square,
Edinburgh, EH3 9SR
Tel: 0131 229 9131

★★★★★ Hotel

Balmore House
34 Gilmore Place,
Edinburgh, Lothian,
EH3 9NQ
Tel: 0131 2211331

★★★★ Guest House

Emerald House
3 Drum Street, Edinburgh,
Lothian, EH17 8GG
Tel: 0131 664 5918

★★ Guest House

The Armadillo Guest House
12 Gilmore Place,
Edinburgh, EH3 9NQ
Tel: 0131 229 6457

★★★ Guest House

Robertson Guest House
5 Hartington Gardens,
Edinburgh, EH10 4LD
Tel: 0131 229 2652

★★★ Guest House

Craigelachie Hotel
21 Murrayfield Avenue,
Edinburgh, EH12 6AU
Tel: 0131 337 4076

★★★★ Guest House

Granville Guest House
13 Granville Terrace,
Edinburgh, EH10 4PQ
Tel: 0131 229 1676

★★ Guest House

Ballarat Guest House
14 Gilmore Place,
Edinburgh, EH3 9NQ
Tel: 0131 2289413

★ Guest House

Parliament House Hotel
15 Calton Hill, Edinburgh,
EH1 3BJ
Tel: 0131 478 4000

★★★ Hotel

Cherry Tree Villa
9 East Mayfield, Edinburgh,
Midlothian, EH9 1SD
Tel: 0131 258 0009

★★★ Guest House

Malmaison Hotel et Brasserie
1 Tower Place, Leith,
Edinburgh, EH6 7DB
Tel: 0131 4685000

★★★★ Hotel

The Glasshouse
2 Greenside Place,
Edinburgh, EH1 3AA
Tel: 0131 5258200

★★★★★ Hotel

Acer Lodge Guest house
425 Queensferry Road,
Edinburgh, Midlothian,
EH4 7NB
Tel: 0131 3362554

★★★★ Guest House

Priestville Guest House
10 Priestfield Road,
Edinburgh, EH16 5HJ
Tel: 0131 667 2435

★★★ Guest House

Radisson SAS Hotel, Edinburgh
80 High Street, The Royal
Mile, Edinburgh, EH1 1TH
Tel: 0131 473 6590

★★★★ Hotel

The Lodge Hotel
6 Hampton Terrace,
Edinburgh, EH12 5JD
Tel: 0131 3373682

★★★★ Small Hotel

Kingsley Guest House
30 Craigmillar Park,
Edinburgh, EH16 5PS
Tel: 0131 667 3177

★★★ Guest House

Ritz Hotel
14-18 Grosvenor Street,
Edinburgh, EH12 5EG
Tel: 0131 337 4315

★★ Hotel

Robb's Guest House
5 Granville Terrace,
Edinburgh, EH10 4PQ
Tel: 0131 229 2086

★★ Guest House

The Laurels
320 Gilmerton Road,
Edinburgh, Midlothian,
EH17 7PR
Tel: 0131 666 2229

★★★ Guest House

Sonas Guest House
3 East Mayfield,
Edinburgh, EH9 1SD
Tel: 0131 667 2781

★★★ Guest House

Thistle House
1 Kilmaurs Terrace,
Edinburgh, EH16 5BZ
Tel: 0131 667 2002

★★ Guest House

Rosehall Hotel
101 Dalkeith Road,
Newington, Edinburgh,
EH16 5AJ
Tel: 0131 667 9372

★★★ Small Hotel

Apex City
61 Grassmarket,
Edinburgh, EH1 2JF
Tel: 0131 300 3456

★★★★ Hotel

Harvest Guest House
33, Straiton Place,
Edinburgh, EH15 2BA
Tel: 0131 657 3160

★ Guest House

The St Valery
36 Coates Gardens,
Edinburgh, EH12 5LE
Tel: 0131 337 1893

★★★ Guest House

Sakura House
18 West Preston Street,
Edinburgh, EH8 9PU
Tel: 0131 668 1204

★ Guest House

Elder York Guest House
38 Elder Street,
Edinburgh, EH1 3DX
Tel: 0131 556 1926

★★★ Guest House

Sandaig Guest House
5 East Hermitage Place,
Leith Links, Edinburgh,
EH6 8AA
Tel: 0131 554 7357

★★★★ Guest House

Sandilands House
25 Queensferry Road,
Edinburgh, EH4 3HB
Tel: 0131 332 2057

★★★ Guest House

Rosevale House
15 Kilmaurs Road,
Edinburgh, EH16 5DA
Tel: 0131 667 4781

★★ Guest House

Melville Castle Hotel
Melville Gate,
Gilmerton Road,
Midlothian,
EH18 1AP
Tel: 0131 6540088
★★★★ Hotel

Abbottshead House
40 Minto Street,
Edinburgh, EH9 2BR
Tel: 0131 668 1658
Awaiting Inspection

Mayville Guest House
5 Minto Street,
Edinburgh, EH9 1RG
Tel: 0131 667 6103
★★★ Guest House

**Ballantrae Hotel
At The West End**
6 Grosvenor Crescent,
Edinburgh, Midlothian,
EH12 5EP
Tel: 0131 225 7033
★★★ Small Hotel

Ballantrae Hotel
8 York Place, Edinburgh,
EH1 3EP
Tel: 0131 478 4748
★★★ Small Hotel

Sheridan Guest House
1 Bonnington Terrace,
Edinburgh, EH6 4BP
Tel: 0131 554 4107
★★★ Guest House

Le Monde Hotel
16 George Street,
Edinburgh, EH3 6EE
Tel: 0131 270 3900
★★★★ Hotel

Relax Guest House
11 Eyre Place, Edinburgh,
Scotland, EH3 5ES
Tel: 0131 5561433
★★ Guest House

Smith's Guest House
77 Mayfield Road,
Edinburgh, EH9 3AA
Tel: 0131 667 2524
★★★ Guest House

Hilton Edinburgh Airport
Edinburgh International
Airport, Edinburgh,
EH28 8LL
Tel: 0131 519 4400
★★★★ Hotel

Joppa Turrets Guest House
1 Lower Joppa(at Beech
end of Morton St),
Edinburgh, EH15 2ER
Tel: 0131 669 5806
★★★ Guest House

St Bernards Guest House
22 St Bernards Crescent,
Edinburgh, EH4 1NS
Tel: 0131 332 2339
★★ Guest House

Merlin Guest House
14 Hartington Place,
Edinburgh, EH10 4LE
Tel: 0131 229 3864
★★ Guest House

Osbourne Hotel
51-59 York Place,
Edinburgh, EH1 3JD
Tel: 0131 556 5577
★ Hotel

Dorstan House
7 Priestfield Road,
Edinburgh, EH16 5HJ
Tel: 0131 667 6721
★★★ Guest House

Richmond House Hotel
20 Leopold Place,
Edinburgh, EH7 5LB
Tel: 0131 556 3556
★★ Small Hotel

Mackenzie Guest House
2 East Hermitage Place,
Edinburgh, EH6 8AA
Tel: 0131 554 3763
★★★★ Guest House

Tania Guest House
19 Minto Street,
Edinburgh, EH9 1RQ
Tel: 0131 667 4144
★ Guest House

Craigmoss Guest House
62 Pilrig Street,
Edinburgh, EH6 4HS
Tel: 0131 554 3885
★★★ Guest House

Express By Holiday Inn
16-22 Picardy Place,
Edinburgh, Lothian,
EH1 3JT
Tel: 0131 5582300
★★★ Hotel

Arrandale Guest House
28 Mayfield Gardens,
Edinburgh, Lothian,
EH9 2BZ
Tel: 0131 622 2232
★★★ Guest House

Ten Hill Place Hotel
10 Hill Place, Edinburgh,
EH8 9DS
Tel: 0131 668 9243
AWAIT INSPECTION

Teviotdale House
53 Grange Loan,
Edinburgh, EH9 2ER
Tel: 0131 667 4376
★★★★ Guest House

Thistle Edinburgh
107 Leith Street,
Edinburgh, EH1 3SW
Tel: 0870 3339153
★★★★ Hotel

Heriott Park Guest House
254/256 Ferry Road,
Edinburgh, EH5 3AN
Tel: 0131 552 3456
★★★ Guest House

Prestonfield
Priestfield Road,
Edinburgh, Lothian,
EH16 5UT
Tel: 0131 668 3346
★★★★★ Hotel

Aaran Lodge Guest House
30 Milton Road East,
Edinburgh, Midlothian,
EH15 2NW
Tel: 0131 657 5615
★★★★ Guest House

The Town House
65 Gilmore Place,
Edinburgh, EH3 9NU
Tel: 0131 229 1985
★★★★ Guest House

Six Marys Place Guest House
Raeburn Place,
Stockbridge,
Edinburgh, EH4 1JH
Tel: 0131 332 8965
★★★ Guest House

Kildonan Lodge Hotel
27 Craigmillar Park,
Edinburgh, EH16 5PE
Tel: 0131 667 2793
★★★★ Small Hotel

Piries Hotel
4-8 Coates Gardens,
Edinburgh, EH12 5LB
Tel: 0131 337 1108
★★★ Hotel

Rowan Guest House
13 Glenorchy Terrace,
Edinburgh, EH9 2DQ
Tel: 0131 667 2463
★★★ Guest House

Ardblair Guest House
1 Duddingston Crescent,
Milton Road, Edinburgh,
Lothian, EH15 3AS
Tel: 0131 6203081
★★★ Guest House

Brae Guest House
119 Willowbrae Road,
Edinburgh, EH8 7HN
Tel: 0131 661 0170
★★★ Guest House

The Walton
79 Dundas Street,
Edinburgh, EH3 6SD
Tel: 0131 556 1137
Guest House

Highfield Guest House
83 Mayfield Road,
Edinburgh, EH9 3AE
Tel: 0131 667 8717
★★★★ Guest House

Stuart House
12 East Claremont Street,
Edinburgh, EH7 4JP
Tel: 0131 557 9030
★★★★ Guest House

Ramada Mount Royal Hotel
53 Princes Street,
Edinburgh, EH2 2DG
Tel: 0131 225 7161
★★★ Hotel

Directory of all VisitScotland Quality Assured Serviced Hotels and Guest Houses

George Hotel
19 / 21 George St.,
Edinburgh, EH2 2PB
Tel: 0131 225 1251
★★★★ Hotel

Claremont Hotel
14a/15 Claremont Crescent,
Edinburgh, EH7 4HX
Tel: 0131 556 1487
★ Small Hotel

Ascot Guest House
98 Dalkeith Road,
Edinburgh, EH16 5AF
Tel: 0131 667 1500
★ Guest House

Rothesay Hotel
Rothesay Place,
Edinburgh, EH3 7SL
Tel: 0131 2254125
★ Hotel

Ben Cruachan
17 McDonald Road,
Edinburgh, Midlothian,
EH7 4LX
Tel: 0131 556 3709
★★★ Guest House

Holiday Inn Edinburgh-North
107 Queensferry Road,
Edinburgh, EH4 3HL
Tel: 8704009025
★★★ Hotel

Salisbury Guest House
43-45 Salisbury Road,
Edinburgh, EH16 5AA
Tel: 0131 667 1264
Awaiting Inspection

MW Guesthouse
94 Dalkeith Road,
Edinburgh, Midlothian,
EH16 5AF
Tel: 0131 662 9265
★★★★ Guest House

MW Town House
11 Spence Street,
Edinburgh, Midlothian,
EH16 5AG
Tel: 0131 662 9265
★★★★ Guest House

Dunedin Guest House
8 Priestfield Road,
Edinburgh, Lothian,
EH16 5HH
Tel: 0131 6681949
Awaiting Inspection

BY EDINBURGH
Dalhousie Castle & Spa
Cockpen Road, Bonnyrigg,
Edinburgh, Midlothian,
EH19 3JB
Tel: 01875 820153
★★★★ Hotel

NR EDINBURGH
The Laird & Dog Hotel
5 High Street, Lasswade,
Midlothian, EH18 1NA
Tel: 0131 663 9219
★★ Inn

GOREBRIDGE
Ivory House
14 Vogrie Road,
Gorebridge, Midlothian,
EH23 4HH
Tel: 01875 820755
★★★★ Guest House

GULLANE
Greywalls
Muirfield, Gullane,
East Lothian, EH31 2EG
Tel: 01620 842144
★★★★ Hotel

Mallard Hotel
East Links Road, Gullane,
East Lothian, EH31 2AF
Tel: 01620 843288
★★ Small Hotel

HADDINGTON
Browns' Hotel
1 West Road,
Haddington,
East Lothian, EH41 3RD
Tel: 01620 822254
★★★ Small Hotel

Maitlandfield House Hotel
24 Sidegate, Haddington,
East Lothian, EH41 4BZ
Tel: 01620 826513
★★★ Hotel

INGLISTON, BY EDINBURGH
Norton House Hotel
Ingliston, Edinburgh,
EH28 8LX
Tel: 0131 333 1275
★★★★ Hotel

KIRKNEWTON
The Marriott Dalmahoy Hotel
and Country Club,
Kirknewton, Midlothian,
EH27 8EP
Tel: 0131 3331845
★★★★ Hotel

LINLITHGOW
The Bonsyde House Hotel
Bonsyde, By Linlithgow,
West Lothian, EH49 7NU
Tel: 01506 842229
★★★ Small Hotel

Aran House
Woodcockdale Farm,
Lanark Road, Linlithgow,
West Lothian, EH49 6QE
Tel: 01506 842088
★★ Guest House

West Port Hotel
West Port, Linlithgow,
West Lothian, EH49 7AZ
Tel: 01506 847456
★★ Small Hotel

LIVINGSTON
Ramada Jarvis Livingston
Almondview,
Livingston, West Lothian,
EH54 6QB
Tel: 01506 431222
★★★ Hotel

LOANHEAD
Aaron Glen Guest House
7 Nivensknowe Road,
Loanhead, Midlothian,
EH20 9AU
Tel: 0131 440 1293
★★★ Guest House

MUSSELBURGH
Arden House
26 Linkfield Road,
Musselburgh,
East Lothian, EH21 7LL
Tel: 0131 665 0663
Awaiting Inspection

Woodside Hotel
30 Linkfield Road,
Musselburgh,
East Lothian, EH21 7LL
Tel: 0131 665 0404
Awaiting Inspection

Carberry Tower
Musselburgh,
East Lothian, EH21 8PY
Tel: 0131 665 3135/3488
★★ Guest House

NORTH BERWICK
**MacDonald Marine
Hotel & Spa**
Cromwell Road, North
Berwick, East Lothian,
EH39 4LZ
Tel: 0870 400 8129
★★★★ Hotel

The Folly
1 Station Hill, North
Berwick, East Lothian,
EH39 4AN
Tel: 01620 895777
★★ Small Hotel

Fenton Tower
Kingston, North Berwick,
East Lothian, EH39 5JH
Tel: 01620 890089
★★★★★ Exclusive Use
Venue

Nether Abbey Hotel
20 Dirleton Avenue,
North Berwick, EH39 4BQ
Tel: 01620 892802
★★ Small Hotel

12 Quality Street
North Berwick,
East Lothian, EH39 4HP
Tel: 01620 892529
Awaiting Inspection

NORTH MIDDLETON
Borthwick Castle Hotel
North Middleton,
Gorebridge, Midlothian,
EH23 4QY
Tel: 01875 820514
★★★ Small Hotel

PENICUIK
Craigiebield House Hotel
Bog Road, Penicuik,
Midlothian, EH26 9BZ
Tel: 01968 672557
Small Hotel

SOUTH QUEENSFERRY
Priory Lodge
8 The Loan, South
Queensferry, West Lothian,
EH30 9NS
Tel: 0131 331 4345
★★★★ Guest House

Dundas Castle
South Queensferry,
Edinburgh, EH30 9SP
Tel: 0131 3192039

★★★★★

Exclusive Use Venue

TRANENT
Rosebank Guest House
161 High Street, Tranent,
East Lothian, EH33 1LP
Tel: 01875 610967

★★★ Guest House

UPHALL
Houstoun House Hotel
Uphall, West Lothian,
EH52 6JS
Tel: 01506 853831

★★★★ Hotel

WHITBURN
Hilcroft Hotel
East Main Street,
Whitburn,
West Lothian, EH47 0JU
Tel: 01501 740818

★★★ Hotel

GREATER GLASGOW AND CLYDE VALLEY

ABINGTON
Abington Hotel
Carlisle Road,
Abington,
Lanarkshire, ML12 6SD
Tel: 01864 502467

★★ Hotel

AIRDRIE
Knight's Rest
150 Clark Street,
Airdrie, Lanarkshire,
ML6 6DZ
Tel: 01236 606193

★★ Guest House

BARRHEAD, GLASGOW
Dalmeny Park Hotel
Lochlibo Road, Barrhead,
Renfrewshire, G78 1LG
Tel: 0141 881 9211

★★★ Small Hotel

BIGGAR
Cornhill House Hotel
Cornhill Road, Coulter,
Biggar, Clyde Valley,
ML12 6QE
Tel: 01899 220001

★★★ Small Hotel

Shieldhill Hotel
Quothquan, Biggar,
Lanarkshire, ML12 6NA
Tel: 01899 220035

★★★★ Small Hotel

BISHOPTON
Mar Hall
Mar Estate, Bishopton,
Renfrewshire, PA7 5NW
Tel: 0141 812 9999

★★★★★ Hotel

CALDERBANK, BY AIRDRIE
Calder Guest House
13 Main Street,
Calderbank, by Airdrie,
Lanarkshire, ML6 9SG
Tel: 01236 769077

★★★ Guest House

COATBRIDGE
The Georgian Hotel
26 Lefroy Street,
Coatbridge, ML5 1LZ
Tel: 01236 421888

★★ Small Hotel

BY COATBRIDGE
Auchenlea
153 Langmuir Road,
Bargeddie, Lanarkshire,
G69 7RT
Tel: 0141 771 6870

★★★ Guest House

CUMBERNAULD
Westerwood Hotel
1 St Andrews Drive,
Cumbernauld,
North Lanarkshire,
G68 0EW
Tel: 01236 457171

★★★ Hotel

EAGLESHAM, BY GLASGOW
Eglinton Arms Hotel
Gilmour Street,
Eaglesham, Glasgow,
G76 0LG
Tel: 01355 302631

★★★ Hotel

EAST KILBRIDE
The Bruce Hotel
35 Cornwall Street,
East Kilbride, G74 1AF
Tel: 01355 229771

★★★ Hotel

Torrance Hotel
135 Main Street,
East Kilbride,
Lanarkshire, G74 4LN
Tel: 013552 25241

★★ Small Hotel

Crutherland House Hotel
Strathaven Road, East
Kilbride, Lanarkshire,
G75 0QJ
Tel: 01355 577000

★★★ Hotel

ERSKINE
Erskine Bridge Hotel
Erskine, Renfrewshire,
PA8 6AN
Tel: 0141 812 0123

★★★ Hotel

GIFFNOCK, GLASGOW
Orchard Park Hotel
2 Park Road, Giffnock,
Glasgow, G46 7LY
Tel: 01416 381044
Small Hotel

GLASGOW
Clifton Hotel
27 Buckingham Terrace,
Glasgow, G12 8ED
Tel: 0141 3348080

★★ Guest House

Albion Hotel
405 North Woodside Road,
Glasgow, G20 6NN
Tel: 0141 339 8620

★★★ Small Hotel

Argyll Hotel
973 Sauchiehall Street,
Glasgow, G3 7TQ
Tel: 0141 337 3313

★★★ Hotel

Botanic Hotel
1 Alfred Terrace,
Glasgow, G12 8RF
Tel: 01413 377007

★★ Guest House

Craigpark Guest House
33 Circus Drive,
Glasgow, G31 2JG
Tel: 0141 554 4160

★★ Guest House

The Town House
4 Hughenden Terrace,
Glasgow, G12 9XR
Tel: 0141 3570862

★★★ Guest House

Devoncove Hotel
931 Sauchiehall Street,
Glasgow, G3 7TQ
Tel: 0141 334 4000

★★★ Hotel

Belgrave Guest House
2 Belgrave Terrace,
Hillhead, Glasgow,
G12 8JD
Tel: 0141 337 1850

★★ Guest House

The Alamo Guest House Ltd
46 Gray Street,
Glasgow, G3 7SE
Tel: 0141 339 2395

★★ Guest House

Bothwell Bridge Hotel
89 Main Street, Bothwell,
Glasgow, G71 8EU
Tel: 01698 852246

★★★ Hotel

Express by Holiday Inn
Theatreland,
165 West Nile Street,
Glasgow, Lanarkshire,
G1 2RL
Tel: 0141 331 6800
★★★ Hotel

Saint Judes
190 Bath Street,
Glasgow, Strathclyde,
G2 4HG
Tel: 0141 3528800
★★★ Small Hotel

Campanile Hotel Glasgow
Tunnel Street, Glasgow,
G3 8HL
Tel: 0141 287 7700
★★★ Hotel

McLays Guest House
268 Renfrew Street,
Glasgow, G3 6TT
Tel: 0141 332 4796
★ Guest House

Glasgow Pond Hotel
Great Western Road,
Glasgow, G12 0XP
Tel: 0141 334 8161
Awaiting Inspection

Kirkland House
42 St Vincent Crescent,
Glasgow, G3 8NG
Tel: 0141 248 3458
★★ Guest House

Willow Hotel
228 Renfrew Street,
Glasgow, G3 6TX
Tel: 0141 332 2332
★★ Guest House

Novotel Glasgow Centre
181 Pitt Street, Glasgow,
G2 4DT
Tel: 0141 222 277
★★★ Hotel

Burnside Hotel
East Kilbride Road,
Rutherglen, Glasgow,
G73 5EA
Tel: 0141 634 1276
★★ Small Hotel

Kelvin Hotel
15 Buckingham Terrace,
Glasgow, G12 8EB
Tel: 0141 339 7143
★★ Guest House

Amadeus Guest House
411 North Woodside Road,
Glasgow, G20 6NN
Tel: 0141 3398257
★★ Guest House

Holiday Inn
161 West Nile Street,
Glasgow, G1 2RL
Tel: 0141 352 8300
★★★★ Hotel

Tulip Inn Glasgow
80 Ballater Street,
Glasgow, G5 0TW
Tel: 0141 429 4233
★★★ Hotel

City Inn Glasgow
Finnieston Quay,
Glasgow, G3 8HN
★★★ Hotel

Glasgow Hilton
1 William Street,
Glasgow, G3 8HT
Tel: 0141 204 5555
★★★★★ Hotel

Carlton George Hotel
44 West George Street,
Glasgow, G2 1DH
Tel: 0141 353 6373
★★★★ Hotel

Corus Hotel Glasgow
377 Argyle Street,
Glasgow,
Dunbartonshire, G2 8LL
Tel: 0141 2482355
★★★ Hotel

The Heritage Hotel
4-5 Alfred Terrace,
Glasgow, G12 8RF
Tel: 0141 339 6955
★★★ Guest House

Holiday Inn Glasgow City West
Bothwell Street,
Glasgow, G2 7EN
Tel: 0870 4009032
★★★ Hotel

Radisson SAS Hotel Glasgow
301 Argyle Street,
Glasgow, G2 8DL
Tel: 0141 204 3333
★★★★★ Hotel

The Arthouse Glasgow Ltd
129 Bath Street,
Glasgow, G2 2SZ
Tel: 0141 2216789
★★★★ Hotel

Langs Hotel
2 Port Dundas Place,
Glasgow, G2 3LB
Tel: 0141 333 1500
★★★★ Hotel

The Belhaven Hotel
15 Belhaven Terrace,
Glasgow, G12 0TG
Tel: 0141 339 3222
★★★ Small Hotel

Busby Hotel
Field Road, Clarkston,
Glasgow, G76 8RX
Tel: 0141 644 2661
★★ Hotel

Buchanan Hotel
185 Buchanan Street,
Glasgow, G1 2JY
Tel: 0141 332 7284
★ Hotel

Lomond Hotel
6 Buckingham Terrace,
Great Western Road,
Glasgow, G12 8EB
Tel: 0141 339 2339
★★ Guest House

Quality Hotel Central
99 Gordon Street,
Glasgow, G1 3SF
Tel: 0141 2219680
★★ Hotel

Manor Park Hotel
28 Balshagray Drive,
Glasgow, G11 7DD
Tel: 0141 339 2143
★★★ Small Hotel

Swallow Hotel
517 Paisley Road West,
Glasgow, G51 1RW
Tel: 0141 427 3146
★★★ Hotel

1 Devonshire Gardens
Glasgow, G12 0UX
Tel: 0141 339 2001
★★★★★ Hotel

The Malmaison
278 West George Street,
Glasgow, G2 4LL
Tel: 0141 5721000
★★★★ Hotel

The Millennium Glasgow Hotel
George Square,
Glasgow, G2 1DS
Tel: 0141 332 6711
★★★★ Hotel

Ibis Hotel Glasgow
220 West Regent Street,
Glasgow, G2 4DQ
Tel: 0141 225 6000
★★ Hotel

Ambassador Hotel
7 Kelvin Drive, Glasgow,
G20 8QG
Tel: 0141 946 1018
★★★ Hotel

Crowne Plaza Hotel
Congress Road,
Glasgow, G3 8QT
Tel: 0870 443 4691
★★★★ Hotel

Menzies Glasgow
27 Washington Street,
Glasgow, G3 8AZ
Tel: 0141 2222929
★★★★ Hotel

Express by Holiday Inn Glasgow
122 Stockwell Street,
Glasgow, G1 4LT
Tel: 0141 548 5000
★★★ Hotel

Thistle Glasgow
36 Cambridge Street,
Glasgow, G2 3HN
Tel: 0141 332 3311
★★★★ Hotel

Kirklee Hotel
11 Kensington Gate,
Glasgow, G12 9LG
Tel: 0141 334 5555
★★★ Guest House

Bewleys Hotel Glasgow
110 Bath Street,
Glasgow, G2 2EN
Tel: 0141 353 0800
★★★ Hotel

Hilton Glasgow Grosvenor
Grosvenor Terrace,
Glasgow, G12 0TA
Tel: 0141 339 8811
★★★★ Hotel

Directory of all VisitScotland Quality Assured Serviced Hotels and Guest Houses

Newton House Hotel
248-252 Bath Street,
Glasgow, G2 4JW
Tel: 0141 3321666
Guest House

The Sandyford Hotel
904 Sauchiehall Street,
Glasgow, G3 7TF
Tel: 0141 334 0000
★★ Lodge

Sherbrooke Castle Hotel
11 Sherbrooke Avenue,
Glasgow, G41 4PG
Tel: 0141 427 4227
★★★ Hotel

Hampton Court Hotel
230 Renfrew Street,
Glasgow, G3 6TX
Tel: 0141 332 6623
★★ Guest House

Artto Hotel
37-39 Hope Street,
Glasgow, G2 6AE
Tel: 0141 2482480
★★★ Hotel

Garfield House Hotel
Cumbernauld Road,
Stepps, Glasgow,
Lanarkshire, G33 6HW
Tel: 0141 779 2111
★★★ Hotel

Smiths Hotel
3 David Donnelly Place,
Kirkintilloch, Glasgow,
G66 1DD
Tel: 0141 775 0398
★★★ Hotel

Kelvingrove Hotel
944 Sauchiehall Street,
Glasgow, G3 7TH
Tel: 0141 339 5011
★★★ Guest House

Hilton Strathclyde
Pheonix Crescent, Bellshill,
North Lanarkshire,ML4 3JQ
Tel: 01698 395500
★★★★ Hotel

Jurys Inn Glasgow
Jamaica Street, Glasgow,
G1 4QE
Tel: 0141 314 4800
★★★ Hotel

The Enterprise Hotel
144 Renfrew Street,
Glasgow, G3 6RF
Tel: 0141 332 8095
★ Guest House

The Ramada Glasgow City
201 Ingram Street,
Glasgow, G1 1DQ
Tel: 0141 248 4401
★★★ Hotel

Glasgow Marriott
500 Argyle Street,
Glasgow, G3 8RR
Tel: 0141 226 5577
★★★★ Hotel

NR GLASGOW

Uplawmoor Hotel
Neilston Road,
Uplawmoor, Glasgow,
G78 4AF
Tel: 01505 850565
★★★ Small Hotel

Wallace Hotel
1 Yieldshields Road,
Carluke, Lanarkshire,
ML8 4QG
Tel: 01555 773000
★★
Restaurant with Rooms

GLASGOW AIRPORT

Ramada Glasgow Airport
Marchburn Drive,
Glasgow Airport
Business Park, Paisley,
PA3 2SJ
Tel: 0141 840 2200
★★★ Hotel

Holiday Inn Glasgow Airport
Abbotsinch, Paisley,
Glasgow, Renfrewshire,
PA3 2TR
Tel: 0870 4009031
★★★ Hotel

GOUROCK

Spinnaker Hotel
121 Albert Road, Gourock,
Renfrewshire, PA19 1BU
Tel: 01475 633107
★★ Small Hotel

Ramada Jarvis Gourock
Cloch Road, Gourock,
Renfrewshire, PA15 1AR
Tel: 01475 634671
★★★ Hotel

GREENOCK

Express by Holiday Inn
Cartsburn, Greenock, PA15
4RT
Tel: 01475 786666
★★★ Hotel

Tontine Hotel
6 Ardgowan Square,
Greenock, Renfrewshire,
PA16 8NG
Tel: 01475 723316
★★★ Hotel

HAMILTON

Thorndale Guest House
Manse Road, Stonehouse,
Lanarkshire, ML9 3NX
Tel: 01698 791133
★★★ Guest House

Avonbridge Hotel
Carlisle Road, Hamilton,
Lanarkshire, ML3 7DG
Tel: 01698 420525
★★★ Hotel

The Villa Hotel
49/51 Burnbank Road,
Hamilton, Lanarkshire,
ML3 9AQ
Tel: 01698 891777
★★★ Small Hotel

HARTHILL, BY SHOTTS

Blairmains Guest House
Harthill, Shotts,
Lanarkshire, ML7 5TJ
Tel: 01501 751278
★★ Guest House

HOWWOOD

Bowfield Hotel & Country Club
Howwood, Renfrewshire,
PA9 1DB
Tel: 01505 705225
★★★ Hotel

INVERKIP

Inverkip Hotel
Main Street, Inverkip,
Renfrewshire, PA16 OAS
Tel: 01475 521478
★★★ Small Hotel

JOHNSTONE

Lynnhurst Hotel
Park Road, Johnstone,
Renfrewshire, PA5 8LS
Tel: 01505 324331
★★★ Hotel

LANARK

**Cartland Bridge
Country House Hotel**
Glasgow Road, Lanark,
ML11 9UE
Tel: 01555 664426
★★★ Small Hotel

LANGBANK

Gleddoch House Hotel
Langbank, Renfrewshire,
PA14 6YE
Tel: 01475 540711
★★★ Hotel

LARKHALL BY

Shawlands Hotel
Ayr Road, Canderside Toll,
by Larkhall, Lanarkshire,
ML9 2TZ
Tel: 01698 791111
★★★ Lodge

MILTON OF CAMPSIE, BY KIRKINTILLOCH

Kincaid House Hotel
Milton of Campsie,
Glasgow, G65 8BZ
Tel: 0141 776 2226
★★★ Small Hotel

MOTHERWELL

The Alona Hotel
Strathclyde Country Park,
Motherwell, North
Lanarkshire, ML1 3RT
Tel: 01698 303031
★★★★ Hotel

The Bentley Hotel
19A High Street,
Motherwell, Lanarkshire,
ML1 3HU
Tel: 01698 265588
★★★ Small Hotel

Motherwell College - Stewart Halls of Residence
Dalzell Drive,
Motherwell,
Lanarkshire, ML1 2DD
Tel: 01698 261890

★ Campus

Moorings Hotel
114 Hamilton Road,
Motherwell, Lanarkshire,
ML1 3DG
Tel: 01698 258131

★★★ Hotel

Dakota Hotel
Eurocentral Business Park,
Motherwell, North
Lanarkshire, ML1 4UD
Tel: 01698 835444

★★★ Hotel

Dalziel Park Hotel and Conference Centre
100 Hagen Drive,
Motherwell, Lanarkshire,
ML1 5RZ
Tel: 01698 862862

★★★ Small Hotel

NEW LANARK, BY LANARK
New Lanark Mill Hotel
New Lanark, Lanarkshire,
ML11 9DB
Tel: 01555 667200

★★★ Hotel

PAISLEY
Dryesdale Guest House
37 Inchinnan Road,
Paisley, Renfrewshire,
PA3 2PR
Tel: 0141 889 7178

★★ Guest House

Watermill Hotel
1 Lonend, Paisley,
Renfrewshire, PA1 1SR
Tel: 0141 889 3201

★★ Hotel

Express by Holiday Inn Glasgow Airport
St Andrews Drive, Paisley,
PA3 2TJ
Tel: 0141 842 1100

★★★ Hotel

Ashtree House
9 Orr Square, Paisley,
Renfrewshire, PA1 2DL
Tel: 0141 8486411

★★★★ Guest House

Ardgowan Town House Hotel
92 Renfrew Road,
Paisley, Renfrewshire,
PA3 4BJ
Tel: 0141 889 4763

★★★ Small Hotel

Ardgowan House
94 Renfrew Road,
Paisley, Renfrewshire,
PA3 4BJ
Tel: 0141 889 4763

★★ Guest House

RENFREW
Glynhill Hotel
169 Paisley Road,
Renfrew, Near Glasgow
Airport, Renfrewshire,
PA4 8XB
Tel: 0141 886 5555

★★★ Hotel

ROSEBANK
Popinjay Hotel
Lanark Road, Rosebank,
Lanarkshire, ML8 5QB
Tel: 01555 860441

★★★★ Hotel

STRATHAVEN
Springvale Hotel
18 Lethame Road,
Strathaven, Lanarkshire,
ML10 6AD
Tel: 01357 521131

★★★ Small Hotel

Strathaven Hotel
Hamilton Road, Strathaven,
Lanarkshire, ML10 6SZ
Tel: 01357 521778

★★★ Hotel

SYMINGTON, BY BIGGAR
Tinto Hotel
Biggar Road, Symington,
Lanarkshire, ML12 6FT
Tel: 01899 308454

★★ Hotel

UDDINGSTON
Redstones Hotel
8-10 Glasgow Road,
Uddingston, Glasgow,
G71 7AS
Tel: 01698 813744

★★★ Small Hotel

WISHAW
Herdshill Guest House
224 Main Street, Bogside,
Wishaw, Lanarkshire,
ML2 8HA
Tel: 01698 381579

★★★ Guest House

WEST HIGHLANDS & ISLANDS, LOCH LOMOND, STIRLING AND TROSSACHS

ABERFOYLE

Crannaig House
Trossachs Road,
Aberfoyle, Stirlingshire,
FK8 3SR
Tel: 01877 382276
★★★ Guest House

Fielbarachan Guest House
Lochard Road, Aberfoyle,
Stirlingshire, FK8 3SZ
Tel: 01877 382536
★★ Guest House

Forest Hills Hotel
Kinlochard, By Aberfoyle,
Stirlingshire, FK8 3TL
Tel: 08701 942105
★★★★ Hotel

Rob Roy Hotel
Aberfoyle, Stirlingshire,
FK8 3UX
Tel: 01877 382245
★★ Hotel

AIRTH, BY FALKIRK
Airth Castle Hotel & Spa Resort
Airth, By Falkirk,
Stirlingshire, FK2 8JF
Tel: 01324 831411
★★★★ Hotel

ALEXANDRIA
De Vere Cameron House
Loch Lomond,
Alexandria,
Dunbartonshire, G83 8QZ
Tel: 01389 755565
★★★★★ Hotel

ALLOA
Gean House
Tullibody Road,
Alloa, Clackmannanshire,
FK10 2EL
Tel: 01259 226400
Awaiting Inspection

ARDEN
Duck Bay Hotel & Marina
Loch Lomond, Arden,
by Alexandria,
Dunbartonshire,
G83 8QZ
Tel: 01389 751234

★★★ Hotel

Polnaberoch
Arden, By Luss, Loch
Lomond, G83 8RQ
Tel: 01389 850615
Awaiting Inspection

ARDEONAIG, BY KILLIN
The Ardeonaig Hotel
South Loch Tay, Killin,
Perthshire, FK21 8SU
★★★ Small Hotel

ARDLUI
Ardlui Hotel
Ardlui, Loch Lomond,
Argyll, G83 7EB
Tel: 01301 704269

★★★ Small Hotel

Beinglas Farm Campsite
Inverarnan, Ardlui,
G83 7DX
Tel: 01301 704281

★★★ Guest House

ARDRISHAIG, BY LOCHGILPHEAD
Allt-Na-Craig House
Tarbert Road,
Ardrishaig, Argyll,
PA30 8EP
Tel: 01546 603245

★★★★ Small Hotel

ARDUAINE
Loch Melfort Hotel
Arduaine, Argyll, PA34 4XG
Tel: 01852 200233

★★★★ Hotel

ARROCHAR
Arrochar Hotel
Arrochar,
Dunbartonshire,
G83 7AU
Tel: 01301 702484
Hotel

Braemor B&B
Braeside, Arrochar,
Dunbartonshire,
G83 7AA
Tel: 1301702535
Awaiting Inspection

Fascadail Country Guest House
Shore Road, Arrochar,
Dunbartonshire,
G83 7AB
Tel: 01301 702344
★★★ Guest House

Claymore Hotel
Arrochar, Argyll & Bute,
G83 7BB
Tel: 01301 702238
★★ Hotel

Loch Long Hotel
Arrochar, Dunbartonshire,
G83 7AA
Tel: 01301 702434
★★★ Hotel

BALLOCH

Anchorage Guest House
31 Balloch Road,
Balloch, Loch Lomond,
G83 8SS
Tel: 01389 753336
★★ Guest House

Gowanlea
Drymen Road,
Balloch, Dunbartonshire,
G83 8HS
Tel: 01389 752456
★★★★ Guest House

Woodvale
Drymen Road, Balloch,
Dunbartonshire, G83
Tel: 01389 755771
★★★ Guest House

Time Out
24 Balloch Road, Balloch,
Dunbartonshire, G83 8LE
Tel: 07957 436731
★★★ Guest House

Norwood Guest House
60 Balloch Road, Balloch,
Dunbartonshire, G83 8LE
Tel: 01389 750309
★★★ Guest House

Palombo's of Balloch
40 Balloch Road, Balloch,
Alexandria, West
Dunbartonshire, G83 8LE
Tel: 01389 756665
Awaiting Inspection

BALQUHIDDER

King's House Hotel
Balquhidder, Perthshire,
FK19 8NY
Tel: 0877 384646
★★ Small Hotel

Monachyle Mhor
Balquhidder,
Lochearnhead, Perthshire,
FK19 8PQ
Tel: 0877 384622
★★★★ Small Hotel

BELLOCHANTUY, BY CAMPBELTOWN

Argyll Hotel
Bellochantuy, by
Campbeltown, Argyll,
PA28 6QE
Tel: 01583 421212
★★ Small Hotel

Hunting Lodge Hotel
Bellochantuy, Kintyre,
Argyll, PA28 6QE
Tel: 01583 421323
★★ Small Hotel

BENDERLOCH, BY OBAN

Dun Na Mara
Benderloch, Oban, Argyll,
PA37 1RT
Tel: 01631 720233
★★★★ Guest House

BO'NESS

Carriden House
Carriden Brae, Bo'ness,
West Lothian, EH51 9SN
Tel: 01506 829811
★★★ Guest House

BRIDGE OF ALLAN

Knockhill Guest House
Bridge of Allan, Stirling,
FK9 4ND
Tel: 01786 833123
Awaiting Inspection

The Queen's Hotel
24 Henderson Street,
Bridge of Allan,
Stirlingshire, FK9 4HP
Tel: 01786 833268
★★★★ Small Hotel

Royal Hotel
55 Henderson Street,
Bridge of Allan,
Stirlingshire, FK9 4HG
Tel: 01786 832284
★★★ Hotel

KILCHATTAN BAY, ISLE OF BUTE

St Blane's Hotel
Kilchattan Bay,
Isle of Bute, PA20 9NW
Tel: 01700 831224
★★ Small Hotel

ROTHESAY

The Ardyne Hotel
38 Mountstuart Road,
Rothesay, Isle of Bute,
PA20 9EB
Tel: 01700 502052
★★★ Hotel

Glendale Guest House
20 Battery Place,
Rothesay,
Isle of Bute, PA20 9DU
Tel: 01700 502329
★★★★ Guest House

Glenburn Hotel
Mount Stuart Road,
Rothesay, Isle of Bute,
PA20 9JB
Tel: 01942 824824
★★★ Hotel

Cannon House Hotel
Battery Place,
Rothesay, Isle of Bute,
PA20 9DP
Tel: 01700 502819
★★★★ Small Hotel

Bayview Hotel
21-22 Mountstuart Road,
Rothesay,
Isle of Bute,
PA20 9EB
Tel: 01700 505411
★★★ Small Hotel

Bute House Hotel
4 West Princess Street,
Rothesay,
Isle of Bute,
PA20 9AF
Tel: 01700 502481
★★★ Guest House

Ardbeg Lodge
23 Marine Place,
Ardbeg, Rothesay,
Isle of Bute, PA20 0LF
Tel: 01700 505448
★★★ Small Hotel

The Regent Hotel
23 Battery Place,
Rothesay, Isle of Bute,
PA20 9DU
Tel: 01700 502006
★★★ Small Hotel

Argyle House
3 Argyle Place,
Rothesay, Isle of Bute,
PA20 0AZ
Tel: 01700 502424
★★ Guest House

Iuybank Villa
Westlands Road,
Rothesay, Isle of Bute,
PA2- 0HQ
Tel: 01700 505064
Awaiting Inspection

The Commodore
12 Battery Place,
Rothesay, Isle of Bute,
PA20 9DP
Tel: 01700 502178
★★★ Guest House

CALLANDER

Annfield Guest House
18 North Church Street,
Callander, Perthshire,
FK17 8EG
Tel: 01877 330204
★★★ Guest House

Roman Camp Hotel
Main Street, Callander,
Perthshire, FK17 8BG
Tel: 01877 330003
★★★★ Small Hotel

Coppice Hotel
Leny Road, Callander,
Perthshire, FK17 8AL
Tel: 01877 330188
★★ Small Hotel

The Crags Hotel
101 Main Street,
Callander, Perthshire,
FK17 8BQ
Tel: 01877 330257
★★★ Guest House

Elmbank Guest House
157 Main Street,
Callander, Perthshire,
FK17 8BH
Tel: 01877 330205
★★★ Guest House

Directory of all VisitScotland Quality Assured Serviced Hotels and Guest Houses

Southfork Villa
25 Cross Street, Callander,
Perthshire, FK17 8EA
Tel: 01877 330831
★★★★ Guest House

Lubnaig House
Leny Feus, Callander,
Perthshire, FK17 8AS
Tel: 01877 330376
★★★★ Guest House

Dunmor House
Leny Road, Callander,
FK17 8AL
Tel: 01877 330756
★★★★ Guest House

Poppies Hotel and Restaurant
Leny Road,
Callander, Perthshire,
FK17 8AL
Tel: 01877 330329
★★★ Small Hotel

Craigburn House
North Church Street,
Callander,
Perthshire, FK17 8EG
Tel: 01877 330332
★★★ Guest House

The Old Rectory Guest House
Leny Road, Callander,
Perthshire, FK17 8AL
Tel: 01877 339215
★★★ Guest House

Arden House
Bracklinn Road,
Callander, Perthshire,
FK17 8EQ
Tel: 01877 330235
★★★★ Guest House

Riverview Guest House
Leny Road, Callander,
Perthshire, FK17 8AL
Tel: 01877 330635
★★★ Guest House

The Knowe
Ancaster Road,
Callander, Perthshire,
FK17 8EL
Tel: 01877 330076
★★★★ Guest House

Dreadnought Hotel
Station Road,
Callander,
Stirlingshire,
FK17 8AN
Tel: 01877 330184
Hotel

CAMPBELTOWN

Ardshiel Hotel
Kilkerran
Road,Campbeltown,
Argyll, PA28 6JL
Tel: 01586 552133
★★ Small Hotel

Dellwood Hotel
Drumore, Campbeltown,
Argyll, PA28 6HD
Tel: 01586 552465
★★ Small Hotel

Craigard House
Low Askomil,
Campbeltown, Argyll,
PA28 6EP
Tel: 01586 554242
★★ Small Hotel

Seafield Hotel
Kilkerran Road,
Campbeltown, Argyll,
PA28 6JL
Tel: 01586 554385
★★ Small Hotel

Westbank Guest House
Dell Road,
Campbeltown, Argyll,
PA28 6JG
Tel: 01586 553660
★★★ Guest House

Janina
George Street, The Walk,
Campbeltown, Argyll,
PA28 6DU
Tel: 01586 553529
Awaiting Inspection

White Hart Hotel
Main Street,
Campbeltown, Argyll,
 PA28
Tel: 01586 552440
Small Hotel

BY CAMPBELTOWN

Dalnaspidal Guest House
Tangy, Kilkenzie, by
Campbeltown, Argyll,
PA28 6QD
Tel: 01586 820466
★★★★★ Guest House

CARRADALE

Carradale Hotel
Carradale, Argyll,
PA28 6RY
Tel: 01583 431223
★★★ Small Hotel

Ashbank Hotel
Carradale, Argyll,
PA28 6RY
Tel: 01583 431650
★★★ Small Hotel

Kiloran Guest House
Carradale, Argyll,
Mull of Kintyre,
PA28 6QG
Tel: 01583 431795
★★★ Bed & Breakfast

Dunvalanree
Portrigh Bay, Carradale,
Argyll, PA28 6SE
Tel: 01583 431226
★★★★ Small Hotel

CASTLECARY VILLAGE, BY CUMBERNAULD

Castlecary House Hotel
Castlecary Road,
Castlecary,
Cumbernauld, G68 0HD
Tel: 01324 840233
★★★ Hotel

CLYDEBANK

Radnor Park Hotel
Kilbowie Road, Clydebank,
Dunbartonshire, G81 2AP
Tel: 0141 9523427
★★ Small Hotel

Beardmore Hotel
Beardmore Street,
Clydebank, Greater
Glasgow, G81 4SA
Tel: 0141 9516000
★★★★ Hotel

COLINTRAIVE

Colintraive Hotel
Colintraive, Argyll, PA22
3AS
Tel: 01700 841207
★★★ Small Hotel

ISLE OF COLL

Coll Hotel
Arinagour, Isle of Coll,
Argyll, PA78 6SZ
Tel: 01879 230334
★★★ Small Hotel

ISLE OF COLONSAY

Isle of Colonsay Hotel
Isle of Colonsay, Argyll,
PA61 7YP
Tel: 01951 200316
★★★ Small Hotel

CONNEL

Greenacre
Connel, by Oban,
Argyll, PA31 1PJ
Tel: 01631 710756
★★ Guest House

Ronebhal Guest House
Connel, by Oban,
Argyll, PA37 1PJ
Tel: 01631 710310
★★★★ Guest House

COVE

Knockderry Hotel
Shore Road, Cove,
Helensburgh, G84 0NX
Tel: 01436 842283
★★★★ Small Hotel

CRIANLARICH

Ben More Lodge
Hotel + Restaurant
Crianlarich, Perthshire,
FK20 8QP
Tel: 01838 300210
★★ Inn

Riverside Guest House
Tigh Na Struith,
Crianlarich, Perthshire,
FK20 8RU
Tel: 01838 300235
★★ Guest House

Inverardran House
A85, Crianlarich,
Perthshire, FK20 8QS
Tel: 01838 300240
★★★ Guest House

Highland Hotel
Crianlarich, Perthshire,
FK20 8RW
Tel: 01838 300272
★★★ Hotel

Ewich House
Strathfillan, Crianlarich,
Perthshire, FK20 8RU
Tel: 01838 300300
★★★ Guest House

The Lodge House
Crianlarich, Perthshire,
FK20 8RU
Tel: 01838 300276
★★★★ Guest House

Glenardran
Crianlarich, Perthshire,
FK20 8QS
Tel: 01838 300236
★★★ Guest House

Directory of all VisitScotland Quality Assured Serviced Hotels and Guest Houses

West Highland Lodge
Crianlarich, Perthshire,
FK20 8RU
Tel: 01838 300283
★★★ Guest House

CRINAN, BY LOCHGILPHEAD

Crinan Hotel
Crinan, Argyll, PA31 8SR
Tel: 01546 830261
★★★★ Small Hotel

DALMALLY

Dalmally Hotel
Dalmally, Argyll, PA33 1AY
Tel: 01838 200444
★★★ Hotel

Craig Villa Guest House
Dalmally, Argyll, PA33 1AX
Tel: 01838 200255
★★★ Guest House

Glenorchy Lodge Hotel
Dalmally, Argyll, PA33 1AA
Tel: 018382 00312
★★★ Small Hotel

DOLLAR

Castle Campbell Hotel
Bridge Street, Dollar,
Clackmannanshire, FK14 7DE
Tel: 01259-742519
★★★ Small Hotel

DRYMEN

Kilmaronock House
Loch Lomond, Near
Drymen, West
Dumbartonshire,
G83 8SB
Tel: 01360 660351
Awaiting Inspection

Hillview
The Square, Drymen,
Stirlingshire,
G63 0BL
Tel: 01360 661000
Awaiting Inspection

**Buchanan Arms
Hotel & Leisure Club**
Main Street, Drymen,
Stirlingshire,
G63 0BQ
Tel: 01360 660588
★★★ Hotel

Winnock Hotel
The Square, Drymen,
Stirlingshire, G63 0BL
★★★ Hotel

DUMBARTON

Dumbuck House Hotel
Glasgow Road,
Dumbarton,
Dunbartonshire,
G82 1EG
Tel: 01389 734336
★★★ Hotel

The Abbotsford Hotel
Stirling Road,
Dumbarton, G82 2PJ
Tel: 01389 733304
★★★ Hotel

DUNBLANE

Dunblane Hydro
Perth Road, Dunblane,
Perthshire, FK15 0HG
Tel: 01786 822551
★★★★ Hotel

BY DUNBLANE

Cromlix House
Kinbuck, Dunblane,
Perthshire,
FK15 9JT
Tel: 01786 822125
★★★★ Small Hotel

DUNOON

Craigen Hotel
85 Argyll Street, Dunoon,
PA23 7DH
Tel: 01369 702307
★★ Guest House

Dhailling Lodge
155 Alexandra Parade,
Dunoon, Argyll, PA23 8AW
Tel: 01369 701253
★★★★ Guest House

Park Hotel
3 Glenmorag Avenue,
Dunoon, Argyll, PA23 7LG
Tel: 01369 702383
★★★ Hotel

Milton Tower Hotel
West Bay, Dunoon, Argyll,
PA23 7LD
Tel: 01369 705785
★★★ Small Hotel

Sebright
41A Alexandra Parade,
Dunoon, Argyll, PA23 8AF
Tel: 01369 702099
★★ Guest House

The Cedars
51 Alexandra Parade, East
Bay, Dunoon, Argyll,
PA23 8AF
Tel: 01369 702425
★★★★ Guest House

Royal Marine Hotel
Hunter's Quay, Dunoon,
Argyll, PA23 8HJ
Tel: 01369 705810
★★★ Hotel

Esplanade Hotel
West Bay, Dunoon,
Argyll, PA23 7HU
Tel: 01369 704070
★★★ Hotel

Craigieburn Hotel
Alexandra Parade, East
Bay, Dunoon, Argyll,
PA23 8AN
Tel: 01369 702048
★★ Guest House

Rosscairn House
51 Hunter Street, Kirn,
Dunoon, Argyll, PA23 8JR
Tel: 01369 704344
★★★ Guest House

Bay House Hotel
West Bay Promenade,
Dunoon, Argyll, PA23 7HU
Tel: 01369 704832/702348
★★★ Small Hotel

Argyll Hotel
Argyll Street, Dunoon,
Argyll, PA23 7NE
Tel: 01369 702059
★ Hotel

Hunters Quay Hotel
Marine Parade, Dunoon,
Argyll, PA23 8HJ
Tel: 01369 707070
★★★★ Small Hotel

West End Hotel
54 Victoria Parade,
Dunoon, Argyll, PA23 7HU
Tel: 01369 702907
★★ Small Hotel

McColl's Hotel
West Bay, Dunoon, Argyll,
PA23 7HN
Tel: 01369 702764/08702
403080
★ Hotel

St Ives Hotel
West Bay, Dunoon, Argyll,
PA23 7HU
Tel: 01369 702400/704825
★★★ Small Hotel

DUNTOCHER, GLASGOW

West Park Hotel
Great Western Road,
Duntocher, Clydebank,
G81 6DB
Tel: 01389 872333
★★ Hotel

FALKIRK

Cladhan Hotel
Kemper Avenue, Falkirk,
Stirlingshire, FK1 1UF
Tel: 01324 627421
★★★ Hotel

Park Hotel Falkirk
Camelon Road, Falkirk,
Stirlingshire, FK1 5RY
Tel: 01324 628331
★★★ Hotel

FINTRY

FORD, BY LOCHGILPHEAD

Ford House
Ford, By Lochgilphead,
Argyll, PA31 8RH
Tel: 01546 810273
★★★ Guest House

Directory of all VisitScotland Quality Assured Serviced Hotels and Guest Houses

GARELOCHHEAD

Rock House
Garelochhead,
Argyll & Bute, G84 0AN
Tel: 01436 810082
★★ Guest House

GARTMORE

Gartmore House
Gartmore, Stirling,
FK8 3SZ
Tel: 01877 382991
Guest House

GARTOCHARN

Badshalloch Farm House
Badshalloch Farm,
Gartocharn, Alexandria,
G83 8SB
Tel: 01360 661167/07795
Awaiting Inspection

ISLE OFGIGHA

Gigha Hotel & Cottages
Isle of Gigha, Argyll,
PA41 7AA
Tel: 01583 505254
★★★ Small Hotel

GRANGEMOUTH

Leapark Hotel
130 Bo'ness Road,
Grangemouth,
Stirlingshire, FK3 9BX
Tel: 01324 486733
★★★ Hotel

Grangeburn House
55 Bo'ness Road,
Grangemouth,
Stirlingshire, FK3 9BJ
Tel: 01324 471301
★★★★ Guest House

The Grange Manor
Glensburgh, Grangemouth,
Stirlingshire, FK3 8XJ
Tel: 01324 474836
★★★★ Hotel

HELENSBURGH

Sinclair House
91/93 Sinclair Street,
Helensburgh,
Argyll & Bute, G84 8TR
Tel: 01436 676301
★★★★ Guest House

INNELLAN, BY DUNOON

The Osborne Hotel
44 Shore Road, Innellan,
By Dunoon, Argyll,
PA23 7TJ
Tel: 01369 830445
★★ Small Hotel

INVERARAY

Swallow Argyll Hotel
Front Street, Inveraray,
Argyll, PA32 8XB
Tel: 01499 302466
★★★★ Hotel

Fernpoint Hotel
By the Pier, Inveraray,
Argyll, PA32 8UX
Tel: 01499 302170
Small Hotel

Creag Dhubh
Inveraray, Argyll,
PA32 8XT
Tel: 01499 302430
★★★★ Guest House

Killean Farm House
Inveraray, Argyll,
PA32 8XT
Tel: 01499 302474
★★★ Guest House

Loch Fyne Hotel
Newtown, Inveraray,
Argyll, PA32 8XJ
Tel: 01499 302148
★★★ Hotel

INVERSNAID

Inversnaid Hotel
Inversnaid, by Aberfoyle,
Stirlingshire, FK8 3TU
Tel: 01877 386223
★★★ Hotel

ISLE OF IONA

Argyll Hotel
Iona, Isle of Iona, Argyll,
PA76 6SJ
Tel: 01681 700334
★★★ Small Hotel

St Columba Hotel
Isle of Iona, Argyll,
PA76 6SL
Tel: 01681 700304
★★★ Hotel

BALLYGRANT

Kilmeny
Ballygrant, Isle of Islay,
PA45 7QW
Tel: 01496 840668
★★★★★ Guest House

BOWMORE

The Harbour Inn and Restaurant
Bowmore, Isle of Islay,
Argyll, PA43 7JR
Tel: 01496 810330
★★★★ Inn

Lochside Hotel
Shore Street, Bowmore,,
Isle of Islay, PA43 7LB
Tel: 01496 810244
★★★ Small Hotel

Lambeth Guest House
Jamieson Street,
Bowmore,
Isle of Islay, Argyll,
PA43 7HL
Tel: 01496 810597
★★★ Guest House

The Bowmore House
Shore Street, Bowmore,
Isle of Islay,
PA43 7LB
Tel: 01496 810324
★★★ Guest House

BRIDGEND

Bridgend Hotel
Bridgend,
Isle of Islay, PA44 7PJ
Tel: 01496 810212
★★★ Small Hotel

BRUICHLADDICH

Loch Gorm House
Bruichladdich, Isle of Islay,
Argyll, PA49 7UN
Tel: 07775 666850
Awaiting Inspection

PORT ASKAIG

Port Askaig Hotel
Port Askaig,
Isle of Islay,
PA46 7RB
Tel: 01496 840 245
★ Small Hotel

PORT CHARLOTTE

The Port Charlotte Hotel
Main Street, Port Charlotte,
Isle of Islay,, PA48 7TU
Tel: 01496 850360
★★★★ Small Hotel

PORT ELLEN

Machrie Hotel & Golf Links
Port Ellen, Isle of Islay,
PA42 7AN
Tel: 01496 302310
★★★ Small Hotel

The Trout Fly Guest House
Charlotte Street, Port Ellen,
Argyll, PA42 7DF
Tel: 01496 302204
★★ Guest House

No 40 Pier Road
Frederick Crescent, Port
Ellen, Isle of Islay,
PA42 7DJ
Tel: 01496 300502
Awaiting Inspection

Glenegedale House
Glenegedale, Port Ellen,
Isle of Islay, Argyll,
PA42 7AS
Tel: 01496 300400
Awaiting Inspection

Glenmachrie
Port Ellen, Isle of Islay,
Argyll, PA42 7AW
Tel: 01496 302560
★★★★ Guest House

ISLE OF JURA

Jura Hotel
Isle of Jura, Argyll,
PA60 7XU
Tel: 01496 820243
★★ Small Hotel

KILCHRENAN

Taychreggan Hotel
Kilchrenan,by Taynuilt,
Argyll, PA35 1HQ
Tel: 01866 833211
★★★ Hotel

Ardanaiseig Hotel
Kilchrenan, by Taynuilt,
Argyll, PA35 1HE
Tel: 01866 833333
★★★★ Small Hotel

KILFINAN

Kilfinan Hotel
Kilfinan, Nr Tighnabruaich,
Argyll, PA21 2EP
Tel: 01700 821201
Awaiting Inspection

KILLIN

Dall Lodge Country House
Main Street, Killin,
Perthshire, FK21 8TN
Tel: 01567 820217
★★★★ Guest House

Invertay House
Main Road, Killin,
Perthshire, FK21 8TN
Tel: 01567 820492
★★★ Guest House

Drumfinn
Country Guest House
Manse Road, Killin,
Perthshire, FK21 8UY
Tel: 01567 820900
★★★ Guest House

Killin Hotel
Main Street, Killin,
Perthshire, FK21 8TP
Tel: 01567 820296
★★ Hotel

Craigbuie Guest House
Main Street, Killin,
Perthshire,
FK21 8UH
Tel: 01567 820439
★★★ Guest House

Bridge of Lochay Hotel
Aberfeldy Road, Killin,
Perthshire, FK21 8TS
Tel: 01567 820272
Awaiting Inspection

Breadalbane House
Main Street, Killin,
Perthshire, FK21 8UT
Tel: 01567 820134
★★★ Guest House

Fairview House
Main Street, Killin,
Perthshire,
FK21 8UT
Tel: 01567 820667
★★★ Guest House

KILNINVER, BY OBAN

Knipoch Hotel
Knipoch, Argyll,
PA34 4QT
Tel: 01852 316251
★★★★ Hotel

LEDAIG, BY OBAN

Isle of Eriska Hotel
Ledaig, Argyll, PA37 1SD
Tel: 01631 720371
★★★★★ Hotel

LOCHAWE

Loch Awe Hotel
Loch Awe, Dalmally,
Argyll, PA33 1AQ
Tel: 01838 200261
★★★ Hotel

LOCHEARNHEAD

Lochearnhead Hotel
Lochside, Lochearnhead,
FK19 8PN
Tel: 01567 830229
★★ Small Hotel

Mansewood Country House
Lochearnhead, Perthshire,
FK19 8NS
Tel: 01567 830213
★★★ Guest House

BY LOCHGILPHEAD

Cairnbaan Hotel
Cairnbaan, by
Lochgilphead, Argyll,
PA31 8SJ
Tel: 01546 603668
★★★★ Small Hotel

LOCHGOIL

Rowan House B&B
The Drey, Carrick Castle,
Loch Goil, Argyll,
PA24 8AF
Tel: 01301 703090
Awaiting Inspection

LOCHGOILHEAD

Drimsynie House Hotel
Lochgoilhead, Argyll,
PA24 8AD
Tel: 01301 703247
★★★ Small Hotel

The Lodge
Lochgoilhead, Argyll,
PA24 8AE
Tel: 01301 703193
★★★★★
Exclusive Use Venue

LUSS

The Lodge on Loch Lomond
Luss, Dunbartonshire,
G83 8NT
Tel: 01436 860201
★★★ Hotel

Colquhoun Arms Hotel
Luss,by Alexandria,
Dunbartonshire,
G83 8NY
Tel: 01436 860282
★★ Small Hotel

ISLE OF MULL, BUNESSAN

Ardachy House Hotel
Uisken, by Bunessan,
Isle of Mull,
Argyll, PA67 6DS
Tel: 01681 700505
★★★ Small Hotel

ISLE OF MULL, CRAIGNURE

Isle of Mull Hotel
Craignure,
Isle of Mull, Argyll,
PA65 6BB
Tel: 01680 812351
★★★ Hotel

Pennygate Lodge
Craignure, Isle of Mull,
Argyll, PA65 6AY
Tel: 01680 812333
★★★ Guest House

Linnhe View
Craignure, Isle of Mull,
Argyll, PA65 6AY
Tel: 01680 812369
Awaiting Inspection

ISLE OF MULL, DERVAIG

Druimnacroish Hotel
Dervaig, Isle of Mull,
PA75 6QW
Tel: 01688 400274
★★★ Small Hotel

ISLE OF MULL, BY DERVAIG

The Calgary Hotel
by Dervaig,
Isle of Mull, Argyll,
PA75 6QW
Tel: 01688 400256
★★★ Small Hotel

ISLE OF MULL, FIONNPHORT

Achaban House
Fionnphort, Isle of Mull,
Argyll, PA66 6BL
Tel: 01681 700205
★★★ Guest House

Seaview
Fionnphort,
Isle of Mull,
PA66 6BL
Tel: 01681 700235
★★★ Guest House

ISLE OF MULL, PENNYGHAEL

Pennyghael Hotel
Pennyghael,
Isle of Mull, Argyll,
PA70 6HB
Tel: 01681 704288
★★★★ Small Hotel

ISLE OF MULL, SALEN, AROS

Ard Mhor House
Pier Road,
Salen, Isle of Mull,
PA72 6JL
Tel: 01680 300255
★★★ Guest House

Salen Hotel
Salen, Isle of Mull,
Argyll, PA72 6JE
Tel: 01680 300324
★★ Small Hotel

ISLE OF MULL, TIRORAN

Tiroran House
Tiroran, Isle of Mull,
Argyll, PA69 6ES
Tel: 01681 705232
★★★★ Small Hotel

ISLE OF MULL, TOBERMORY

Failte Guest House
Main Street, Tobermory,
Isle of Mull, Argyll,
PA75 6NU
Tel: 01688 302495
★★★ Guest House

Sunart View Guest House
Eas Brae, Tobermory,
Isle of Mull, Argyll, PA75
6QA
Tel: 01688 302439
★★★ Guest House

Highland Cottage
Breadalbane Street,
Tobermory, Isle of Mull,
PA75 6PD
Tel: 01688 302030
★★★★ Small Hotel

The Western Isles Hotel
Tobermory, Isle of Mull,
Argyll, PA75 6PR
Tel: 01688 302012
★★★ Hotel

Tobermory Hotel
Main Street, Tobermory,
Isle of Mull, PA75 6NT
Tel: 01688 302091
★★★ Small Hotel

Fairways Lodge
Erray Road, Tobermory,
Isle of Mull, Argyll,
PA75 6PS
Tel: 01688 302792
★★★★ Guest House

NORTH CONNEL

Lochnell Arms Hotel
North Connel, Argyll,
PA37 1RP
Tel: 01631 710239
★★★ Small Hotel

OBAN

Sutherland Hotel
Corran Esplanade,
Oban, Argyll,
PA34 5PN
Tel: 01631 562539
★★★ Guest House

Thornloe Guest House
Albert Road, Oban,
Argyll, PA34 5JD
Tel: 01631 562879
★★★★ Guest House

Glenara Guest House
Rockfield Road, Oban,
Argyll, PA34 5DQ
Tel: 01631 563172
★★★★ Guest House

Lower Soroba Farmhouse
Oban, Argyll,
PA34 4LE
Tel: 01631 565349
Awaiting Inspection

Roseneath Guest House
Dalriach Road, Oban,
Argyll, PA34 5EQ
Tel: 01631 562929
★★★ Guest House

Alexandra Hotel
The Esplanade, Oban,
Argyll, PA34 5AA
Tel: 1838200444
★★★ Hotel

Regent Hotel
Esplanade, Oban,
Argyll, PA34 5PZ
Tel: 01631 562341
Hotel

Corriemar House
6 Corran Esplanade,
Oban, Argyll,
PA34 5AQ
Tel: 01631 562476
★★★★ Guest House

Kilchrenan House
Corran Esplanade,
Oban, Argyll,
PA34 5AQ
Tel: 01631 562663
★★★★ Guest House

Wellpark House
Esplanade, Oban,
Argyll, PA34 5AQ
Tel: 01631 562948
★★★ Guest House

Don-Muir Guest House
Pulpit Hill, Oban,
Argyll, PA34 4LX
Tel: 01631 564536
★★★★ Guest House

Maridon House
Dunuaran Road, Oban,
Argyll, PA34 4NE
Tel: 01631 562670
★★★ Guest House

Foxholes Country Hotel
Cologin, Lerags, Oban,
Argyll, PA34 4SE
Tel: 01631 564982
★★★★ Small Hotel

Glenbervie Guest House
Dalriach Road, Oban,
Argyll, PA34 5JD
Tel: 01631 564770
★★★★ Guest House

Alt Na Craig
Glenmore Road, Oban,
Argyll, PA34 4PG
Tel: 01631 563637
★★★★ Guest House

Ulva Villa
Soroba Road, Oban,
Argyll, PA34 4JF
Tel: 01631 563042
★★★ Guest House

Great Western Hotel
Corran Esplanade, Oban,
Argyll, PA34 5PP
Tel: 01942 824824
★★★ Hotel

Greencourt Guest House
Benvoullin Road, Oban,
Argyll, PA34 5EF
Tel: 01631 563987
★★★★ Guest House

Alltavona
Corran Esplanade, Oban,
Argyll, PA34 5AQ
Tel: 01631 565067
★★★★ Guest House

Gramarvin Guest House
Breadalbane Street, Oban,
Argyll, PA34 5PE
Tel: 01631 564622
★★★ Guest House

Sgeir Mhaol Guest House
Soroba Road, Oban,
Argyll, PA34 4JF
Tel: 01631 562650
★★★ Guest House

Oban Bay Hotel
Esplanade, Oban, Argyll,
PA34 5AE
Tel: 0870 950 6273
★★★ Hotel

[DThe Barriemore
Corran Esplanade, Oban,
Argyll, PA34 5AQ
Tel: 01631 566356
★★★★ Guest House

Kathmore Guest House
Soroba Road, Oban,
Argyll, PA34 4JF
Tel: 01631 562104
★★★ Guest House

**The Kimberley Hotel,
Bachler's Conservatory**
3 Dalriach Road, Oban,
Argyll, PA34 5EQ
Tel: 01631 571115
★★★★ Small Hotel

Kings Knoll Hotel
Dunollie Road, Oban,
PA34 5JH
Tel: 01631 562536
★★★ Small Hotel

Ayres Guest House
3 Victoria Crescent,
Corran Esplanade,
Oban, Argyll,
PA34 5JL
Tel: 01631 562 260
★★ Guest House

Glenrigh Guest House
The Esplanade, Oban,
Argyll, PA34 5AQ
Tel: 01631 562991
★★★ Guest House

Strathnaver Guest House
Dunollie Road, Oban,
Argyll, PA34 5JQ
Tel: 01631 63305
★★★ Guest House

St Anne's Guest House
Dunollie Road, Oban,
Argyll, PA34 5PH
Tel: 01631 562743
★★★ Guest House

Glengorm
Dunollie Road, Oban,
Argyll, PA34 5PH
Tel: 01631 564386
★★★ Guest House

The Manor House
Gallanoch Road, Oban,
Argyll, PA34 4LS
Tel: 01631 562087
★★★★ Small Hotel

Hawthornbank Guest House
Dalriach Road, Oban,
Argyll, PA34 5JE
Tel: 01631 562041
★★★★ Guest House

The Town House
George Street, Oban,
Argyll, PA34 5NX
Tel: 01631 562954
Awaiting Inspection

Kelvin Hotel
Shore Street, Oban,
Argyll, PA34 4LQ
Tel: 01631 562150
★ Guest House

Viewbank
Breadalbane Lane, Oban,
Argyll, PA34 5PF
Tel: 01631 562328
★★★★ Guest House

Beech Grove Guest House
Croft Road, Oban,
Argyll, PA34 5JL
Tel: 01631 66111
★★★★ Guest House

Royal Hotel
Argyll Square, Oban,
Argyll, PA34 4BE
Tel: 01631 563021
★★ Hotel

Herbridean Princess
South Pier, Oban
★★★★★ Cruise Ship

The Old Manse
Dalriach Road, Oban,
Argyll, PA34 5JE
Tel: 01631 564886
★★★★ Guest House

Dungallan House Hotel
Gallanach Road, Oban,
Argyll, PA34 4PD
Tel: 01631 563799
★★★★ Small Hotel

Glenburnie
Esplanade, Oban,
Argyll, PA34 5AQ
Tel: 01631 562089
★★★★ Guest House

The Caledonian Hotel
Station Square, Oban,
Argyll, PA34 5RT
Tel: 01631 563133
★★★★ Hotel

Queens Hotel
Esplanade, Oban,
Argyll, PA34 5AG
Tel: 01631 562505
Hotel

Glenroy Guest House
Rockfield Road, Oban,
Argyll, PA34 5DQ
Tel: 01631 562 585
★★★ Guest House

BY OBAN
Falls of Lora Hotel
Connel Ferry, by Oban,
Argyll, PA37 1PB
Tel: 01631 710483
★★★ Hotel

Ards House
Connel, Oban, Argyll,
PA37 1PT
Tel: 01631 710255
★★★★ Guest House

Willowburn Hotel
Clachan Seil, by Oban,
Argyll, PA34 4TJ
Tel: 01852 300276
★★★★ Small Hotel

POLMONT, BY FALKIRK
Inchyra Grange Hotel
Grange Road, Polmont,
Stirlingshire, FK2 0YB
Tel: 01324 711911
★★★★ Hotel

PORT APPIN
The Pierhouse Hotel
Port Appin, Appin,
Argyll, PA38 4DE
Tel: 01631 730302
★★★ Small Hotel

The Airds Hotel
Port Appin, Appin,
Argyll, PA38 4DF
Tel: 01631 730236
★★★★ Small Hotel

ROSNEATH
Easter Garth
The Clachan, Rosneath,
Argyll & Bute,
G84 0RF
Tel: 01436 831007
★★★ Guest House

ROWARDENNAN
Rowardennan Hotel
Rowardennan,
By Drymen, Stirlingshire,
G63 0AR
Tel: 01360 870273
★★★ Small Hotel

ST CATHERINES
Thistle House
St Catherines, Argyll,
PA25 8AZ
Tel: 01499 302209
★★★★ Guest House

STIRLING
Stillrovin In Scotland
Stillrovin, Bannockburn
Road, Cowie,
Stirlingshire, FK7 7BG
Tel: 01786 818899
Awaiting Inspection

Munro Guest House
14 Princes Street,
Stirling, FK8 1HQ
Tel: 01786 472685
★★★ Guest House

156 Bannockburn Road
Stirling, FK7 0EW
Tel: 01786 812098
Awaiting Inspection

Garfield Guesthouse
12 Victoria Square,
Stirling, Stirlingshire,
FK8 2QZ
Tel: 01786 473730
★★★ Guest House

Stirling Management Centre
University of Stirling,
Stirling, FK9 4LA
Tel: 01786 451666
★★★ Hotel

**Harviestoun Country
Hotel & Restaurant**
Dollar Road, Tillicoultry,
Clackmannanshire,
FK13 6PQ
Tel: 01259 752522
★★★ Small Hotel

The Whitehouse
13 Glasgow Road,
Stirling, Stirlingshire,
FK7 0PA
Tel: 01786 462636
★★★ Guest House

Cambria Guest House
141 Bannockburn Road,
Stirling, FK7 0EP
Tel: 01786 814603
★★★★ Guest House

King Robert Hotel
Glasgow Road,
Bannockburn, Stirling,
FK7 0LJ
Tel: 01786 811666
★★★ Hotel

Allan Park Hotel
20 Allan Park,
Stirling, Stirlingshire,
FK8 2QG
Tel: 01786 473598
★★ Small Hotel

Linden Guest House
22 Linden Avenue,
Stirling, Stirlingshire,
FK7 7PQ
Tel: 01786 448850
★★★★ Guest House

Castlecraig
50 Causewayhead Road,
Stirling,
Stirlingshire, FK9 5EY
Tel: 01786 475452
★★★ Guest House

Wallaceview
4 Causewayhead Road,
Stirling, Stirlingshire,
FK9 5EN
Tel: 01786 475447
★★★ Guest House

**Express by
Holiday Inn - Stirling**
Springkerse Business Park,
Stirling, Stirlingshire,
FK7 7XH
Tel: 01786 449922
★★★ Hotel

**Paramount Stirling
Highland Hotel**
Spittal Street, Stirling,
FK8 1DU
Tel: 01786 272727
★★★★ Hotel

**The Park Lodge Country
House Hotel**
32 Park Terrace,
Stirling, FK8 2JS
Tel: 01786 474862
★★★ Small Hotel

Terraces Hotel
4 Melville Terrace,
Stirling, Stirlingshire,
FK8 2ND
Tel: 01786 472268
★★★ Small Hotel

**The Royal Hotel and Royal
Lodge Conference Centre**
55 & 103 Henderson Street,
Bridge of Allan,
Stirlingshire,
FK9 4HG
Tel: 01786 832284
★★★ Small Hotel

No 8 Deroran Place
Stirling, Stirlingshire,
FK8 2PG
Tel: 01786 475225
Awaiting Inspection

Burns View
1 Albert Place, Stirling,
Stirlingshire,
FK8 2QL
Tel: 01786 451002
★★★ Guest House

STRACHUR
The Creggans Inn
Strachur, Argyll,
PA27 8BX
Tel: 01369 860279
★★★ Small Hotel

Directory of all VisitScotland Quality Assured Serviced Hotels and Guest Houses

STRATHYRE

Creagan House Restaurant with Accommodation
Strathyre, Callander,
Perthshire, FK18 8ND
Tel: 01877 384638

★★★★

Restaurant with Rooms

TARBERT, LOCH FYNE

Balinakill Country House Hotel
Clachan, by Tarbet,
Kintyre, PA29 6XL
Tel: 01880 740206

★★★ Small Hotel

The Columba Hotel
East Pier Road, Tarbert,
Argyll, PA29 6UF
Tel: 01880 820808

★★★ Small Hotel

Stonefield Castle Hotel
Tarbert, Loch Fyne,
Argyll, PA29 6YJ
Tel: 01880 820836

★★★ Hotel

TARBET, BY ARROCHAR

Tarbet Hotel
Tarbert, Arrochar, Loch
Lomond, Argyll & Bute,
G83 7DE
Tel: 01942 824824

★★ Hotel

TIGHNABRUAICH

The Royal at Tighnabruaich
Shore Road,
Tighnabruaich, Argyll,
PA21 2BE
Tel: 01700 811239

★★★★ Small Hotel

GOTT BAY

Kirkapol Guest House
Gott Bay, Isle of Tiree,
Argyll, PA77 6TW
Tel: 01879 220729

★★★ Guest House

ISLE OF TIREE

Glebe House Tiree
Gott Bay, Isle of Tiree,
Argyllshire, PA77 6TN
Tel: 01879 220758

★★★★ Guest House

TROSSACHS, BY CALLANDER

Loch Achray Hotel
by Callander,
Stirlingshire, FK17 8HZ
Tel: 01877 376229

★★★ Hotel

TYNDRUM, BY CRIANLARICH

Ben Doran Hotel
Tyndrum, Perthshire,
FK20
Tel: 01838 400373

★★★ Hotel

Royal Hotel
Tyndrum, by Crianlarich,
Perthshire, FK20 8RZ
Tel: 01838 400272

★★★ Hotel

Invervey Hotel
Tyndrum, by Crianlarich,
Perthshire, FK20 8RY
Tel: 01838 400219

★★ Small Hotel

Dalkell Cottages
Lower Station Road,
Tyndrum, Perthshire,
FK20 8RY
Tel: 01838 400285

★★★ Guest House

PERTHSHIRE, ANGUS AND DUNDEE AND THE KINGDOM OF FIFE

ABERDOUR

Aberdour Hotel
38 High Street,
Aberdour, Fife, KY3 0SW
Tel: 01383 860325

★★★ Small Hotel

The Cedar Inn
20 Shore Road, Aberdour,
Fife, KY3 0TR
Tel: 01383 860310

★★ Inn

The Woodside Hotel
High Street, Aberdour,
Fife, KY3 0SW
Tel: 01383 860328

★★★ Small Hotel

ABERFELDY

Balnearn House
Crieff Road, Aberfeldy,
Perthshire, PH15 2BJ
Tel: 01887 820431

★★★ Guest House

Fortingall Hotel
Fortingall, Aberfeldy,
Perthshire, PH15 2NG,
Te/Fax:01887 830367

★★★★ Small Hotel

The Moness House Hotel & Country Club
Crieff Road, Aberfeldy,
Perthshire, PH15 2DY
Tel: 0870 4431460

★★★ Small Hotel

BY ABERFELDY

The Weem Hotel
Weem, By Aberfeldy,
Perthshire, PH15 2LD
Tel: 01887 820381

★★★ Small Hotel

ALYTH

Tigh Na Leigh
22-24 Airlie Street, Alyth,
Perthshire, PH11 8AD
Tel: 01828 632372

★★★★ Guest House

Lands of Loyal Hotel
Loyal Road, Alyth,
Blairgowrie, PH11 8JQ
Tel: 01828 633151

★★★★ Small Hotel

Airlie Mount Mansion House
2 Albert Street,
Alyth, Blairgowrie,
Perthshire,
PH11 8AX
Tel: 01828 632986

★★ Guest House

ANSTRUTHER

The Spindrift
Pittenween Road,
Anstruther,
Fife, KY10 3DT
Tel: 01333 310573

★★★★ Guest House

ARBROATH

Blairdene Guest House
216 High Street,
Arbroath, Angus,
DD11 1HY
Tel: 01241 872380

★★ Guest House

Harbour Nights Guest House
4 Shore,
Arbroath, Angus,
DD11 1PB
Tel: 01241 434343

★★★★ Guest House

Rosely Country House Hotel
Forfar Road, Arbroath,
Angus, DD11 3RB
Tel: 01241 876828

★★ Small Hotel

Cliffburn Hotel
Cliffburn Road, Arbroath,
Angus, DD11 5BT
Tel: 01241 873432

★ Small Hotel

Towerbank Guest House
9 James Street,
Arbroath, Angus,
DD11 1JP
Tel: 01241 431343

★★★ Guest House

AUCHTERARDER

Cairn Lodge Hotel
Orchil Road,
Auchterarder,
Perthshire, PH3 1LX
Tel: 01764 662634

★★★★ Small Hotel

The Gleneagles Hotel
Auchterarder,
Perthshire, PH3 1NF
Tel: 01764 662231

★★★★★

International Resort

Collearn House Hotel
High Street, Auchterarder,
Perthshire, PH3 1DF
Tel: 01764 663553

★★★★ Small Hotel

Duchally Country Estate
Duchally Country Estate,
Duchally, Auchterarder,
Perthshire, PH3 1PN
Tel: 01764 663071

★★★ Small Hotel

AUCHTERMUCHTY

Myres Castle
Auchtermuchty, Fife,
KY14 7EW
Tel: 01337 828350

★★★★★

Exclusive Use Venue

BALLINLUIG, BY PITLOCHRY

Cuil -an- Daraich
2 Cuil -an- Daraich,
Logierait, Pitlochry,
Perthshire, PH9 0LH
Tel: 01796 482750
★★★ Guest House

BLACKFORD

Blackford Hotel
Moray Street, Blackford,
Perthshire, PH4 1QF
Tel: 01764 682497
★★★ Small Hotel

BLAIR ATHOLL

Atholl Arms Hotel
Old North Road,
Blair Atholl, by Pitlochry,
Perthshire, PH18 5SG
Tel: 01796 481205
★★★ Hotel

Bridge of Tilt Hotel
Bridge of Tilt, Blair Atholl,
Perthshire, PH18 5SU
Tel: 01796 481333
★★ Hotel

Ptarmigan House
Bridge of Tilt, Blair Atholl,
Perthshire, PH18 5SZ
Tel: 01796 481269
★★★ Guest House

Dalgreine Guest House
Bridge of Tilt, Blair Atholl,
Perthshire, PH18 5SX
Tel: 01796 481276
★★★★ Guest House

BLAIRGOWRIE

Broadmyre Motel
Carsie, Blairgowrie,
Perthshire, PH10 6QW
Tel: 01250 873262
★★ Guest House

Rosebank House
Balmoral Road,
Blairgowrie,
Perthshire, PH10 7AF
Tel: 01250 872912
★★★ Guest House

Glensheiling House
Hatton Road, Blairgowrie,
Perthshire, PH10 7HZ
Tel: 01250 874605
★★★★ Guest House

Ivybank Guest House
Boat Brae, Blairgowrie,
Perthshire, PH10 7BH
Tel: 01250 873056
★★★★ Guest House

Miramichi
Golf Course Road,
Blairgowrie, Perthshire,
PH10 6LQ
Tel: 01250 873310
Awaiting Inspection

Duncraggan
Perth Road, Blairgowrie,
Perthshire, PH10 6EJ
Tel: 01250 872082
★★★★ Guest House

Altamount House Hotel
Coupar Angus Road,
Blairgowrie, Perthshire,
PH10 6JN
Tel: 01250 873512
★★★ Small Hotel

The Laurels
Golf Course Road,
Blairgowrie,
Perthshire, PH10 6LH
Tel: 01250 874920
★★★ Guest House

Royal Hotel
53 Allan Street,
Blairgowrie,
Perthshire, PH10 6AB
Tel: 01250 872226
Hotel

Victoria Hotel
Lower Mill Street,
Blairgowrie,
Perthshire, PH10 6NG
Tel: 01250 876669
Awaiting Inspection

Angus Hotel
Wellmeadow,
Blairgowrie,
Perthshire, PH10 6NQ
Tel: 01250 872455
★★★ Hotel

Drumkilbo House
Meigle, Blairgowrie,
Perthshire, PH12 8QS
Tel: 01828 640445
Awaiting Inspection

BY BLAIRGOWRIE

Kinloch House Hotel
Blairgowrie, Perthshire,
PH10 6SG
Tel: 01250 884237
★★★★★ Hotel

Moorfield House Hotel
Myreriggs Road,
Coupar Angus,
Perthshire, PH13 9HS
Tel: 01828 627303
★★★ Small Hotel

BRECHIN

Northern Hotel
2 Clerk Street,
Brechin, Angus,
DD9 6AE
Tel: 01356 625400
★★★ Small Hotel

BRIDGE OF CALLY

Bridge of Cally Hotel
Bridge of Cally,
Blairgowrie,
Perthshire, PH10 7JJ
Tel: 01250 886231
★★★ Small Hotel

BRIDGE OF EARN

The Last Cast Hotel
Main Street,
Bridge of Earn,
Perthshire, PH2 9PL
Tel: 01738 812578
★★ Guest House

BROUGHTY FERRY

Redwood Guest House
89 Monifieth Road,
Broughty Ferry,
Dundee, DD5 2SB
Tel: 01382 736550
★★★★ Guest House

BURNTISLAND

Kingswood Hotel
Kinghorn Road,
Burntisland, Fife,
KY3 9LL
Tel: 01592 872329
★★★ Small Hotel

Burntisland Sands Hotel
Lochies Road,
Burntisland, Fife,
KY3 9JX
Tel: 01592 872230
★★★ Small Hotel

CARNOUSTIE

Lochtybank House
20 High Street,
Carnoustie, Angus,
DD7 6AQ
Tel: 01241 854849
★★★ Guest House

Seaview Private Hotel
29 Ireland Street,
Carnoustie, Angus,
DD7 6AS
Tel: 01241 851092
★★★★ Small Hotel

Station Hotel
Station Road,
Carnoustie, Angus,
DD7 6AR
Tel: 01241 852447
★★ Small Hotel

Carnoustie Golf Course Hotel & Resort
The Links,
Carnoustie, Angus,
DD7 7JE
Tel: 01241 411999
★★★★ Hotel

Lochlorian House Hotel
13 Philip Street,
Carnoustie, Angus,
DD7 6ED
Tel: 01241 852182
★★★ Small Hotel

Kinloch Arms Hotel
27 High Street,
Carnoustie, Angus,
DD7 6AN
Tel: 01241 853127
★★ Small Hotel

CHARLESTOWN, BY DUNFERMLINE

The Elgin Hotel and Restaurants
Charlestown, by
Dunfermline, Fife,
KY11 3EE
Tel: 01383 872257
★★★ Small Hotel

COMRIE

The Royal Hotel
Melville Square, Comrie,
Perthshire, PH6 2DN
Tel: 01764 679200
★★★★ Small Hotel

COUPAR ANGUS

Red House Hotel
Station Road, Coupar
Angus, Blairgowrie,
PH13 9AL
Tel: 01828 628500
★★★ Hotel

COWDENBEATH

Struan Bank Hotel
74 Perth Road,
Cowdenbeath, Fife,
KY4 9BG
Tel: 01383 511057
★★ Guest House

CRAIL

Balcomie Links Hotel
Balcomie Road, Crail,
Anstruther, Fife,
KY10 3TN
Tel: 01333 450237
★★ Small Hotel

Caiplie House
53 High Street, Crail,
Fife, KY10 3RA
Tel: 01333 450564
★★★ Guest House

Marine Hotel
54 Nethergate, Crail,
Fife, KY10 3TZ
Tel: 01333 450207
★★★ Guest House

The Hazelton
29 Marketgate, Crail,
Fife, KY15 4HF
Tel: 01333 450250
★★★ Guest House

Golf Hotel
4 High Street, Crail,
Fife, KY10 3TD
Tel: 01333 450206
★★ Small Hotel

The Honeypot Guest House
6 High Street South,
Crail, Fife, KY10 3TD
Tel: 01333 450935
★★★ Guest House

CRIEFF

Glenearn House
Perth Road,
Crieff, Perthshire,
PH7 3EQ
Tel: 01764 650000
★★★★ Guest House

Murraypark Hotel
Connaught Terrace,
Crieff, Perthshire,
PH7 3DJ
Tel: 01764 653731
★★★ Hotel

Crieff Hydro Hotel
Crieff, Perthshire,
PH7 3LQ
Tel: 01764 655555
★★★★ Hotel

The Crieff Hotel
45-47 East High Street,
Crieff,
Perthshire, PH7 3HY
Tel: 01764 652632
★★ Small Hotel

Fendoch Guest House
Sma' Glen,
Crieff, Perthshire,
PH7 3LW
Tel: 01764 653446
★★★ Guest House

Galvelbeg House
Perth Road, Crieff,
Perthshire, PH7 3EQ
Tel: 01764 655061
★★★ Guest House

Drummond Arms Hotel
James Square, Crieff,
Perthshire, PH7 3HX
Tel: 01764 652151
★★ Hotel

Roundelwood Health Spa
Drummond Terrace, Crieff,
Perthshire, PH7 4AN
Tel: 01764 653806
★★★ Small Hotel

Kingarth
Perth Road, Crieff,
Perthshire, PH7 3EQ
Tel: 01764 652060
★★★ Guest House

Leven House Hotel
Comrie Road, Crieff,
PH7 4BA
Tel: 01764 652529
★★ Small Hotel

Comely Bank Guest House
32 Burrell Street,
Crieff, Perthshire,
PH7 4DT
Tel: 01764 653409
★★★ Guest House

Arduthie House
Perth Road, Crieff,
Perthshire, PH7 3EQ
Tel: 01764 653113
★★★ Guest House

CUPAR

Craigsanquhar House Hotel
Logie, Cupar, Fife,
KY15 4PZ
Tel: 01334 653426
★★★ Small Hotel

DUNDEE

Anderson's Guest House
285 Perth Road,
Dundee, Tayside,
DD2 1JS
Tel: 01382 668585
★★★ Guest House

Apex City Quay Hotel & Spa
1 West Victoria Dock Road,
Dundee, DD1 3JP
Tel: 0845 365 0000
★★★★ Hotel

Auld Steeple Guest House
94 Nethergate, Dundee,
Angus, DD1 4EL
Tel: 01382 200302
★ Guest House

Grosvenor Hotel
1 Grosvenor Road,
Dundee, Angus,
DD2 1LF
Tel: 01382 642991
★★★ Guest House

Taychreggan Hotel
4 Ellieslea Road, Broughty
Ferry, Dundee, Angus,
DD5 1JG
Tel: 01382 778626
★★★ Small Hotel

The Craigtay Hotel
101 Broughty Ferry Road,
Dundee, Angus,
DD4 6JE
Tel: 01382 451142
★★ Small Hotel

The Fort Hotel
58-60 Fort Street, Broughty
Ferry, Dundee,
Angus, DD5 2AB
Tel: 01382 737999
★★ Small Hotel

St Leonard B&B
22 Albany Terrace,
Dundee, Angus,
DD3 6HR
Tel: 01382 227146/227461
★ Guest House

Shaftesbury Hotel
1 Hyndford Street,
Dundee, Angus,
DD2 1HQ
Tel: 01382 669216
★★★ Small Hotel

The Grampian
295 Perth Road,
Dundee, DD2 1JS
Tel: 01382 667785
★★★ Guest House

Hilton Dundee
Earl Grey Place,
Dundee, DD1 4DE
Tel: 01382 229271
★★★★ Hotel

Invercarse Hotel
371 Perth Road,
Dundee, Angus,
DD2 1PG
Tel: 01382 669231
★★★ Hotel

Park House Hotel
40 Coupar Angus Road,
Dundee, Angus,
DD2 3HY
Tel: 01382 611151
★★★ Small Hotel

Strathdon Guest House
277 Perth Road, Dundee,
Angus, DD2 1JS
Tel: 01382 665648
★★★ Guest House

Alcorn Guest House
5 Hyndford Street,
Dundee, Angus,
DD2 1HQ
Tel: 01382 668433
★★★ Guest House

Dunlaw House Hotel
10 Union Terrace,
Dundee, Angus,
DD3 6JD
Tel: 01382 221703
★★ Small Hotel

Abertay Guest House
65 Monifieth Road,
Broughty Ferry, Dundee,
DD5 2RW
Tel: 01382 731453
★★ Guest House

Queens Hotel
160 Nethergate, Dundee,
Angus, DD1 4DU
Tel: 01382 322515
★★★ Hotel

Hotel Broughty Ferry
16 West Queen Street,
Broughty Ferry, Dundee,
DD5 1AR
Tel: 01382 480027
★★★★ Small Hotel

The Fishermans Tavern Hotel
10-16 Fort Street,
Broughty Ferry, Dundee,
Angus, DD5 2AD
Tel: 01382 775941
★★ Small Hotel

Swallow Hotel
Kingsway West,
Invergowrie, Dundee,
Angus, DD2 5JT
Tel: 01382 641122
★★ Hotel

Cullaig Guest House
1 Rosemount Terrace,
Dundee, Tayside, DD3 6JQ
Tel: 01382 322154
★★★ Guest House

Woodlands Hotel
13 Panmure Terrace,
Barnhill, Dundee,
Angus, DD5 2QL
Tel: 01382 480033
★★★ Hotel

DUNFERMLINE

Best Western Keavil House Hotel
Crossford, Fife,
KY12 8QW
Tel: 01383 736258
★★★ Hotel

Clarke Cottage Guest House
139 Halbeath Road,
Dunfermline, Fife,
KY11 4LA
Tel: 01383 735935
★★★ Guest House

Davaar House Hotel
126 Grieve Street,
Dunfermline, Fife,
KY12 8DW
Tel: 01383 721886
★★★ Small Hotel

Garvock House Hotel
St Johns Drive,
Dunfermline, KY12 7TU
Tel: 01383 621067
★★★★ Small Hotel

Rooms at 29 Bruce Street
29-35 Bruce Street,
Dunfermline, Fife,
KY12 7AG
Tel: 01383 840041
★★★ Small Hotel

King Malcolm Hotel
Queensferry Road,
Dunfermline,
Fife, KY11 8DS
Tel: 01383 722611
★★★ Hotel

Pitbauchlie House Hotel
Aberdour Road,
Dunfermline, KY11 4PB
Tel: 01383 722282
★★★ Hotel

Queensferry Hotel
St Margarets Head, North
Queensferry, Fife, KY11 1HP
Tel: 01383 410000
★★ Hotel

Merchant House
44 East Quality Street,
Dysart, Fife,
KY1 2PN
Tel: 01592 659177
Awaiting Inspection

Pitreavie Guest House
3 Aberdour Road,
Dunfermline, Fife,
KY11 4PB
Tel: 01383 724244
★★★★ Guest House

DUNKELD

Atholl Arms Hotel
Bridgehead,
Dunkeld, Perthshire,
PH8 0AQ
Tel: 01350 727219
★★★ Small Hotel

Hilton Dunkeld
Dunkeld, Perthshire,
PH8 0HX
Tel: 01350 727771
★★★★ Hotel

The Birnam Guest House
4 Murthly Terrace,
Birnam, By Dunkeld,
Perthshire, PH8 0BG
Tel: 01350 727201
★★★ Guest House

Waterbury Guest House
Murthly Terrace,
Birnam, by Dunkeld,
Perthshire, PH8 0BG
Tel: 01350 727324
★★★★ Guest House

Royal Dunkeld Hotel
Atholl Street,
Dunkeld, PH8 0AR
Tel: 01350 727322
★★★ Hotel

BY DUNKELD

Kinnaird
Kinnaird Estate,
Dalguise,
by Dunkeld, Perthshire,
PH8 0LB
Tel: 01796 482440
★★★★★ Small Hotel

EDZELL
Glenesk Hotel
High Street, Edzell,
Tayside, DD9 7TF
Tel: 01356 648319
★★★ Hotel

Panmure Arms Hotel
52 High Street, Edzell,
Angus, DD9 7TA
Tel: 01356 648950
★★★ Small Hotel

FORFAR
Royal Hotel
Castle Street, Forfar,
Angus, DD8 3AE
Tel: 01307 462691
★★ Hotel

The Chapelbank House Hotel
69 East High Street,
Forfar, Angus, DD8 2EP
Tel: 01307 463151
★★★ Small Hotel

FREUCHIE
Lomond Hills Hotel and Leisure Centre
Parliament Square,
Freuchie, Cupar, Fife,
KY15 7EY
Tel: 01337 857329
★★ Hotel

GLAMIS
Castleton House Hotel
Glamis, Angus, DD8 1SJ
Tel: 01307 840340
★★★★ Small Hotel

GLEN CLOVA, BY KIRRIEMUIR
Glen Clova Hotel
Glen Clova,
by Kirriemuir, Angus,
DD8 4QS
Tel: 01575 550350
★★★ Small Hotel

GLENISLA
Glenmarkie Guest House
Glenisla, by Blairgowrie,
Perthshire, PH11 8QB
Tel: 01575 582295
★★★ Guest House

GLENROTHES
Express by Holiday Inn
Leslie Road, Glenrothes,
KY7 6XX
Tel: 01592 745509
★★★ Hotel

Directory of all VisitScotland Quality Assured Serviced Hotels and Guest Houses

Balgeddie House Hotel
Balgeddie Way,
Glenrothes, Fife,
KY6 3ET
Tel: 01592 742511
★★★ Hotel

The Gilvenbank Hotel
Huntsman's Road,
Glenrothes, Fife,
KY7 6RA
Tel: 01592 742077
★★★ Hotel

GLENSHEE

Dalmunzie
Spittal of Glenshee,
Blairgowrie, Perthshire,
PH10 7QG
Tel: 01250 885224
★★★ Small Hotel

INVERKEILOR, BY ARBROATH

Balnabrechan Lodge
Inverkeilor by Arbroath,
Angus, DD11 5SS
Tel: 01241 830462
Awaiting Inspection

KENMORE

Kenmore Hotel
The Square, Kenmore,
Perthshire, PH15 2NU
Tel: 01887 830205
★★★ Hotel

KILLIECRANKIE

Killiecrankie House Hotel
Pass of Killiecrankie,
by Pitlochry, PH16 5LG
Tel: 01796 473220
★★★★ Small Hotel

KINLOCH RANNOCH

Dunalastair Hotel
The Square, Kinloch
Rannoch, Perthshire,
PH16 5PW
Tel: 01882 632218
★★★ Hotel

Loch Rannoch Hotel
Kinloch Rannoch,
Perthshire, PH16 5PS
Tel: 01882 632201
★★★ Hotel

KINNESSWOOD, BY KINROSS

Park House
Main Street, Kinnesswood,
Perth & Kinross,
KY13 9HN
Tel: 01592 840237
Awaiting Inspection

KINROSS

The Green Hotel
2 The Muirs, Kinross,
KY13 8AS
Tel: 01577 863467
★★★★ Hotel

Kirklands Hotel
20 High Street,
Kinross, Perthshire,
KY13 8AN
Tel: 01577 863313
★★★ Small Hotel

Windlestrae Hotel
The Muirs,
Kinross, Perthshire,
KY13 8AS
Tel: 01577 863217
★★ Hotel

Roxburghe Guest House
126 High Street,
Kinross,
KY13 8DA
Tel: 01577 862498
★★ Guest House

The Well Country Inn
Main Street,
Scotlandwell, Kinross,
KY13 9JA
Tel: 01592 840444
★★★ Small Hotel

BY KINROSS

Gartwhinzean Hotel
Powmill, By Dollar,
Clackmannanshire,
FK14 7NW
Tel: 01577 840595
★★ Hotel

KIRKCALDY

Dean Park Hotel
Chapel Level,
Kirkcaldy, Fife,
KY2 6QW
Tel: 01592 261635
★★★ Hotel

Auld Post Hotel
1 Hunter Street,
Kirkcaldy, Fife,
KY1 1ED
Tel: 01592 204040
★★ Small Hotel

Dunnikier House Hotel
Dunnikier Park,
Kirkcaldy, Fife,
KY1 3LP
Tel: 01592 268393
★★★ Hotel

Swallow Parkway Hotel
6 Abbotshall Road,
Kirkcaldy, Fife,
KY2 5PQ
Tel: 01592 262 143
★★ Hotel

Mintella
38 Bennochy Road,
Kirkcaldy, Fife,
KY2 5RB
Tel: 01592 593446
★★ Guest House

KIRKMICHAEL

The Log Cabin Hotel
Glen Derby, Kirkmichael,
Blairgowrie, Perthshire,
PH10 7NA
Tel: 01250 881288
★★ Small Hotel

KIRRIEMUIR

Thrums Hotel
25 Bank Street, Kirriemuir,
Angus, DD8 4BE
Tel: 01575 572758
★★★ Small Hotel

LADYBANK

Redlands Country Lodge
Pitlessie Road, By
Ladybank, Fife, KY7 7SH
Tel: 01337 831091
★★★ Guest House

LESLIE

Rescobie House Hotel
6 Valley Drive, Leslie,
Fife, KY6 3BQ
Tel: 01592 749555
★★★ Small Hotel

LEUCHARS BY

Drumoig Hotel & Golf Resort
Drumoig, Leuchars,
by St Andrews, Fife,
KY16 0BE
Tel: 01382 541800
★★★ Hotel

LEVEN

Dunclutha Guest House
16 Victoria Road,
Leven, Fife,
KY8 4EX
Tel: 01333 425515
★★★★ Guest House

LOCH EARN

Achray House Hotel
St Fillans, Perthshire,
PH6 2NF
Tel: 01764 685231
★★★ Small Hotel

The Four Seasons Hotel
St Fillans, Perthshire,
PH6 2NF,
info@thefourseasonshotel.
co.uk,
www.thefourseasonshotel.
co.uk
Tel: 01764 685333
★★★ Small Hotel

LOCH RANNOCH

Talladh-a-Bheithe Lodge
Loch Rannoch,
by Pitlochry,
Perthshire, PH17 2QW
Tel: 01882 633203
★★★ Guest House

LOWER LARGO

Crusoe Hotel
2 Main Street, Lower Largo,
Fife, KY8 6BT
Tel: 01333 320759
★★★ Small Hotel

LUNDIN LINKS

Lundin Links Hotel
Leven Road, Lundin Links,
Fife, KY8 6AP
Tel: 01333 320207
★★★ Hotel

Swallow Old Manor Hotel
55 Leven Road, Lundin
Links, Fife, KY8 6AJ
Tel: 01333 320368
★★★★ Hotel

MARKINCH

Balbirnie House Hotel
Balbirnie Park, Markinch,
by Glenrothes, Fife,
KY7 6NE
Tel: 01592 610066
★★★★ Hotel

MEIKLEOUR, BY PERTH

Meikleour Hotel
Meikleour, Perthshire,
PH2 6EB
Tel: 01250 883206
★★★★ Inn

MONIFIETH, BY DUNDEE

Panmure Hotel
Tay Street, Monifieth,
Angus, DD5 4AX
Tel: 01382 532911
★★ Small Hotel

MONIKIE

Craigton House B&B
Craigton Road,
Monikie, Angus,
DD5 3QN
Tel: 01382 370570
Awaiting Inspection

MONTROSE

36 The Mall
Montrose, Angus,
DD10 8SS
Tel: 01674 673646
★★★★ Bed & Breakfast

Best Western Links Hotel
Mid Links, Montrose,
Angus, DD10 8RL
Tel: 01674 671000
★★★★ Hotel

Park Hotel
61 John Street, Montrose,
Angus, DD10
Tel: 01674 663400
★★★ Hotel

George Hotel
22 George Street,
Montrose, Angus,
DD10 8EW
Tel: 01674 675050
★★ Hotel

The Limes Guest House
15 King Street, Montrose,
Angus, DD10 8NL
Tel: 01674 677236
Awaiting Inspection

PERTH

Achnacarry Guest House
3 Pitcullen Crescent,
Perth,
PH2 7HT
Tel: 01738 621421
★★★★ Guest House

Ackinnoull Guest House
5 Pitcullen Crescent,
Perth, PH2 7HT
Tel: 01738 634165
★★★★ Guest House

The Royal George
Tay Street, Perth,
PH1 5LD
Tel: 01738 624455
★★★ Hotel

The Bield at Blackruthven
Blackruthven House,
Tibbermore, Perthshire,
PH1 1PY
Tel: 01738 583238
★★★ Guest House

Arisaig Guest House
4 Pitcullen Crescent,
Perth, PH2 7HT
Tel: 01738 628240
★★★★ Guest House

**Ballathie House
Sportsman's Lodge**
Kinclaven, Stanley,
Perthshire, PH1 4QN
Tel: 01250 883268
★★★ Lodge

Queens Hotel
105 Leonard Street,
Perth, Perthshire,
PH2 8HB
Tel: 01738 442222
★★★ Hotel

Dunallan
10 Pitcullen Crescent,
Perth, Perthshire,
PH2 7TH
Tel: 01738 622551
★★★★ Guest House

Aberdeen Guest House
13 Pitcullen Terrace,
Perth, Perthshire,
PH2 7HT
Tel: 01738 633183
★★★★ Guest House

Cherrybank Inn
210 Glasgow Road,
Perth, PH2 0NA
Tel: 01738 624349
★★★ Inn

Clunie Guest House
12 Pitcullen Crescent,
Perth, PH2 7HT
Tel: 01738 623625
★★★ Guest House

Almond Villa Guest House
51 Dunkeld Road,
Perth, PH1 5RP
Tel: 01738 629356
★★★★ Guest House

Rowanlea
87 Glasgow Road,
Perth, Perthshire,
PH2 0PQ
Tel: 01738 621922
★★★★ Guest House

Parklands Hotel
2 St Leonards Bank,
Perth, Perthshire,
PH2 8EB
Tel: 01738 622451
★★★★ Small Hotel

The Gables
24-26 Dunkeld Road,
Perth, PH1 5RW
Tel: 01738 624717
★★★ Guest House

Lorne Villa Guest House
65 Dunkeld Road,
Perth, Perthshire,
PH1 5RP
Tel: 01738 628043
★★★ Guest House

Huntingtower Hotel
Crieff Road, Perth,
PH1 3JT
Tel: 01738 583771
★★★ Hotel

Iona Guest House
2 Pitcullen Crescent,
Perth, Perthshire,
PH2 7HT
Tel: 01738 627261
★★★ Guest House

WoodLea Hotel
23 York Place,
Perth, Perthshire,
PH2 8EP
Tel: 01738 621744
★★★ Small Hotel

Ardfern House
15 Pitcullen Crescent,
Perth, Perthshire,
PH2 7HT
Tel: 01738 637031
★★★★ Guest House

The New County Hotel
22-30 County Place,
Perth, PH2 8EE
Tel: 01738 623355
★★★ Hotel

Newton House Hotel
Glencarse, Perth,
PH2 7LX
Tel: 01738 860250
★★★ Small Hotel

Ramada Hotel Perth
West Mill Street,
Perth, PH1 5QP
Tel: 01738 628281
★★★ Hotel

Pitcullen Guest House
17 Pitcullen Crescent,
Perth, Perthshire,
PH2 7HT
Tel: 01738 626506
★★★ Guest House

Salutation Hotel
34 South Street, Perth,
PH2 8PH
Tel: 01738 630066
★★ Hotel

Hazeldene Guest House
Strathmore Street,
Perth, Perthshire,
PH2 7HP
Tel: 01738 623550
★★★ Guest House

Clifton House
36 Glasgow Road,
Perth, Perthshire,
PH2 0PB
Tel: 01738 621997
★★★★ Guest House

Rosebank Guest House
53 Dunkeld Road,
Perth, PH1 5RP
Tel: 01738 621737
★★★ Guest House

Kinnaird Guest House
5 Marshall Place,
Perth, Perthshire,
PH2 8AH
Tel: 01738 628021
★★★★ Guest House

Heidl Guest House
43 York Place,
Perth, Perthshire,
PH2 8EH
Tel: 01738 635031
★★★ Guest House

Westview Bed & Breakfast
49 Dunkeld Road, Perth,
PH1 5RP
Tel: 01738 627787
★★★★ Bed & Breakfast

Adam Guest House
6 Pitcullen Crescent,
Perth, PH2 7HT
Tel: 01738 627179
★★★ Guest House

Lovat Hotel
Glasgow Road,
Perth, Perthshire,
PH2 0LT
Tel: 01738 636555
★★★ Hotel

Sunbank House Hotel
50 Dundee Road,
Perth, Perthshire,
PH2 7BA
Tel: 01738 624882
★★★★ Small Hotel

BY PERTH

Ballathie House Hotel
Kinclaven, Stanley,
Perthshire, PH1 4QN
Tel: 01250 883268
★★★★ Hotel

Tayside Hotel
51 Mill Street, Stanley,
Perthshire, PH1 4NL
Tel: 01738 828249
★★★ Small Hotel

Murrayshall Hotel
Scone, Perth,
Perthshire, PH2 7PH
Tel: 01738 551171
★★★★ Hotel

Glencarse Hotel
Glencarse, by Perth,
Perthshire, PH2 7LX
Tel: 01738 860206
Awaiting Inspection

PITLOCHRY

Claymore Hotel
162 Atholl Road,
Pitlochry, Perthshire,
PH16 5AR
Tel: 01796 472888
★★★ Small Hotel

Atholl Palace Hotel
Pitlochry, Perthshire,
PH16 5LY
Tel: 01796 472400
★★★★ Hotel

Balrobin Hotel
Higher Oakfield,
Pitlochry, PH16 5HT
Tel: 01796 472901
★★★ Small Hotel

Bendarroch House
Strathtay, Pitlochry,
PH9 0PG
Tel: 01887 840420
★★★ Guest House

Tir Aluinn
10 Higher Oakfield,
Pitlochry, Perthshire,
PH16 5HT
Tel: 01796 473811
★★★ Guest House

Westlands Hotel
160 Atholl Road,
Pitlochry, Perthshire,
PH16 5AR
Tel: 01796 472266
★★★ Hotel

Craigvrack Hotel
38 West Moulin Road,
Pitlochry, Perthshire,
PH16 5EQ
Tel: 01796 472399
★★★ Small Hotel

Strathgarry Hotel
113 Atholl Road,
Pitlochry, Perthshire,
PH16 5AG
Tel: 01796 472469
★★★ Small Hotel

Dundarach Hotel
Perth Road,
Pitlochry, Perthshire,
PH16 5DJ
Tel: 01796 472862
★★★ Hotel

Almond Lee
East Moulin Road,
Pitlochry, Perthshire,
PH16 5HU
Tel: 01796 474048
★★★ Guest House

The Green Park Hotel
Clunie Bridge Road,
Pitlochry, Perthshire,
PH16 5JY
Tel: 01796 473248
★★★★ Hotel

Birchwood Hotel
2 East Moulin Road,
Pitlochry, Perthshire,
PH16 5DW
Tel: 01796 472477
★★★ Small Hotel

Annslea Guest House
164 Atholl Road,
Pitlochry, Perthshire,
PH16 5AR
Tel: 01796 472430
★★★ Guest House

Easter Croftinloan Farmhouse
Croftloan Farm,
Pitlochry, Perthshire,
PH16 5TA
Tel: 01796 473 454
★★★★ Guest House

Knockendarroch House Hotel
Higher Oakfield,
Pitlochry, Perthshire,
PH16 5HT
Tel: 01796 473473
★★★★ Small Hotel

Loch Tummel Inn
Queens View,
Strathtummel,
Pitlochry, Perthshire,
PH16 5RP
Tel: 01882 634272
★★ Inn

**Macdonald's
Restaurant & Guest House**
140 Atholl Road,
Pitlochry, Perthshire,
PH16 5AG
Tel: 01796 472170
★★★ Guest House

Buttonboss Lodge
27 Atholl Road,
Pitlochry, Perthshire,
PH16 5BX
Tel: 01796 472065
★★★ Guest House

Craigmhor Lodge
27 West Moulin Road,
Pitlochry, Perthshire,
PH16 5EF
Tel: 01796 472123
★★★★ Guest House

Rosehill
47 Atholl Road,
Pitlochry, Perthshire,
PH16 5BX
Tel: 01796 472958
★★★ Guest House

Atholl Villa Guest House
29/31 Atholl Road,
Pitlochry, Perthshire,
PH16 5BX
Tel: 01796 473820
★★★ Guest House

**East Haugh House
Country Hotel & Restaurant**
East Haugh, by Pitlochry,
Perthshire, PH16 5JS
Tel: 01796 473121
★★★★ Small Hotel

Acarsaid Hotel
8 Atholl Road,
Pitlochry, Perthshire,
PH16 5BX
Tel: 01796 472389
★★★ Hotel

Pine Trees Hotel
Strathview Terrace,
Pitlochry, Perthshire,
PH16 5QR
Tel: 01796 472121
★★★★ Small Hotel

Pitlochry Hydro Hotel
Knockard Road,
Pitlochry, Perthshire,
PH16 5JH
Tel: 01942 824824
★★★ Hotel

Rosemount Hotel
12 Higher Oakfield,
Pitlochry, PH16 5HT
Tel: 01796 472302
★★★ Hotel

Sunnybank B&B
19 Lower Oakfield,
Pitlochry, Perthshire,
PH16 5DS
Tel: 01796 473014
★★★ Bed & Breakfast

The Poplars
27 Lower Oakfield,
Pitlochry, Perthshire,
PH16 5DS
Tel: 01796 472911
★★★ Guest House

Torrdarach House
Golf Course Road,
Pitlochry, Perthshire,
PH16 5AU
Tel: 01796 472136
★★★★ Guest House

Wellwood House
13 West Moulin Road,
Pitlochry, Perthshire,
PH16 5EA
Tel: 01796 474288
★★★★ Guest House

The Well House
11 Toberargan Road,
Pitlochry, Perthshire,
PH16 5HG
Tel: 01796 472239
★★★★ Guest House

Southwood
East Haugh,
by Pitlochry, Perthshire,
PH16 5TA
Awaiting Inspection

Tigh Na Cloich Hotel
Larchwood Road, Pitlochry,
Perthshire, PH16 5AS
Tel: 01796 472216
★★★ Small Hotel

Craigatin House & Courtyard
165 Atholl Road, Pitlochry,
Perthshire, PH16 5QL
Tel: 01796 472478
★★★★ Guest House

Dunmurray Lodge Guest House
72 Bonnethill Road,
Pitlochry, Perthshire,
PH16 5ED
Tel: 01796 473624
★★★★ Guest House

Fishers Hotel
75-79 Atholl Road,
Pitlochry, Perthshire,
PH16 5BN
Tel: 01796 472000
★★★ Hotel

Scotlands Hotel
40 Bonnethill Road,
Pitlochry, Perthshire,
PH16 5BT
Tel: 01796 472292
Awaiting Inspection

ST ANDREWS

The Albany Hotel
56 North Street,
St Andrews, Fife,
KY16 9AH
Tel: 01334 477737
★★★ Small Hotel

Brooksby House
Queens Terrace,
St Andrews, Fife,
KY16 9ER
Tel: 01334 470723
★★★★ Guest House

The White Lodge
94 Hepburn Gardens,
St Andrews, Fife,
KY16 9LN
Tel: 01334 475710
Awaiting Inspection

Amberside
4 Murray Park,
St Andrews, Fife,
KY16 9AW
Tel: 01334 474644
★★★ Guest House

Cleveden House
3 Murray Place,
St Andrews, Fife,
KY16 9AP
Tel: 01334 474212
★★★ Guest House

Lorimer House
19 Murray Park,
St Andrews, Fife,
KY16 9AW
Tel: 01334 476599
★★★★ Guest House

Craigmore Guest House
3 Murray Park,
St Andrews, Fife,
KY16 9AW
Tel: 01334 472142
★★★★ Guest House

Burness House
1 Murray Park,
St Andrews, Fife,
KY16 9AW
Tel: 01334 474314
★★★★ Guest House

The Russell Hotel
26 The Scores,
St Andrews, Fife,
KY16 9AS
Tel: 01334 473447
FAX 0334 478279
★★★ Small Hotel

Feddinch Mansion Country Guest House
St Andrews, Fife,
KY16 8NR
Tel: 01334 470888
★★★★ Guest House

Annandale Guest House
23 Murray Park,
St Andrews, Fife,
KY16 9AW
Tel: 01334 475310
★★★ Guest House

Hazelbank Hotel
28 The Scores,
St Andrews, Fife,
KY16 9AS
Tel: 01334 472466
★★★ Small Hotel

Shandon House
10 Murray Place,
St Andrews, Fife,
KY16 9AP
Tel: 01334 472412
★★★ Guest House

Five Pilmour Place
North Street,
St Andrews, Fife,
KY16 9HZ
Tel: 01334 478665
★★★★ Guest House

Macdonald Rusacks Hotel
Pilmour Links,
St Andrews, Fife,
KY16 9JQ
Tel: 0870 4008128
★★★★ Hotel

Yorkston House
68-70 Argyle Street,
St Andrews, Fife, KY16 9BU
Tel: 01334 472019
★★★ Guest House

Scores Hotel
76 The Scores,
St Andrews, Fife,
KY16 9BB
Tel: 01334 472451
★★★ Hotel

Arran House
5 Murray Park,
St Andrews, Fife,
KY16 9AW
Tel: 01334 474 724
Awaiting Inspection

Ardgowan Hotel
2 Playfair Terrace,
St Andrews, Fife,
KY16 9HX
Tel: 01334 472970
★★★ Small Hotel

Hoppity House
38 Market Street,
St Andrews, Fife,
KY16 9NT
Tel: 01334 461192
Awaiting Inspection

Greyfriars Hotel
29 North Street,
St Andrews, Fife,
KY16 9AG
Tel: 01334 474906
Awaiting Inspection

Charlesworth House
9 Murray Place,
St Andrews, Fife,
KY16 9AP
Tel: 01334 476528
★★★ Guest House

Montague Guest House
21 Murray Park,
St Andrews, Fife,
KY16 9AW
Tel: 01334 479 287
★★★ Guest House

New Hall, University of St Andrews
North Haugh,
St Andrews, Fife,
KY16 9XW
Tel: 01334 467000
★★★ Hotel

Old Course Hotel, Golf Resort & Spa
St Andrews, Fife,
KY16 9SP
Tel: 01334 474371
★★★★★
International Resort

Directory of all VisitScotland Quality Assured Serviced Hotels and Guest Houses

The Old Station Country Guest House
Stravithie Bridge,
St Andrews, KY16 8LR
Tel: 01334 880505
★★★★ Guest House

Cameron House
11 Murray Park,
St Andrews, Fife,
KY16 9AW
Tel: 01334 72306
★★★★ Guest House

Aslar House
120 North Street,
St Andrews, Fife,
KY16 9AF
Tel: 01334 473460
★★★★ Guest House

Glenderran Guest House
9 Murray Park,
St Andrews, Fife,
KY16 9AW
Tel: 01334 477951
★★★★ Guest House

Whitecroft Guest House
33 Strathkinness
High Road,
St Andrews, Fife,
KY16 9UA
Tel: 01334 474448
★★★★ Guest House

Riverview Guest House
Edenside, St Andrews,
Fife, KY16 9SQ
Tel: 01334 838009
★★★ Guest House

Doune House
5 Murray Place,
St Andrews, Fife,
KY16 9AP
Tel: 01334 475195
★★★ Guest House

Rufflets Country House Hotel
Strathkinness Low Road,
St Andrews, Fife,
KY16 9TX
Tel: 01334 472594
★★★★★ Hotel

St Andrews Bay Golf Resort & Spa
St Andrews, Fife,
KY16 8PN
Tel: 01334 837000
★★★★★★
International Resort

St Andrews Golf Hotel
40 The Scores,
St Andrews, Fife,
KY16 9AS
Tel: 01334 472611
★★★★ Hotel

Nethan House
17 Murray Park,
St Andrews, Fife,
KY16 9AW
Tel: 01334 472104
★★★★ Guest House

Bell Craig
8 Murray Park,
St Andrews, Fife,
KY16 9AW
Tel: 01334 472962
★★★ Guest House

Brownlees
7 Murray Place,
St Andrews, Fife,
KY16 9AP
Tel: 01334 473868
★★★★ Guest House

Dunvegan Hotel
7 Pilmour Place,
North Street, St Andrews,
Fife, KY16 9HZ
Tel: 01334 473105
★★★ Small Hotel

BY ST ANDREWS

Pinewood Country House
Tayport Road,
St Michaels, Fife,
KY16 0DU
Tel: 01334 839860
★★★★ Guest House

The Inn At Lathones
By Largoward,
St Andrews, Fife,
KY9 1JE
Tel: 01334 840494
★★★★ Inn

Edenside House
Edenside,
By St Andrews, Fife,
KY16 9QS
Tel: 0133483 8108
★★★ Guest House

TUMMEL BRIDGE

Kynachan Loch Tummel Hotel
Tummel Bridge,
Perthshire, PH16 5SB
Tel: 01796 484848
★★★ Hotel

UPPER LARGO

Monturpie Guest House
Monturpie,
Upper Largo, Fife,
KY8 5QS
Tel: 01333 360254
★★★ Guest House

ABERDEEN AND GRAMPIAN HIGHLANDS – SCOTLAND'S CASTLE AND WHISKY COUNTRY

ABERDEEN

Abbotswell Guest House
28 Abbotswell Crescent,
Aberdeen, AB12 5AR
Tel: 01224 871788
★★★ Guest House

Aberdeen Patio Hotel
Beach Boulevard,
Aberdeen, AB24 5EF
Tel: 01224 633339
★★★★ Hotel

Aberdeen Springdale Guest House
404 Great Western Road,
Aberdeen, AB10 6NR
Tel: 01224 316561
★★★ Guest House

Arkaig Guest House
43 Powis Terrace,
Aberdeen, AB25 3PP
Tel: 01224 638872
★★★ Guest House

Allan Guest House
56 Polmuir Road,
Aberdeen, AB11 7RT
Tel: 01224 584484
★★★★ Guest House

Albany Guest House
18 Whinhil Road,
Aberdeen, Aberdeen-shire,
AB11 7XH
Tel: 01224 571703
★★★ Guest House

Atholl Hotel
54 Kings Gate,
Aberdeen, AB15 4YN
Tel: 01224 323505
★★★★ Hotel

Water Wheel Toby Hotel
203 North Deeside Rd,
Bieldside, Aberdeen,
AB15 9EQ
Tel: 01224 861659
Hotel

Thistle Aberdeen Airport Hotel
Argyll Road,
Aberdeen, Aberdeenshire,
AB21 0AF
Tel: 01224 725252
★★★★ Hotel

Thistle Aberdeen Caledonian
10-14 Union Terrace,
Aberdeen, Aberdeenshire,
AB10 1WE
Tel: 01224 640233
★★★ Hotel

Beeches Private Hotel
193 Great Western Road,
Aberdeen, AB10 6PS
Tel: 01224 586413
★★★ Guest House

Cloverleaf Hotel
Kepplehills Road,
Bucksburn, Aberdeen,
AB21 9DG
Tel: 01224 714294
★ Hotel

Granville Guest House
401 Great Western Road,
Aberdeen, AB10 6NY
Tel: 01224 313043
★★★ Guest House

Brentwood Hotel
101 Crown Street,
Aberdeen, AB11 6HH
Tel: 01224 595440
★★★ Hotel

Simpson's Hotel
59 Queens Road,
Aberdeen, Aberdeen-shire,
AB15 4YP
Tel: 01224 327777
★★★★ Hotel

Burnett Guest House
75 Constitution Street,
Aberdeen, AB24 5ET
Tel: 01224 647995
★★★ Guest House

Crown Guest House
10 Springbank Terrace,
Aberdeen, AB11
Tel: 01224 586842
★★★ Guest House

Butler's Islander Guest House
122 Crown Street,
Aberdeen, Aberdeenshire,
AB11 6HJ
Tel: 01224 212411
★★★ Guest House

Dyce Skean Dhu Hotel
Farburn Terrace, Dyce,
Aberdeenshire, AB21 7DW
Tel: 01224 723101
★★★ Hotel

Armadale Guest House
605 Holburn Street,
Aberdeen, AB10 7JN
Tel: 01224 580636
★★★ Guest House

Copthorne Hotel Aberdeen
122 Huntly Street,
Aberdeen, AB10 1SU
Tel: 01224 630404
★★★★ Hotel

Northern Hotel
1 Great Northern Road,
Aberdeen, AB24 3PS
Tel: 01224 483342
★★★ Hotel

Craighaar Hotel
Waterton Road, Bucksburn,
Aberdeen, AB21 9HS
Tel: 01224 712275
★★★ Hotel

Brentwood Villa
560 King Street, Aberdeen,
Grampian, AB24 5SR
Tel: 01224 480633
★★★ Guest House

Cults Hotel
328 North Deeside Road,
Aberdeen, AB15 9SE
Tel: 01224 867632
★★★ Small Hotel

Dunrovin Guest House
168 Bon-Accord Street,
Aberdeen, AB10 2TX
Tel: 01224 586081
★★★ Guest House

Holiday Inn
Claymore Drive, Aberdeen,
AB23 8GP
Tel: 08704 009046
★★★ Hotel

Cragganmore Guest House
63 Springbank Terrace,
Aberdeen, AB11 6JZ
Tel: 01224 572867
★★★ Guest House

Mariner Hotel
349 Great Western Road,
Aberdeen, AB10 6NW
Tel: 01224 588901
★★★ Hotel

Ellenville Guest House
50 Springbank Terrace,
Aberdeen, AB11 6LR
Tel: 01224 213334
★★★ Guest House

Ardoe House Hotel
South Deeside Road,
Blairs, Aberdeen,
Aberdeenshire, AB12 5YP
Tel: 01224 867355
★★★★ Hotel

Furain Guest House
92 North Deeside Road,
Peterculter, Aberdeen,
AB14 0QN
Tel: 01224 732189
★★★ Guest House

Greyholme Guest House
35 Springbank Terrace,
Aberdeen, AB11 6LR
Tel: 01224 587081
★★★ Guest House

Britannia Hotel
Malcolm Road,
Aberdeen, Grampian,
AB21 9LN
Tel: 01224 409988
★★★ Hotel

Antrim Guest House
157 Crown Street,
Aberdeen, AB11 6HT
Tel: 01224 590987
★★ Guest House

The Jays Guest House
422 King Street,
Aberdeen, AB24 3BR
Tel: 01224 638295
★★★★ Guest House

Arden Guest House
61 Dee Street, Aberdeen,
Aberdeenshire, AB10 2EE
Tel: 01224 580700
★★★ Guest House

Queens Hotel
51-53 Queens Road,
Aberdeen, AB15 4YP
Tel: 01224 209999
★★★★ Hotel

Norwood Hall Hotel
Garthdee Road,
Aberdeen, AB15 9NX
Tel: 01224 868951
★★★★ Hotel

St Ola Guest House
421 Great Western Road,
Aberdeen, AB10 6NJ
Tel: 01224 317186
★★★ Guest House

Royal Crown Guest House
111 Crown Street,
Aberdeen, AB11 2HN
Tel: 01224 586461
★★★ Guest House

Aberdeen Douglas Hotel
43-45 Market Street,
Aberdeen, AB11 5EL
Tel: 01224 582255
★★★ Hotel

Maryculter House Hotel
South Deeside Road,
Maryculter, Aberdeenshire,
AB12 5GB
Tel: 01224 732124
★★★ Hotel

Kildonan Guest House
410 Great Western Road,
Aberdeen, AB10 6NR
Tel: 01224 316115
★★★ Guest House

Cedars Private Hotel
339 Great Western Road,
Aberdeen, AB10 6NW
Tel: 01224 583225
★★★ Guest House

Strathisla Guest House
408 Great Western Road,
Aberdeen, AB10 6NR
Tel: 01224 321026
★★★ Guest House

Palm Court Hotel
81 Seafield Road,
Aberdeen, AB15 7YX
Tel: 01224 310351
★★★ Hotel

Hilton Aberdeen Treetops
161 Springfield Road,
Aberdeen, AB15 7AQ
Tel: 01224 313377
★★★★ Hotel

Aldersyde Guest House
138 Bon Accord Street,
Aberdeen, AB11 6TX
Tel: 01224 580012
Awaiting Inspection

Roselea House
12 Springbank Terrace,
Aberdeen, AB10 2LS
Tel: 01224 583060
★★★ Guest House

Aberdeen Guest House
218 Great Western Road,
Aberdeen, AB10 6PD
Tel: 01224 211733
★★★ Guest House

Bimini Guest House
69 Constitution Street,
Aberdeen, AB24 5ET
Tel: 01224 646912
★★★ Guest House

Directory of all VisitScotland Quality Assured Serviced Hotels and Guest Houses

Adelphi Guest House
8 Whinhill Road,
Aberdeen, AB11 7XH
Tel: 01224 583078
★★★ Guest House

Aberdeen Marriott Hotel
Riverview Drive,
Farburn, Dyce,
Aberdeenshire,
AB21 7AZ
Tel: 0870 400 7291
★★★★ Hotel

376 Great Western Road
Aberdeen, Aberdeenshire,
AB10 6PH
Tel: 01224 313678
★★★ Guest House

Penny Meadow
189 Great Western Road,
Aberdeen, AB10 6PS
Tel: 01224 588037
★★★★ Guest House

Ashgrove Guest House
34 Ashgrove Road,
Aberdeen, AB25 3AD
Tel: 01224 484861
★★★ Guest House

Royal Hotel
1-3 Bath Street,
Aberdeen, AB11 6BJ
Tel: 01224 585152
★★ Hotel

St Elmo
64 Hilton Drive,
Aberdeen, AB24 4NP
Tel: 01224 483065
★★★★ Guest House

Skene House HotelSuites
96 Rosemount Viaduct,
Aberdeen, AB25 1NX
Tel: 01224 645971
★★★★★★★ Serviced Apartments

The Angel Islington Guest House
191 Bon Accord Street,
Aberdeen, AB11 6AU
Tel: 01224 587043
★★★ Guest House

Speedbird Inn
Argyll Road,
Aberdeen Airport,
Dyce, AB21 0AF
Tel: 01224 772883
★★★ Hotel

Marcliffe at Pitfodels
North Deeside Road,
Pitfodels, Aberdeen,
AB15 9YA
Tel: 01224 861000
★★★★★ Hotel

Merkland Guest House
12 Merkland Road East,
Aberdeen, AB24 5PR
Tel: 01224 634451
★★ Guest House

Thistle Aberdeen Altens
Soutarhead Road,
Altens, Aberdeen,
Aberdeenshire, AB12 3LF
Tel: 01224 877000
★★★ Hotel

Express by Holiday Inn
Chapel Street,
Aberdeen, AB10 1SQ
Tel: 01224 623500
★★★ Hotel

University of Aberdeen, Crombie Johnston Hall
University of Aberdeen,
Aberdeen, AB24 3TT
Tel: 01224 273444
★ Campus

University of Aberdeen, King's Hall
College Bounds,
Aberdeen, AB24 3TT
Tel: 01224 273444
★★ Campus

Dunnydeer Guest House
402 Great Western Road,
Aberdeen, AB10 6NR
Tel: 01224 312821
★★★ Guest House

West Lodge Guest House
Norwood Hall,
Garthdee Road, Cults,
Aberdeen, AB15 9FX
Tel: 01224 861936
★★★ Guest House

NR ABERDEEN

The Belvedere Hotel
41 Evan Street,
Stonehaven,
Aberdeenshire, AB39 2ET
Tel: 01569 762672
★★ Small Hotel

Old Mill Inn
South Deeside Road,
Maryculter, Aberdeen,
AB12 5FX
Tel: 01224 733212
★★★ Small Hotel

Strathburn Hotel
Burghmuir Drive,
Inverurie, Aberdeenshire,
AB51 4GY
Tel: 01467 624422
★★★★ Hotel

ARCHIESTOWN

Archiestown Hotel
The Square, Archiestown,
Morayshire, AB38 7QL
Tel: 01340 810218
★★★ Small Hotel

AUCHENBLAE

Netherton House Bed and Breakfast
Kintore Street,
Auchenblae, Laurencekirk,
Kincardineshire,
AB30 1XP
Tel: 01561 320587
Awaiting Inspection

BALLATER

Glen Lui Hotel
14 Invercauld Road,
Ballater, Aberdeenshire,
AB35 5PP
Tel: 01339 755402
★★★ Small Hotel

Cambus O'May Hotel
nr Ballater,
Aberdeenshire, AB35 5SE
Tel: 013397 55428
★★★ Small Hotel

Morvada House
28 Braemar Road,
Ballater, Deeside,
AB35 5RL
Tel: 013397 56334
★★★★ Guest House

Loirston Hotel
Victoria Road,
Ballater, Aberdeenshire,
AB35 5RA
Tel: 01339 755413
Hotel

Moorside Guest House
26 Braemar Road,
Ballater, Aberdeenshire,
AB35 5RL
Tel: 01339 755492
★★★★ Guest House

Balgonie Country House
Braemar Place,
Ballater, Aberdeenshire,
AB35 5NQ
Tel: 013397 55482
★★★★ Small Hotel

Darroch Learg Hotel
Braemar Road,
Ballater, Aberdeenshire,
AB35 5UX
Tel: 013397 55443
★★★★ Small Hotel

Alexandra Hotel
12 Bridge Square,
Ballater, Aberdeenshire,
AB35 5QJ
Tel: 01339 755376
★★★ Small Hotel

School House
Anderson Road,
Ballater, Aberdeenshire,
AB35 5QW
Tel: 01339 756333
Awaiting Inspection

Hilton Craigendarroch Hotel
Braemar Road,
Ballater, Aberdeenshire,
AB35 5RQ
Tel: 013397 55858
★★★ Hotel

Deeside Hotel
Braemar Road,
Ballater, Aberdeenshire,
AB35 5RQ
Tel: 013397 55420
★★★ Small Hotel

Netherley Guest House
2 Netherley Place,
Ballater, Aberdeenshire,
AB35 5QE
Tel: 013397 55792
★★★ Guest House

The Gordon Guest House
Station Square, Ballater,
Aberdeenshire, AB35 5QB
Tel: 013397 55996
★★★★ Guest House

BY BALLATER

Loch Kinord Hotel
Ballater Road, Dinnet,
Royal Deeside,
Aberdeenshire, AB34 5JY
Tel: 013398 85229
★★★ Hotel

BANCHORY

The Burnett Arms Hotel
25 High Street, Banchory,
Aberdeenshire, AB31 5TD
Tel: 01330 824944
★★★ Small Hotel

Douglas Arms Hotel
22 High Street, Banchory,
Aberdeenshire, AB51 5SR
Tel: 01330 822547
★★ Small Hotel

Banchory Lodge Hotel
Off Dee Street, Banchory,
Kincardineshire, AB31 5HS
Tel: 01330 822625
★★★ Hotel

Raemoir House Hotel
Banchory, Aberdeenshire,
AB31 4ED
Tel: 01330 824884
★★★★ Hotel

BANCHORY BY

Learney Arms Hotel
The Square, Torphins,
Kincardineshire, AB31 4JP
Tel: 01339 882202
★★ Small Hotel

BANFF

Banff Springs Hotel
Golden Knowes Road,
Banff, Banffshire, AB45 2JE
Tel: 01261 812881
★★★ Hotel

Carmelite House Hotel
Low Street, Banff,
AB45 1AY
Tel: 01261 812152
★★ Small Hotel

Fife Lodge Hotel
Sandyhill Road,
Banff, AB45 1BE
Tel: 01261 812436
★★★ Small Hotel

Banff Links Hotel
Swordanes, Banff,
Aberdeenshire, AB45 2JJ
Tel: 01261 812414
★★ Small Hotel

BRAEMAR

Callater Lodge Guest House
9 Glenshee Road, Braemar,
Aberdeenshire, AB35 5YQ
Tel: 013397 41275
★★★★ Guest House

Cranford Guest House
15 Glenshee Road,
Braemar, Aberdeenshire,
AB35 5YQ
Tel: 01339 741675
★★★ Guest House

Clunie Lodge Guest House
Cluniebank Road, Braemar,
Aberdeenshire, AB35 5ZP
Tel: 013397 41330
★★★ Guest House

Invercauld Arms
Main Street, Braemar,
Aberdeenshire, AB35 5YR
Tel: 01942 824824
★★★ Hotel

Braemar Lodge Hotel
Glenshee Road, Braemar,
Aberdeenshire, AB35 5YQ
Tel: 013397 41627
★★★ Small Hotel

Schiehallion House
10 Glenshee Road,
Braemar, Aberdeenshire,
AB35 5YQ
Tel: 013397 41679
★★★ Guest House

BUCKIE

The Old Coach House Hotel
26 High Street, Buckie,
Banffshire, AB56 1AR
Tel: 01542 836266
★★★ Hotel

CRAIGELLACHIE

Craigellachie Hotel
Victoria Street,
Craigellachie, Aberlour,
Banffshire, AB38 9SR
Tel: 01340-881 204
★★★★ Hotel

CRUDEN BAY

Kilmarnock Arms Hotel
Bridge Street, Cruden Bay,
by Peterhead, AB42 0HD
Tel: 01779 812213
★★★ Small Hotel

CULLEN

Seafield Arms Hotel
19 Seafield Street, Cullen
, Moray, AB56 4SG
Tel: 01542 840791
★★★ Hotel

DUFFTOWN

**Tannochbrae Guest House &
Scotts Restaurant**
22 Fife Street, Dufftown,
Banffshire, AB55 4AL
Tel: 01340 820541
★★★ Guest House

Gowan Brae B&B
19 Church Street, Dufftown,
Banffshire, AB55 4AR
Tel: 01340 821344
Awaiting Inspection

ELGIN

The Mansion House Hotel
The Haugh, Elgin, Moray,
IV30 1AW
Tel: 01343 548811
★★★ Hotel

The Pines Guest House
East Road, Elgin, Moray,
IV30 1XG
Tel: 01343 552495
★★★★ Guest House

**Eight Acres Hotel &
Leisure Club**
Morriston Road, Elgin,
Moray, IV30 6UL
Tel: 01343 543077
★★★ Hotel

Ardvorlich
125 South Street, Elgin,
Moray, IV30 1JB
Awaiting Inspection

Laichmoray Hotel
Maisondieu Road, Elgin,
Moray, IV30 1QR
Tel: 01343 540045
★★★ Hotel

The Mansefield Hotel
Mayne Road, Elgin, Moray,
IV30 1NY
Tel: 01343 540883
★★★★ Hotel

Royal Hotel
Station Road, Elgin,
Moray, IV30 1QW
Tel: 01343 542320
★★★ Small Hotel

Southbank Guest House
36 Academy Street, Elgin,
Moray, IV30 1LP
Tel: 01343 547132
★★★ Guest House

Moraydale
276 High Street, Elgin,
Morayshire, IV30 1AG
Tel: 01343 546381
★★★ Guest House

The Lodge
Duff Avenue, Elgin,
Moray, IV30 1QS
Tel: 01343 549981
★★★★ Guest House

Auchmillan
12 Reidhaven Street,
Elgin, IV30 1QG
Tel: 01343 549077
★★★ Guest House

Sunninghill Hotel
Hay Street, Elgin,
Moray, IV30 1NH
Tel: 01343 547799
★★★ Hotel

West End Guest House
282 High Street, Elgin,
IV30 1AQ
Tel: 01343 549629
★★★ Guest House

ELLON

Station Hotel
Station Brae, Ellon,
Aberdeenshire, AB41 9BD
Tel: 01358 720209
★★ Small Hotel

FORDYCE

Academy House
School Road, Fordyce,
nr Portsoy, Banffshire,
AB45 2SJ
Tel: 01261 842743
★★★★★
Bed & Breakfast

FORRES

Mayfield Guest House
Victoria Road, Forres,
Moray, IV36 3BN
Tel: 01309 676931
Awaiting Inspection

Cluny Bank Hotel
St Leonards Road, Forres,
Morayshire, IV36 1DW
Tel: 01309 674304
★★★★ Small Hotel

Directory of all VisitScotland Quality Assured Serviced Hotels and Guest Houses

Knockomie Hotel
Grantown Road, Forres,
Moray, IV36 2SG
Tel: 01309 673146
★★★★ Small Hotel

Ramnee Hotel
Victoria Road, Forres,
Moray, IV36 3BN
Tel: 01309 672410
★★★ Hotel

GLENLIVET

Minmore House Hotel
Glenlivet, Ballindalloch,
Banffshire, AB37 9DB
Tel: 01807 590378
★★★ Small Hotel

HUNTLY

Dunedin Guest House
17 Bogie Street,
Huntly, Aberdeenshire,
AB5 5DX
Tel: 01466 794162
★ Guest House

Huntly Hotel
No 18, The Square,
Huntly, Aberdeenshire,
AB54 8BR
Tel: 01466 792703
★★ Small Hotel

Castle Hotel
Huntly, Aberdeenshire,
AB54 4SH
Tel: 01466 792696
★★★★ Small Hotel

Gordon Arms Hotel
The Square,
Huntly, Aberdeenshire,
AB54 8AF
Tel: 01466 792288
★★ Small Hotel

INVERURIE

The Steading B&B
T[DFisherford, Inverurie,
Aberdeenshire, AB51 8YS
Tel: 01464 841476
Awaiting Inspection

Ardennan House Hotel
Kemnay Road, Port
Elphinstone, Inverurie,
Aberdeenshire, AB51 3XD
Tel: 01467 621502
★★★ Small Hotel

Breaslann Guest House
Old Chapel Road,
Inverurie, Aberdeenshire,
AB51 4QN
Tel: 01467 621608
★★★ Guest House

Swallow Thainstone House Hotel
Thainstone Estate,
Inverurie Road, Inverurie,
Aberdeenshire, AB51 5NT
Tel: 01467 621643
★★★★ Hotel

W[DSwallow Kintore Arms Hotel
High Street, Inverurie,
Aberdeenshire, AB51 3QJ
Tel: 01467 621367
Small Hotel

BY INVERURIE

Pittodrie House Hotel
Chapel of Garioch,
by Inverurie, Aberdeen,
AB51 5HS
Tel: 01467 681444
★★★ Hotel

KEMNAY

Bennachie Lodge Hotel
Victoria Terrace, Kemnay,
Aberdeenshire, AB51 5RL
Tel: 01467 642789
★★ Small Hotel

Burnett Arms Hotel
Bridge Street, Kemnay,
Aberdeenshire, AB51 5QT
Tel: 01467 642208
★★ Small Hotel

KILDRUMMY

Kildrummy Castle Hotel
Kildrummy, Alford,
Aberdeenshire, AB33 8RA
Tel: 019755 71288
★★★★ Hotel

KINTORE

Torryburn Hotel
School Road, Kintore,
Aberdeenshire, AB51 0XP
Tel: 01467 632269
★★★ Small Hotel

LAURENCEKIRK

Marykirk Hotel
Main Street, Marykirk,
Laurencekirk,,
Aberdeenshire, AB30 1UT
Tel: 01674 840239
★★★ Inn

LOSSIEMOUTH

Stotfield Hotel
Stotfield Road,
Lossiemouth, Moray,
IV31 6QS
Tel: 01343 812011
Hotel

MACDUFF

The Park Hotel
Fife Street, Macduff,
Banffshire, AB44 1YA
Tel: 01261 832265
★★★ Guest House

NEWBURGH

Ythan Hotel
Main Street, Newburgh,
Aberdeenshire, AB41 6BP
Tel: 01358 789257
★★★ Small Hotel

Swallow Udny Arms Hotel
Main Street, Newburgh,
Aberdeenshire,
AB41 0BL
Tel: 01358 789444
Hotel

OLD DEER, BY PETERHEAD

Saplinbrae House Hotel
Old Deer, Mintlaw,
Aberdeenshire,
AB42 4LP
Tel: 01771 623 515
Awaiting Inspection

OLD MELDRUM

Meldrum House Hotel
Golf Country Estate
Old Meldrum,
Aberdeenshire, AB51 0AE
Tel: 01651 872294
★★★ Small Hotel

OLDMELDRUM

Meldrum Arms Hotel
The Square, Old Meldrum,
Aberdeenshire, AB51 0DS
Tel: 01651 872238
★ Small Hotel

The Redgarth
Kirk Brae, Old Meldrum,
Aberdeenshire, AB51 0DJ
Tel: 01651 872353
★★★★ Inn

OLD RAYNE

The Lodge Hotel
Old Rayne, Insch,
Aberdeenshire, AB52 6RY
Tel: 01464 851205
★★ Small Hotel

PETERHEAD

Invernettie Guest House
South Road Burnhaven,
Peterhead, Aberdeenshire,
AB42 0YX
Tel: 01779 473530
★★★ Guest House

Carrick Guest House
16 Merchant Street,
Peterhead, Aberdeenshire,
AB42 1DU
Tel: 01779 470610
★★ Guest House

Waterside Inn
Fraserburgh Road,
Peterhead, Aberdeenshire,
AB42 3BN
Tel: 0779 471121
★★★ Hotel

Palace Hotel
Prince Street, Peterhead,
Aberdeenshire, AB42 6PL
Tel: 01779 474821
★★★ Hotel

PORT ELPHINSTONE

Ashdon Guest House
Old Kemney Road, Port
Elphinstone, Inverurie,
Aberdeenshire, AB51 5XJ
Tel: 01467 620980
★★★ Guest House

PORTSOY

The Boyne Hotel Portsoy
2 North High Street,
Portsoy, Aberdeenshire,
AB45 2PA
Tel: 01261 842242
★ Small Hotel

Station Hotel
Seafield Street, Portsoy,
Aberdeenshire, AB45 2QT
Tel: 01261 842327
★★ Small Hotel

ROTHES

The Ben Aigen Hotel
51 New Street, Rothes,
Moray, AB38 7BJ
Tel: 01340 831240
★★ Small Hotel

ROTHIENORMAN

Rothie Inn
Main Street, Rothienorman,
Aberdeenshire, AB51 8UD
Tel: 01651 821206
★★★ Inn

ST COMBS, BY FRASERBURGH

The Tufted Duck Hotel
Corsekelly Place, St Combs, Aberdeenshire, AB43 8ZS
Tel: 01346 582481
★★★ Small Hotel

STONEHAVEN

Johnston Lodge
26 Ann Street, Stonehaven, Aberdeenshire, AB39 2DA
Tel: 01569 763586
Awaiting Inspection

Arduthie Guest House
Ann Street, Stonehaven, Kincardineshire, AB39
Tel: 01569 762381
★★★★ Guest House

Heugh Hotel
Westfield Road, Stonehaven, Aberdeenshire, AB39 2EE
Tel: 01569 762379
★★★ Small Hotel

STRATHDON

The Colquhonnie Hotel
Strathdon, Aberdeenshire, AB36 8UN
Tel: 01975 651210
Small Hotel

TOMINTOUL

The Gordon Hotel
The Square, Tomintoul, Aberdeenshire, AB37 9ET
Tel: 01807 580206
★★★ Hotel

Richmond Hotel
The Square, Tomintoul, Aberdeenshire, AB37 9ET
Tel: 01807 580777
★ Hotel

TURRIFF

Union Hotel
Main Street, Turriff, Aberdeenshire, AB53 7AA
Tel: 01888 563704
Hotel

Fife Arms Hotel
The Square, Turriff, Aberdeenshire, AB53 4AE
Tel: 01888 563124
★★★ Small Hotel

Deveron Lodge B&B Guesthouse
Bridgend Terrace, Turriff, Aberdeenshire, AB53 4ES
Tel: 1888563613
★★★★ Guest House

WESTHILL

Kilnhall
Strawberry Field Road, Westhill, Aberdeenshire, AB32 6TB
Tel: 01224 279640
Awaiting Inspection

THE HIGHLANDS AND SKYE

ACHARACLE

Loch Shiel House Hotel
Salen Road, Acharacle, Argyll, PH36 4JL
Tel: 01967 431224
★★ Small Hotel

ACHNASHEEN

Ledgowan Lodge Hotel
Ledgowan, Achnasheen, Ross-shire, IV22 2EJ
Tel: 01445 720252
★★★ Small Hotel

ARDELVE, BY DORNIE

Conchra House
Sallachy Road, Ardelve, by Kyle, Ross-shire, IV40 8DZ
Tel: 01599 555 233
★★★ Guest House

Caberfeidh House
Caberfeidh House, Upper Ardelve, by Kyle of Lochalsh, Ross-shire, IV40 8DY
Tel: 01599 555293
★★★ Guest House

ARDGOUR, BY FORT WILLIAM

The Inn at Ardgour
Ardgour, by Fort William, Inverness-shire, PH33 7AA
Tel: 01855 841225
★★★ Small Hotel

ARDROSS

Kildermorie Estate
Ardross, Easter Ross, IV17 0YH
Tel: 020 7352 6248
Awaiting Inspection

ARISAIG

The Arisaig Hotel
Arisaig, Inverness-shire, PH39 4NH
Tel: 01687 450210
Small Hotel

Cnoc-na-Faire Hotel
Back of Keppoch, Arisaig, Inverness-shire, PH39 4NS
Tel: 01687 450249
★★★★ Small Hotel

AULTBEA

Aultbea Hotel
Aultbea, Ross-shire, IV22 2HX
Tel: 01445 731201
★★★ Small Hotel

Mellondale Guest House
47 Mellon Charles, Aultbea, Ross-shire, IV22 2JL
Tel: 01445 731326
★★★★ Guest House

Cartmel Guest House
Birchburn Road, Aultbea, Ross-shire, IV22 2HZ
Tel: 01445 731375
★★★★ Guest House

Drumchork Lodge Hotel
Drumchork Estate, Aultbea, Wester Ross, IV22 2HU
Tel: 01445 731242
★★ Small Hotel

AVIEMORE

Cairngorm Guest House
Grampian Road, Aviemore, Inverness-shire, PH22 1RP
Tel: 01479 810630
★★★ Guest House

Cairngorm Hotel
Grampian Road, Aviemore, PH22 1PE
Tel: 01479 810233
★★★ Hotel

Aviemore Four Seasons
Aviemore, Inverness-shire, PH22 1PJ
Tel: 01479 815100
★★★ Hotel

Kinapol Guest House
Dalfaber Road, Aviemore, Inverness-shire, PH22 1PY
Tel: 01479 810513
★★ Guest House

Junipers
5 Dellmhor, Aviemore, Inverness-shire, PH22 1QW
Tel: 01479 810405
★★★ Guest House

MacDonald Highlands Hotel
Aviemore Centre, Aviemore, Inverness-shire, PH22 1PJ
Tel: 01479 810771
★★★★ Hotel

Hilton Coylumbridge Hotel
Coylumbridge, by Aviemore, Inverness-shire, PH22 1QN
Tel: 01479 810661
Hotel

Ravenscraig Guest House
Grampian oad, Aviemore, Inverness-shire, PH22 1RP
Tel: 01479 810278
★★★ Guest House

The Rowan Tree Country Hotel
Loch Alvie, by Aviemore, Inverness-shire, PH22 1QB
Tel: 01479 810207
★★★ Small Hotel

Directory of all VisitScotland Quality Assured Serviced Hotels and Guest Houses

Corrour House
Inverdruie, Aviemore,
Inverness-shire, PH22 1QH
Tel: 01479 810220
★★★★ Guest House

Ardlogie Guest House
Dalfaber Road, Aviemore,
Inverness-shire, PH22 1PU
Tel: 01479 810747
★★★ Guest House

BALLACHULISH

Craiglinnhe House
Lettermore,
Ballachulish, Argyll,
PH49 4JD
Tel: 01855 811270
★★★★ Guest House

Lyn Leven Guest House
Ballachulish, Argyll,
PH49 4JP
Tel: 01855 811392
★★★★ Guest House

The Ballachulish Hotel
Ballachulish, Argyll,
PH49 4JY
Tel: 01855 821582
★★★ Hotel

Isles of Glencoe Hotel & Leisure Centre
Ballachulish, Argyll,
PH49 4HL
Tel: 01855 821582
★★★★ Hotel

Ballachulish House
Ballachulish, Argyll,
PH49 4JX
Tel: 01855 811266
★★★★★ Small Hotel

Strathassynt Guest House
Loan Fern, Ballachulish,
Argyll, PH49 4JB
Tel: 01855 811261
★★★ Guest House

BEAULY

Archdale Guest House
High Street, Beauly,
Inverness-shire,
IV4 7BT
Tel: 01463 783043
★★ Guest House

BOAT OF GARTEN

The Boat Hotel
Boat of Garten,
Inverness-shire,
PH24 3BH
Tel: 01479 831258
★★★★ Hotel

Moorfield House
Deshar Road,
Boat of Garten,
Inverness-shire, PH24 3BN
Tel: 01479 831646
★★★★ Guest House

Granlea House
Deshar Road, Boat of
Garten, Inverness-shire,
PH24 3BN
Tel: 01479 831601
★★★ Guest House

Heathbank House
Drumuillie Road,
Boat of Garten,
Inverness-shire, PH24 3BD
Tel: 01479 831234
★★★ Guest House

BRACKLA, LOCH NESS-SIDE

Loch Ness Clansman Hotel
Brackla, Loch Ness Side,
Inverness-shire, IV3 8LA
Tel: 01456 450326
★★★ Hotel

BRORA

Royal Marine Hotel
Golf Road, Brora,
Sutherland, KW9 6GS
Tel: 01408 621252
★★★★ Hotel

CARRBRIDGE

The Cairn Hotel
Main Road, Carrbridge,
Inverness-shire,
PH23 3AS
Tel: 01479 841212
★★★ Inn

Dalrachney Lodge Hotel
Carrbridge,
Inverness-shire,
PH23 3AT
Tel: 01479 841252
★★★★ Small Hotel

Craigellachie House
Main Street, Carrbridge,
Inverness-shire, PH23 3AS
Tel: 01479 841641
★★★ Guest House

Cairdeas Guest House
Main Street, Carrbridge,
Inverness-shire, PH23 3AA
Tel: 01479 841271
★★★★ Guest House

Fairwinds Hotel
Carrbridge, Inverness-
shire, PH23 3AA
Tel: 01479 841240
★★★★ Small Hotel

Carrmoor Guest House
Carr Road, Carrbridge,
Inverness-shire, PH23 3AD
Tel: 01479 841244
★★★ Guest House

CASTLETOWN, BY THURSO

Greenland House
Main Street, Castletown,
Caithness, KW14 8TU
Tel: 01847 821694
★★★ Guest House

St Clair Arms Hotel
Main Street, Castletown,
Caithness, KW14 8TP
Tel: 01847 821656
★★ Hotel

CONTIN

Coul House Hotel
Contin, By Strathpeffer,
Ross-shire, IV14 9ES
Tel: 01997 421487
★★★ Hotel

CORPACH, BY FORT WILLIAM

Braeburn
Badabrie, Fort William,
Inverness-shire, PH33 7LX
Tel: 01397 77 772047
★★★★ Guest House

CROMARTY

Royal Hotel
Marine Terrace, Cromarty,
Ross-shire, IV11 8YN
Tel: 01381 600217
★★★ Small Hotel

DINGWALL

Tulloch Castle Hotel
Tulloch Castle Drive,
Dingwall, Ross-shire,
IV15 9ND
Tel: 01349 861325
★★★★ Hotel

BY DINGWALL

Kinkell Country House
Easter Kinkell,
by Conon Bridge,
Ross-shire, IV7 8HY
Tel: 01349 861270
★★★ Small Hotel

DORNIE, BY KYLE OF LOCHALSH

Dornie Hotel
Francis Street, Dornie,
Ross-shire, IV40 8DT
Tel: 01599 555205
★★★ Small Hotel

Eilean A-Cheo
Dornie, by Kyle of Lochalsh,
Ross-shire, IV40 8DY
Tel: 01599 555485
★★★ Guest House

Loch Duich Hotel & Seafood Restaurant
Ardelve, By Kyle of
Lochalsh, Ross-shire,
IV40 8DY
Tel: 01599 555213
★★ Small Hotel

DORNOCH

Dornoch Hotel
Grange Road,
Dornoch, IV25 3LD
Tel: 01942 824824
★★ Hotel

The Eagle Hotel
Castle Street, Dornoch,
Sutherland, IV25 3SR
Tel: 01862 810008
★★★ Small Hotel

Royal Golf Hotel
Grange Road, Dornoch,
Sutherland, IV25 3LD
Tel: 01667 452301
★★★ Hotel

Burghfield House Hotel
Dornoch, Sutherland,
IV25 3HN
Tel: 01862 810212
★★ Hotel

Dornoch Castle Hotel
Castle Street,
Dornoch, Sutherland,
IV25 3SD
Tel: 01862 810216
★★★ Hotel

Directory of all VisitScotland Quality Assured Serviced Hotels and Guest Houses

.DRUMNADROCHIT

Cruachan
Milton, Drumnadrochit,
Inverness-shire, IV63 6UA
Tel: 01456 450574
Awaiting Inspection

Drumnadrochit Hotel
Drumnadrochit,
Inverness-shire,
IV63 6TU
Tel: 01456 450218
Hotel

Polmaily House Hotel
Glenurquhart,
Drumnadrochit,
Inverness-shire,
IV63 6XT
Tel: 01456 450343
★★ Small Hotel

Clunebeg Lodge Guest House
Clunebeg Estate,
Drumnadrochit,
Inverness-shire,
IV63 6US
Tel: 01456 450387
★★★ Guest House

Loch Ness Lodge Hotel
Drumnadrochit,
Inverness-shire,
IV63 6TU
Tel: 01456 450342
★★★ Hotel

**DULNAIN BRIDGE,
BY GRANTOWN-ON-SPEY**

**Tigh Na Sgiath
Country House Hotel**
Skye of Curr, Dulnain
Bridge, Inverness-shire,
PH26 3PA
Tel: 01479 851345
★★★ Small Hotel

Rosegrove Guest House
Skye of Curr Road,
Dulnain Bridge,
Grantown on Spey,
PH26 3PA
Tel: 01479 851335
★★★ Guest House

DURNESS

MacKays
Durness, Sutherland, IV27
4PN
Tel: 01971 511209
★★★★ Small Hotel

DUROR

Stewart Hotel
Glen Duror, Appin,
Argyll, PA38 4BW
Tel: 01631 740268
★★ Hotel

EVANTON BY

Kiltearn House
Kiltearn House, Kiltearn,
by Evanton, Ross-shire,
IV16 9UY
Tel: 01349 830 617
★★★★ Guest House

FARR, BY INVERNESS

The Steadings Hotel
Flichity, Farr,
Inverness-shire, IV2 6XD
Tel: 01808 521314
★★★ Small Hotel

FESHIE BRIDGE, BY KINCRAIG

March House Guest House
Feshiebridge,
Kincraig, Inverness-shire,
PH21 1NA
Tel: 01540 651388
★★★ Guest House

FORSS, BY THURSO

Forss House Hotel
Forss, by Thurso,
Caithness, KW14 7XY
Tel: 01847 861201
★★★★ Small Hotel

FORT AUGUSTUS

Caledonian Hotel
Fort Augustus, Inverness-
shire, PH32 4BQ
Tel: 01320 366256
★★★ Small Hotel

The Lovat Arms Hotel
Fort William Road, Fort
Augustus, Inverness-shire,
PH32 4DU
Tel: 01320 366366
Awaiting Inspection

Inchnacardoch Hotel
Fort Augustus, Inverness-
shire, PH32 4BL
Tel: 01456 450900
★★★ Small Hotel

FORT WILLIAM

Guisachan Guest House
Alma Road, Fort William,
Inverness-shire, PH33 6HA
Tel: 01397 703797
★★★ Guest House

Lochan Cottage Guest House
Lochyside, Fort William,
Inverness-shire, PH33 7NX
Tel: 01397 702695
★★★★ Guest House

Caledonian Hotel
Achintore Road, Fort
William, Inverness-shire,,
PH33 6RW
Tel: 01942 824824
★★★ Hotel

Clan MacDuff Hotel
Achintore Road, Fort
William, Inverness-shire,,
PH33 6RW
Tel: 01397 702341
★★★ Hotel

Cruachan Hotel
Achintore Road, Fort
William, Inverness-shire,,
PH33 6RQ
Tel: 01397 702022
★★ Hotel

Distillery Guest House
Nevis Bridge, Fort William,
Inverness-shire,, PH33 6LR
Tel: 01397 700103
★★★★ Guest House

Glenlochy Guest House
Nevis Bridge, Fort William,
Inverness-shire,, PH33 6LP
Tel: 01397 702909
★★★ Guest House

Highland Hotel
Union Road, Fort William,
Inverness-shire, PH33 6QT
Tel: 01397 702291
★★ Hotel

Grand Hotel
Gordon Square, Fort
William, Inverness-shire,,
PH33 6DX
Tel: 01397 702928
★★★ Hotel

Balcarres
Seafield Gardens, Fort
William, Inverness-shire,
PH33 6RJ
Tel: 01397 702377
Awaiting Inspection

Alexandra Hotel
The Parade, Fort William,
Inverness-shire, PH33 6AZ
Tel: 01397 702241
★★ Hotel

Lochview House
Heathercroft, off Argyll
Terrace, Fort William,
Inverness-shire, PH33 6RE
Tel: 01397 703149
★★★ Guest House

Inverlochy Castle Hotel
Torlundy, Fort William,
Inverness-shire, PH33 6SN
Tel: 01397 702177
★★★★★ Hotel

The Moorings Hotel
Banavie, by Fort William,
Inverness-shire, PH33 7LY
Tel: 01397 772797
★★★★ Hotel

Constantia House
Costantia, Fassifern Road,
Fort William, Inverness-
shire, PH33 6BD
Tel: 01397 702893
Awaiting Inspection

Berkeley House
Belford Road, Fort William,
Inverness-shire, PH33 6BT
Tel: 01397 701185
★★★ Guest House

Mansefield Guest House
Corpach, Fort William,
Inverness-shire, PH33 7LT
Tel: 01397 772262
★★★ Guest House

Nevis Bank Hotel
Belford Road, Fort William,
Inverness-shire, PH33 6BY
Tel: 01397 705721
★★ Hotel

Stronchreggan View Guest House
Achintore Road, Fort William, Inverness-shire, PH33 6RW
Tel: 01397 704644
★★★ Guest House

Ben Nevis Hotel & Leisure Club
North Road, Fort William, Inverness-shire, PH33 6TG
Tel: 01397 702331
★★ Hotel

Craig Nevis West
Belford Road, Fort William, Inverness-shire, PH33 6BU
Tel: 01397 702023
★★ Guest House

Orchy Villa Guest House
Alma Road, Fort William, Inverness-shire, PH33 6HA
Tel: 01397 702445
★ Guest House

Glentower Lower Observatory
Achintore Road, Fort William, Inverness Shire, PH33 6PQ
Tel: 01397 704007
★★★★ Guest House

The Imperial Hotel
Fraser Square, Fort William, Inverness-shire, PH33 6DW
Tel: 01397 702040
★★★ Hotel

Glenaladale House
Achintore Road, Fort William, Inverness-shire, PH33 6RQ
Tel: 01397 708609
Awaiting Inspection

Lochiel Villa Guest House
Achintore Road, Fort William, Inverness-shire, PH33 6RQ
Tel: 01397 703616
★★★ Guest House

West End Hotel
Achintore Road, Fort William, PH33 6ED
Tel: 01397 702614
★★★ Hotel

Lime Tree Studio
Achintore Road, Fort William, Inverness-shire, PH33 6RQ
Tel: 01397 701806
★★★ Small Hotel

FORT WILLIAM BY

Dailanna Guest House
Kinlocheil, Fort William, Inverness-shire, PH33 7NP
Tel: 01397 722253
★★★★ Bed & Breakfast

Carinbrook
Banavie, Fort William, Inverness-shire, PH33 7LX
Tel: 01397 772318
★★★ Guest House

Glen Loy Lodge
Banavie, Fort William, Inverness-shire, PH33 7PD
Tel: 01397 712 700
★★ Guest House

Old Pines Hotel & Restaurant
Spean Bridge, by Fort William, PH34 4EG
Tel: 01397 712324
★★★★ Small Hotel

NR FORT WILLIAM

The Tailrace Inn
Riverside Road, Kinlochleven, Argyll, PH50 4QH
Tel: 01855 831777
★★★ Inn

FOYERS

Foyers Bay House
Foyers, Loch Ness, Inverness-shire, IV2 6YB
Tel: 01456 486624
★★★ Guest House

GAIRLOCH

Gairloch Hotel
Gairloch, Highland Region, IV21 2BL
Tel: 01942 824824
★★★ Hotel

Myrtle Bank Hotel
Low Road, Gairloch, Ross-shire, IV21 2BS
Tel: 01445 712004
★★ Small Hotel

Millcroft Hotel
Gairloch, Ross-shire, IV21 2BT
Tel: 01445 712376
AWAITING INSPECTION

The Old Inn
Gairloch, Ross-shire, IV21 2BD
Tel: 01445 712006
★★★ Inn

Shieldaig Lodge Hotel
Gairloch, Ross-shire, IV21 2AN
Tel: 01445 741 250
★★★ Small Hotel

GLENCOE

Dunire
Glencoe, Argyll, PH49 4HS
Tel: 01855 811305
★★★ Guest House

Clachaig Inn
Glencoe, Argyll, PH49 4HX
Tel: 01855 811252
★★ Inn

Dorrington Lodge
6 Tigh Phuirst, Glencoe, Argyll, PH49 4HN
Tel: 01855 811653
★★★ Guest House

MacDonald Hotel
Fort William Road, Kinlochleven, Argyll, PH50 4QL
Tel: 01855 831539
★★★ Small Hotel

Scorrybreac Guest House
Glencoe, Argyll, PH49 4HT
Tel: 01855 811354
★★★ Guest House

GLENFINNAN

The Princes' House Hotel
Glenfinnan, Inverness-shire, PH37 4LT
Tel: 01397 722246
★★★ Small Hotel

GLENMORISTON

Cluanie Inn
Glenmoriston, Inverness-shire, IV63 7YW
Tel: 01320 340238
★★★ Small Hotel

GLEN NEVIS, BY FORT WILLIAM

Corrie Duff Guest House
Glen Nevis, Fort William, Inverness-shire, PH33 6AB
Tel: 01397 701412
★★★ Guest House

Glenfer
Glen Nevis, Fort William, Inverness-shire, PH33 6PF
Tel: 01397 705848
★★★ Guest House

GLENSHIEL, BY KYLE OF LOCHALSH

Kintail Lodge Hotel
Glenshiel, Ross-shire, IV40 8HL
Tel: 01599 511275
★★★ Small Hotel

GLEN URQUHART

Glenurquhart House
Glenurquhart, Drumnadrochit, Inverness-shire, IV63 6TJ
Tel: 01456 476234
★★★ Small Hotel

GOLSPIE

Granite Villa Guest House
Fountain Road, Golspie, Sutherland, KW10 6TH
Tel: 01408 633146
★★★ Guest House

The Golf Links Hotel
Church Street, Golspie, Sutherland, KW10 6TT
Tel: 01408 633 408
★★ Small Hotel

GRANTOWN-ON-SPEY

Grant Arms Hotel
The Square, Grantown-on-Spey, Morayshire, PH21 3HF
Tel: 01479 872526
★★ Hotel

An Cala Guest House
Woodlands Terrace,
Grantown on Spey, Moray,
PH26 3JU
Tel: 01479 873293
★★★★ Guest House

Rosehall Guest House
13 The Square, Grantown
On Spey, Morayshire,
PH26 3HG
Tel: 01479 872721
★★★★ Guest House

Ben Mhor Hotel
53-57 High Street,
Grantown on Spey, Moray,
PH26 3EG
Tel: 01479 872056
★★★ Hotel

Strathallan House
Grant Road,
Grantown-on-Spey,
Moray, PH26 3LD
Tel: 01479 872165
★★★ Guest House

Holmhill House
Woodside Avenue,
Grantown on Spey,
Morayshire, PH26 3JR
Tel: 01479 873977
★★★★ Guest House

Ravenscourt House Hotel
Seafield Avenue,
Grantown-on-Spey,
Morayshire, PH26 3JG
Tel: 01479 872286
★★★★ Small Hotel

Garden Park Guest House
Woodside Avenue,
Grantown-on-Spey,
Moray, PH26 3JN
Tel: 01479 873235
★★★★ Guest House

Craiglynne Hotel
Woodlands Terrace,
Grantown-on-Spey,
Morayshire, PH26 3JX
Tel: 01479 872597
★★★ Hotel

Parkburn Guest House
High Street,
Grantown-on-Spey,
Moray, PH26 3EN
Tel: 01479 873116
★★★ Guest House

Willowbank
High Street,
Grantown on Spey,
Morayshire, PH26 3EN
Tel: 01479 872089
★★★ Guest House

Seafield Lodge Hotel
Woodside Avenue,
Grantown-on-Spey,
Morayshire, PH26 3JN
Tel: 01479 872152
★★★ Small Hotel

Muckrach Lodge Hotel
Dulnain Bridge, Grantown-
on-spey, Moray, PH26 3LY
Tel: 01479 851257
★★★★ Small Hotel

Culdearn House
Woodland Terrace,
Grantown-on-Spey,
Morayshire, PH26 3JU
Tel: 01479 872106
★★★★ Small Hotel

Kinross Guest House
Woodside Avenue,
Grantown-on-Spey, Moray,
PH26 3JR
Tel: 01479 872042
★★★★ Guest House

Westhaven
South Street,
Grantown On Spey,
Morayshire, PH26 3HZ
Tel: 01479 872471
Awaiting Inspection

Rossmor Guest House
Woodlands Terrace,
Grantown on Spey, Moray,
PH26 3JU
Tel: 01479 872201
★★★★ Guest House

The Pines
Woodside Avenue,
Grantown-on-Spey,
Moray, PH26 3JR
Tel: 01479 872092
★★★★ Small Hotel

Garth Hotel
The Square,
Grantown-on-Spey, Moray,
PH26 3HN
Tel: 01479 872836
★★★ Small Hotel

HELMSDALE

Kindale House
5 Lilleshall Street,
Helmsdale,
Sutherland, KW8 6JF
Tel: 01431 821415
★★★★ Guest House

INVERGARRY

Glengarry Castle Hotel
Invergarry, Inverness-shire,
PH35 4HW
Tel: 01809 501254
★★★★ Hotel

Forest Lodge
South Laggan, Invergarry,
Inverness-shire, PH34 4EA
Tel: 01809 501219
★★★ Guest House

INVERGORDON

Kincraig House Hotel
Invergordon, Ross-shire,
IV18 0LF
Tel: 01349 852587
★★★ Hotel

INVERNESS

Ballifeary House Hotel
10 Ballifeary Road,
Inverness, IV3 5PJ
Tel: 01463 235572
★★★★ Guest House

Crown Guest House
19 Ardconnel Street,
Inverness, Inverness-shire,
IV2 3EU
Tel: 01463 231135
★★★ Guest House

Thistle Inverness
Millburn Road, Inverness,
Inverness-shire, IV2 3TR
Tel: 01463 239666
★★★ Hotel

Talisker House
25 Ness Bank, Inverness,
Inverness-shire, IV2 4SF
Tel: 01463 236221
★★★ Guest House

Bunchrew House Hotel
Bunchrew, Inverness,
IV3 8TA
Tel: 01463 234917
★★★★ Small Hotel

Acorn House
Bruce Gardens, Inverness,
Inverness-shire, IV3 5ED
Tel: 01463 717021
★★★ Guest House

Alban House
Bruce Gardens,
Inverness, IV3 5EN
Tel: 01463 714301
★★★ Guest House

Ivybank Guest House
28 Old Edinburgh Road,
Inverness, IV2 3HJ
Tel: 01463 232796
★★★★ Guest House

Castle View Guest House
2A Ness Walk,
Inverness, IV3 5NE
Tel: 01463 241443
★★★ Guest House

Cedar Villa Guest House
33 Kenneth Street,
Inverness, IV3 5DH
Tel: 01463 230477
★★★ Guest House

Culloden House Hotel
Milton of Culloden,
Inverness, IV1 2NZ
Tel: 01463 792181
★★★★ Hotel

Dunain Park Hotel
Inverness, IV3 8JN
Tel: 01463 230512
AWAITING INSPECTION

Glen Mhor Hotel
9-12 Ness Bank, Inverness,
Inverness-shire, IV2 4SG
Tel: 01463 234308
Awaiting Inspection

Beaufort Hotel
11 Culduthel Road,
Inverness, IV2 4AG
Tel: 01463 222897
★★★ Hotel

Glasphein Bed and Breakfast
Glasphein, Easter
Muckovie, Westhill,
Inverness, IV2 5BN
Tel: 01463 790561
Awaiting Inspection

Maple Court Hotel
Ness Walk, Inverness,
IV3 5SQ
Tel: 01463 230330
★★★ Small Hotel

Lochardil House Hotel
Stratherrick Road,
Inverness, Inverness-shire,
IV2 4LF
Tel: 01463 235995
★★★★ Hotel

Inverness Marriott Hotel
Culcabock Road, Inverness,
IV2 3LP
Tel: 01463 237166
★★★★ Hotel

Ramada Jarvis Inverness
Church Street, Inverness,
Inverness-shire, IV1 1DX
Tel: 01463 235181
★★★ Hotel

Craignay House
16 Ardross Street,
Inverness, IV3 5NS
Tel: 01463 226563
★★★ Guest House

Larchfield House
15 Ness Bank, Inverness,
IV2 4SF
Tel: 01463 233874
★★★ Guest House

Glenmoriston Town House
20 Ness Bank, Inverness,
Inverness-shire,
IV2 4SF
Tel: 01463 223777
★★★★ Hotel

Eden House
8 Ballifeary Road,
Inverness, Inverness-shire,
IV3 5PJ
Tel: 01463 230278
★★★★ Guest House

Ach Aluinn Guest House
27 Fairfield Road,
Inverness, IV3 5QD
Tel: 01463 230127
★★★★ Guest House

MacDougall Clansman Hotel
103 Church Street,
Inverness, IV1 1ES
Tel: 01463 713702
★ Small Hotel

Avalon Guest House
79 Glenurquhart Road,
Inverness, Inverness-shire,
IV3 5PB
Tel: 01463 239075
★★★★ Guest House

Abermar Guest House
25 Fairfield Road,
Inverness, IV3 5QD
Tel: 01463 239019
★★★ Guest House

Malvern
54 Kenneth Street,
Inverness, Inverness-shire,
IV3 5PZ
Tel: 01463 242251
★★★ Guest House

Kessock Hotel
North Kessock, Ross-shire,
IV1 1XN
Tel: 01463 731208
★★★ Small Hotel

St Ann's House
37 Harrowden Road,
Inverness, Inverness-shire,
IV3 5QN
Tel: 01463 236157
★★★ Guest House

White Lodge
15 Bishops Road,
Inverness, IV3 5SB
Tel: 01463 230693
★★★★ Guest House

New Drumossie Hotel
Perth Road, Inverness,
Inverness-shire, IV1 2BE
Tel: 01463 236451
★★★★ Hotel

Waterside Hotel
Ness Bank, Inverness,
Inverness-shire, IV2 4SF
Tel: 01463 233065
★★★ Hotel

Eskdale House
41 Greig Street, Inverness,
IV3 5PX
Tel: 01463 240933
★★★ Guest House

Royston Guest House
16 Millburn Road,
Inverness, IV2 3PS
Tel: 01463 231243
★★★ Guest House

Ness Bank Guest House
7 Ness Bank, Inverness,
Inverness-shire, IV2 4SF
Tel: 01463 232939
★★★ Guest House

Loch Ness House Hotel
Glenurquhart Road,
Inverness, Inverness-shire,
IV3 8JL
Tel: 01463 231248
★★★ Hotel

Winston Guest House
10 Ardross Terrace,
Inverness, Inverness-shire,
IV3 5NQ
Tel: 01463 234477
★★★ Guest House

Whinpark Guest House
17 Ardross Street,
Inverness, Inverness-shire,
IV3 5NS
Tel: 01463 232549
★★★ Guest House

Moray Park House
Island Bank Road,
Inverness, IV2 4SX
Tel: 01463 233528
★★★ Guest House

Roseneath Guest House
39 Greig Street, Inverness,
IV3 5PX
Tel: 01463 220201
★★★ Guest House

The Alexander
16 Ness Bank, Inverness,
Inverness-shire, IV2 4SF
Tel: 01463 231151
★★★ Guest House

The Old Royal Guest House
10 Union Street, Inverness,
IV1 1PL
Tel: 01463 230551
★ Guest House

Best Western Inverness Palace Hotel & Spa
Ness Walk, Inverness,
IV3 5NG
Tel: 01463 223243
★★★ Hotel

Parkhill Guest House
17 Ardconnel Street,
Inverness, IV2 3EU
Tel: 01463 223300
★★★ Guest House

Rocpool Reserve Hotel
14 Culduthel Road,
Inverness, Inverness-shire,
IV2 4AG
Tel: 01463 240089
★★★★ Small Hotel

Pitfaranne Guest House
57 Crown Street,
Inverness, IV2 3AY
Tel: 01463 239338
★★★ Guest House

Melrose Villa
35 Kenneth Street,
Inverness, IV3 5DH
Tel: 01463 233745
★★★ Guest House

The Priory Hotel
The Square, Beauly,
Inverness-shire, IV4 7BX
Tel: 01463 782309
★★★ Hotel

Craigmonie Hotel
9 Annfield Road, Inverness,
Inverness-shire, IV2 3HX
Tel: 01463 231649
★★★ Hotel

Ardconnel House
21 Arconnel Street,
Inverness, Inverness-shire,
IV2 3EU
Tel: 01463 240455
★★★★ Guest House

Inverglen
7 Abertarff Road,
Inverness, IV2 3NW
Tel: 01463 236281
★★★ Guest House

Riverview Guest House
2 Moray Park, Island Bank
Road, Inverness,
Inverness-shire,
IV2 4SX
Tel: 01463 235557
★★★ Guest House

Copperfield
Culloden Road, Westhill,
Inverness, IV2 5BP
Tel: 01463 792251
★★★ Guest House

Glencairn and Ardross House
18-19 Ardross Street,
Inverness, IV3 5NS
Tel: 01463 232965
★★★ Guest House

Glendruidh House
Old Edinburgh Road,
Inverness, IV1 2AA
Tel: 01463 226499
★★★★ Small Hotel

Tower Hotel
4 Ardross Terrace,
Inverness, IV3 5NQ
Tel: 01463 232765
Awaiting Inspection

Eildon Guest House
29 Old Edinburgh Road,
Inverness, Inverness-shire,
IV2 3HJ
Tel: 01463 231969
★★ Guest House

Cuchullin Lodge Hotel
43 Culduthel Road,
Inverness, Inverness-shire,
IV2 4HQ
Tel: 01463 231945
★★★★ Small Hotel

Felstead House
18 Ness Bank, Inverness,
Inverness-shire, IV2 4SF
Tel: 01463 231634
★★★★ Guest House

Columba Hotel
Ness Walk,
Inverness, IV3 5NF
Tel: 01463 231391
★★★ Hotel

Aberfeldy Lodge Guest House
11 Southside Road,
Inverness, Inverness-shire,
IV2 3BG
Tel: 01463 231120
★★★ Guest House

Crown Court Hotel
25 Southside Road,
Inverness, IV2 3BG
Tel: 01463 234816
★★★ Small Hotel

JOHN O'GROATS

Caber Feidh Guest House
John O'Groats, Wick,
Caithness, KW1 4YR
Tel: 01955 611219
★★ Guest House

Seaview Hotel
John O'Groats, Caithness,
KW1 4YR
Tel: 01955 611220
★★ Small Hotel

KENTALLEN, BY APPIN

Holly Tree Hotel
Kentallen, Appin,
Argyll, PA38 4BY
Tel: 01631 740292
★★★ Small Hotel

KINCRAIG, BY KINGUSSIE

Braeriach Guest House
Braeriach Road, Kincraig,
by Kingussie, Inverness-
shire, PH21 1NA
Tel: 01540 651369
★★★★ Guest House

Suie Hotel
Kincraig, Inverness-shire,
PH21 1NA
Tel: 01540 651 344
★★★ Guest House

KINGUSSIE

Homewood Lodge
Newtonmore Road,
Kingussie, Inverness-shire,
PH21 1HD
Tel: 01540 661507
★★★★ Guest House

The Osprey Hotel
Ruthven Road, Kingussie,
Inverness-shire, PH21 1EN
Tel: 01540 661510
Awaiting Inspection

Columba House Hotel & Garden Restaurant
Manse Road, Kingussie,
Inverness-shire, PH21 1JF
Tel: 01540 661402
★★★ Small Hotel

Sonnhalde Guest House
East Terrace, Kingussie,
Inverness-shire, PH21 1JS
Tel: 015401 661 266
★★★ Guest House

Arden House
Newtonmore Road,
Kingussie, Inverness-shire,
PH21 1HE
Tel: 01540 661369
Awaiting Inspection

The Scot House Hotel
Newtonmore Road,
Kingussie, Inverness-shire,
PH21 1HE
Tel: 01540 661351
★★★ Small Hotel

The Hermitage Guest House
Spey Street, Kingussie,
Inverness-shire, PH21 1HN
Tel: 01540 662137
★★★★ Guest House

Duke of Gordon Hotel
Kingussie, Inverness-shire,
PH21 1HE
Tel: 01540 661302
★★★ Hotel

KINLOCHBERVIE

The Kinlochbervie Hotel
Kinlochbervie,
Sutherland, IV27 4RP
Tel: 01971 521275
★★ Small Hotel

**Old School
Restaurant & Rooms**
Inshegra, Kinlochbervie,
Sutherland, IV27 4RH
Tel: 01971 521383
★★★ Guest House

KINLOCHEWE

Kinlochewe Hotel
Kinlochewe, By
Achnasheen, Wester Ross,
IV22 2PA
Tel: 01445 760253
Small Hotel

KINLOCHLEVEN

Mamore Lodge Hotel
Kinlochleven, Argyll,
PH50 4QN
Tel: 01855 831 213
★ Small Hotel

Tigh-Na-Cheo
Garbien Road,
Kinlochleven, Argyll,
PH50 4SE
Tel: 01855 831434
★★★ Guest House

KYLE OF LOCHALSH

Tingle Creek Hotel
Erbusaig, Kyle,
Ross-shire, IV40 8BB
Tel: 01599 534430
Awaiting Inspection

Kyle Hotel
Main Street, Kyle of
Lochalsh, Ross-shire,
IV40 8AB
Tel: 01599 534204
★★★ Hotel

KYLESKU

Newton Lodge
Kylesku, Sutherland,
IV27 4HW
Tel: 01971 502070
★★★★ Small Hotel

Directory of all VisitScotland Quality Assured Serviced Hotels and Guest Houses

LAGGAN BRIDGE, BY NEWTONMORE

Laggan Country Hotel
Laggan, Inverness-shire, PH20 1BS
Tel: 01528 544250
★★★ Hotel

Monadhliath Hotel
Laggan Bridge, nr Newtonmore, Inverness-shire, PH20 1BT
Tel: 01528 544276
★★★ Small Hotel

LAIRG

The Nip Inn
Main Street, Lairg, Sutherland, IV27 4DB
Tel: 01549 402243
★★★ Small Hotel

Altnaharra Hotel
Altnaharra, By Lairg, Sutherland, IV27 4UE
Tel: 01549 411222
★★★ Small Hotel

BY LAIRG

The Overscaig House Hotel
Loch Shin, Sutherland, IV27 4NY
Tel: 01549 431203
★★★ Small Hotel

LOCHBROOM

Clachan Farmhouse
Lochbroom, Ullapool, Ross-shire, IV23 2RZ
Tel: 01854 655209
Awaiting Inspection

LOCHINVER

The Albannach
Baddidarroch, Lochinver, Sutherland, IV27 4LP
Tel: 01571 844407
★★★★ Small Hotel

Inver Lodge Hotel
Lochinver, Sutherland, IV27 4LU
Tel: 01571 844496
★★★★ Hotel

Kylesku Hotel
Kylesku, by Lochinver, Sutherland, IV27 4HW
Tel: 01971 502231
★★★ Small Hotel

Polcraig Guest House
Lochinver, Sutherland, IV27 4LD
Tel: 01571 844429
★★★★ Guest House

Ardglas
Lochinver, Lairg, Sutherland, IV27 4LJ
Tel: 01571 844257
★★ Guest House

LOCH NESS

Whitebridge Hotel
Whitebridge, Inverness-shire, IV2 6UN
Tel: 01456 486226
★★ Small Hotel

LOCH NESS (SOUTH)

Craigdarroch House Hotel
South Loch Ness Side, Foyers, Inverness-shire, IV2 6XU
Tel: 01456 486400
★★★★ Small Hotel

BY LOCH TORRIDON

Tigh an Eilean Hotel
Shieldaig, by Strathcarron, Ross-shire, IV54 8XN
Tel: 01520 755251
★★★★ Small Hotel

LYBSTER

Portland Arms Hotel
Lybster, Caithness, KW3 6BS
Tel: 01593 721721
★★★ Small Hotel

MALLAIG

The Moorings
East Bay, Mallaig, Inverness-shire, PH41 4PQ
Tel: 01687 462225
★★★ Guest House

Marine Hotel
Station Road, Mallaig, Inverness-shire, PH41 4PY
Tel: 01687 462217
★★ Hotel

Garramore House
South Morar, Mallaig, Inverness-shire, PH40 4PD
Tel: 01687 450268
★★ Guest House

Western Isles
East Bay, Mallaig, Inverness-shire, PH41 4QG
Tel: 01687 462320
★★★ Guest House

West Highland Hotel
Mallaig, Inverness-shire, PH41 4QZ
Tel: 01687 462210
★★★ Hotel

MARYBANK

Fairburn Activity Centre
Urray, Muir of Ord, Ross-shire, IV6 7UT
Tel: 01997 433397
★★★ Small Hotel

MELVICH

Melvich Hotel
Melvich, Sutherland, KW14 7YJ
Tel: 01641 531206
★★ Small Hotel

Bighouse Lodge
Melvich, by Thurso, Sutherland, KW14 7YJ
Tel: 01641 531207
★★★★ Small Hotel

MEY

Castle Arms Hotel
Mey, by Thurso, Caithness, KW14 8XH
Tel: 01847 851244
★★ Small Hotel

MORAR

Morar Hotel
Morar, By Mallaig, Inverness-shire, PH40 4PA
Tel: 01687 462346
★★ Hotel

MUIR OF ORD

Ord House Hotel
Muir of Ord, Ross-shire, IV6 7UH
Tel: 01463 870492
★★ Small Hotel

NAIRN

Sunny Brae Hotel
Marine Road, Nairn, Inverness-shire, IV12 4AE
Tel: 01667 452309
★★★★ Small Hotel

Claymore House Hotel
Seabank Road, Nairn, IV12 4EY
Tel: 01667 453731
★★★★ Small Hotel

Brighton House
Grant Street, Nairn, Inverness-shire, IV12 4NN
Tel: 01667 454670
Awaiting Inspection

Directory of all VisitScotland Quality Assured Serviced Hotels and Guest Houses

Ascot House
7 Cawdor Street, Nairn,
Inverness-shire, IV12 4QD
Tel: 01667 455855
★★★ Guest House

Invernairne Guest House
Thurlow Road, Nairn,
Inverness-shire, IV12 4EZ
Tel: 01667 452039
★★★ Guest House

Bracadale House
Albert Street, Nairn,
IV12 4HF
Tel: 01667 452547
★★★★ Guest House

Napier
60 Seabank Road, Nairn,
IV12 4HA
Tel: 01667 453 330
Awaiting Inspection

Golf View Hotel
Seabank Road, Nairn,
Inverness-shire, IV12 4HD
Tel: 01667 452301
★★★★★ Hotel

Newton Hotel
Nairn, Inverness-shire,
IV12 4RX
Tel: 01667 453144
★★★★ Hotel

Glen Lyon Lodge
19 Waverley Road, Nairn,
Nairnshire, IV12 4RH
Tel: 01667 452780
★★★ Guest House

Aurora Hotel
2 Academy Street, Nairn,
Nairn-shire, IV12 4RJ
Tel: 01667 453551
★★ Small Hotel

Windsor Hotel
Albert Street, Nairn,
IV12 4HP
Tel: 01667 453108
★★★ Hotel

NETHY BRIDGE
Coire Choille B&B
Lynstock, Nethy Bridge,
Inverness-shire, PH25 3DY
Tel: 01479 821716
Awaiting Inspection

Nethybridge Hotel
Nethybridge, Inverness-
shire, PH25 3DP
Tel: 01479 821203
★★★ Hotel

Mount View Hotel
Nethy Bridge,
Inverness-shire,
PH25 3EB
Tel: 01479 821 248
★★★ Small Hotel

NEWTONMORE
Balavil Sport Hotel
Main Street, Newtonmore,
Inverness-shire, PH20 1DL
Tel: 01540 673220
★★ Hotel

Alvey House Hotel
Golf Course Road,
Newtonmore, Inverness-
shire,, PH20 1AT
Tel: 01540 673260
★★★ Small Hotel

Crubenbeg House
Falls of Truim, By
Newtonmore, PH20 1BE
Tel: 01540 673300
★★★★ Guest House

Coig Na Shee
Fort William Road,
Newtonmore,
Inverness-shire, PH20 1DG
Tel: 01540 670109
★★★★ Guest House

ONICH, BY FORT WILLIAM
Creag Mhor Lodge
Onich, Fort William,
Inverness-shire,
PH33 6RY
Tel: 01855 821379
★★★★ Guest House

Camus House
Lochside Lodge, Onich,
Inverness-shire,
PH33 6RY
Tel: 01855 821200
★★★ Guest House

Allt-Nan-Ros Hotel
Main Road, Onich,
Inverness-shire, PH33 6RY
Tel: 01855 821462
★★★ Small Hotel

Onich Hotel
Onich, Inverness-shire,
PH33 6RY
Tel: 01855 821214
★★★★ Hotel

Cuilcheanna House
Onich, Inverness-shire,
PH33 6SD
Tel: 01855 821226
★★★★ Small Hotel

PLOCKTON
Duncraig Castle
By Plockton, Ross-shire,
IV52 8TZ
Tel: 01599 544295
Awaiting Inspection

The Haven Hotel
Innes Street, Plockton,
Ross-shire, IV52 8TW
Tel: 01599 544 223
★★★ Small Hotel

POOLEWE
Pool House
Poolewe, Rosshire, IV22
2LD
Tel: 01445 781272
★★★★ Small Hotel

Poolewe Hotel
Main Street, Poolewe,
IV22 2JX
Tel: 01445 781241
★★★ Small Hotel

ISLE OF RAASAY
Isle of Raasay Hotel
Raasay, Kyle of Lochalsh,
Ross-shire, IV40 8PB
Tel: 01478 660222
★★★ Small Hotel

RHICONICH
Rhiconich Hotel
Rhiconich, Sutherland,
IV27 4RN
Tel: 01971 521224
★★★ Small Hotel

ROTHIEMURCHUS
The Old Ministers House
Rothiemurchus,
Aviemore, Inverness-shire,
PH22 1QH
Tel: 01479 812181
★★★★ Guest House

ROY BRIDGE
Glenspean Lodge Hotel
Roy Bridge, Inverness-
shire, PH31 4AW
Tel: 01397 712223
★★★★ Small Hotel

SCOURIE
Eddrachilles Hotel
Badcall Bay, Scourie,
Sutherland, IV27 4TH
Tel: 01971 502080
★★★ Small Hotel

Scourie Hotel
Scourie, Sutherland,
IV27 4SX
Tel: 01971 502396
★★★ Small Hotel

Scourie Guest House
55 Scourie Village,
By Lairg, Sutherland,
IV27 4TE
Tel: 01971 502001
★★★ Guest House

**ISLE OF SKYE,
ARDVASAR, SLEAT**
Ardvasar Hotel
Ardvasar, Isle of Skye,
IV45 8RS
Tel: 01471 844223
★★★ Small Hotel

**ISLE OF SKYE,
BERNISDALE, BY PORTREE**
52 Aird
Bernisdale, By Portree,
Isle of Skye, IV51 9NU
Tel: 01470 532471
Awaiting Inspection

ISLE OF SKYE, BROADFORD

Slapin View
Torrin, Broadford,
Isle of Skye, IV49 9BA
Tel: 01471 822672
Awaiting Inspection

Seaview
Main Street, Broadford,
Isle of Skye, IV49 9AB
Tel: 01471 820308
Awaiting Inspection

Dunollie Hotel
Broadford, Isle of Skye,
Inverness-shire, IV49 9AE
Tel: 01471 822253
Hotel

Broadford Hotel
Broadford, Isle of Skye,
Inverness-shire, IV49 9AB
Tel: 01471 822414
Awaiting Inspection

ISLE OF SKYE, DUNVEGAN

The Tables Hotel
Main Street, Dunvegan,
Isle of Skye, Inverness-
shire, IV55 8WA
Tel: 01470 521404
★★ Small Hotel

Dunorin House Hotel
2 Herebost, Dunvegan,
Isle of Skye, Inverness-
shire, IV55 8GZ
Tel: 01470 521488
★★★★ Small Hotel

Dunvegan Hotel
Main Street, Dunvegan,
Isle of Skye, IV55 8WA
Tel: 01470 521497
★★★ Small Hotel

ISLE OF SKYE, KYLEAKIN

King's Arms Hotel
Kyleakin, Isle of Skye,
Inverness-shire, IV41 8PH
Tel: 01599 534109
Hotel

Glenarroch
Main Street, Kyleakin,
Isle of Skye, IV41 8PH
Tel: 01599 534845
★★★ Guest House

Mackinnon Country House Hotel
Old Farm Road, Kyleakin,
Isle of Skye, Inverness-
shire, IV41 8PQ
Tel: 01599 534180
★★★ Small Hotel

ISLE OF SKYE, ORD, SLEAT

Ord House
Ord, Sleat, Isle of Skye,
IV44 8RN
Tel: 01471 822180
Awaiting Inspection

ISLE OF SKYE, PORTREE

Givendale Guest House
Heron Place, Portree,
Isle of Skye, IV51 9GU
Tel: 01478 612183
★★★ Guest House

The Pink Guest House
1 Quay Street, Portree,
Isle of Skye, Inverness-
shire, IV51 9BT
Tel: 01478 612263
★★★ Guest House

Balloch
Viewfield Road, Portree,
Isle of Skye, Inverness-
shire, IV51 9ES
Tel: 01478 612093
★★★★ Guest House

Corran House
Kensaleyre, Portree,
Isle of Skye,
Inverness-shire,
IV51 9XE
Tel: 01470 532311
★★★★ Guest House

Cuillin Hills Hotel
Portree, Isle of Skye, IV51 9QU
Tel: 01478 612003
★★★★ Hotel

Orasay
14 Idrigill, Uig,
Portree, Isle Of Skye,
IV51 9XU
Tel: 01470 542316
Awaiting Inspection

Peinmore House
By Portree, Isle of Skye,
IV51 9LG
Tel: 01478 612 574
★★★★ Guest House

Viewfield House Hotel
Portree, Isle of Skye,
IV51 9EU
Tel: 01478 612217
★★★ Guest House

Quiraing Guest House
Viewfield Road, Portree,
Isle of Skye,
Inverness-shire,
IV51 9ES
Tel: 01478 612870
★★★★ Guest House

Rosebank House
Springfield Road, Portree,
Isle of Skye,
Inverness-shire,
IV51 9QX
Tel: 01478 612282
★★★ Guest House

The Bosville Hotel
10 Bosville Terrace,
Portree, Isle of Skye,
Inverness-shire, IV51 9DG
Tel: 01478 612846
★★★★ Hotel

An Airidh
6 Fisherfield, Portree,
Isle of Skye, IV51 9EU
Tel: 01478 612250
★★★ Guest House

Green Acres Guest House
Viewfield Road, Portree,
Isle of Skye, IV51 9EU
Tel: 01478 613175
★★★★ Guest House

Royal Hotel
Bank Street, Portree,
Isle of Skye, Inverness-
shire, IV51 9BU
Tel: 01478 61 2525
★★★ Hotel

Marmalade
Home Farm Road, Portree,
Isle of Skye, IV51 9LX
Tel: 01478 611711
★★★★ Small Hotel

Meadowbank House
Seafield Place, Portree,
Isle of Skye, IV51 9ES
Tel: 01478 612059
★★★ Guest House

Rosedale Hotel
Beaumont Crescent,
Portree, Isle of Skye,
IV51 9DB
Tel: 01478 613131
★★★ Hotel

ISLE OF SKYE, BY PORTREE

Greshornish House Hotel
Edinbane, By Portree,
Isle of Skye, IV51 9PN
Tel: 01470 582266
★★★ Small Hotel

ISLE FO SKYE, SCONSER

Sconser Lodge Hotel
Sconser, Isle of Skye,
Inverness-shire, IV48 3TD
Tel: 01478 650333
★★★ Small Hotel

ISLE OF SKYE, SLEAT

Kinloch Lodge
Sleat, Isle of Skye,
IV43 8QY
Tel: 01471 833214
★★★★ Small Hotel

Eilean Iarmain
Camus Cross, Sleat,
Isle of Skye, IV43 8QR
Tel: 01471 833332
★★★ Small Hotel

Toravaig House Hotel & Iona Restaurant
Knock Bay, Sleat,
Isle of Skye, IV44 8RE
Tel: 01471 833231
★★★★ Small Hotel

ISLE OF SKYE, STAFFIN

Flodigarry Country House Hotel
Flodigarry, Staffin,
Isle of Skye, IV51 9HZ
Tel: 01470 552203
★★★ Small Hotel

Glenview Hotel
Culnacnoc,
Staffin, Isle of Skye,
IV51 9JH
Tel: 01470 562248
★★ Small Hotel

ISLE OF SKYE, STRUAN, BY DUNVEGAN

Ullinish Lodge Hotel
Struan,
Isle of Skye, IV56 8FD
Tel: 01470 572214
★★★★ Small Hotel

Grianan
One Balmeanach,
by Struan,
Isle of Skye,
IV56 8FH
Tel: 01470 572374
Awaiting Inspection

ISLE OF SKYE, TREASLANE

Auchendinny
Treaslane, Portree,
Isle of Skye,
Inverness-shire,
IV51 9NX
Tel: 01470 532470
★★★ Guest House

ISLE OF SKYE, UIG

Woodbine House
Uig, Portree,
Isle of Skye,
IV51 9XP
Tel: 01470 542243
★★★ Guest House

Uig Hotel
Uig, Isle of Skye,
Inverness-shire,
IV51 9YE
Tel: 01470 542205
★★★ Small Hotel

ISLE OF SKYE, WATERNISH

Stein Inn
Macleod's Terrace,
Waternish, Isle of Skye,
Inverness-shire,
IV55 8GA
Tel: 01470 592362
★★★ Inn

SPEAN BRIDGE

The Heathers
Invergloy Halt,
Spean Bridge,
Inverness-shire,
PH34 4DY
Tel: 01397 712077
★★★★ Guest House

Corriegour Lodge Hotel
Loch Lochy,
by Spean Bridge,
Inverness-shire,
PH34 4EA
Tel: 01397 712685
★★★★ Small Hotel

The Braes Guest House
Spean Bridge,
Inverness-shire,
PH34 4EU
Tel: 01397 71243
★★★ Guest House

Aonach Mor Hotel
North Road, Spean Bridge,
Inverness-shire,
PH34 4ES
Tel: 01397 712351
★★ Small Hotel

Inverour Guest House
Roy Bridge Road,
Spean Bridge,
Inverness-shire,
PH34 4EU
Tel: 01397 712218
★★★ Guest House

Coire Glas Guest House
Roybridge Road, Spean
Bridge, Inverness-shire,
PH34 4EU
Tel: 01397 712272
★★★ Guest House

Distant Hills Guest House
Roybridge Road, Spean
Bridge, Inverness-shire,
PH34 4EU
Tel: 01397 712452
Guest House

Spean Bridge Hotel
Main Road, Spean Bridge,
Inverness-shire, PH34 4ES
Tel: 01397 712250
★★ Hotel

Smiddy House Guest House
Spean Bridge,
Inverness-shire, PH34 4EU
Tel: 01397 712335
★★★★ Guest House

STOER

Cruachan Guest House
Stoer, by Lochinver,
Sutherland, IV27 4JE
Tel: 01571 855303
★★★ Guest House

STRATHPEFFER

Brunstane Lodge Hotel
Golf Road, Strathpeffer,
Ross-shire, IV14 9AT
Tel: 01997 421261
★★★ Small Hotel

Richmond Hotel
Church Brae, Golf Course
Road, Strathpeffer,
Ross-shire, IV14 9AW
Tel: 01997 421300
Awaiting Inspection

Highland Hotel
Strathpeffer, Highland
Region, IV14 9AN
Tel: 01942 824824
★★★ Hotel

Ben Wyvis Hotel
Strathpeffer, Ross-shire,
IV14 9DN
Tel: 01997 421323
★★★ Hotel

Garden House
Garden House Brae,
Strathpeffer, Ross-shire,
IV14 9BJ
Tel: 01997 421242
★★★ Guest House

STRONTIAN

Kilcamb Lodge Hotel
Strontian, Argyll,
PH36 4HY
Tel: 01967 402257
★★★★ Small Hotel

Ben View Hotel
Strontian, Acharacle,
Argyll, PH36 4HY
Tel: 01967 402333
★★★ Small Hotel

Tom an Sighean
Upper Scotstown,
Strontian, Argyll, PH36 4JB
Tel: 01967 402464
Awaiting Inspection

STRUY, BY BEAULY

Cnoc Hotel
Struy, By Beauly,
Inverness-shire,
IV4 7JU
Tel: 01463 761 264
★★★ Small Hotel

TAIN

Pitcalzean House
Pitcalnie, Nr Tain,
Ross-shire,
IV19 1QT
★★★ Guest House

Dunbius Guest House
Morangie Road, Tain,
Ross-shire,
IV19 1HP
Tel: 01862 894902
★★★ Guest House

Swallow Morangie House Hotel
Morangie Road,
Tain, Ross-shire,
IV19 1PY
Tel: 01862 892281
★★★★ Hotel

Mansfield Castle
Scotsburn Road,
Tain, Ross-shire,
IV19 1PR
Tel: 01862 892052
★★★★ Hotel

Golf View Guest House
13 Knockbreck Road,
Tain, Ross-shire,
IV19 1BN
Tel: 01862 892856
★★★★ Guest House

THURSO

Pentland Hotel
Princes Street,
Thurso, Caithness,
KW14 7AA
Tel: 01847 893202
★★★ Hotel

Park Hotel
Thurso, KW14 8RE
Tel: 01847 893251
★★★ Small Hotel

Directory of all VisitScotland Quality Assured Serviced Hotels and Guest Houses

Station Hotel and Apartments
54-58 Princes Street,
Thurso, Caithness,
KW14 7DH
Tel: 01847 892003
★★★ Hotel

Pentland Lodge House
Granville Street, Thurso,
Caithness, KW14 7LG
Tel: 01847 8611206
Awaiting Inspection

Weigh Inn Hotel
Burnside, Thurso,
KW14 7UG
Tel: 01847 893722
★★★ Hotel

Royal Hotel
Trail Street, Thurso,
Caithness, KW14 8EH
Tel: 01847 893251
★★★ Hotel

TOMICH

Tomich Hotel
Tomich, by Cannich, near
Beauly, Inverness-shire,
IV4 7LY
Tel: 01456 415399
★★★ Small Hotel

TONGUE

Ben Loyal Hotel
Main Street, Tongue,
Sutherland, IV27 4XE
Tel: 01847 611216
★★★ Small Hotel

Tongue Hotel
Tongue, Sutherland,
IV27 4XD
Tel: 01847 611206
★★★★ Small Hotel

TORRIDON

Loch Torridon Hotel
Torridon, Achnasheen,
Ross-shire, IV22 2EY
Tel: 01445 791242
★★★★ Small Hotel

ULLAPOOL

Ardvreck House
North Road, Morefield,
Ullapool, IV26 2TH
Tel: 01854 612028
★★★★ Guest House

The Argyll Hotel
18 Argyle Street, Ullapool,
IV26 2UB
Tel: 01854 612422
Awaiting Inspection

Harbour Lights Hotel
Garve Road, Ullapool,
Ross-shire, IV26 2SX
Tel: 01854 612222
★★ Small Hotel

Glenfield Hotel
North Road, Ullapool,
Ross-shire, IV26 2XL
Tel: 01854 612314
★★ Hotel

Ullapool Hotel
g[DGarve Road, Ullapool,
Wester Ross, IV26 2SX
Tel: 01854 612905
★★ Small Hotel

Caledonian Hotel
Ullapool, Ross-shire,
IV26 2UG
Tel: 01854 612306
★★ Hotel

Westlea Guest House
2 Market Street, Ullapool,
Ross-shire, IV26 2XE
Tel: 01854 612594
★★★★ Guest House

Eilean Donan Guest House
14 Market Street, Ullapool,
Ross-shire, IV26 2XE
Tel: 01854 612524
★★★ Guest House

Riverside
Quay Street, Ullapool,
Ross-shire, IV26 2UE
Tel: 01854 612239
★★★ Guest House

Strathmore House
Morefield, Ullapool, Ross-
shire, IV26 2TH
Tel: 01854 612423
★★★ Guest House

WICK

Wellington Guest House
41-43 High Street, Wick,
Caithness, KW1 4BS
Tel: 01955 603287
★★★ Guest House

Nethercliffe Hotel
Louisburgh Street, Wick,
Caithness, KW1 4NS
Tel: 01955 602044
★★ Small Hotel

Mackays Hotel
46 Union Street, Wick,
Caithness, KW1 5ED
Tel: 01955 602323
★★★ HotelImpala Craigie

Highland Home
Broadhaven Road, Wick,
Caithness, KW1 4RF
Tel: 01955 602194
★★★ Guest House

Queens Hotel
16 Francis Street, Wick,
Caithness, KW1 5PZ
Tel: 01955 602992
★★ Small Hotel

Norseman Hotel
Riverside, Wick,
Caithness,
KW1 4NL
Tel: 01955 603344
★★ Hotel

ISLE OF BARRA, CASTLEBAY

Castlebay Hotel
Castlebay,
Isle of Barra,
HS9 5XD
Tel: 01871 810223
★★★ Small Hotel

Craigard Hotel
Castlebay, Barra,
Outer Hebrides,
HS9 5XD
Tel: 01871 810200
★★★ Small Hotel

ISLE OF BARRA, TANGASDALE

Isle of Barra Hotel
Tangusdale, Barra,
Western Isles,
HS9 5XW
Tel: 01871 810383
★★ Hotel

ISLE OF BENBECULA, CREAGORRY

**The Isle of Benbecula
House Hotel**
Creagorry,
Isle of Benbecula,
Western Isles,,
HS7 5PG
Tel: 01870 602024
★★★ Hotel

ISLE OF BENBECULA, LINICLATE

Lionacleit Guest House
27 Liniclate,
Benbecula,
Western Isles, HS7 5PY
Tel: 01870 602179
★★ Guest House

Dark Island Hotel
Liniclate,
Isle of Benbecula, Western
Isles,
HS7 5PJ
Tel: 0870 602414
★★★ Hotel

ISLE OF BENBECULA, TORLUM

Borve Guest House
5 Torlum,
Benbecula,
Western Isles,
HS7 5PP
Tel: 01870 602685
★★★★ Guest House

ISLE OF HARRIS, AMHUINNSUIDHE

Amhuinnsuidhe Castle
Isle of Harris,
Western Isles,
HS3 3AS
Tel: 01859 560200
★★★★★
Exclusive Use Venue

ISLE OF HARRIS, ARDHASAIG

Ardhasaig House
Ardhasaig,
Isle of Harris,
HS3 3AJ
Tel: 0185950 2066
★★★★ Small Hotel

ISLE OF HARRIS, KYLES HARRIS

Rodel Hotel
Rodel, Isle of Harris,
HS5 3TW
Tel: 01859 520 210
★★★ Small Hotel

Rodean
Ceann Dibig, Isle Of Harris,
Western Isles, HS3 3HQ
Tel: 01859 502079
Awaiting Inspection

ISLE OF HARRIS, LEVERBURGH

Grimisdale
Leverburgh,
Isle of Harris,
Western Isles,
HS5 3TS
Tel: 01859 520460
★★★★ Guest House

ISLE OF HARRIS, SCARISTA

Scarista House
Scarista, Isle of Harris,
HS3 3HX
Tel: 01859 550238
★★★★ Guest House

ISLE OF HARRIS, TARBERT

MacLeod Motel
Pier Road, Tarbert,
Isle of Harris,
HS3 3DG
Tel: 01859 502364
★★ Inn

Ceol Na Mara Guest House
7 Direclete, Tarbert,
Isle of Harris, HS3 3DP
Tel: 01859 502464
★★★★ Guest House

Harris Hotel
Tarbert, Isle of Harris,
Western Isles, HS3 3DL
Tel: 01859 502154
★★ Hotel

ISLE OF LEWIS, ACHMORE

Cleascro House
Achmore,,
Isle of Lewis,
HS2 9DU
Tel: 01851 860302
★★★★ Guest House

ISLE OF LEWIS, BACK

Banagher House
43 Vatisker, Back,
Isle of Lewis,
HS2 0LF
Awaiting Inspection

ISLE OF LEWIS, BREASCLEIT

Eshcol Guest House
21 Breasclete, Callanish,
Lewis, Outer Hebrides,
HS2 9DY
Tel: 01851 621357
★★★★ Guest House

Loch Roag Guest House
22A Breasclete, Isle of
Lewis, Western Isles,
HS2 9EF
Tel: 01851 621357
★★★★ Guest House

ISLE OF LEWIS, CALLANISH

Leumadair Guest House
7 Callanish,
HS2 9DY
Tel: 01857 621706
★★★★ Guest House

ISLE OF LEWIS, LOCHS

Claitair Hotel
Shieldinish, Isle of Lewis,
HS2 9RA
Tel: 01851 830473
Awaiting Inspection

ISLE OF LEWIS, SOUTH GALSON

Galson Farm Guest House
South Galson, Lewis,
Western Isles,
 HS2 0SH
Tel: 01851 850492
★★★★ Guest House

ISLE OF LEWIS, STORNOWAY

Cuanna House
29 Francis Street,
Stornoway,
Isle of Lewis,
HS1 2NF
Tel: 01851 703482
★★★★ Guest House

Park Guest House
30 James Street,
Stornoway,
Isle of Lewis,
HS1 2QN
Tel: 01851 702485
★★★ Guest House

Cabarfeidh Hotel
Manor Park,
Stornoway,
Isle of Lewis,
HS1 2EU
Tel: 01851 702604
★★★ Hotel

Caladh Inn
James Street, Stornoway,
Isle of Lewis, HS1 2QN
Tel: 01851 702604
★★ Hotel

Braighe House
20 Braighe Road,
Stornoway, Isle Of Lewis,
HS2 0BQ
Tel: 01851 705287
★★★★ Guest House

Hebridean Guest House
61 Bayhead,
Stornoway,
Isle of Lewis,
HS1 2DZ
Tel: 01851 702268
★★★ Guest House

Hal-O The Wynd
2 Newton Street,
Stornoway, Isle of Lewis,
HS1 2RE
Tel: 01851 706073
★★★ Guest House

Greenacres
8 Smith Avenue,
Stornoway,
Isle of Lewis,
Western Isles,
HS1 2PY
Tel: 01851 706383
★★★ Guest House

ISLE OF LEWIS, TIMSGARRY

Baile-Na-Cille
Timsgarry, Uig, Isle of
Lewis, HS2 9SD
Tel: 01851 672242
★★ Guest House

ISLE OF NORTH UIST, CARINISH

Temple View Hotel
Carinish,
Isle of North Uist,
Western Isles,,
HS6 5EJ
Tel: 01876 580676
★★★★ Small Hotel

ISLE OF NORTH UIST, LOCHEPORT

Langass Lodge
Locheport,
North Uist,
Western Isles, HS6 5HA
Tel: 01876 580285
★★★ Small Hotel

ISLE OF NORTH UIST, LOCHMADDY

Lochmaddy Hotel
Lochmaddy,
North Uist,
Western Isles,
HS6 5AA
Tel: 01876 500331
★★ Hotel

Tigh Dearg Hotel
Lochmaddy,
Isle of North Uist,
Western Isles,
HS6 5AE
Tel: 01876 500700
★★★★ Small Hotel

ORKNEY, BIRSAY

Barony Hotel
Birsay, Orkney,
KW17 2LS
Tel: 01856 721327
★★ Small Hotel

ORKNEY, BURRAY

Sands Hotel
Burray, Orkney,
KW17 2SS
Tel: 01856 731298
★★★★ Small Hotel

ORKNEY, DOUNBY

Ashleigh
Howaback Road,
Dounby, Orkney,
KW17 2JA
Tel: 01856 771378
Awaiting Inspection

ORKNEY, EDAY

Roadside
Eday, Orkney,
KW17 2AA
Tel: 01857 622303
Awaiting Inspection

ORKNEY, EVIE

Woodwick House
Evie, Orkney,
KW17 2PQ
Tel: 01856 751330
★★★ Small Hotel

Stoo Bed & Breakfast
Stoo Costa, Evie,
Orkney,
KW17 2NN
Tel: 01856 751761
Awaiting Inspection

Directory of all VisitScotland Quality Assured Serviced Hotels and Guest Houses

ORKNEY, HARRAY

Merkister Hotel
Loch Harray,
Orkney,
KW17 2LF
Tel: 01856 771366
★★★ Small Hotel

ORKNEY, HOY

Stromabank
Hoy, Orkney,
KW16 3PA
Tel: 01856 701494
★★★ Small Hotel

ORKNEY, KIRKWALL

Brekkness Guest House
Muddisdale Road, Kirkwall,
Orkney, KW15 1RS
Tel: 01856 874317
★★★ Guest House

Royal Oak Guest House
Holm Road,
Kirkwall, Orkney,
KW15 1PY
Tel: 01856 873487
★★★ Guest House

Foveran Hotel
St Ola, Kirkwall,
Orkney,
KW15 1SF
Tel: 01856 872389
★★★ Small Hotel

Narvik
Weyland Terrace, Kirkwall,
Orkney, KW15 1LS
Tel: 01856 879049
Awaiting Inspection

Albert Hotel
Mounthoolie Lane,
Kirkwall,
Orkney,
KW15 1JZ
Tel: 01856 876000
Hotel

West End Hotel
14 Main Street, Kirkwall,
Orkney, KW15 1BU
Tel: 01856 872368
★★ Small Hotel

No 5 Ingale
Kirkwall, Orkney, KW15 1UY
Tel: 01856 875721
Awaiting Inspection

Ayre Hotel
Ayre Road, Kirkwall,
Orkney, KW15 1QX
Tel: 01856 873001
★★★ Hotel

Orkney Hotel
Victoria Street, Kirkwall,
Orkney, KW15
Tel: 01856 873477
★★★ Hotel

Kirkwall Hotel
Harbour Street, Kirkwall,
Orkney, KW15 1LF
Tel: 01856 872232
★★★ Hotel

Queens Hotel
Shore Street, Kirkwall,
Orkney, KW15 1DN
Tel: 01856 872200
★★ Small Hotel

Lynnfield Hotel
Holm Road,
Kirkwall,
Orkney,
KW15 1SU
Tel: 01856 872505
★★★ Small Hotel

Polrudden Guest House
Peerie Sea Loan, Kirkwall,
Orkney, KW15 1UH
Tel: 01856 874761
★★★ Guest House

Lav'rockha Guest House
Inganess Road, Kirkwall,
Orkney, KW15 1SP
Tel: 01856 876103
★★★★ Guest House

ORKNEY, NORTH RONALDSAY

ORKNEY, ORPHIR

Scorrabrae Inn
Orphir, Orkney, KW17 2RF
Tel: 01856 811262
Awaiting Inspection

ORKNEY, PAPA WESTRAY

Beltane House
Papay Community
Cooperative Ltd, Papa
Westray, Orkney, KW17 2BU
Tel: 01857 644321
★★ Guest House

ORKNEY, SHAPINSAY

Balfour Castle
Balfour Village,
Shapinsay, Orkney,
KW17 2DY
Tel: 01856 711282
★★★ Small Hotel

ORKNEY, STENNESS

ORKNEY, STROMNESS

Millers House & Harbourside B&B
7 & 13 John Street,
Stromness, Orkney,
KW16 3AD
Tel: 01856 851969
★★★ Guest House

Orca Hotel
76 Victoria Street,
Stromness, Orkney,
KW16 3BS
Tel: 01856 850447
★★ Guest House

Stromness Hotel
Victoria Street,
Stromness,
Orkney,
KW16 3AA
Tel: 01856 850298
★★★ Hotel

The Ferry Lodge
15 John Street,
Stromness,
Orkney,
KW16 3AD
Tel: 01856 850109
Awaiting Inspection

Royal Hotel
55-57 Victoria Street,
Stromness,
Orkney,
KW16 3BS
Tel: 01856 850342
★★ Small Hotel

ORKNEY, WESTRAY

Cleaton House
Cleaton, Westray,
Orkney,
KW17 2DB
Tel: 01857 677508
★★★★ Small Hotel

SHETLAND, BRAE, NORTH MAINLAND

Busta House Hotel
Busta,
North Mainland,
Shetland,
ZE2 9QN
Tel: 01806 522506
★★★ Hotel

SHETLAND, FAIR ISLE

Fair Isle Bird Observatory Lodge
Fair Isle, Shetland,
ZE2 9JU
Tel: 01595 760258
★★ Guest House

SHETLAND, LERWICK

Lerwick Hotel
15 South Road, Lerwick,
Shetland, ZE1 0RB
Tel: 01595 692166
★★★ Hotel

Shetland Hotel
Holmsgarth Road,
Lerwick,
Shetland,
ZE1 0PW
Tel: 01595 695515
★★★ Hotel

Breiview
43 Kanterstead Road,
Lerwick, Shetland, ZE1 0RJ
Tel: 01595 695956
★★★ Guest House

Glen Orchy Guest House
20 Knab Road, Lerwick,
Shetland,
ZE1 0AX
Tel: 01595 692031
★★★ Guest House

Grand Hotel
Commercial Street,
Lerwick, Shetland,
ZE1 0HX
Tel: 01595 692826
★★★ Hotel

Queen's Hotel
Commercial Street,
Lerwick,
Shetland,
ZE1 0AB
Tel: 01595 692826
★★★ Hotel

Alderlodge Guest House
6 Clairmont Place,
Lerwick, Shetland,
ZE1 0BR
Tel: 01595 695705
★★★ Guest House

Solheim Guest House
34 King Harald Street,
Lerwick, Shetland,
ZE1 0EQ
Tel: 01595 695275
★★★ Guest House

Eddlewood Guest House
8 Clairmont Place,
Lerwick, Shetland,
ZE1 0BR
Tel: 01595 692772
★★★ Guest House

Westhall
Ness of Sound, Lerwick,
Shetland,
ZE1 0RN
Tel: 01595 694247
Awaiting Inspection

Fort Charlotte Guest House
1 Charlotte Street,
Lerwick, Shetland,
ZE1 0JL
Tel: 01595 692140
★★★ Guest House

Kveldsro House Hotel
Greenfield Place, Lerwick,
Shetland, ZE1 0AN
Tel: 01595 692195
★★★★ Small Hotel

SHETLAND, SCOUSBURGH
Spiggie Hotel
Scouseburgh, Shetland
Isles, ZE2 9JE
Tel: 01950 460409
★★★ Small Hotel

SHETLAND, SUMBURGH
Sumburgh Hotel
Sumburgh, Virkie,
Shetland, ZE3 9JN
Tel: 01950 60201
★★★ Hotel

SHETLAND, TINGWALL
Herrislea House
Veensgarth, Tingwall,
Shetland, ZE2 9SB
Tel: 01595 840208
★★★★ Small Hotel

SHETLAND, ISLAND OF UNST
Ordale Guest House
Baltasound, Unst,
Shetland, ZE2 9DT
Tel: 01957 711867
★★ Guest House

The Baltasound Hotel
Baltasound, Unst,
Shetland, ZE2 9DS
Tel: 01957 711334
★★ Hotel

SHETLAND, WALLS
Burrastow House
Walls, Shetland, ZE2 9PD
Tel: 01595 809307
★★★★ Guest House

SOUTH UIST, DALIBURGH
Borrodale Hotel
Daliburgh, South Uist,
Western Isles, HS8 5SS
Tel: 01878 700444
★★★ Small Hotel

SOUTH UIST, EOCHDAR
Anglers Retreat
1 Ardmore, Iochdar,
South Uist, HS8 5QY
Tel: 01870 610325
★★ Guest House

SOUTH UIST, LOCHBOISDALE
Lochboisdale Hotel
Lochboisdale, South Uist,
HS8 5TH
Tel: 01878 700332
Small Hotel

Brae Lea House
Lasgair, Lochboisdale, Isle
of South Uist, HS8 5TH
Tel: 01878 700497
★★★ Guest House

SOUTH UIST, LOCHCARNAN
Orasay Inn
Lochcarnan, South Uist,
Outer Hebrides, HS8 5PD
Tel: 01870 610298
★★★ Small Hotel

Index

By location

**

want to know
where to eat and drink in Scotland?

Perhaps you feel like dining in a beautiful restaurant, with first-class ingredients carefully prepared by talented chefs. Or you might be looking for something quicker, simpler. You might be on holiday, or maybe you live in Scotland and you like to eat out now and then.

Where do you turn to for advice?

VisitScotland has come up with the answer and launched EatScotland the food quality assurance scheme for Scotland (branded as Scottish Tourist Board). And, of course, only places offering good quality food can participate in the scheme. Hundreds of restaurants, tea-rooms, coffee shops, pubs, self-service restaurants and takeaways across the length and breadth of Scotland have already been assessed ensuring these businesses offer you good quality food, ambience and service.

We want you to enjoy a quality eating experience in Scotland. With this in mind, businesses that participate in the EatScotland quality assurance scheme must reach and maintain high standards not only once, but year after year. Each business receives an annual incognito assessment by a dedicated food quality advisor who takes many things into account, including:

- hospitality
- staff appearance
- culinary skills
- fresh ingredients
- appearance of food
- quality of the main ingredients, including any sauce or accompaniment
- appearance, quality, flavour and selection of accompanying vegetables
- balance and flavour of the food
- sundries such as water, bread and butter, complimentary courses and quality of beverages served at the end of a meal
- wine and other alcoholic drinks
- housekeeping and hygiene
- toilets

Wherever you see the EatScotland logo you can be assured of a quality eating experience, so look out for this logo in brochures, websites and on windows.

To give you the widest possible choice of places to eat and drink, EatScotland's website lists both assessed and non-assessed businesses, and it's easy to serach by business type, business name, by area or town. You can soon identify those in the EatScotland food quality assurance scheme as they have the logo beside their name, and these are the places where you will find consistently high standards.

From tea rooms to fish and chip shops, from bistros to fine dining, a range of mouth-watering options are on offer. So why wait? Choose your eating experience by logging on to:

Live it. Visit *Scotland*.
visitscotland.com   0845 22 55 121
The No.1 booking and information service for Scotland.

www.eatscotland.com